I0762817

SOVIET FACTOGRAPHY

SOVIET

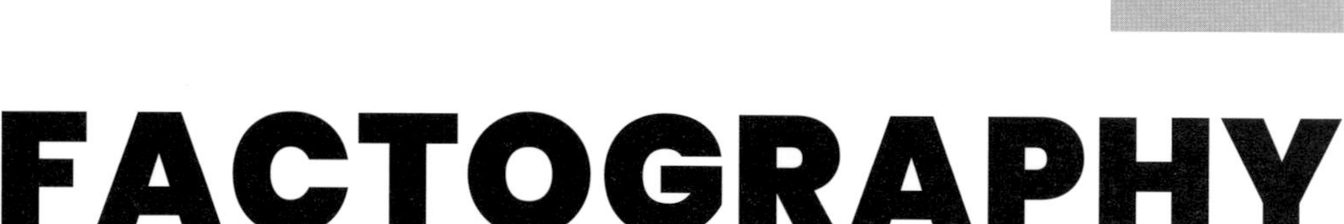

FACTOGRAPHY

REALITY WITHOUT REALISM

DEVIN FORE

The University of Chicago Press / Chicago and London

The University of Chicago Press, Chicago 60637
The University of Chicago Press, Ltd., London

Published 2024
Printed in the United States of America

33 32 31 30 29 28 27 26 25 24   1 2 3 4 5

ISBN-13: 978-0-226-23486-1 (cloth)
ISBN-13: 978-0-226-83102-2 (e-book)
DOI: https://doi.org/10.7208/chicago/9780226831022.001.0001

This publication is made possible in part by the Barr Ferree Foundation Fund for Publications, Department of Art and Archaeology, Princeton University.

Library of Congress Cataloging-in-Publication Data

Names: Fore, Devin, 1972– author.
Title: Soviet factography : reality without realism / Devin Fore.
Description: Chicago : The University of Chicago Press, 2024. | Includes bibliographical references and index.
Identifiers: LCCN 2023053656 | ISBN 9780226234861 (cloth) | ISBN 9780226831022 (ebook)
Subjects: LCSH: Documentary mass media—Soviet Union. | Documentary photography—Soviet Union. | Reportage literature, Russian—Soviet Union. | Modernism (Aesthetics)—Soviet Union.
Classification: LCC P96.D622 S65 2024 | DDC 070.10947/09042—dc23/eng/20240130
LC record available at https://lccn.loc.gov/2023053656

♾ This paper meets the requirements of ANSI/NISO Z39.48-1992 (Permanence of Paper).

Contents

The Now moves and propels itself through each day, whenever. It is pulsing in all that happens with its shortest time, and it is knocking on the door. But not every present opens up for it.
—ERNST BLOCH[1]

Introduction

FACTOGRAPHY'S FORTUNES

Any study of factography first has to deal with the strangeness of the word itself, an awkwardly technicist, distinctly non-Russian neologism that, as the lexical roots of *fakto-grafiia* would suggest, named a certain method for inscribing facts. Readers familiar with the early Soviet zeal for linguistic invention might suspect that factography is just another word for documentary. First coined in 1928, factography was actually but one of a host of terms used to identify a broad field of related practices that were emerging at that time in Soviet Russia and that bore various names like factism, chronicalism, *ocherkizm*, the cinema of fact, documentation, and so on. The diversity of words used to designate this kind of work in the 1920s collectively testifies to the absence of any single aesthetic or conceptual model capable of encompassing all manifestations of this militantly experimental technique. Whenever they were asked to explain what they do, practitioners of factography provided concrete examples of their work rather than nomothetic definitions or generic labels for the things they made.[2] "We still have not found a common language for 'nonfictional' things, and we still, as in the realm of literature, have no methodology whatsoever for the cinema of fact," proclaimed one leader of the movement in 1928.[3] They would never actually make any real advances on this front.

Indeed, as they approached the apogee of their influence the following year, the factographers stopped publishing programmatic statements and instead dedicated themselves entirely to their operative practice. For them, there was no general theory of factography, nor should there be.

Nor for that matter were there any obvious precedents to this method in the lineage of valorized cultural forms. There was no great tradition of factography. In contrast to our own understanding of documentary, a genre that now encompasses a familiar array of conventions for faithfully signifying reality, in the 1920s the diverse strategies of factography had not yet been consolidated into a fixed repertoire of aesthetic devices. Formalizing that system would be a project of the 1930s, when the panoply of experimental techniques operating loosely under the rubric of factography was reinvented as a finite set of legible generic markers specific to each medium. From voice-of-God overdubbing in cinema to the linear style of literary reportage and the post-montage narrativization of the photo-essay, almost all of the devices of modern documentary were a creation of this decade. Outfitted with this arsenal of reality effects, documentary was transformed on the eve of the Second World War into the quintessential expression of cultural authority and objective truth that we recognize today.

This book examines a body of work that was made before the generic stabilization of these practices under the rubric of documentary. Less a performance of authority than a protocol of inquiry, Soviet factography was far more tentative, more contingent, than the high documentary of the 1930s. Georg Lukács, who championed enduring, monumental literary genres like the realist novel, was understandably skeptical of this kind of work, which he dismissed as an unstable and open-ended "experiment in form" (*Formexperiment*).[4] Before the creation of documentary as such, techniques of documentation were indeed formally promiscuous, cropping up in the 1920s in outwardly dissimilar and genetically unrelated avant-garde projects that ranged from the ethnographic researches of the French *Documents* circle to the anti-hermeneutic positivism of the German dadaists. The striking reach and diversity of this international experiment in form was partly a consequence of the avant-garde's turn in those years to photography, cinematography, stenography, and other technologies of mechanical inscription. As scholars have pointed out, these indexical recording devices erased the distinctions between individual artistic genres and eroded the very premise of medium specificity.[5] The proliferation of technical media in the 1920s, which broke down the boundary between word and image and which gave rise to any number of hybrid cultural practices, made it difficult to maintain the long-standing aesthetic classifications and hierarchies of knowledge that anchored the thinking of traditionalists like Lukács. A case in point: the Russian word most often used to label factographic production, *ocherk* (sketch), can apply not just to prose, cinema, and photography but also to work that is both literary and scientific. The practice of documentation—which this book will rigorously distinguish from the genre of documentary—inevitably dissolves the borders between cultural forms and discourses. As the philosopher Michel de Certeau explained, "the movement of documentation . . . brings about a slow erosion of organizing concepts," since it entails a "wearing out of the classificatory divisions that cement the foundation of the textual system."[6]

Nowhere was the document's assault on artistic categories and conceptual taxonomies more robust and sophisticated than in Soviet Russia, where factography surpassed its European counterparts in rigor, inventiveness, and sheer scale. In the era of the Cultural Revolution (1928–31), this practice found fertile ground in the institutions of mass journalism and the worker-correspondence movement, where a commitment to aesthetic and epistemic deskilling posed unprecedented challenges to established conventions of art and hierarchies of truth. Technology's erosion of traditional classificatory systems was compounded in the Soviet context by a prevalent skepticism toward prerevolutionary culture and by the widespread impulse to establish the canons of thought upon more inclusive, democratic grounds. The efforts of the factographers to automate artistic creation and set up lateral peer-to-peer networks between amateur producers made vital contributions to this project of cultural transvaluation. In the historical phase of the revolution known as the transitional period, cultural workers had to unlearn all they knew about art and start over again from the beginning, rebuilding the basic structures of human expression and communication from the ground up. At the Orphean moment that followed the revolution, poets and artists along with everyday citizens were asked to invent languages and symbolic forms adequate to the strange new reality inaugurated in October 1917. The writer and photographer Ilya Ehrenburg observed in 1929 that "the traditions have been forgotten, the craft no longer exists, the language is young and new, and the various themes, too, have never been addressed before. At the present, writing is almost as difficult as it was in the first centuries of the written word." The First World War, the Bolshevik Revolution, and the Civil War had decimated not just the national economy but literature and art as well. And reconstructing the latter, Ehrenburg added, was "far more difficult than the mere reconstruction of industry."[7]

Leading the factographic crusade at this moment of cultural renovation was Sergei Mikhailovich Tret'iakov (1892–1937), a lawyer, poet, and playwright who began in the mid-1920s to work by turns as a reporter, photographer, editor, activist, ocherkist, translator, and scenarist. For Tret'iakov, the zero-hour of transitional society represented a singular opportunity to intervene at the most basic strata of human consciousness and experience. "The revolution has fundamentally changed the way in which he views, feels, and names all of the objects that surround him," he enthused about the Soviet subject.[8] Initially drawn to poetry as a means to engage with this new reality, Tret'iakov had started composing Futurist lyrics while he was still studying law in Moscow during the First

World War and, after moving eastward in 1919, assumed a leading role in the Vladivostok-based group Creation. Upon returning to the capital city in 1922, Tret'iakov joined the Moscow division of the mass organization Proletkul't, where he worked alongside members of the avant-garde such as the production theorist Boris Arvatov and the theater director Sergei Eisenstein. It was during these years in the Proletkul't studios that Tret'iakov began to distance himself from Ego-Futurist poetry and to develop forms and strategies of cultural work better suited to mass-political activism. From its founding in 1923 to its final issue in 1925, Tret'iakov was a core contributor to the journal *Lef*, Vladimir Mayakovsky's showcase for constructivist and productivist work as well as an important theoretical organ for the Moscow Linguistic Circle. In 1924 and 1925, Tret'iakov served as a foreign correspondent for *Pravda* in Beijing, where he first began to cultivate the popular, document-based practice that would soon come to be known as factography. Indeed, when *Lef* was relaunched in 1927 as *Novyi Lef* (New Lef), the face of Mayakovsky's journal had been completely transformed by Tret'iakov's influence from an occasional venue for the utopian, at times quixotic, aesthetic experiments of the Futurists into a monthly periodical specializing in fact-based reportage and photography. Supported by the institutions and ethos of the Cultural Revolution, the practice of mass documentation pioneered by Tret'iakov enjoyed a meteoric career in the late 1920s as the most successful rival to the school of proletarian realism. The latter impulse would triumph in the next decade, of course, but for a few brief years until 1931, the literature, cinema, and photography of fact were major, even defining, forces in Soviet culture.

Tret'iakov himself reported on diverse topics ranging from political protests in Beijing and the modernization of Svanetia's infrastructure to silicate mining in Siberia and Moscow's electrical industry. Each of these assignments required the factographer to attend a different "university," as Tret'iakov put it, in order to acquire the specialized knowledge and skills necessary to carry out his work, whether in political economy, cultural history, geology, or engineering.[9] In turn, each dispatch from the field was formulated in a different voice, written as if by a different hand, so that critics would often remark that Tret'iakov had no distinctive style of his own.[10] The Orphean factographer had to reinvent the conditions of language with every new assignment.

Tret'iakov's most sustained and renowned work was at the Communist Lighthouse, a remote kolkhoz (collective farm) in the Caucasus region where he served in an astonishing variety of roles over six years from 1928 to 1933. He looked back on that period: "I carried out the most diverse kinds of work. I coordinated the mass social labor of 18 kolkhozes, built cultural trucks, taught shepherds how to make wall newspapers, edited a print newspaper, served as an examiner for young people who wanted to pass a course on tractors, had discussions with accountants about different methods of bookkeeping, wrote scripts to be performed in the clubs of the kolkhoz, offered consultations in collective homes for infants, was cursed out by peasants at assemblies whenever the work wasn't completely satisfactory, showed peasants from other places the demonstration sections of the commune."[11] If the testimonies of the locals are to be believed, Tret'iakov excelled at each of these tasks, integrating himself so successfully that the farmers often forgot that he was there as a reporter from *Pravda*.[12] In 1930 they even elected him to serve on the leadership council of the kolkhoz. Resourceful, pliant, and adaptive by character, Tret'iakov tirelessly pursued the "biographical inclusion" of his assignments into his own vita, as he called his practice of embedded journalism.[13] This "rangy, six-foot, bespectacled, head-shaved dynamo" was a master of continuous self-reinvention, a talent particularly suited for the rapid tempo and ever-changing conditions of life after the revolution.[14] "Today, almost from the moment you go on the attack, you are already running for cover; one minute you're basing your work on one sociobiological type, and the next minute this type is declared unsuitable and antirevolutionary," he wrote in 1927.[15] Like so many living in the transitional period, Tret'iakov tacked back and forth between changing directives, always in response to the latest resolution. As a result, his biography cuts a zigzag line across diverse, often discontinuous, frameworks of experience and political positions.

But this book is not about the life and work of Tret'iakov. While his case may offer the best introduction to the factographic method, the impulses that he channeled can be observed in any number of cultural producers of the period. During the years of its peak around 1928–31, factography was a ubiquitous practice that united a variety of figures from the writer Boris Kushner and the artist Aleksandr Rodchenko to the filmmaker Dziga Vertov and the Formalist Viktor Shklovsky. The group of producers assembled under the aegis of factography was so heterogeneous, and their platform seemingly so incoherent, that one critic declared them guilty of "monstrous double duty" (*чудовищное совместительство*), since each of these figures appeared to endorse different, mutually incompatible practices.[16] Although they could hardly be counted among the key practitioners, Eisenstein, Mayakovsky, and Andrei Platonov also experimented with techniques of documentation at various points in the late 1920s, albeit with differing levels of commitment and degrees of success. As the method became more widespread, other factographic organs beyond *Novyi Lef* were founded, such as the important Siberian journal *The Present* (*Настоящее*). Enticed by the immense popularity of the movement, even rival organizations like the Russian Association of Proletarian Writers (RAPP) tried to assimilate features of factography into their own program for proletarian realism.

While this book prospects a suitably broad range of sources, it focuses in particular on the work of two lesser-known figures who, alongside the more famous Tret'iakov, contributed decisively to the factographic movement: the dialectician Nikolai Chuzhak (born Nasimovich), who was known among his peers as "the Russian thinker with the German devices" and who was distinguished within the avant-garde for his unblemished Bolshevik pedigree;[17] and the critic Viktor Pertsov, who began his career as the secretary to the Soviet Taylorist Aleksei Gastev and who consequently understood more about art's relationship to industrial technology than any other member of Lef save, perhaps, Arvatov.[18] Tret'iakov, Chuzhak, and Pertsov together formed the core of the factographic secession that broke in 1928 not just with traditional art practices, but with all art as such.[19] Contemporaries likened Tret'iakov to Plato, the ancient philosopher who had called for the eradication of imagery and who demanded the expulsion of the poets from the republic.[20]

The ruthless campaign that Tret'iakov, Chuzhak, and Pertsov launched against the aesthetic as a sphere of autonomous sensory experience and a preserve of timeless cultural value was driven by three convergent insights, one political, one epistemological, and one technological. First was the trio's shared commitment to disbanding the professional caste of art-makers, democratizing the means of personal expression, and unleashing the forces of popular creativity on a mass scale. To do this, the three former Proletkul'tists promoted photography, stenography, and other inscription technologies that required no particular talent or specialized knowledge of aesthetic craft. In the end, their campaign to deskill, rationalize, and collectivize artistic creation did in fact succeed in driving out the poets: increasing tensions within Lef culminated in a schism with Mayakovsky, who declared "amnesty to Rembrandt" and abandoned *Novyi Lef* in mid-1928, taking half of the journal's editorial board with him. ("Not every boy who can press the button on a camera is a member of Lef," protested the Futurist.[21]) Even after Mayakovsky's departure, the factographers still came to the conclusion that Lef could not be saved from the inherent "aesthetic aristocratism" that was built into the avant-garde organization and dissolved the group at the end of the year in order to dedicate themselves more fully to mass technics of the document. "Our work is worthless if we don't empty into the sea—into the sea of the masses," stated Tret'iakov's final editorial for *Novyi Lef*.[22]

The factographers' rejection of art expressed, secondly, their conviction that the mediation of experience through imagery—and indeed, the very act of representing the world—had become superfluous if not deleterious in the phase of revolutionary transition. Looking back on their work, Pertsov would later explain that they strove "for recording and protocoling reality instead of artistic generalization and comprehension of life. . . . By equating the 'fact' with its 'mirror' reflection in literature, by negating the role of thinking in images, by schematically opposing fact to fiction, [we] oversimplified the role of the artist."[23] Pertsov's assessment might sound extreme, and yet it actually underplays the agenda of the factographers, who sought not just to simplify the role of the artist but to eliminate it entirely, along with the category of autonomous art. For the factographers, the hiatus of aesthetic reflection only distanced consciousness from world and delayed the subject's encounter with the present. Hoping to cut through the tangle of mental associations and imagery that impeded the perception of reality, they pursued a zero-degree writing free of trope and a formless photography without figural content. Chuzhak explained that art becomes an obstacle to knowledge at intervals of rapid historical change such as their own. "At moments when the entire creativity of a nation shifts into the realm of reality—such are the moments of revolutions and wars—it is especially difficult to gain awareness of phenomena through art."[24] At worst, complex aesthetic mediation actively foreclosed access to real experience. At best, this process was simply unnecessary. As Platonov observed, the epistemological divide that separated poetry from reality in nonrevolutionary phases of history had contracted dramatically, so much that signs now began to converge with the objects that they designated. The distinction between object and symbol—and with it the line between nature and artifice—had grown all too tenuous: "In our society the separation between art and life has decreased. Art lies on the surface of reality in readymade form, because our reality is so unusual that the distance between art and reality is already close."[25] Under these conditions, decoding reality required no particular contrivance, no act of aesthetic transfiguration or feat of ideological exfoliation. Nor did it even require any skill. All that the artist or writer needed to do was go about harvesting readymade documents from the surface of reality.

To be sure, the situation in Russia after 1917 was not unique in this respect. The proximity of art to reality has been a signature of revolutionary episodes throughout the modern era. These political conjunctures have always supercharged language and endowed cultural symbols with concrete force. At such moments in history, poetry's modality shifts from the depictive to the operative. Art too is desublimated, transformed from a passive reflection into an instrument for leveraging reality. Translated instantaneously into effect, language and image begin to intervene in the events that they purport to describe, triggering a delirious spiral of feedback between the witness and the agent of history. "Follow your slogans to the point at which they become embodied," enjoins the French revolutionary in Georg Büchner's play *Danton's Death*. "Look around you, it is everything that you have spoken, a mimic translation of your words."[26] As the distance closes between *logos* (language) and *ergon* (action)—a distinction fundamental to the poetics of realism since antiquity—symbols come to inflect and direct life rather than just reflecting and recording it.[27] In such conjunctures, no utterance can be considered apolitical nor any sign nonpartisan, since every phrase and picture is already influencing the course of events from the moment of its expression. This muscular, even coercive, language was the desideratum of modernity's Ur-revolutionary Faust, whom Tret'iakov paraphrased: "The word has become a deed."[28]

In the specific case of Soviet Russia, though, there was also a third factor, absent in other modern revolutions, that rendered art superfluous. This was the primary industrial explosion of the reconstruction period. As Lenin made clear in his famous definition of communism as "Soviet power plus electrification," the Party's political agenda was inseparable from the technical modernization of Russia. For the Bolsheviks, it would be a mistake to pursue either of these two programs without the other: politics without industrialization would lapse into what Marx called "political superstition," while industrialization without politics would result in a technocratic pseudo-revolution.[29] These two dimensions were likewise inseparable for the factographers, who combined the democratizing impulses of Proletkul't with a productivist enthusiasm for machinery. The expansion of the industrial milieu into a full-blown lifeworld, into a second nature built out of technology, was indeed an indispensable condition for the emergence of factography. It explains why this approach to documenting reality did not yet appear in 1917 or during the Civil War, but flourished only in the phase of rapid industrial growth that followed these crises, when the initial revolutionary impulse was augmented and amplified by the technological Prometheanism of the late 1920s. Looking back at the ascent of the factographic sketch as a cultural form, Tret'iakov later confirmed that "the real flowering of the ocherk began in the epoch of the reconstruction."[30]

It is indeed impossible to understand the factographic episode without taking into account the explosion of technical media and the attending mass-cultural formations that resulted from the industrialization campaigns of the 1920s. Not only did this decade experience the advent of radio broadcasting, the introduction of sound into film, advances in photomechanical reproduction that produced the modern illustrated press, and the automation of image-making through handheld, high-speed, roll-film cameras such as the Ermanox or the Leica (Tret'iakov's brand of choice). It also witnessed the proliferation of popular photography organizations, widespread literacy campaigns, and a peer-to-peer worker-correspondent movement that aspired to transform the consumer of information into its active producer. It is no accident that factography began to reach the apogee of its influence and praxeological cogency in 1927, the birth-year of the society of the spectacle.[31] Echoing Platonov, Fredric Jameson has written that Russians of this generation confronted "the spectacle of a world in which nature as such has been eliminated, a world saturated with messages and information, whose intricate commodity network may be seen as the very prototype of a system of signs."[32] As technically mediated forms of communication became increasingly ubiquitous and the spaces of spontaneously given nature contracted, the factographers came to see the activity of signifying as an elementary, constitutive force that shaped and textured the fabric of reality itself, rather than just a secondary reflection of primary experience. Factography was, in Chuzhak's famous formulation, a "literature of life-construction" (*литература жизнестроения*).

New technologies underwrote factography as both content and technique. At the same time that the industrialization campaigns of the 1920s provided novel subject matter for Tret'iakov and his colleagues, who documented colossal enterprises such as the construction of the Dnieper dam, the agricultural collectivization of the countryside, and the development of Russia's railway infrastructure (to list just a few sites of their engagement), this emerging technical civilization also equipped the factographers with instruments for rationalizing and mechanizing art. They brought cameras, block notebooks, and stopwatches on their journeys to factories and collective farms. They examined the world through optical lenses, wrote in the managerial idiom of the bureaucratic enterprise, and formulated their conclusions in technical charts and diagrams. In the visual arts they replaced easelism with photography, and in prose they endorsed stenography over storytelling. One critic aptly called the factographers "Spenglerians in reverse" because they enthused about all the industrial machines that cultural traditionalists so despised.[33] "Lef wants to be on the front line of contemporary construction," Pertsov confirmed: "It directs the graphic skills of the artist toward the powerful means of the latest technical machine and apparatus for recording."[34]

The impulse to document has always flourished at moments of crisis when the telos of history becomes remote and the logic of lived experience inscrutable. In France the surveys of the Missions Héliographiques photographed the decaying monuments of a nation undergoing modernization in the 1850s; the Mass Observationists in England established an archive of everyday life and social mores after the Abdication Crisis of 1936, when the king renounced the throne and a rift opened in the symbolic order of authority; in the United States the Farm Security Administration recorded premodern existence in the rural towns that were approaching extinction in the era of the New Deal reforms. In all of these cases, the experience of loss triggered by modernization launched projects to memorialize cultures and values perceived to be on the cusp of disappearance. Each time, the response to social upheaval was backward-looking, if not outright nostalgic. The photography and writing of Mass Observation and the FSA traffic in primitivist cliché and pastoralist fantasy. Even when nostalgia is not explicit in the work itself, the same retrospectivism is baked into the organizational architectures that shore up these projects: the thousands of diaries and questionnaires collected by Mass Observation are to this day held in deep storage in a facility called the Keep, and most of the negatives produced by the Missions Héliographiques were immediately filed away, never to be printed or viewed. Imagining an indeterminate moment in the future when the records of all that was lost would once again be of interest to historians, melancholic projects like these sought to preserve the soon-to-be past for a yet-to-come generation. In the introduction to his 1924 autobiography, one working-class writer in Germany dreamt of a time when all of the documents of his own era, still tentative and shapeless at the present moment, might finally make sense:

> Our historical turning point will take on a significance in the cultural history of humanity similar to the great upheavals in the ages of invention and discovery, of the Renaissance and the Reformation, and of the French Revolution. And in the same way that people have searched carefully each time for sources that might explain the causes and circumstances of these great upheavals, so too in the near future we will place special value on everything that helps to illuminate the becoming and the essence [*das Werden und Wesen*] of our own pivotal moment, everything that conveys accurate information about the labors and sufferings, the hopes and desires of our generation. . . . Right at this moment we are seeing an abundant variety of memory-works emerging from conscious and unconscious feelings.[35]

For proletarian writers like this one, what actually took place in the traumatic years after World War I could be reconstructed with certainty only at a later date, by a reader situated outside the tumultuous events of the present. For similar reasons, interwar critics and journalists like Erich Auerbach and Egon Erwin Kisch argued that the prototype for the modern reporter was Dante Alighieri, the medieval poet who had traveled to the *Futurum* of the afterlife in order to dispel the fog that veiled his own chaotic present. Only from a vantage at the end of time could the divine logic of history and the truth of the poet's own moment finally be revealed.[36] Clarity was a gift of hindsight.

Herein lies another crucial difference between European documentary and Soviet factography, which turned emphatically and uncompromisingly toward its own present moment. Factography found its home in the journalistic ephemera of daily press, not the deep storage of the archive. According to the second-generation factographer Boris Agapov, their movement had been a response to Lenin's injunction to compose "a history of the contemporary," one that was written for coevals, not a future generation.[37] The factographers didn't care if nothing remained of their work for posterity. They joined in the Futurist assault on the past, but unlike their forward-looking comrades, the factographers renounced the future as well. They disdained arcadias and utopias alike. Already in 1924 Tret'iakov had been identified as the leader of a "presentist" deviation within Lef that foregrounded the "momentary" and refused to look "beyond the confines of the present."[38] Films made in the factographic mode would be assessed similarly: "Neither the past nor the future is accessible to Vertov."[39] As a rule, the Soviet enthusiasts of fact always focused on the slim and elusive interval of the Now.

This disregard for the future put the factographers at odds with the growing appetite for planning and prognosticating that followed the launch of the first Five-Year Plan in 1928. As paradoxical as this position might seem, the factographers believed that any effort to organize the future actively thwarted its arrival. In hastily telescoping history forward, socialist planners would fail to discern random mutations in their own present moment, those embryonic forms of communism that were arising spontaneously and unbidden in transitional society. Following a ready-made blueprint reduced the future to an extension of the present, inhibited the emergence of those unforeseeable phenomena that exceed the imagination of the current generation, and ultimately precluded the novelty that is essential to all genuine political and cultural transformation. For this reason, Marx is alleged to have remarked that "whoever draws up a program for the future is a reactionary."[40] The syndicalist Georges Sorel thus cautioned revolutionaries against the temptations of premeditation, since "there is no process by which the future can be predicted scientifically, nor even one which enables us to discuss whether one hypothesis about it is better than another; innumerable memorable examples have shown that the greatest men have committed prodigious errors in thus desiring to make predictions about even the least distant futures."[41] As we will see, the factographers likewise considered visions of the future just as hostile to the advancement of communism as attachments to the past. They believed that cultural revolutionaries must pledge themselves to a future that is beyond the ken of the present, one that is fundamentally other, alien, and unknowable.

The commitment to a present that was uncoupled from both the past and the future suffused all aspects of factography, down to its formal devices. The basic technique of documentation takes discontinuity to be a foundational structural principle of the work. As Michel Foucault and other postwar philosopher-historians explained, the document invokes a different temporality than the monument, a locus of cultural memory whose steady, resting existence presumes the stability of collective experience and knowledge over time.[42] Documents, by contrast, are discrete, mobile, and can be rearranged from one moment to the next depending on shifting needs and contingencies. De Certeau consequently described documentary collections as a "'gigantic machine' that will make an entirely different history possible."[43] Practices of writing that utilize documents such as factography perturb the older models of historiography that view time as an "aprioristic schema" striving toward closure and finality.[44] "The documentary revolution . . . tends to promote a new unit of information. Instead of the fact that leads to the event and to a linear history, to a progressive memory, the privileged position passes to the datum, which leads to a series and a discontinuous history."[45] Along these lines, the Weimar journalist Erik Reger characterized reportage as a "vivisection of time," a method that cuts into the flow of events and extracts moments that are still warm and alive, still pulsing with the blood of the present.[46] The factographers used nonlinear montage in their work to arrest the forward thrust of history and make room for a revolutionary process whose final outcome could change at any moment. In contrast to the monumental arts of Socialist Realism, whose chiliastic fantasy of real existing socialism looked forward to the end of history, factographic documentation embraced the conditions of a transitional society whose laws were provisional and whose developmental trajectory shifted from one day to the next. Time appeared to the factographers not as a continuous line but as a constellation of points, an array of individual moments each of which opened logically onto a different future. Transitional society inaugurates a temporality without diachrony and a history without a theory of stages, writes Étienne Balibar. Its motto: "Against evolutionism, for the revolutionary dialectic."[47] In the words of one contemporary, the factographers believed that "the development of life comes to a standstill, that history under socialism stops its movement forward."[48] They inhabited a world of unfinished instants, one devoid of accumulation or momentum in which history could still veer at any moment in an unanticipated direction.

The factographers focused their work on the present, but they quickly discovered that current events resist capture, analysis, and conceptualization. Unlike the past and the future, two dimensions of experience that are clearly contoured in the mind as recollection and anticipation, the present remains inaccessible to perception, not to speak of higher thought. Shklovsky characterized consciousness as a blind monad cut off from events around it: "We live in a poor and enclosed world. We do not feel the world in which we live, just as we do not feel the clothes we wear. We fly through the world as Jules Verne's heroes fly 'through the atmosphere in a cannonball.' But our cannonball has no windows."[49] For Shklovsky and other structuralists, the gap between the sensible and the intelligible condemned us to encounter the world only elliptically, through its symbolic translations. It is as if "by some statutory exclusion, what is alive cannot signify," wrote Roland Barthes.[50] But the factographers would not abide the structuralist exclusion of the living or the reduction of reality to an effect. Proclaiming that "the present must be alive" (*настоящее живым*), Tret'iakov sought to breach the enclosure around the mind and awaken consciousness to a revolutionary history that was unfolding at a speed that was both exhilarating and profoundly disorienting.[51]

Doing this required new protocols of inquiry and structures of knowledge that were more dynamic and responsive to current events than the categorical reasoning of Enlightenment philosophy. More than just a conduit for information, factography constituted its own particular mode of thought, a unique method for synthesizing experience in the present. As Peter Sloterdijk observed, practices of life-writing in the 1920s thrived "wherever a gap arose between an experience and the end result, between learning and the lesson."[52] From the moment of its emergence, the factographic movement was indeed driven by an incessant desire to span the chasm between event and understanding. It was an "epistephilic" form:[53] Tret'iakov professed a "longing for knowledge" and a "colossal thirst to know everything";[54] Agapov characterized the ocherk as a "means of humanity's self-knowledge," just as Osip Brik wrote of the "cognitive orientation" of factography;[55] even Maxim Gorky, hardly a fan of the factographers, had to concede that the ocherk was "the most successful form for the cognition of life."[56] During the historical hiatus of transitional society, when the tsarist past had been razed and the communist future had not yet been established, the factographers seized hold of current events "in flagrante," as Tret'iakov put it, and tried to fashion these experiences into usable, if highly tentative, pivots of thought.[57]

The daily newspaper provided a platform for this presentist system of knowledge. Tret'iakov stated that he could not work, or even think, without the newspaper.[58] The daily press followed a principle of rigorous periodicity, bracketing off what came before from what came next and focusing the full scope of the reader's attention on the immediate moment at hand. Twice a day, at twelve-hour intervals, it erased the past and refreshed consciousness. European philosophers consequently associated journalism with "a time marked by the crisis of the philosophy of history" and understood the newspaper, in turn, as "a place where all teleological and totalizing representations of history are destined to founder, together with the conceptions of progress and development that sustain them." With each new edition, the newspaper announces "a transition that never quite comes to a conclusion."[59] The disavowal of universal history and the synchronization of consciousness to the rhythmic beat of the present was especially pronounced in the early Soviet press, which advised correspondents to avoid the longer news "stories" typical of American journalism and instead submit terse telegraphic dispatches.[60] Lenin called for newspapers to publish hundreds of tiny, punctual facts instead of a dozen well-developed articles.[61] In this respect, Soviet journalism pursued a prose of discrete data: correspondents resisted speculating about the causes of events and refrained from longer narrative syntagma with a beginning, middle, and end; editors in turn used montage methods to arrange these disparate facts into a nonlinear mosaic of events. Shklovsky explained that the journalist, "thinking logically, ignores genesis [*не считается с генезисом*], compares 'distant things,' and picks out individual facts through reconnaissance."[62] The facts of the day were presented not in their continuity with previous events, but in the constellation of forces that prevailed at the current moment. The result was a strikingly anti-genetic, even ahistorical view of the news.

The proximity of sign and thing in factography presumed a world transparent to thought. Using photography, stenography, and other mechanical techniques that converted the stuff of material reality directly into symbolic language, the factographers retired the hoary philosophical dualism of semblance and essence, and with it, the psychotechnical distinction between perception and consciousness. Their romance with experimental instruments, their skepticism toward interpretive commentary, and their faith in immediate sensory experience caused the factographers to be denounced as a "pitiful mongrel of positivism."[63] In both Russia and Europe, the movement was routinely attacked as a cultural expression of Machism, the strain of scientific positivism named after the Viennese physicist Ernst Mach that Lenin had ruthlessly pilloried with *Materialism and Empirio-criticism*.[64] So many practices and theories were branded as "Machist" in the 1920s that the term is largely meaningless, but in the case of factography the epithet had purchase: like Mach, who held that even the most abstract concept or ideological system was just an elaborate assembly of physical sensations, and who advocated the method of empirio-criticism for breaking down these psychic compounds into their constituent units of experience, the factographers believed that all mental phenomena were built out of observable facts. Following the Russian Machist Alexander Bogdanov, whose thought they had assimilated during their years working in Proletkul't in the early 1920s, the factographers maintained that thought and matter differed from one another only in their organizational structure and degree of patterning. Machist principles were rehearsed constantly in the writings of Tret'iakov, Arvatov, and other members of Lef who embraced Bogdanov's Universal Organizational Science as a means to overcome the legacy of bourgeois dualism.[65] For these Soviet monists, who asserted "the equivalence between everyday existence and consciousness, between object and subject," the mind would enjoy no special privilege over empirical experience.[66]

While some contemporaries conceded that Lef's positivism was at least "progressive in its struggle against metaphysics," most felt that the factographers had taken this program too far, abandoning critical reflection and even consciousness itself.[67] Rival writer Aleksandr Fadeev noted that the "'precise recording of facts' . . . rejects all forms of philosophy."[68] In response to these accusations, the factographers pointed out that abstract principles and categorical reasoning were hardly reliable guides in the historically singular context of transitional society. Instead they followed industrial monists like Gastev, whose *Uprising of Culture* from 1923 proclaimed: "In order to kill all 'philosophical' tendencies, we have to teach people to be empiricists with a limited scope, but the most important thing is to firmly and microscopically fix all observations with precision."[69] There was no place for vagueness, generality, and speculation in the 1920s, once the revolution had entered the phase that Lenin famously designated a "concrete situation." Luminaries in the new field of newspaper studies (*газетоведение*) celebrated the positivist rigor of journalism as a welcome relief from the universalist pretensions of Idealism. "The daily press has the exact opposite tasks of philosophy," wrote Iakov Shafir. "It deals only with material that is transitory, quotidian, and if possible, based entirely in sensation."[70] Embracing the anti-philosophy of the newspaper, the factographers pursued thinking that was evidential rather than axiomatic, and bottom-up rather than top-down.

This explains why, after an initial outburst of programmatic statements, Tret'iakov's theoretical output dropped off precipitously at the height of factography's influence in 1929. Right at the moment that the movement reached its apogee, its most articulate champion suddenly had nothing to say about it.[71] This was not because the factographer stopped writing, of course, but because Tret'iakov stopped writing about writing. He renounced the conceit of any discourse that, like philosophy, would claim to speak about and above other discourses. "The concrete analysis of the concrete situation is not an opposite of 'pure' theory, but—on the contrary—it is the culmination of genuine theory, its consummation—the point where it breaks into practice," Lukács wrote about Lenin's thought in 1924.[72] Analyzing the "concrete situation" demanded factual data and specific cases taken from existing circumstances, not philosophical prattle about truth and essence. Inverting Hegel's Idealist dictum "all the worse for the facts," Shklovsky quipped in *Novyi Lef* that "if facts destroy theory, then all the better for theory."[73] For Shklovsky and Tret'iakov, facts were valuable precisely because they pushed back against the overweening subjectivism—and ultimately, the tedious predictability—of bourgeois philosophers. Indeed, ever since the word "fact" first took on its modern meaning in the sixteenth century, it had thwarted abstract categorization and mocked forecasting. "Facts were angular, even truculent entities, sturdily resisting all attempts to ignore them or bend them to fit the Procrustean bed of theory," writes Lorraine Daston about the early usages of the term.[74] Lenin put it succinctly: "Facts are an obstinate thing."[75]

Belief in the fidelity of facts and in the reliability of empirical sensation made factography a target of the major schools of critical thought in the twentieth century. Structural linguistics dismissed the premise of direct correspondence between sign and thing as semiotically primitive, and Marxist ideological criticism ridiculed the presumption that appearance (*Wesen*) corresponded to essence (*Erscheinung*). In response, the factographers argued that skeptics like these were the actual dupes, since the underlying belief that truth was lurking somewhere behind the surface of reality was itself the oldest ruse of metaphysics. Even Lenin, despite his fierce polemics against empirio-criticism before the revolution, came to embrace positivist methods after 1917, when he placed an embargo on theory and enjoined cultural producers to document and study the individual features of the concrete situation that they had entered. What transitional society needed was not philosophical conjecture but vigilant observation and careful, inductive experimentation.

While *Soviet Factography* thus defends the legitimacy, and even necessity, of positivist methods in transitional Russia, it nonetheless acknowledges that the same strategies lead to a reactionary aesthetics of pseudo-realism in non-revolutionary contexts. Outside of the conjunctural alignment, reality is not spontaneously intelligible, as the factographers claimed. Tret'iakov's reception in Weimar Germany turns out to be highly instructive on this point. Although scholars today like to recall the German intelligentsia's enthusiastic response to Tret'iakov's 1931 book tour, many of the most insightful reactions were actually quite disparaging.[76] The factographer was rebuked not only by right-wing authors like Gottfried Benn but also by committed communists like Johannes Becher. Only Walter Benjamin, a thinker himself inclined to "the wide-eyed presentation of mere facts," would manage a meaningful defense of Tret'iakov's program, and even then only very belatedly.[77] Most of the criticisms in 1931 objected to the factographer's claim to have directly connected life and literature without the mediation of aesthetic form, effectively eradicating art. Tret'iakov's faith in the spontaneous transparency of the world to consciousness struck many Europeans as either naïve in its literalism or irrelevant in its sheer redundancy. To them, the proposal to record reality without symbolic translation—not to speak of aesthetic transfiguration—was a project doomed just to replicate the status quo. For those living in the capitalist West, the human senses were not epistemologically reliable, nor could phenomenalism become a basis for revolutionary science. Against Tret'iakov, German Leftists thus insisted on the continued need for critical methods to decrypt the truths behind the world of appearances and for artistic devices to give these truths concrete sensuous form.

Both sides were right. The German reception of Tret'iakov offers a concise lesson in the dialectic of cultural forms, reminding us that the same strategies that are progressive in one historical context might prove to be reactionary in another. This was the verdict of Siegfried Kracauer, who wrote three penetrating reviews after Tret'iakov's visit that voiced admiration for the project of collectivizing art in Soviet Russia, but nonetheless concluded that factography finds "no immediate application in our conditions because of course we don't find ourselves in the stage of socialist construction."[78] As Kracauer saw it, European writers and artists of the Left were still in the business of semiotic disruption and perceptual estrangement, not life-construction and state-building. As such, they still needed the distance that was afforded by aesthetic autonomy. "The entire lecture showed one thing," Kracauer wrote: "just how specific current developments in Russia are to their national conditions."[79] Kracauer's assessment would soon be confirmed by the development of European documentary, a practice whose positivistic pretense to show life "as it is" gave rise in the 1930s to some of the most beguiling and tenacious reality effects of twentieth-century art. Worse still, outside of the context of revolutionary transition, the fusion of sign and deed gave rise to a totalitarian mentality in which the act of naming became indistinguishable from the act of judging. The journalism of wartime Europe created a "realism of the order of presence" that led to a "collapse of language and reality" and blurred "facticity and legitimacy." The result was a condition in which "what counts as real is the 'fait accompli,' the 'positive fact,' the 'objective situation'—which is, in the political as in every other respect, also a situation brought about by force."[80] Indeed, one review of Chuzhak's 1929 anthology *The Literature of Fact* presciently warned against the positivism of the sign that was beginning to take hold in the West: surveying the latest trends in European literature, this critic expressed concern that all of the domestic "clamor around 'factography,' 'factograms,' 'documentary sketches' and so on" had mutated abroad into "clearly pronounced fascist tendencies."[81] Outside of the concrete situation of Soviet Russia, factography lapsed into myth, transformed from materialism into "metaphysics," Kracauer wrote.[82]

In sum, the techniques pioneered by Tret'iakov cannot simply be transposed into other contexts, for the efficacy of factographic work presumes specific geopolitical conditions and, equally, a specific historical conjuncture. Positivism may prove to be progressive at revolutionary moments, but it is instead reflection and critique that are needed in phases of political stagnation, when consciousness is out of phase with historical events and when reality must be refracted through the prism of art and theory in order to be understood. As Maurice Merleau-Ponty observed about the European Left during the interwar period: "They had to learn the slowness of mediations."[83] This is why, despite formal resemblances, Western documentary was largely a matter of regressive ontologizing while Soviet factography was not. Tret'iakov's mixed reception in Germany also delivers an important caveat about the viability of factographic methods today, for our own moment is not one of spontaneous truths but of oblique logics, when reality cannot be perceived directly but must instead be approximated asymptotically. Ours is once again an era of mediated connections and attenuated causalities, a theoretical moment. Despite superficial resemblances between these two societies of the spectacle, one revolutionary and one capitalist, we must thus resist the temptation to conflate them. The "broad present" of the digital media has a different material basis than the revolutionary presentism of transitional society;[84] the dismantling of objectivity and authority in the mass correspondence movement of the Cultural Revolution cannot be compared to the pseudo-populist post-truthism that proliferates on the internet today; and the psychotechnical methods of the factographers, who always insisted on the social origins of physical reflexes, must be distinguished from the strains of affect theory and empirical neuroaesthetics that now seek to naturalize structures of perception and somatic responses as universal anthropological givens. Readers seeking a general theory of factography will therefore be disappointed by this book, for while *Soviet Factography* does not eschew theoretical analysis, it does assume that any study of factography must in the end be bounded historically. If there is one thing that the work of artists and filmmakers like Kevin Jerome Everson, Allan Sekula, Hito Steyerl, and Harun Farocki forcefully demonstrates, it is that engaging with reality today requires methods that are more refined and devices that are more elliptical than those of Soviet factography. Now is not a time to expel the poets.

One aspect of Tret'iakov's platform that was enthusiastically welcomed by Kracauer, however, was the operative goal to "transform matter in the process of presenting it."[85] In contrast to European reporters who hid behind the pretense of journalistic neutrality, the factographers readily acknowledged that every newspaper article had concrete repercussions and that every act of reporting was also a vector of force.[86] "For us factists there is no such thing as a fact 'as such.' There is the fact-as-effect and the fact-as-defect . . . the fact-as-friend and the fact-as-enemy" ("To Be Continued," 56). Tret'iakov explained to his German audiences that the bourgeois public sphere's conceit of objectivity exists only "within the boundaries of a basic position that is itself established by class." Writing without concern for its impact belongs to "a position that is allegedly beyond class, but one that in reality is all too favorable to the existing social order, i.e., a position that is ultimately that of the bourgeoisie."[87] Rejecting European journalism's policy of noninvolvement and its pathos of indifference, Tret'iakov foregrounded the ethical dimensions of his practice and emphasized the close, existential bond he had with his subjects. Operative writers like him refused to stand on the sidelines watching events unfold "like tourists," he insisted.[88] Thus, when Alfred H. Barr Jr. met up with Tret'iakov in Moscow in 1927 and asked, "How soon will it be possible to write objectively of the revolution?," he received a blunt reply: "Objectivity is bad."[89] For the factographer, the very premise of Barr's question was flawed since it presupposed an axiomatically neutral space of communication and the possibility of detached contemplation outside the crucible of history. Tret'iakov believed it was better to risk the dangers of theoretical relativism and political ad hocism than to cling to a nondialectical metaphysics of truth.[90] As Bogdanov had explained, "Marxism entails the rejection of the absolute objectivity of any truth whatsoever, the rejection of any eternal truths."[91]

In renouncing objectivity, the factographers also undermined the very premise of any aesthetics of representationalism (*отображательство*), reflectionism (*отражательство*), or pictorialism (*изображательство*)—in sum, any art that might purport to depict the world faithfully and accurately. Scholars today often situate factography as a transitional practice between the experimental avant-garde of the early 1920s and the Socialist Realism of the 1930s, but this narrative is contradicted by the factographers themselves, who insisted in essay after essay that their work was fundamentally incompatible with all realist art, no matter how radical its content.[92] For Chuzhak, an artwork that depicts revolutionary themes will always remain "a gun that doesn't shoot" because it substitutes an image of the world for actual, direct engagement with life.[93] In his first survey of factography from 1928, Chuzhak thus insisted that their own practice must be distinguished from the great forms of nineteenth-century literature and art that aspired to portray reality, which he derided as "naive and lying verisimilitude" ("Literatura zhiznestroeniia," 38). This categorical rejection of representation would lead to frequent skirmishes with RAPP and the Association of Artists of Revolutionary Russia (AKhRR), two rival groups that were seeking to revive the mimetic strategies of the previous century under the banner of "proletarian realism." With respect to device and technique, the factographers are actually more closely related to the German dadaists who celebrated the positivistic chaos of "naked facts" or the French Documents group who renounced the poetics of resemblance and proclaimed a "tyranny of the particular"—even if the factographers' incorruptible faith in rationalism set them apart from these two movements ideologically.[94] The disdain for objectivist depiction also explains why so many signal works of the factographers, from Tret'iakov's *Den Shi-Khua* to Vertov's *Man with a Movie Camera*, flaunt their madeness, as Formalists would say, and exhibit a degree of self-reflexivity unknown in the documentary of the West until the 1960s. During the reconstruction period, when the process of industrialization seemed to be transforming all aspects of the lifeworld, the very idea that a work of art might aspire to be spontaneous, natural, or unprocessed struck the factographers as risible. The technical explosion of the 1920s had returned the discourse of facticity to the "sphere of non-originarity and making" and restored the etymological root of "fact" in the Latin *facere*, "to make" or "to do."[95] They were living in a "factory of facts," as Vertov put it.

Tret'iakov grew impatient with artists and critics who debated endlessly about whether the content or the form of an artwork was more important, since, to him, this distinction just rehashed the age-old dualism of mind and matter. Neither the what (*что*) nor the how (*как*) of a work was as important as the why (*зачем*), which was "the link that transforms an 'artwork' into an 'thing,' i.e., into an instrument of expedient effect."[96] As rigorous positivists, the factographers believed that the empirical parameters and effects of all art-things could be measured and quantified using laboratory instruments. Every psychological feature of a film or a text, no matter how subjective or seemingly immaterial, had a corresponding physiological value. Metaphysicians of art were wrong to claim that "psychic exertion is not extensional—that it has no volume, no weight, etc."[97] Everything, thought and emotion included, had a tangible magnitude and force that could be determined with chronometers, plethysmographs, and other instruments. The results of these scientific assays were uncompromisingly materialist but also bewilderingly literal: instead of reconstructing the artwork's meaning, the factographers recorded variations in the pulse rate of the spectator; instead of analyzing the style of a sketch, they diagrammed the patterns of reflexes that it provoked; instead of exploring the symbolism of a story, they gauged its speed and velocity.

Of the many empirical dimensions of art, one was the master metric of all factographic work: time. Inspired by the program for cultural rationalization proposed by the League of Time, Tret'iakov was determined to calibrate art and literature with absolute chronometric precision, since, as he reasoned, making operative work meant intervening in history and intervening in history, in turn, requires punctuality. Operativity demands not just political commitment and media savvy but actuality and speed. As the philosopher of the conjuncture Louis Althusser once noted, the most impactful materialist thinkers—the ones who succeed in bringing the mind into contact with the world—are not the ones who have worked out the right doctrines but the ones who are alert and agile enough to hoist themselves onto the locomotive of history as it flies past.[98] For Althusser, correct thinking demands good timing. Artmaking too requires *kairos*, a sense for the opportune moment. No matter how radical an artist's commitments, she will miss the opportunity to engage with current events if her reflexes are off. For the factographers, sluggish, unwieldy genres like easel painting and the novel were disqualified because they take too long to produce and, as a consequence, suffer from a structural belatedness (*отставание*). They rejected fiction less because it was untrue than because it was simply too slow and always missed its deadline. They likewise objected to the use of figures in art and tropes in literature not because they were false per se, but because imagery and metaphor ensnared the viewer or reader in a tangle of mental associations, inhibiting his physical reactions and causing him to fall out of sync with current events. Fiction and figuration are inoperative by nature.

By contrast, prompt facts cut through the web of connotation and connect the mind directly with the present. But this timeliness came with an expiration date. The lifespan of the snapshots and sketches that were made by the factographers could be measured in mere hours. Nothing endured of this writing, not just because the constellation of facts changed from one day to the next, or because it was often printed on cheap paper stock that disintegrated with exposure to light and air, but also, as this book demonstrates, because every aspect of its language, from its syntax and its rhetoric to its lexicon, was engineered for the shortest possible life. But, as theorists of the newspaper argued, the ephemerality of factical language was not a defect but a source of unmatched phenomenological intensity. The renowned organizer, activist, and editor Platon Kerzhentsev wrote that "although the newspaper lives only for a single day—more precisely: for several hours in total—and although the lines of the newspaper are read just once never to be reread again, there is not a single printed word that could act more powerfully upon the reader than the material of the newspaper."[99] Reflecting on the evanescence of their work, Pertsov compared the psychic structure of factography to that of the joke, a speech genre that exists only for the brief instant in which it triggers an explosive convulsion of laughter, after which it fades quickly from consciousness. Jokes never have the same impact the second time around. According to Pertsov, factographic art aspired to a similar degree of volatility and force, for "there is nothing more contemporary and coercive."[100] The evaporative writing of the factographers disappeared quickly, but for the brief moment of its existence, it was omnipotent.

Facts are transient, labile phenomena. The typographer Ilia Zdanevich pointed this out (literally) in his cover for Igor' Terent'ev's booklet *Fact*, where two printer's manicules invade from the margins and set the letters aflight, causing the title to quiver and evanesce. The hands dislodge the *Ф* to reveal the fleeting *акт* that lies behind every *Факт* (fig. 0.1). Zdanevich's cover reminds us that facts are related not just to paper documents (the Russian word *akt* also means certificate) but also to transitory events like feats and deeds. "In Latin and the major European vernaculars the word 'fact' and its cognates derives from the verb 'to do' or 'to make,' and originally referred to a deed or action, especially one remarkable for either valor or malevolence: *facere/factum*, *faire/fait*, *fare/fatto*, *tun/Tatsachen*."[101] Facts are contingent and fleeting, and for this reason must be distinguished from generalities and laws. One essay in the 1931 anthology *Studies in the Nature of Facts* accordingly defined facts as "concrete events" and as "charactered and related occurrences" that must be strictly distinguished from philosophical truths.[102] Whereas the latter reflect laws that are permanent and eternal, facts are short lived and often accidental. There are no facts in general or for all time.

The Bolshevik Revolution had inaugurated an era of facts, a historical period full of feats and actions that eluded attempts at forecasting. Indeed, October 1917 was itself an event that was never supposed to happen. If there was one takeaway from the success of a proletarian revolution in an underdeveloped agricultural nation with virtually no industrial working class—and, conversely, from the historico-philosophical truancy of this revolution in the European nations where Hegelian Marxists had predicted its success—it was the lesson that facts do not adhere to a foreseeable logical scheme. Daston points out that the word "fact" was first used to designate marvelous phenomena such as prodigies and miracles, and then, with Enlightenment secularization, came to apply to surprising anomalies, exceptions, and errors.[103] The fact of the Bolshevik Revolution likewise took everyone by surprise, its own instigators above all. Lenin often described the revolution as a "miracle" (*чудес*), although he rejected the theological resonances of this word. "There are no miracles in nature or history, but every abrupt turn in history, and this applies to every revolution, presents such a wealth of content, unfolds such unexpected and specific combinations of forms of struggle and alignment of forces of the contestants, that to the lay mind there is much that must appear miraculous."[104] This world-

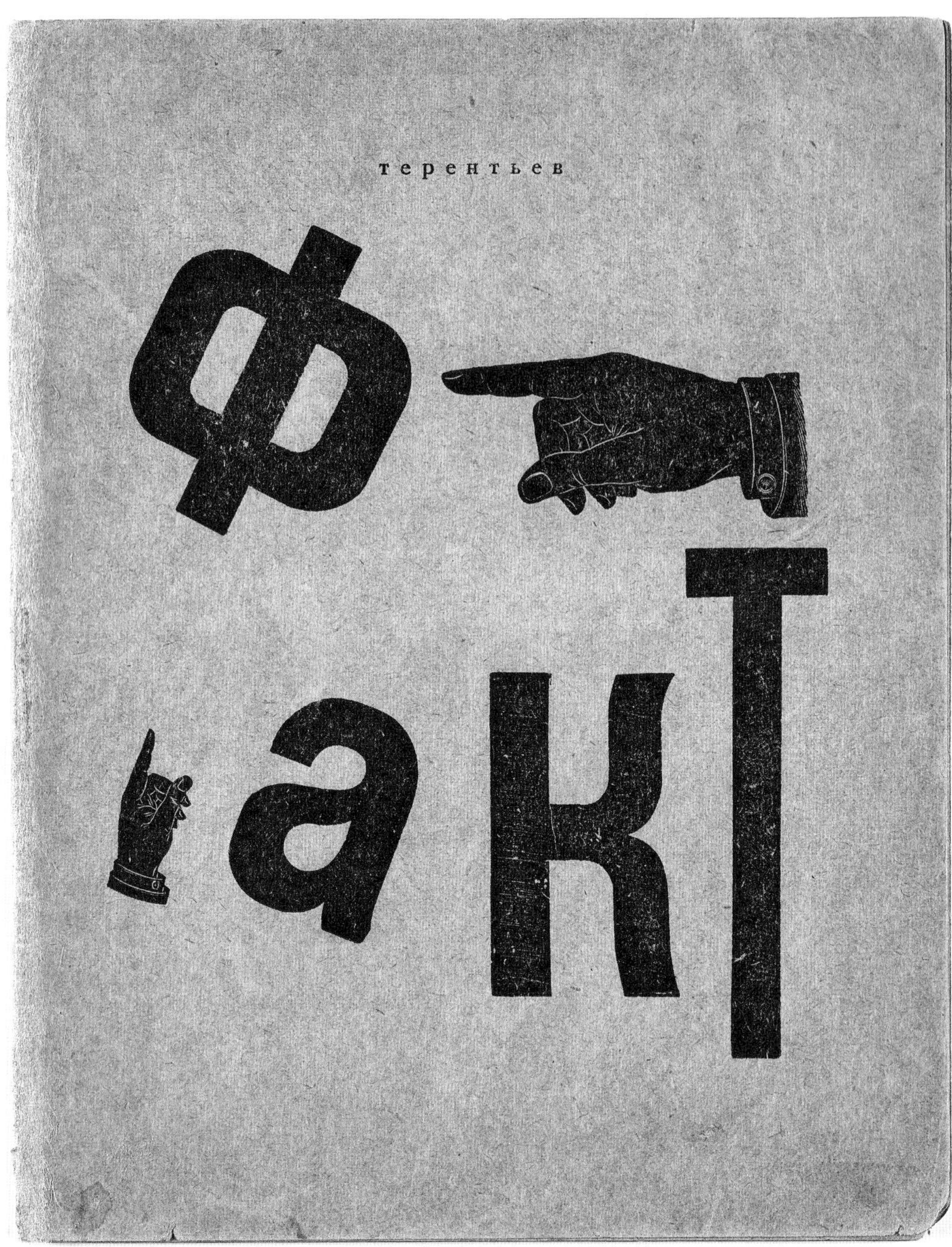

0.1 Ilia Zdanevich, cover for Igor' Terent'ev, *Fakt* (1919). Getty Research Institute, Los Angeles (88-B29294).

historical accident, which exceeded the foresight even of professional Party strategists, suddenly put the Bolsheviks at the helm of a revolutionary engine whose controls were obscure and whose destination was unknown.

Althusser situated Lenin's conception of the miracle within a lineage of materialist thought that reached back to Epicurus, the ancient philosopher who had claimed that the universe began with the random, unforeseen swerve of an atom.[105] According to Epicurus, prior to this deviation, there was just a vertical cascade of particles that never came into contact with each other. It was only when, through some transcendental contingency, a single atom drifted infinitesimally from this downward trajectory and collided with its neighbor that atoms interlocked and began to pile up, causing matter to accumulate irreversibly. For thinkers like Lenin and Marx (who wrote his 1841 dissertation on Epicurus), this model from ancient physics described the structure of history as well, in particular the mechanism by which the new comes into the world. At the origin of every miraculous fact-event is an accident, a clinamen that breaks with the sequence of mechanical causality and the deterministic schemes of formal logic. Marx quoted Lucretius, who insisted that a moment of deviation is necessary "so as to originate some new movement that will snap the bonds of fate, the everlasting sequence of cause and effect."[106] Political swerves such as revolutions interrupt the teleological connection of past to future, inserting an interval of freedom into the inexorable chain of necessity. Althusser subsequently observed that *fortuna* turns out to be "the pre-Marxian concept that comes closest to what Lenin calls the encounter of the objective and subjective conditions of any practice whatsoever" (*Philosophy of the Encounter*, xl). At this moment of chance contact between subjective and objective conditions, when mind and reality fall into fleeting alignment, it becomes possible to breach the closed sequence of destiny. With the swerve of the fact—what Lenin called the "abrupt turn in history"—fortune suspends the law of fate and pushes history in a different direction.

Tret'iakov and his cohort embraced the contingency of facts. They cherished irruptions of error, whether the random noise that crops up in photographic snapshots or the unnecessary detail that defies narrative motivation. Tret'iakov called on his contemporaries to be more forgiving of failures (*неудачи*), the experimental swerves that did not take.[107] Unlike the ideologues of the Plan, he assumed that the transition to communism would demand extravagant expenditure and waste, and that only an art that was open to accident could bring about the new reality. Shklovsky pointed out that every great cultural and scientific invention had come about as the result of error.[108] He echoed Andrei Shingarev, a minister in the Provisional Government where he once served, who wrote that "the best science is our own mistakes."[109] Indeed, it would seem that the practice of factography was ultimately distinguished not by any particular aesthetic device or ideological message but by its capacity to sensitize the reader or viewer to the experience of change and to open her mind to the dividends of errancy. For all the depictions of industrial factories, collective farms, and other spectacular innovations of the reconstruction period, the real content of factography turns out to be novelty itself, historical difference as such. Tret'iakov and his circle referenced contemporary research in newspaper studies that claimed anomaly and surprise to be the characteristic features of journalistic discourse and which accordingly defined the modern information unit as a "degree of non-recurrence" (*неповторимое качество*) within a finite series. Anticipating developments in the information aesthetics of the postwar period, the factographers elaborated this insight into a full-blown probabilistics of art.[110] This celebration of contingency and chance operations would align the factographers with the French Surrealists, although the two movements differed in one crucial regard: whereas the Surrealists used accident to expose the irrational core of modern life, the factographers mobilized chance procedures for the controlled randomization of revolutionary culture. Anything but anarchic, their method was inspired by the heuristics of the scientific experiment, a "difference machine" that courts error in order to produce "knowledge that lies beyond what one has been able to imagine and anticipate at a particular point in time."[111] For the factographers, unlike the Surrealists, contingency was entirely compatible with rationalization.

At the height of factography's influence in 1928, the critic Il'ia Dukor wrote that Tret'iakov "deliberately refuses to 'wager on eternity.'"[112] His phrase invoked Pascal's wager, the famous proof by which the seventeenth-century mathematician and theologian claimed to demonstrate the soundness of belief in God. According to the decision matrix that Pascal laid out in his proof, the person who denies the existence of God might gain finite pleasure (comforts in this world) but risks infinite loss (eternal damnation), while the man of faith sacrifices finite pleasure but wins in exchange the possibility of infinite gratification. Pascal concluded that any rational agent who was motivated by "maximum expectation" would naturally choose the unlimited pleasures of the afterlife.[113] But as Dukor observed, Tret'iakov refused to place his bet on eternity in this way. The materialist factographer was oriented not toward the afterlife but toward the Now. Instead of accepting the chiliastic visions of a communist future that were being peddled by the proletarian realists, he wagered on his own contingent and flawed present, and instead of subscribing to a Plan with a foreseeable path, he courted risk. "What we need instead of solitaire [*пасьянс*] is a fierce game of chance," Tret'iakov declared ("To Be Continued," 55).[114] According to his admirer Benjamin, the true political revolutionary is not a planner but a gambler who plays the odds.[115] Having lived through the First World War, the October Revolution, the Civil War, the New Economic Policy, and shock industrialization—all in just over a decade—members of the first Soviet generation like Tret'iakov knew that if there was one thing that they could count on, one thing that was entirely predictable, it was the unpredictability of history itself. Under these circumstances, the factographer did not just prepare for the possibility that tomorrow might differ from today. He banked on it.

In 1937 Tret'iakov was arrested and murdered on charges of spying for the

Japanese in order to pay off debts from gambling, of all things. But factography had already ceased to be a defining cultural practice half a decade before. Moving deeper into the first Five-Year Plan, the fierce games of chance started to abate, and by the middle of the 1930s, they were replaced entirely by rounds of solitaire. Cultural producers who had previously worked with punctual documents had to recalibrate their practice to the vast timescale of the monument and readjust to the slowness of mediations. Factography disappeared in these years, its retreat proceeding in step with the dwindling of opportunities to intervene operatively. Tret'iakov's revolutionary aleatorics, once essential to the evolution of transitional culture, had no purpose in a society whose future was entirely programmable. Nonetheless, many elements of his practice did find their way into the aesthetic programs of other, often rival movements. The 1930s are actually full of partial and incomplete appropriations of factographic devices by Gorky, RAPP, and other architects of Socialist Realism. But the strange eclecticism of these later docu-fictions only confirms that the original impulse had by then ceased to constitute an internally consistent movement and that the techniques once pioneered by Tret'iakov were now reduced to a colorful palette of reality effects. The era of factography was over and documentary was born.

Taking shorthand on a train at full speed is really a heroic task.
—LEON TROTSKY[1]

1

THE FACTS AGAINST THE IMAGE

At some point every revolution must articulate not just a new conception of history but a new relationship to mundane, empirical time. The puzzle of "chronological dislocation" is a defining feature of the transitional phase from capitalism to communism, as Étienne Balibar explains: calendars have to be updated, workweeks reorganized, clocks adjusted, and the hours of the day reapportioned. But what becomes of art and literature under the new temporal regime? Rejecting paintings, novels, and other monumental cultural forms that hoard and encumber time, the factographers turned to swift, punctual techniques of documentation that promised to rationalize and redistribute this valuable resource along more egalitarian lines. Through close readings of their practice, this chapter explains that the program to democratize time demanded a literature without figures and a photography without images. It was only through a strategy of "image-destruction" (*образоборчество*) that the factographers would succeed in synchronizing art with the revolutionary present. Pivoting from aesthetics to the philosophy of mind, the chapter concludes by asking what kind of consciousness was produced by their imageless, this-worldly art. Factographic subjectivity renounced the utopian imagination for positivistic, prompt fantasy.

HOW I BECAME A LEAGUIST

The first collection of factographic sketches by Sergei Mikhailovich Tret'iakov, "Moscow–Beijing (A Travel Film)," appeared in the final issue of *Lef* in 1925. Written on the six-thousand-mile train journey between the two capital cities, it began with a commission:

> *What Osia Said*
> "You are going to Beijing. You should write down travel notes. But they shouldn't be notes for you. No, they should have a public value. Orient yourself in accordance with NOT [the Scientific Organization of Labor] and record what you see with a keen, watchful eye. Cultivate the faculty of observation. Do not allow a single detail to slip by. You are in a train car: then kodak every detail and conversation. You are at a station: then make note of everything down to the posters that have been washed away by the rain."
>
> Understood. I will kodak. If that is what Osia says. It is hard to contradict him; he has razor-sharp logic and a sense of utility. I went to the store and bought a sturdy block notebook. This is what TsIT [the Central Institute of Labor] teaches. It also teaches that everyone must have a watch. Alas, I do not have a watch. Which is why I shamefully tricked the journal *Time* by leaving on the 14th of February when they were expecting my story by the 15th.[2]

In the text that follows, Tret'iakov obeys the instructions of this Osia scrupulously, recording every event, encounter, and thought the minute it takes place. The Soviet "Marco Polo," as Shklovsky once called Tret'iakov, jots furiously in his notebook, hoping to keep pace with the scenes that unspool as his train races eastward. The resulting collection of sketches, possibly meant as source material for a film to be made with his friend Eisenstein, makes no effort to connect these discrete episodes to one another. Each of the thirty scenes breaks with the one before it, inaugurating each time a new point of departure for his writing. Rather than compose a story with a beginning, middle, and end, Tret'iakov directs his "faculty of observation," his *nabliudatel'nost'*, toward what is immediately in front of him at any given moment, whether that be the layout of the coupé, the variety of books sold at a station kiosk, or the gestures of the customs officer at the border. Some of the people sharing Tret'iakov's itinerary resurface repeatedly across the sketches, but every time the fleeting silhouette evaporates just as quickly as it arose. There are no developed, rounded characters in "Moscow–Beijing," nor even a causal sense of before and after. There is only the experience of remainderless contemporaneity that the sociologist Georg Simmel described in "The Philosophy of Adventure" as an "unconditional presentness [*unbedingte Gegenwärtigkeit*], the quickening of the process of life to a point that possesses neither past nor future and therefore contains life within itself with an intensity that is often relatively indifferent to the content of the event."[3]

Many of the sketches in "Moscow–Beijing" are named after the stations that Tret'iakov passes on his journey, giving the collection the overall appearance of a train schedule. The resemblance is no accident. For Russians like Tret'iakov who hailed from a barely industrialized country that was famously decried for its belatedness (*отсталость*), locomotives exemplified not just mechanical force but the promise of punctuality. As historians of technology have explained, the construction of railway networks in the mid-nineteenth century was a key infrastructural determinant of the experience of contemporaneity that became central to the fabric of modern life. In order to coordinate train traffic between distant stations, railway companies had to synchronize the clocks across their lines, giving rise in 1847 to the standard Greenwich mean time to which all localities would henceforth be subordinated. The possibility of a uniform architecture of time, indeed, the very concept of a universal present that could be shared by people dispersed across space, was effectively a product of train travel. Aleksei Gastev, founder of the institute for industrial rationalization that is invoked at the beginning of "Moscow–Beijing," the Central Institute of Labor, thus concluded that the railway system was nothing other than an "enormous . . . chronometer."[4] At the end of the first sketch, Tret'iakov might lament that he doesn't own a watch, but this is of little consequence since he is in fact sitting inside a gigantic timepiece. In his particular case, the railway's promise of contemporaneity was even more extreme: one unique feature of the Trans-Siberian line that takes Tret'iakov from Moscow to Beijing is that all of the local stations operate on Moscow time, so that even the station clock in distant Chita continues to show the same time as one in the Russian capital thousands of miles to the west. Boarding the train, Tret'iakov steps into a corridor of time that cuts across vast geographical expanse, an artery of shared presence that pulses from European Moscow all the way to the Chinese border.

From the outset of "Moscow–Beijing," Tret'iakov strives to be as prompt in his writing as the locomotive that conveys him. He races to keep up with this itinerary, although he quickly learns that flesh is not as punctual as machine. After sheepishly acknowledging that he already failed to meet the deadline for *Time* (the house journal for an organization called the League of Time), Tret'iakov is constantly running late, just behind his assignations, hoping to seize on paper an ephemeral present that always threatens to elude capture. In all of its diverse instantiations, factography will fight in this way against the peril of Russian belatedness. It is always struggling to overcome the lag of consciousness, to align the time of events with the time of their inscription, and through this convergence, to achieve a condition of presence that abrogates representation as such.[5] As Tret'iakov will discover in "Moscow–Beijing," closing the gap between event and writing requires abandoning the specular system of realist prose along with honored literary devices such as figural language and plot construction. Over the course of the thirty sketches, he starts to record each encounter in an increasingly mechanical fashion, developing a quasi-journalistic practice of writing whose choppy staccato is unlike anything found in the archives of mimetic fiction.

"Moscow–Beijing" begins under the sign of belatedness, with the watchless author missing the deadline for *Time* and then struggling to keep up with an elusive Now, but by the concluding sketch Tret'iakov has at last achieved promptness in language. To accomplish this, the factographer has had to invent a way of writing that is timely and succinct, one whose paratactic brevity gives the word unprecedented velocity. His notations have accelerated over the course of the collection, becoming lighter and swifter, more compact and stenographic, so that by the end he is finally able to connect with the present. He arrives punctually in the last sketch:

> A pagoda like a grey fir tree of stone, with bells hanging at either end like sharp petals. Beijing's first wall enclosing the city in a square: so wide that gardens are arranged upon it and that six carts ride along it side-by-side easily, all serried in a square. Behind that: the tip of the Temple of Heaven's blue funnel pierces the Beijing sky, blue like the clothing of the Chinese. Behind the temple: the steel covering of the radio towers. A cylinder visible over the city: the upper stories of the enormous building Hotel de Beijing. The second wall, with gigantic six-story barracks at the corners and multi-tiered blue-and-gold towers that are intricately constructed overhead.
>
> Station. Beijing. ("Moskva–Pekin," 58)

As Tret'iakov's train pulls into the station, language comes to a standstill. The loss of epic breadth and the contraction of time is underscored by the striking lack of movement or action at the very end. Of the seventy-nine words in the last paragraph, only two are verbs. The nominalization of language is a process that has been gradually unfolding over the course of "Moscow–Beijing": the first sketches are written in the traditional preterite of the storyteller ("What Osia said"; "I fumbled about with the suitcase"; "I rode in the international car"), then the factographer gradually shifts to verbs in the present tense ("On the rack sits the German's suitcase"; "The train runs precisely and efficiently"; "A traveler bargains for boots from a shoemaker"), and by the time his train finally arrives in Beijing, the writing has been drained almost entirely of verbs. In Russian, a language that forgoes the copula *is* in the present tense, verbless constructions like these tacitly express presence and immediacy. As "Moscow–Beijing" also attests, deverbative writing robs the text of the temporal indicators conveyed by verb conjugation. Past and future, *was* and *will be*, are absorbed into the sheer facticity of present-day Beijing. Tradition and modernity coexist side by side on a single plane of occurrence, exemplified by Tret'iakov's juxtaposition of the centuries-old Temple of Heaven with the metal radio tower. With the factographer's arrival, the *before* and *after* of narrative storytelling, like the *old* and *new* of historical sequence, are replaced by a complex of nouns that are welded together into a schema of spatial relations: *at*, *above*, *upon*, *behind*, *along*. Tret'iakov's first factographic collection concludes not with an ending to the story, but with a static diagram.

"Moscow–Beijing" contains no actual photographs, but the absent medium can be felt throughout the text. As it happens, the last paragraph of the collection is an exact description of a snapshot taken from the Beijing train station, which Tret'iakov had published just a few months earlier in the illustrated journal *Searchlight* (fig. 1.1). In a canny acknowledgment of the camera's mediating function, the *Lef* version prints the two final words "Station. Beijing" in a slightly smaller font, as if captioning an illustration (fig. 1.2). In this way, Tret'iakov ends the collection by "kodaking" the scene, just as Osia had instructed. All factographic prose must indeed be read with its subtending photographic conditions in mind.[6] But this was not because the factographers aspired to write eidetically vivid, visual prose. Photography was for them not an optical medium, at least not foremost. They were instead drawn to the camera's unique capacity to bring time to a standstill, to arrest life and lift a single instant out of its organic flow. For the factographers, all photography was snapshot photog-

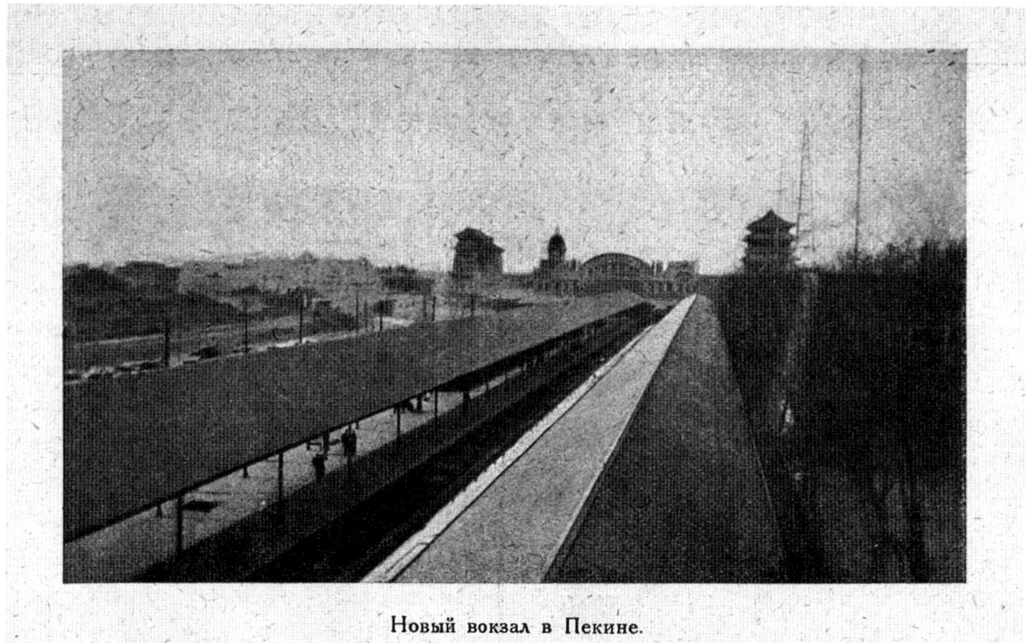

Новый вокзал в Пекине.

1.1 Photograph of the Beijing train station. From Sergei Tret'iakov, "Beijing," *Prozhektor*, no. 11 (1924): 12.

Пагода, как каменная серая елка; по концам увешанная остролепестными колокольцами. Первая пекинская стена, в квадрат охватившая город, толстая такая, что на ней разбиты сады, и шесть повозок в ряд свободно едут по ней, вся в квадратных зубцах. За нею—синяя воронка Храма Неба ткнулась своим острием в пекинское небо, синее, как одежда китайцев. За храмом—стальной переплет радио-башен. Над городом видна труба, верхние этажи громадины дома Отель де Пекин. Вторая стена с гигантскими шестиэтажными угловыми казармами и сине-золотыми многоярусными сложно-строительными надворотными башнями.

Вокзал. Пекин.

1.2 The final paragraph of Sergei Tret'iakov, "Moscow–Beijing," *Lef*, no. 7 (1925): 58.

raphy. To quote the philosopher of durée Henri Bergson, "instantaneous photography isolates any moment," "puts them all in the same rank," and thereby facilitates "the indefinite breaking up of time."[7] Snapshot photography flattens and deterritorializes events, rendering all moments in time as interchangeable equivalents. Starting with "Moscow–Beijing," Tret'iakov would strive to achieve a comparable degree of ontological thinness in all of his factographic sketches. Renouncing fluent storytelling, these static prose snapshots present discrete and discontinuous cross-sections of time, punctual instants that are devoid of all narrative momentum, mnemonic sedimentation, and psychological coloring.

"Moscow–Beijing" abounds in references to the mass organization known as the League of Time. Tret'iakov misses the deadline for the League's house journal *Time* in the first sketch, but in the following, titled "A Watch," he acquires a chronometer and declares "That is how I became a Leaguist." Similarly, the "Osia" whose directive sets the entire factographic enterprise in motion in the first paragraph is none other than Osip Brik, the fellow editor of *Lef* who had just written *The Adventures of a Leaguist*, a film scenario for a comedy about a man racing against the clock to keep up with the breakneck pace of postrevolutionary life.[8] Indeed, the debt of the factographers to the League of Time's program for cultural rationalization cannot be overstated. For a largely preindustrialized country in which everyone seemed to be out of sync—falling behind or, less often, running ahead, but in either case still missing the appointed rendezvous—the League of Time promised to usher Russia into a shared present. The Proletkul't organizer and newspaper theorist Platon Kerzhentsev had been inspired to found the League after once waiting for two hours for speakers to arrive to a conference. According to the calculations of the person sitting next to him, who reckoned 3,500 people present, two airplanes could have been built with the 7,000 work hours that were lost that day.[9] Kerzhentsev's notorious account of this incident, the 1923 *Pravda* article "Time Builds Airplanes," lamented the impact of such production blockages on the national economy and proposed a number of strategies for overcoming these delays. But the scope of his article extended far beyond the industrial sector to touch upon numerous social and cultural causes for Russia's asynchrony. Kerzhentsev's League of Time decried everything from the endless queues in which shoppers wasted their days to the slow turnaround of books at the press. A favorite target of the League were pleonastic speech patterns that failed to get to the point. Gastev, who welcomed the new organization enthusiastically, published a *Pravda* article "The Clock Strikes," which complained that "instead of simple words—'I'm listening,' 'yes,' 'no'—you get an entire philosophy. It is no accident that we have so many psychologists and philosophers in Russia."[10] Members of the League denounced inefficient habits of communication that resulted in endless deliberation at meetings and conferences. Political organizers might succeed in gathering people in a shared space, but that was only half of the job: if the assembled were unable to convey their ideas succinctly and promptly, the group would still fail to unite around a common platform and forge a shared will.[11] The mechanical montage of airplanes in factories required coordinating schedules, but so did the psycho-montage of collective consciousness.

In many cases, the asynchrony of the Russian population was outwardly visible. Gastev pointed out that factory workers and mental laborers, for example, start and end their days on different schedules, segment their labor differently (eight hours for the former; six for the latter), and even take different trains to and from work. As a consequence of this temporal sequestration, the movement of the hands and the minds of Soviet Russia remained uncoordinated ("Vremia," 63–64). This class asynchrony had profound psychological origins that were rooted in the technical mode of production. In the essay "Time and Culture," which appeared in *Time* in 1924, the industrial theorist Iosif Kan explained that the diversification of labor forms in the modern world had led to the desynchronization of subjective experience. Building on the work of the statistician Stanislav Strumilin, whose classic 1924 study *The Time-Budget of the Russian Worker and Peasant in 1922–1923* was gospel in the League, Kan argued that each mode of production generates a corresponding time-architecture that structures the labor activities, everyday routines, and even social horizon of its operator. The temporality of the peasant, for example, is subordinated to "natural clocks" such as the turnover of the seasons, the rhythms of day and night, and natural reproductive cycles. Primitive societies measure time not in hours, minutes, and seconds but in "the ripening of seed, the thawing of snow, and the appearance of fish on shores," Kan wrote. This changed with the advent of industrial manufacture, the introduction of the division of labor, and the growth of modern cities, all of which uncoupled the time-patterns of existence from the organic periods of the natural world and gave rise to multiple, often mutually incompatible, experiences of time that were localized within particular socioeconomic groups.[12]

Ever since Faust first pined for "the fruit that rots before 'tis broken, / And trees that day by day their green repair," people have reflected on the quickening of life in modernity, although few noticed what so obsessed members of the League: that acceleration did not usher people into a shared present but, to the contrary, threw them out of sync. It is well known that the industrial mode of production uprooted the peasant from the organic life-rhythms of the countryside and forced him to internalize the mechanical time of the factory clock.[13] For members of the League, this reformatting of time-consciousness was not deleterious in and of itself, since, as Kan observed, every society must invariably impress some particular "style and application of time" upon its members anyway. Peasant time is no less or more tyrannical per se than proletarian time. For the Leaguists, the issue was not that capitalism accelerates and restructures time, but that it does this in order to balkanize its subjects, dividing social groups temporally so as to exploit them economically and neutralize them politically. The capitalist mode of production quickens life, but it does so in a way that actively inhibits the emergence of collective time and forecloses the threat of a revolutionary alignment. As the historian Reinhart Koselleck noted, modernity's acceleration *in* history never produced the acceleration *of* history.[14] For this reason, the sociologist Hartmut Rosa has recently observed that "experiences of the 'non-simultaneity of the simultaneous' clearly seem to be on the rise between as well as within specific societies," so that "social groups or individuals following very different temporal rhythms frequently coexist in any given territory." The result, he writes, is a condition of "frenetic standstill."[15] Industrial capitalism's insidious combination of technical instantaneity with psycho-temporal atomization means that, even in densely populated cities, individuals may occupy the same spaces and walk the same streets but they do not ever encounter each other because they are always out of phase.

Divergence in the temporalities of modern life was all too plain to see in the 1920s, when the consequences of the systemic desynchronization of experience reached a crisis. The operations of financial markets accelerated beyond the threshold of human perception so that an entire world economy crashed nearly overnight in October 1929 at the same time that political processes slowed down and ground to a halt in the deliberative paralysis of parliamentary democracy.[16] Beyond economic and political institutions, the jarring contrast between speed and stasis was manifest also in the phenomenology of everyday life in the 1920s, when the loss of continuity made it increasingly difficult for people to navigate smoothly between disjunctive temporal contexts. "In functionally differentiated societies, wherever goings-on must be synchronized with one another or temporally geared to each other, a temporal change like the acceleration of processes leads to potential friction problems at the synchronization points . . . In some situations this desynchronization leads (temporarily) to massive real slowdowns, as when complicated chains of work fall so far out of step that blockages occur."[17] This conflictual multitemporality was evident in a number of geopolitical contexts, but in revolutionary Russia above all. As Trotsky had pointed out, Russia's combined economy—part agrarian, part industrial, part nomadic—offered a particularly salient object lesson in the laws of non-synchronous development. European visitors were struck by the dramatic contrast between fast and slow, ultra-modern and archaic, that they saw in Soviet Russia. Upon arriving in Moscow in 1926, Walter Benjamin, for example, was startled by the many "time catastrophes" and "time collisions" that he witnessed. There the rhythms of village life and premodern modes of artisanal production still flourished in the heart of the industrial capital, while peasant populations in the countryside were learning to operate technologies of mass communication like radio before they had ever even learned to read.[18]

Leaguists hoped to coordinate these disparate temporalities and gather Russia's diverse demography together within the horizon of a shared Now. Denouncing the capitalist entrepreneurs who distributed the resource of time unevenly among workers in order to exploit the differentials for their own profit, the League demanded the "synchrony and coordination" of individual time frames.[19] They pursued a variety of remedies to socialize time. Leaguists pared speech down to achieve maximal laconism and used photocyclograms to eliminate uneconomical movements. They conducted psychotechnical experiments to hone reaction time, redesigned commercial interiors to make transactions more efficient, and developed polytechnical pedagogies to coordinate movements of the hands with the progression of thought. Every act and gesture, every idea and interpersonal exchange, was measured, analyzed, and regimented chronometrically.

The League's subordination of all aspects of life to the clock provoked protest from cultural romantics who lamented the loss of psychologically textured, organic time, but these criticisms failed to grasp the deeply social, even existential dimensions of clock-time. As Martin Heidegger explained in 1924, the technical time of the clock overwrites the spontaneous rhythms of the body, but in so doing it also weaves people into a shared fabric of concern (*Sorge*). Clocks enable individuals to connect within an integrated and uniform Now. Dasein, he wrote, "is the time in which one is with another: 'one's' time. The clock that one has, every clock, shows the time of being-with-one-another-in-the-world."[20] In this respect, the clock is a communication medium more primary than any printing press or telephone because it builds a universal architecture of time that can be inhabited by multiple individuals. The clock transmits no message, but is itself the prerequisite for contact and connection. It is a "machine that coordinate[s] the collective actions of people, creating the public grid for their common world."[21] Through the chronometric structuring of existence, the League sought to transform time from a private good into social weal. "'Being-in-the-world' is a society of clocks. One is only 'being-with-others,' in Heideggerian terms, if one can switch on one's radio set at exactly the same time when all others are doing it—for instance, when the news program or the broadcast of a soccer game starts. This is the so-called public time, or world time. Since clocks can be synchronized, they can warrant that several people can say 'Now' together in different places."[22] For the League of Time, punctuality was a fundamental social qualification, and clock-time, in turn, was the technical infrastructure for all communal—if not all communistic—existence. "To be human, one must have a watch," proclaimed the famous advertisement that Mayakovsky and Rodchenko made for *Time* (fig. 1.3).

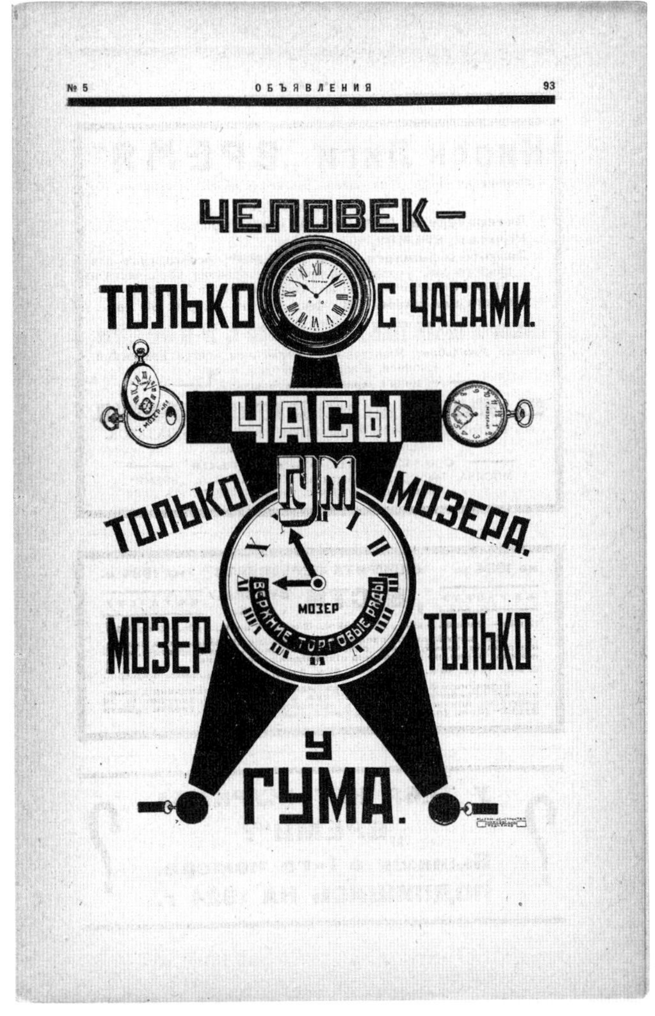

1.3 Aleksander Rodchenko and Vladimir Mayakovsky, advertisement for Moser watches, *Vremia*, no. 5 (1923): 93. Getty Research Institute, Los Angeles (85-S956). © 2024 Estate of Alexander Rodchenko / UPRAVIS, Moscow / Artists Rights Society (ARS), NY.

In order to reintegrate the divergent temporalities of Russia, Gastev proposed a two-front program for the "objective" and the "subjective" coordination of time ("Vremia," 63–66).[23] Objective coordination—which encompassed such things as the timely provision of materials to factories, the judicious scheduling of work shifts, the punctual dispatch of trains, and other activities that today fall under the rubric of organizational logistics—was a relatively straightforward technical matter that could be accomplished by industrial engineers and managers. More challenging was the subjective coordination of time, especially given the notoriously underdeveloped sense for time among Russians. When the Slovakian art critic Ivan Matsa first moved to Moscow in 1923, he was struck by the ubiquitous use of the word *seichas* ("at once"), which, he quickly learned, meant the exact opposite of what it promised. *Seichas* did not mean now, but eternal delay. In an editorial published in *Time*, Matsa explained that the adverb was a holdover from Russia's "patriarchal" past, when the tyrannical lord invoked *seichas* on a whim according to his own needs and desires.[24] Even after the revolution, the Russian Now remained erratic, arbitrary, and divisive in nature—a "subjectified occasionalism," to borrow Carl Schmitt's apt characterization of the temporality of the sovereign.[25] It belonged to a decisionistic, fundamentally anti-democratic time that isolated people and inhibited collaboration. Benjamin too was struck by the emptiness of the *seichas*, a word that he heard everywhere during his winter in Moscow and that he, like Matsa, linked to the earlier "Asiatic" (or despotic) mode of production.[26] Even to the casual visitor, it was clear that subjective time in Soviet Russia was hopelessly out of joint.

In a *Time* essay titled "The Psychology of Belatedness," the organizational engineer F. Dunaevskii concluded that just getting trains to operate on time would not suffice to cure the epidemic of delays in Russia. Correcting the "psychological aberrations in the time-sense" required that people develop what Dunaevskii called *vremiamer*, an instinct for intuiting units of time. In general, Russian workers had a decent sense for gauging physical extension and mass, but they were unable to estimate minutes and seconds as accurately as an *arshin* or a meter.[27] "We need to implement the 'chronization' of life using measures whose effect is above all subjective in nature," Gastev had explained ("Vremia," 64). As a primitive but effective strategy for refining the time-sense, Dunaevskii cited the village bell tower whose hourly report synchronizes everyone in earshot throughout the day, summoning them into a shared present. But the League aspired to a time-sense that was far more precise. They distributed timepieces among their members, enjoining them to note the exact duration of every activity and event in the day. "The watch that you carry in your pocket becomes an indispensable instrument for recording," wrote Gastev. "Capture the hour and the minute in your sketches. The watch is simultaneously your chronometer."[28] Timekeeping needed to be practiced constantly, refined and habituated, so that the psyche would be more prompt and present.

The politics of micro-time embraced all aspects of life, public and private, economic and reproductive. No topic was beyond the purview of the League's journal *Time*. In addition to the predictable stream of articles about labor and administration, this lifestyle magazine for the punctual also featured pieces on subjects ranging from the virtues of shorthand and efficiency in commercial transactions to bibliographic classification, architecture, and hygiene. Through rigorous chronometric regimentation, the League strove to synchronize the internal clocks of the population and bring these subjective times into alignment, transforming an anarchy of isolated individuals into an integrated revolutionary body poised for collective action. "For us manager-revolutionaries, the coordinate of time turns out to be the decisive Revolutionary," wrote Gleb Krzhizhanovskii, director of the State Commission for the Electrification of Russia (GOELRO). "It is an expediter of reality, an agent-accelerator of reality's elemental processes in time."[29]

For Leaguists, time was not the universal a priori that Kant had assumed it to be, but a mutable quasi-substance, a material value (*материальная ценность*) that was shaped by the topological particularities of space.[30] It was amassed in objects and redistributed through activities. All physical things, no matter how dissimilar qualitatively or outwardly incommensurable, could be rendered as concrete magnitudes of time (*величины времени*) that could be measured and compared.[31] When Kerzhentsev envisioned an airplane, for example, he did not see an engine, fuselage, and wings, but 3,500 labor hours, and when students in the League cell at Moscow State University considered a professor with "solid qualifications," they likewise reckoned: "52,500 hours, or 8,750 workdays, which equals 29 years of mental labor."[32] Marx argued in *Capital* that all commodities are essentially congealed labor-time, but so are infrastructures, books, and philosophical systems. Whether considering the weeks necessary to build a stretch of railway track, the hours required to consume a piece of fiction, or the seconds that the mind needs to work through a logical problem, Leaguists insisted that all things and processes embodied a determinate quantity of duration that could be established empirically. A leader of Soviet industry thus concluded: "It is no more possible to seriously argue against chronometrics as a global method for measuring the temporality of all phenomena (including labor processes) than it is to dispute the superiority of measuring the physical dimensions of bodies using precise instruments rather than just estimating it."[33]

Of the diverse means that the League promoted for leading a punctual life, the most notorious were the chronocards. From Kerzhentsev and Gastev to the psychotechnician Isaak Shpil'rein, each theorist in the organization advanced a distinctive format for this system of life-logging, although all of these proposals were essentially variations on the same model: the train timetable (fig. 1.4). Card users were enjoined to record the hours and minutes they spent at various "stations" of the day such as sleeping, working, eating, commuting, meeting, relaxing, grooming, reading, and so on. In addition to regimenting and thereby collectivizing the time-sense of the individual members, the chronocards also supplied valuable data to the League's time managers, who were able to see which users were in temporal alignment at any moment in the twenty-four-hour cycle. On the basis of this information, Gastev proposed establishing "belts of time" (*пояса времени*) in the day when temporal conspecifics would enter into a shared present ("Vremia," 64). And yet the League's objective was never to subordinate all members to a single uniform rhythm—an idea that made as much sense as having all trains in a network pull into a station simultaneously. Rather, the goal was to establish an integrated system that would allow people to interface and sync up like so many different gears rotating at their own speed. Even within her or his own body, the individual is not fully integrated temporally but is instead an interlocking assembly of distinct times and rhythms: tellingly, the clock in the head of the figure in Mayakovsky and Rodchenko's advertisement shows a different time than the ones that are in the hands, which in turn diverges from the one in the viscera (fig. 1.3). For members of the League, every activity and pastime, from philosophizing to factory work to romancing, has its own speed and periodicity. Even with everyone following their own schedule, the League believed that the rational organization of these individual subroutines by the time managers would be able to transform

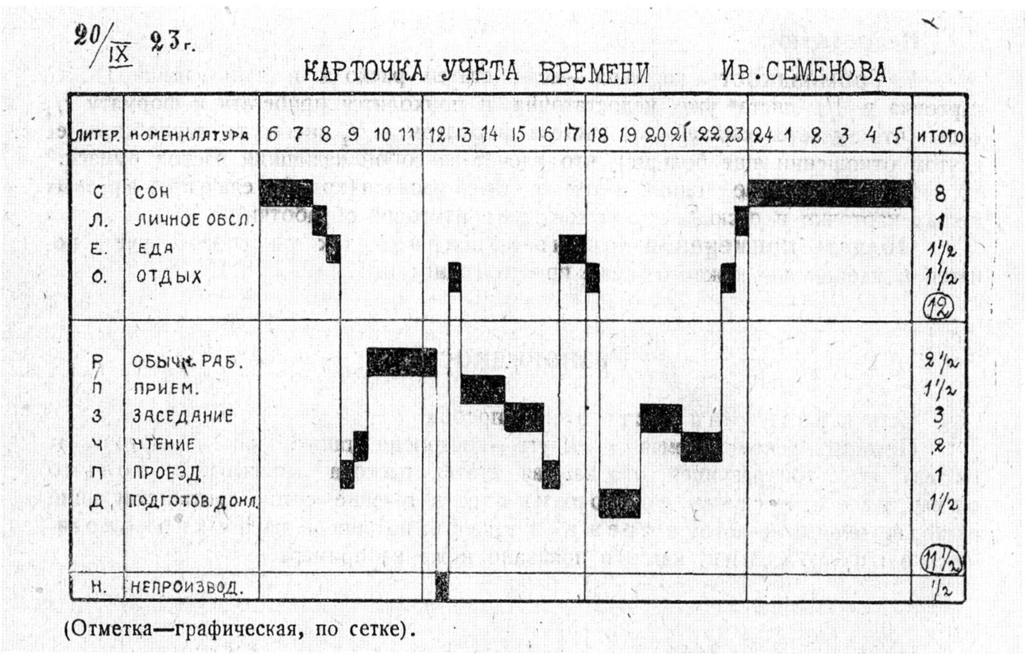

1.4 A. Ivanov, "Cards for Time-Accounting," *Vremia*, no. 1 (1923): 46. Getty Research Institute, Los Angeles (85-S956).

the anarchy of personal impulses into a giant machinery of collective endeavor. Through the precise engineering of time, people would meet, liaise, and uncouple punctually, and Russia would be enveloped in a vast choreography of coordinated movement.

One striking feature of the chronocard is its manifest discontinuity. After waking up at 8 a.m. sharp, the activities of the Leaguist begin to flicker all over the chart. This "photograph of a day" (*фотография дня*) presents a remarkably dynamic portrait of the new Soviet subject, one whose countenance and bearing changes from one moment to the next in response to each encounter. In contrast to the confessional, diary-writing, and other techniques of the self that took root in the West, the League's chronocard did not presume or perform a stable psyche. Rather than linking episodes together into a developmental scheme of *bildung*, the chronocard depicts a life that has been patched together out of discrete instants. The League's embrace of discontinuity reflected the lessons of a revolution that had taught that inflexible adherence to a particular political program or class ontology inhibited the ability to adapt on the fly to rapidly changing conditions. Looking at the situation in 1920, Lenin drew two conclusions from recent events: "First, that in order to accomplish its task the revolutionary class must be able to master all forms or aspects of social activity without exception . . . second, that the revolutionary class must be prepared for the most rapid and brusque replacement of one form by another."[34] Under mutable circumstances such as these, the baggage of psychological identity would only encumber the revolutionary subject. One contributing editor to *Time*, the influential psychoanalyst-turned-schizoanalyst Aron Zalkind, predicted that the psyche of the future Soviet subject would accordingly be based not on "stagnation" but on "condensation" (*сгущение*). Fundamentally unstable and highly reactive, this ideal communist could be seen reading quietly at one moment, laboring intensively at the next, and agitating fervently at another. Her psyche was a "cold bomb" that could be "either peaceful or explosive," depending on the needs of the moment, Zalkind wrote.[35] The non-identitarian Leaguist self fulfilled Marx's famous prediction in *The German Ideology* that the communist of the future would "hunt in the morning, fish in the afternoon, rear cattle in the evening, practice critique after dinner . . . without ever becoming a hunter, a fisherman, a herdsman or a critic."[36] The mission of the League, as outlined by its leaders, was to prime the psyche for this discontinuous existence. Gastev promised that "training makes it possible to adopt a new mental orientation quickly," without losing time to slow adaptation ("Vremia," 79). Moving from one activity to another, leaping from time-belt to time-belt, Leaguists learned to adjust swiftly and efficiently to each new circumstance without clinging to old mental orientations (*установки*).

The factographers delivered the cultural practice that corresponded to this prompt, revolutionary self. Indeed, Tret'iakov attributes the directives of

"Moscow–Beijing" to Osip Brik, but they turn out to be taken verbatim from a recent essay by the Leaguist Gastev:

> Affix your observations: they must be recorded. Write quickly. Don't go anywhere without a note pad and pencil. Of course it would be best if everyone learned stenography. But if that's not possible, then master cursive. You have to be able to make sketches, produce outlines quickly, know symbols and conventional signs; you have to get used to basic scheduling (always giving preference to notebooks with graph paper). When recording you have to get used to designating everything in units: in centimeters, meters, pounds, and so on. Use the watch that you carry in your pocket as an indispensable instrument of recording. Write down the hour and minutes in your notes. Your watch is also your chronometer. If you don't have a watch in your pocket, look at the clock on the wall. If there is none on the wall, gauge the time by the sun in the sky; if there is no sun, gauge the time by the traffic in the streets.

Clocks are everywhere: in your pocket, on the wall, in the sky, on the streets. By paying attention to these ubiquitous chronometers, "you will become recorders [*фиксаторами*], nimble reporters of life," Gastev writes.[37] The Central Institute of Labor "teaches that everyone must have a watch," echoes Tret'iakov, who then proceeds in "Moscow–Beijing" to hone his inner clock and to focus the full powers of his consciousness on each fleeting moment before him. He sets out as a storyteller, but by the time he arrives in China he is writing prompt and verbless telegraphic dispatches. Seeking to align his subjective time-sense with objective events, Tret'iakov adopts a new "mental orientation" in each episode, per Gastev's instructions. There is little psychic accumulation across the sketches, no carryover from one event to the next. Though factographic texts are, as a rule, always composed in the first person, the *I* that speaks in them is a hollow one, a mere conduit for relaying surrounding events and phenomena.

This tabula rasa of selfhood, initiated thirty times over in "Moscow–Beijing," explains the inconsistent tone of the sketches, each of which appears to be written by a different author. One reviewer would thus characterize Tret'iakov's style as a "multi-style" (*многостилье*), clarifying that "every book resounds in a different tonality, is written by a new hand."[38] One sketch in "Moscow–Beijing" presents a stenographic transcription of a conversation between two Americans, a second describes going through border customs, and a third comments on the movement theories of Émile-Jaques Dalcroze and Rudolf Bode. Still another, titled "2:55" per the convention of the Central Institute of Labor, offers a thought experiment inspired by the League's efforts to regiment all aspects of private life, including acts of love and intimacy:

Kiss each other at this time. In 6 minutes it will be too late.

In one minute it is possible to manufacture 12 acts of kissing, each composed of 5 smacks of the lips apiece.

In the case of a larger assembly of participants (more than a company), it is possible to organize mass production up to 60 kisses per minute.

Kiss each other in perfect time.

NOT says: don't kiss at all. ("Moskva–Pekin," 33)

It would be easy to dismiss this Chaplinesque factory of kissing as a parody of the League's hyper-productivism if only Tret'iakov weren't dead serious about similar proposals in other works such as the play *I Want a Baby*, which explored the rationalization of sex and desire with the icy aloofness of an "anatomical atlas."[39] The shifting tone of "Moscow–Beijing," which expresses enthusiasm at one point, irony at another, and disregard at still another, offers no clue about Tret'iakov's own feelings about these matters. The author's inscrutability does not indicate a lack of conviction, however, but submission to the changing exigencies of the present. Borrowing a phrase from Montaigne, whose autoscopic *Essays* likewise sought to examine selfhood under conditions of continuous change, we could say that the factographer portrays passing rather than being, and that if he regularly contradicts himself as a result, he nonetheless never contradicts the facts. The sheer positivity of the act of inscription results in an endless variety of personal dispositions.[40] As Tret'iakov explains in the eighth sketch, "I am not mocking. I am only recording" ("Moskva–Pekin," 36).

The neutral and colorless idiom of factography derives from journalism, the form of discourse that Barthes later identified as the model of all degree-zero writing.[41] Like the constative prose of the reporter, Tret'iakov neither judges nor opines but merely registers a constellation of facts that changes from one minute to the next. His Orphean writing bears no trace of past usage. With each pen stroke, the factographer creates the conditions of literature anew. In the 1924 essay "In Praise of the Newspaper," Czech author Karel Čapek described how this "press consciousness" is continuously refreshed in real time: "The newspaper world, like that of wild beasts, exists solely in the present; Press consciousness (if one can speak of consciousness) is circumscribed by simple present time extending from the morning on to the evening edition, or the other way around. If you read a paper a week old you feel as if you were turning the pages of Dalimil's chronicle: no longer is it a newspaper but a memorial. The noetic system of the newspaper is actualized realism: what is just now exists; *Extra praesentiam non est existencia: ergo bibamus*."[42] These last words—"So let us drink," taken from a Goethe poem that became a popular drinking song—capture both the cheerful abandon of giving oneself over to a liquid present as well as the oblivion that results from this intoxication. A continuous stream of events flows through the newspaper, Lethe-like, obliterating the past and returning language over and over to its degree-zero origins. For Weimar Germany's raging reporter Egon Erwin Kisch, there was a powerful undercurrent of nihilism in this flux: "The newspaper never tackles what is eternally the same: it wants something that changes from day to day, something that is always current—something that is nothing."[43] The words that appear in the newspaper are consumed only once, on the spot, leaving behind no mnemonic residue. In this respect, the newspaper more closely resembles a live broadcast technology such as radio than durable print media such as the book, as one might expect. Newspapers are "contradictorily bivalent," writes media historian Lisa Gitelman: materially, they consist of words on paper, but these words are fleeting and impermanent like a speech act.[44] "A newspaper lives only for a single day," noted one Soviet editor. "And it also reports about what happened only on a single day. This is why you have to read the newspaper every day."[45] For a press consciousness that exists only for the present moment, missing just one edition leaves the mind unmoored and disoriented in the world.

The factographers' turn to newspapers and mass periodicals in the mid-1920s realized the Russian avant-garde's long-standing dream of language as presence and positivity. Siegfried Kracauer aptly characterized Tret'iakov as the kind of writer "who is unwilling to serve the 'absolute,' but who instead takes it upon himself to provide an account of our current situation." In contrast to traditional authors who are "enveloped by the odor of eternity" and who safeguard experience so it can be "preserved in this form for later times," the factographers were indifferent to posterity. No lingering thought or memory, no vivid mental impression, was meant to survive the onetime event of the factographic sketch, which "exhausts its meaning in being published in 'the moment.'" Such writing "fundamentally refutes the transcendental stratum of existence," Kracauer concluded.[46] Tret'iakov refused monumentality even at the level of material support: he proposed to print his artbook on John Heartfield on cheap newspaper stock, guaranteeing that the lavishly illustrated monograph would disintegrate over time and leave nothing behind but dust. Neither the ideas nor even the physical stuff of this evanescent writing was meant to endure.

Already long before Tret'iakov's heyday, the elder Futurist Chuzhak had foretold the arrival of the factographer when in 1910 he called for a writer who was not just physically agile enough to capture the barrage of stimuli emitted by urban life, but also ideologically astute enough to organize these sensory impressions into systems of logical correspondence. In a likely reference to Charles Baudelaire's poem "À une passante," Chuzhak endorsed the strategy of aesthetic "presentification": "'A minute, no longer!' the city says to us. And we, its grains, submit. You walk along the street; you are lost in thought for a minute. A beautiful face flashes past; you fall in love for a minute. Someone shoves you; you get angry for a minute. Someone smiles at you; you are happy for a minute."[47] Anticipating the discontinuous grid of the League's chronocard and the thirty discrete episodes of "Moscow–Beijing," Chuzhak celebrated the punctual encounter that lasts for an instant and then evaporates without leaving a trace on the psyche. Fifteen years later, the factographers renounced the hermeticism of modernist poetry, although they radicalized its pledge to the contemporary.

The factographers recognized that the actual content of the newspaper is not information but temporality. Even before it reports anything about what is happening in the world, even prior to conveying any determinate message at all, the daily press generates an awareness of time at a primary experiential level, a temporal horizon of eventfulness from which the individual event can emerge. From political summits to natural catastrophes, everything that appears on the pages of the newspaper presumes this master referent, the Now. It is no coincidence that Kerzhentsev, the founder of the League of Time, also wrote one of the foundational texts of newspaper studies. For him, the newspaper was the most punctual, most chronometrically regimented form of writing available. One chapter of his popular multi-edition study broke down the twenty-four-hour newspaper cycle (*газетные сутки*) with clockwork precision, reconstructing how the text was assembled hour by hour within the rhythmic period that he designated the "newspaper day" (*газетный день*). "This means that the precise work must be carried out by a strictly appointed time, not a moment later, and that certain fixed times . . . must be observed with strict pedantism" (*Gazeta*, 32). Every aspect of newspaper labor is subordinated to a scheme of mechanical time in which "number rules the world" (*Gazeta*, 37). It is often noted that the newspaper affirms this clock-time whether or not any newsworthy events have even taken place: editors do not wait until something important has happened to print a new edition, but mark time regardless. For this reason, the great critical theorists of the last century often complained that the newspaper is contentless and redundant, a "great pleonasm" characterized by an "insistent prolixity that says and shows nothing."[48] But these objections are based on a fundamental generic misprision that sees the newspaper as a form of failed literature. Leaguists like Kerzhentsev recognized, however, that the newspaper descended not from the book but from the clock. It conveys time and rhythms, not scenes and stories.

The newspaper may not itself say anything, but in synchronizing and connecting people, it enables communication and coordinates movement. Like the report of the village bell tower or the blast of the factory whistle, the appearance of the broadsheet assembles everyone in its radius several times a day. More important than the specific topics that appear in the newspaper is the simple fact that everyone who reads the newspaper will soon be discussing and debating these topics. This phatic speech primes the channels of communication by establishing a "mental set for contact" in its reader.[49] Newspaper day after newspaper day, it produces the present as a shared, public framework of experience. "The mass media are . . . behind the much-debated characteristics of modern temporal structures, such as the dominance of the past/future schema, the uniformization of world time, acceleration, the extension of simultaneity to non-simultaneous events. They generate the time they presuppose, and society adapts itself accordingly."[50] However phenomenologically primary it might appear, the experience of actuality and contemporaneity that is so central to the fabric of modern life is neither spontaneously given nor universal, but is itself an artifact that must be produced. In the late nineteenth century, this present was the product of railway travel; in the twentieth century, this function was taken over by the mass media.

According to the English journalist and sociologist Charles Madge, founder of the popular documentary movement Mass Observation, the media's formatting of time was indeed the only thing differentiating contemporary civilizations from traditional cultures. His essay "Press, Radio, and Social Consciousness," which came out just a few months after the launch of Mass Observation in 1937, argued that "social homogeneity in our day" is distinguished less by the sheer number of people that it embraces than by the fact that these collectives inhabit a common present that has been created by the media. For Madge, what makes today's masses distinct is that they all "read and hear the same thing *on the same day*." Like Heidegger, who considered the clock to be a technical precondition for a shared world of concern, Madge believed that news periodicals were the glue holding modern society together. Whereas older cultures were founded upon "a traditional set of texts, whose influence made itself felt over the course of centuries," technical civilizations use newspapers and radio to "ensure that everyone should read, and everyone should hear, a statement about the world which is valid for a day, and only for a day." Industrial man "has a new Bible every day, in the form of a newspaper."[51] In contrast to the Christian Bible, however, the modern newspaper does not unite its readers through binding axioms or foundational myths. It generates a shared realm of experience independently of doctrine, ideology, or worldview. This insight was fundamental to the practical work of Mass Observation: building upon the precedent of Mikhail Kol'tsov's *Day of the World*, which compiled items from around the globe that were all written on September 27, 1935, Madge's organization would become famous for its annual "day-surveys," which solicited impressions from thousands of contributors on a single day of the year, May 12, in order to create quasi-synchronic "weather-maps of public feeling in a crisis."[52] Like the daily newspaper, the day-surveys of Mass Observation reflected, but also actively produced, the temporal coherence of the modern world.

Tret'iakov too heralded the newspaper as the "bible of the present day" ("New Leo Tolstoy," 50).[53] The factographer strove to facilitate a mass literature that was "born out of actuality," as he put it, but he recognized that the conditions for such a project in Russia were also singularly inhospitable.[54] It was a society of "time collisions" (Benjamin) and "patriarchal" temporizing (Matsa), one whose journalistic public sphere was organized around so-called thick journals that appeared intermittently whenever its editor decided he had something important to say. Faced with temporal aberrations like these, Tret'iakov proposed to restructure literary production like a "conveyer belt"—a model for him not just because assembly-line production allowed an entire collective of writers to work together on a single text but also because working on a conveyer belt presumed rigorous chronometric regimentation. Just as factory work requires everyone to submit to a common time, writers too must learn to coordinate schedules. When *Lef* was reborn in 1927 as *Novyi Lef*, the physiognomy of the new periodical reflected both the format and the temporality of the newspaper. Whereas its predecessor had been a classic thick journal that came out irregularly and that varied in length between 144 and 256 pages, *Novyi Lef* appeared punctually every month and was always exactly forty-eight pages long. *Novyi Lef* would be sent to the printer whether or not Mayakovsky felt inspired to put out a new issue. To meet the deadline, the factographers would sometimes fill out the tabloid with résumés of recent lectures, gossip that was overheard in the hall, and letters not to the editor but to each other. The new factographic publication was markedly chattier than its predecessor, but this empty phaticism established a temporality that was truly egalitarian, not set by the capricious *seichas* of the editorial board. The collective present had to be maintained and the channels of communication kept open, even at the cost of quality.

Meeting deadlines demanded prompt writing. Just as they turned to photography to automate their graphic work, the factographers turned to stenography to reduce the production time of prose to an absolute minimum. Already as a Futurist poet Tret'iakov had practiced writing telegrammatic "compacts,"[55] a strategy that would lead several years later to the so-called auto-correspondence (*авто-корреспонденция*) of factography.[56] Here too Lef followed the lead of cultural rationalizers like Gastev and Kerzhentsev, who promoted cursive and stenography as basic cultural competencies for all Russians.[57] One injunction in the first issue of *Time* recommended factography as the journal's house style: "*Leaguists*! Stay in continuous contact with the journal *Time*. Write to the journal concisely but clearly: *more facts* and fewer general meditations."[58] Mass stenography was also endorsed by prominent Party figures such as Trotsky, who believed that mechanical writing democratized knowledge by expediting the movement of information. An essay that Trotsky wrote for the journal *Questions of Stenography* in 1924 attributed the achievements of the Bolshevik Revolution to notational techniques that had eliminated the lag between historical events and writing. He predicted that popular stenography initiatives would soon expand to encompass nearly every dimension of public life. "In the first Soviet years, stenography mainly served politics . . . [but] it will increasingly serve economic tasks, science, art, and all branches of socialist culture. In a certain sense it can be said that the cultural growth of our society will be measured by the place that stenography has in it."[59] Without stenography there could be no socialism. As Liubov' Popova's cover for *Questions of Stenography* suggested later that year, this "writing of the future" was just as indispensable to the progress of revolutionary modernity as celebrated technologies such as the dynamo and the airplane (fig. 1.5).

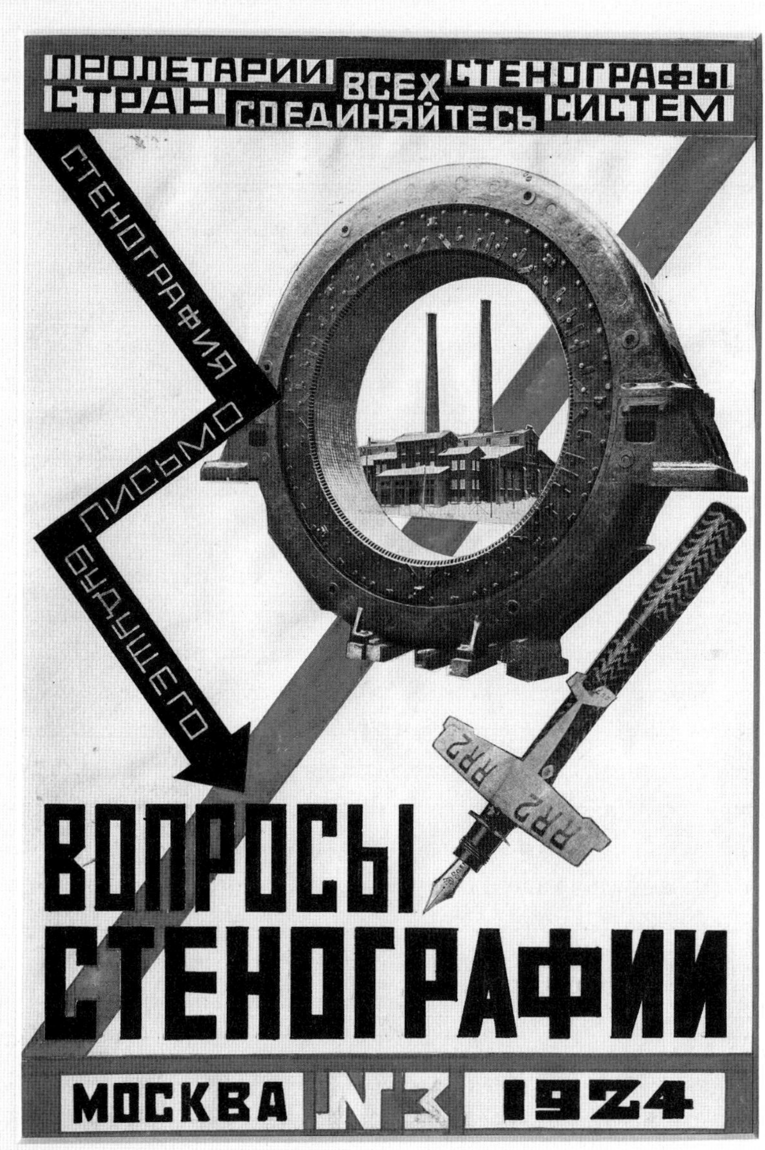

1.5 Liubov' Popova, cover design for *Questions of Stenography*, no. 3 (1924). Tsaritsyno Museum, Moscow. © Tsaritsyno State Museum-Reserve.

Proponents of stenography believed that accelerated writing would not just enhance the information infrastructure of Russia but would even resolve the mind-body dualism that they had inherited from bourgeois philosophy. Stenography was the script of revolutionary monism. According to Trotsky, the practice of rhythmic mechanical writing coordinates the gestures of the hands with the movement of thought, bringing the mind into alignment with the activity of the nerves and muscles. "Thought becomes disciplined and works more rhythmically in harmony with the stenographer's pencil," he observed.[60] Through measured, cadenced script, the physical impulses of the body come to shape those of thought and vice versa.

For similar reasons, Barthes would later identify the "speed of the graphic act" as a "cultural issue" with profound repercussions not just for the transmission of knowledge but for the texture of experience itself. Like Trotsky, he considered the ideal practice of writing to be one that established a rhythmic harmony between thought and inscription. "Perhaps writing consists in not thinking any faster than your hand can write, in mastering that relationship, in making it optimal." This insight led Barthes to a poetological imperative: "We could risk defining the work in general terms as a kinetic relationship between the head and the hand." While Barthes had once perceived an insuperable chasm to exist between event and sign in his earlier structuralist phase, later in life he came to believe that quickening the act of writing made it possible to overcome this hiatus, "to reconcile—dialecticize—the *distance* implied by the *enunciation of writing* and the *proximity*, the transportation of the present experienced as it happens."[61] In contrast to the longhand of traditional literature, whose sluggish pace dragged behind reality and doomed the writer to retrospection, the prompt writing of the stenographer promised contact with the present.

Seen in this way, an author's relationship to reality is less a matter of ideology, class, or worldview than of timing, dexterity, and choice of writing instrument. In the 1920s, Soviet journalists debated different techniques of notation, supporting their positions with information about which writers composed by hand, which ones dictated, which used a notebook, which used a typewriter (and what kind of typewriter). (One contribution by Kol'tsov, which discussed the habits of prominent figures from Bukharin to Radek, also mentioned a worker-correspondent who still wrote by hand, quipping that "As soon as he gets used to dictating, then we will have the literal 'dictatorship of the proletariat' to the editorial board."[62]) Using cursive rather than a script that breaks contact with the writing surface; the degree of resistance or glide established by the paper stock; sartorial conventions like pockets that make a notebook ready-to-hand: all of these factors, Barthes would later point out, determine the speed of inscription and, in turn, the ability of the writer to connect with reality in a timely fashion. "All of literature, all of culture, all of 'psychology' would be different had the hand not moved at a slower pace than the inside of our heads." As the act of writing accelerates, the journalist nears the "asymptotic rapprochement of the manual (the muscles) and the mental (the affective): the hand seems plugged directly into the mental." Barthes thus cited the pivotal role that techniques of notation have played in the attempts of philosophers to overcome dualist epistemologies. The experimental shorthand that Edmund Husserl invented in order to write "at a gallop," for example, eliminated the time-delay that separated the moments of apperception, inscription, and introspection (*Preparation of the Novel*, 265). Recognizing that the mind would never be able to touch the world using longhand, the German phenomenologist transformed philosophy into reportage.

SPECIFIC THROUGH AND THROUGH

Cultural critics in the League of Time quickly determined that punctuality was incompatible with depictive mimesis. Henceforth they would measure the success of the artist or writer not against transcendental criteria like truth and veracity but against empirical metrics such as velocity and reaction time. It was the speed of the creative act—rather than any particular skill manipulating reality effects—that ultimately determined whether an artwork was faithful to life. This was the conclusion reached by diverse research of the League, both historical and experimental. One essay by the critic Iakov Tugendkhol'd that appeared in *Time*, "Laconism in Art," surveyed the evolution of art from primitive cave drawing to Futurism, assessing each of the stages according to the speed of the image-making act. Applying methods of chronometric analysis to works of culture in this way was "one of the most important and interesting tasks of the day, which will lead to the program of NOT," he wrote. For Tugendkhol'd, the perennial debates of critics about verisimilitude and abstraction just diverted attention from the more fundamental distinction between slow and fast art. As he saw it, realism was nothing more than a processing delay between manual and mental operations.[63]

The conflict between realism and speed was most obvious in the practices of contemporary photography. In 1924 the production theorist, Proletkul't organizer, and contributing editor to *Time* Nikolai Tarabukin conducted a series of experiments with the GAKhN photographer Nikolai Svishchev-Paolo demonstrating how the momentary snapshot (*снимок*) dismantled the "school of naturalism." This research first appeared in *Time* in 1924 and was then expanded the following year into a longer contribution for the *Proletkul't Almanac* that was edited by Chuzhak. One of the experimental photographs that Tarabukin published presents a succinct emblem for the League's entire project: in it, a man reaches forward and flashes the organization's logo like the badge of a policeman, freezing time in a gesture of arrest (fig. 1.6). A second focuses the camera lens on the soles of a reclining man's shoes (fig. 1.7). In each of these anti-portraits, extremities of the body have displaced the face as the usual locus of visual interest. According to Tarabukin, who emphasized the camera's use as an epistemological device and as an instrument of scientific investigation rather than as a means for making images, the collision of planes in the first photograph and the extreme foreshortening of the second illustrated the snapshot's capacity to suspend the habits of vision. He explained that the denaturalization of realism was a direct consequence of the automation and acceleration of the image-making process, which subordinated verisimilitude to the contingencies of the moment. "Photography, which creates the possibility of deforming representationalism in the snapshot, advances a series of mechanical procedures that replace the manual, slow, costly labor of the artist."[64] Not only did speed and mechanization make the artist obsolete, but they also dis-figured the subject of the photograph and rendered him unrecognizable.

Tarabukin's observations illuminate the photographic practice of Aleksandr Rodchenko, whose use of raking angles and extreme foreshortening ceded resemblance to chance appearance. In Rodchenko's snapshots, the fleeting instant hijacks likeness and estranges the identity of the subject. In his key 1928 text "Against the Synthetic Portrait, For the Snapshot," an essay that was cel-

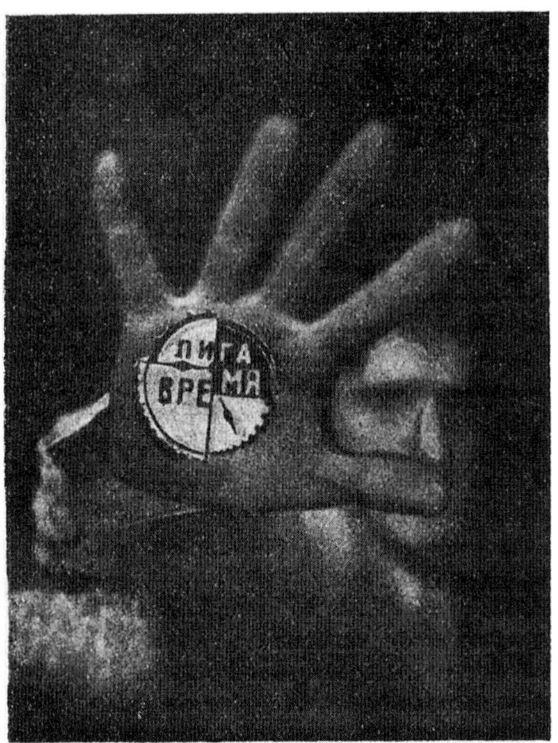

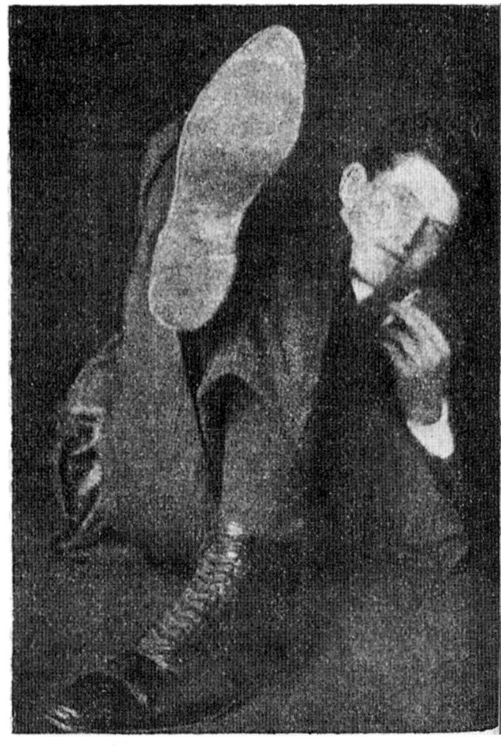

1.6–1.7 Snapshot experiments. From Nikolai Tarabukin and Nikolai Svishchev-Paolo, "Foto-reklama i foto-plakat," *Vremia*, no. 10–11 (1924): 44. Getty Research Institute, Los Angeles (85-S956).

ebrated by factographers like Tret'iakov, the photographer rejected easelism's "sum total of moments" in favor of the camera's "0.001 of a moment." As Rodchenko explained there, the distinction between realist painting and photography represented a "collision . . . between eternity and the moment." The haphazard vantages that are enabled by handheld snapshot photography—aptly called a "momentary photo" (*моментальное фото*) in Russian—undermine the visual "stereotype" of the synthetic image.[65] Building on this insight, Rodchenko developed his signature method of compressing, folding, and otherwise distorting the bodies and objects before his lens, showing them from eccentric angles rather than from their familiar frontal view (figs. 1.8 and 1.9). These de-

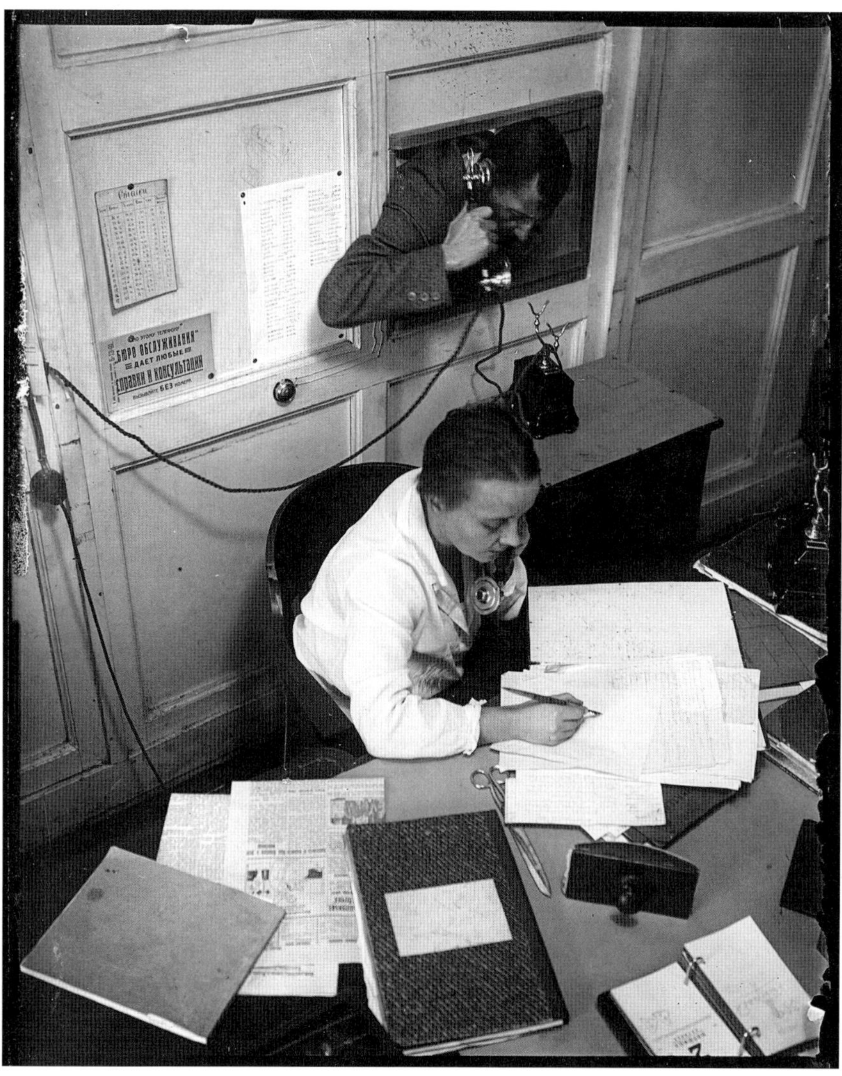

1.8 Aleksandr Rodchenko, secretary at the newspaper *Gudok* (The Whistle), 1928. Rodchenko-Stepanova Archive, Moscow. © 2024 Estate of Alexander Rodchenko / UPRAVIS, Moscow / Artists Rights Society (ARS), NY.

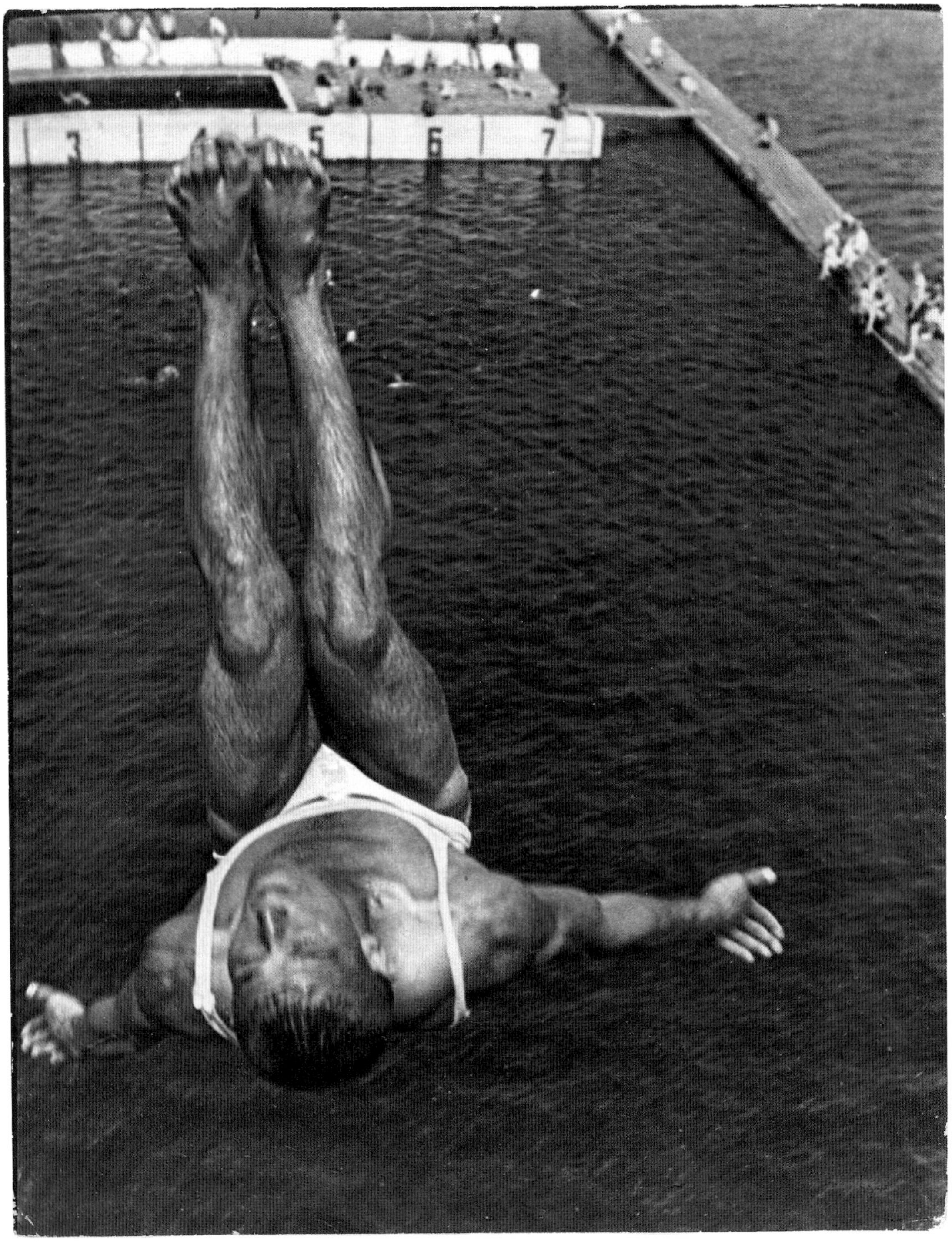

1.9 Alexander Rodchenko, "Dive," 1934. Museum of Modern Art, New York (1826.2001). Thomas Walther Collection, Gift of Shirley C. Burden, by exchange. © 2024 Estate of Alexander Rodchenko / UPRAVIS, Moscow / Artists Rights Society (ARS), NY. Digital Image © The Museum of Modern Art / Licensed by SCALA / Art Resource, NY.

formations open a rift between the factual object and the viewer's mental image of it. Photography would be celebrated in the nineteenth and twentieth centuries as the highest achievement of pictorial naturalism and the consummate technological suture of mind and eye, but Rodchenko's snapshots demonstrate, to the contrary, that "there is nothing to prevent the photograph from being separated from the image."[66] As Kracauer explained in his 1927 essay on photography, the snapshot is indeed inimical to the "memory-image" (*Gedächtnisbild*) because it pries the superficial and contingent expression of an object away from our habituated mental model of it. Tret'iakov would likewise characterize the snapshot as "a kind of infinitely thin scale [*чешуйка*] that has been peeled off the surface of reality" ("From the Photo-Series," 75). In high-speed photography, chance and superficial appearance contradict resemblance and essence. At the end of "Against the Synthetic Portrait, For the Snapshot," Rodchenko thus marvels at a recent 1927 photo album of Lenin that aggressively dismantles the spectator's memory-image of the Bolshevik leader rather than shoring it up. Snapshot photography refracts the one monumental Lenin into countless documentary Lenins.

The League of Time's presentist directive eventually led the factographers to a full-scale assault on the dilatory poetics of realism. Of all of their rivals, Lef pilloried none more relentlessly than the Association of Artists of Revolutionary Russia (AKhRR) and the Russian Association of Proletarian Writers (RAPP), two groups that repackaged the aesthetic conventions of the previous century under the brand of "proletarian realism." To the factographers, this project was pure metaphysics, a "spiritism" designed to dupe the spectator or reader into believing a spectral version of life.[67] They rejected all art that was based on representationalism (*изобразительность*) as inherently antirevolutionary, even when it gave voice to progressive political worldviews. Chuzhak explained: "So-called realism ('so-called' because in reality it was idealism) was a definitively conventional language that allowed [the imitators of life] to avoid the obstacles then facing them. All our realist criticism, including that of Plekhanov, is, moreover, based upon this language, and to this day no one has exposed its conventionality."[68] Chuzhak considered it perverse that the school of art that called itself Realism was the very one that was most disconnected from reality.[69] At least mannerism and modernism had the honesty to flaunt their distance from the world and, in the best cases, the conviction to use this autonomy as a lever with which to critique and transform it. As he saw matters, "all of the chatter about reflectionism [*отображательстве*] in literature is not only theoretically vapid, but deleterious in practice since it diverts attention away from the most important thing: construction."[70] Abandoning aesthetic reflection in this way put the Lefists in direct conflict not just with emerging currents of proletarian realism but also with the dominant school of theoretical Marxism that, per Second International orthodoxy, had defined cultural phenomena as secondary expressions of primary material reality. For the factographers, this doctrine of base-superstructural reflectionism was intrinsically flawed because it presumed a hiatus that was both epistemological and temporal in nature. All mediation entails a delay that precludes direct intervention, explained Tret'iakov. "Reflectionism can negate [even] the most vital issue" ("To Be Continued," 55).

Critics may have denounced factography as a "cult of description," but the writing itself was anything but vivid, lifelike, or descriptive.[71] At those moments when the ocherk comes closest to achieving the ideals of mechanicity and instantaneity, its language turns abstract and colorless. The degree-zero austerity of the scene in "Moscow–Beijing" when Tret'iakov and the German Blinch arrive at the border is typical: "Customs inspection. Question: Are you carrying furs or gold currency? I cannot translate the words for the German. 'Fur': I point out the sheepskin lining of my coat. The German does not understand. It is funny to me; it is suspicious to the customs officials. It too ends. Manchuria in 15 minutes. The steppe stretches out there, into the distance, into the Gobi desert. The longest thing on the horizon is the ditch that has been hammered into it. This is the border between China and Russia" ("Moskva–Pekin," 45). The passage delivers no imagery to the mind's eye, nothing for the reader to visualize. Tret'iakov withholds all stylistic flourishes and qualitative shading that might distinguish one particular moment as more pivotal or dramatic than any other. Predicates are rare in his telegraphic shorthand: the customs agent here is little more than a disembodied voice, the fur is devoid of tactile properties, and the landscape is a simple geometric plane. Without qualities to ballast objects with sensuous attributes, language begins to shed its weight and thin out. Like the train that propels Tret'iakov eastward, the stream of words grows light and accelerates, darting past without leaving traces behind in the memory of the reader. Tret'iakov ponders whether methods of literary description are compatible with this Leaguist stenography: "It is possible to describe Mr. Blinch?" he asks. The answer is definitive: "You cannot describe him in accordance with NOT" ("Moskva–Pekin," 41).[72] The lack of vivid imagery in the factographic sketch thus confirms the Formalist Iurii Tynianov's observation that all truly "concrete" words—those that hew most tightly to actual physical existence—perforce have no "visual analogue."[73] The stratum of language closest to reality is experienced psychologically as the most abstract and elusive, indeed, as the most unreal.

Maxim Gorky's rich and vivid reportage from the same years offers an instructive contrast to the eidetically impoverished prose snapshots of Tret'iakov. In the multipart series "In and About the Soviet Union" (1929), which took Gorky from the Ukrainian steppe to the labor camps of Solovki, the celebrated novelist assumes the "elevated point of view" typical of realist prose, a transcendental posture high above the fray of events.[74] As living, breathing flesh, Gorky is absent in these texts, replaced by a vertical eye/I that surveys the world at a remove. His travelogue pursues the "structural reduction of the body as a privileged perceptual field of self-presence nearly to the point of disappearance."[75] Bracketing off the pressing sensations of the body and distancing himself from reality in this way enables Gorky to weave a vibrant and colorful tapestry for his reader. At a practical level, he attributed the exceptional vividness of this prose to the particular technique that he used to write: Gorky boasted that he never took notes while he was underway but instead tried to remember everything without the use of mnemonic aids. "I never write down what I hear and see, relying instead on my visual memory [*зрительную память*] and my general ability to recall."[76] Gorky's method as a reporter was first to distill his experiences into distinct images and then to commit these recollections to writing only later, when he was back at the comfort of his desk. As a rule, realist writers internalize experience mentally before externalizing it on paper.

Factographers proceed in the reverse order, first recording events directly into a notebook without encoding them mnemonically and then pausing to reflect on their significance only later. Tret'iakov's very first act in "Moscow–Beijing," even before he gets a watch, is to purchase the sturdy block notebook in which he will store everything that he hears and sees, all the conversational snippets that he overhears on the train and the fading posters that fly past him at the stations. The notebook became so indispensable to Tret'iakov's practice that one contemporary even described it as a prosthetic extension of the factographer's own body, a kind of artificial sensory organ through which he perceived the world. "Tret'iakov fills his block notebooks on the run, amongst activities . . . The block notebook devours everything caught by the eye of the journalist."[77] Unlike Gorky, the factographer does not wait for the event to conclude before beginning to write, but instead starts jotting down details and facts while he is still in the immediacy of the encounter, the movements of his hand working in rhythmic coordination with those of his mind. His strategy of monistic auto-correspondence recalls the *écriture automatique* of the French Surrealists, another avant-garde that shared the factographers' aversion to reflection and retrospection: "Write quickly, without any preconceived subject, fast enough so that you will not remember what you're writing and be tempted to reread what you have written."[78] Such strategies of instantaneous notation were promoted on the pages of *Time*, where correspondents were told to replace organic memory with mechanical inscription. One essay promoted the mnemotechnologies used by modern professionals who "refuse on principle to rely on their own memory and instead use its surrogates, various forms of recording."[79] Not only were these technologies more accurate and reliable than natural memory, but they allowed the writer to remain in direct contact with events around him. Whereas realist writers like Gorky withdrew to the comfort of the study to practice their craft, the stenographic method took the factographer onto the street and into the churn of history. "The ocherkist is a writer on wheels," explained Pertsov, who argued that physical mobilization was in fact a defining generic feature of their method: "The movement of the ocherkist in space is a prerequisite of the ocherk as a literary movement."[80] When asked his opinion about contemporary fiction, Tret'iakov's close friend Oskar Maria Graf put it simply: "Too much of the writing is happening at desks."[81]

Chuzhak took Gorky to task for the tardiness of realism in his 1928 broadside "An Essay on Learning from a Classic." While the factographer conceded there that the great "teacher of life" (as the novelist was known) might possess valuable knowledge, he pointed out that these insights were always hindsights, the result of belated reflection rather than concrete perception. Gorky is always "instructing life after the fact." Like a pharmacist who labels and arranges all of his inventory on shelves before mixing his concoctions, the teacher of life plans out every move before setting to work. In the inaugural year of the Five-Year Plan, Chuzhak thus declares Gorky to be "the most 'plan-oriented' writer of our day." The problem with this approach, Chuzhak continues, is that writing according to plan has left the realist ill equipped to deal with messy and volatile matters that cannot be organized as tidily as flasks on a shelf. According to Chuzhak, these limitations come to the fore in *The Artamonov Business* (1925), the recent novel in which Gorky finally attempted for the first time to depict the Bolshevik Revolution. Sitting at his desk in Italy eight years after the events of October, Gorky managed to write only a dozen pages on the subject. The revolution found its way into *Artamonov*, "but judging by the twelve pages it is given in the thick novel, the matter is clearly not settled. Gorky hasn't investigated the revolution enough to be able to show it. He hasn't yet affixed the necessary labels or arranged everything on the correct shelves." Although the novel was written "at a distance from the facts that is both territorial (Sorrento) and chronological," the events of the revolution elude depiction because they remain unfinished and ongoing in the transitional period. The realist method of "refracting through time" (*преломления во времени*) that Gorky learned from nineteenth-century classics has left the novelist at a loss for words. To this day he still has not "become aware" (*осознал*) of the revolution: "Gorky studied the classics of the nobility, which don't allow our teacher to fraternize too closely with life's urgent issues. According to this aesthetic, events should be 'settled' enough in the 'soul' and in the 'time' of the artist, who has filtered them through the 'prism' of his 'consciousness.' The consciousness of the artist is the highest law. If the facts contradict consciousness, then all the worse for the facts! In the best case they can then . . . wait a bit."[82]

Gorky exemplifies what Chuzhak calls a "realist-retrospectivist" (*реалист-осознаватель*), a species of writer who suffers from chronic "lagging behind life." According to the factographer, all mimetic art suffers structurally from a "belated retrospectivism" (*осознавательство задним умом*: literally, a "coming into awareness in hindsight") that causes consciousness to fall out of sync with the present and that precludes operative intervention. "*Belated retrospectivism*. We made the revolution, we fought in the civil war, we are regenerating the national economy, we are building socialism. That is us: builders. We don't have any time. But you: you are observers, you are cognizers [*познаватели*]. You are writers and witnesses. You become aware of *yesterday*! (Awareness of the present day is not possible for you, since it is proscribed by the old aesthetics: the event must wait. Becoming aware of 'today' is life-construction, not life-cognition)" ("Literatura zhiznestroeniia," 45). Distance from events and refraction through time are what give the realist novel its remarkable vividness and timeless monumentality—the lifelike characters and places of *Artamonov* are "illuminated by the soul" and painted in "festively epic" colors—but lifelike is not the same as alive. (In a discussion of the mythical contest between Zeuxis and Parrhasius, the two artists who competed to outdo the other in painterly illusionism, Chuzhak pointed out that commentators never see the incident from the perspective of the hungry birds that were duped by the fake fruit.[83]) Gorky's overreliance on imagery precludes concrete reference to reality. In a single short but exemplary passage from *The Artamonov Business*, Chuzhak thus counts no fewer than seven occurrences of the word *like* (*как*) but only one specific designation (*определение*): "Look at how disconcertedly and helplessly [Gorky] runs from 'image' to 'image' (such are the means of traditional artistic thought!)."[84] The realist writer cannot escape from the imagination's machinery of likeness, a hermetic world of resemblance and association in which images continuously beget more images.

Chuzhak's essay on Gorky identifies a structural law at the heart of all factographic work: the opposition of fact to image (*образ*). Whether in literature, film, or photography, the factographic assault on the metaphysics of representation always begins with the eradication of mental imagery. The editors of the journal *The Present* declared, for example, that their acts of documentation "opposed the fact as such to the artistic image," just as Eisenstein characterized the chronicle film as "the negation of the image in the name of the fact."[85] This antagonism became the movement's enduring cultural legacy so that even forty years later, in the midst of the second factographic wave, one critic would still trace "the fact's current assault on the image" back to the work of *Novyi Lef*.[86] From literary "representationalism" (*из-образительность*, or "imaging forth") to cognitive "reflectionism" (*от-ображательство*, or "imaging back"), any method of artistic creation or modality of consciousness that utilized imagery became a target of the factographers. "Are the tasks of the revolution in the realm of art resolved by *representation* and *reflection*, or is art faced with *organizational* and *constructive* tasks that have not been fulfilled by the forms that have existed up to our time?" ("Art in the Revolution," 14). The fundamental opposition between fact and image opened onto any number of further theoretical distinctions that were taken up by the factographers, whether that was the epistemological distinction between truth and fiction, the discursive distinction between journalism and fiction, the ontological distinction between reality and illusion, or the dromological distinction between fast and slow. As we will see, the factographers rehearsed the antagonism between fact and image in every possible conceptual key.

In an echo of the Russian word for "iconoclasm" (*иконоборчество*), Tret'iakov christened their work an act of "image-destruction" (*образоборчество*).[87] Like Protestants who smashed the idols that blocked access to their god, the factographers would shatter the tropes and figures that obscured direct perception of reality. They were not alone. Assaults on imagery in art and literature were in fact so widespread in these years that some have characterized late modernism broadly as a project to "abolish the mediation of the image."[88] The Russian Formalists, to cite a famous example, denounced neo-Aristotelian critics who equated art with "thinking in images." This prohibition on imagining was not limited to art and literature, but so pervaded all levels of culture that the leading scholar of visual cognition Allan Paivio lamented the early twentieth century as a "most arid period" for mental imagery in general.[89] Even the sciences of mind rejected the centuries-old precept of thinking in images. In Germany, laboratory experiments identified cognitive processes that unfolded entirely without introspection, leading psychologists to conclude that many features of inner life originated in so-called imageless thoughts (*unanschauliche Gedanken*) and general affective dispositions (*Bewußtseinslagen*). Meanwhile, Russian researchers were investigating how the mind came to know and navigate the world through embodied sensorimotor action-schemas, prompting psychologists like Vygotsky to argue that many higher cognitive functions were actually based on nonrepresentational somatic orientations and situational capacities rather than on mental pictures of the world. In both art and science, the mind went dark in the early twentieth century.

The factographers traced their own practice of imageless writing back to the 1860s. In "The Literature of Life-Construction," the programmatic essay in which the term "factography" made its debut, Chuzhak explained that their movement descended from journalistic practices that challenged the poetics of the realist novel in the mid-nineteenth century. If the latter monumental line in Russian literature stemmed from Ivan Turgenev, whose *Fathers and Sons* fashioned an aesthetic totality in which all personal fates were intertwined, all events were illuminated by destiny, and, by the conclusion of the novel, all emotional conflicts were resolved, the line of the factographers derived instead from the little-known radical journalist Fedor Reshetnikov (1841–71), whose "uncannily artless records" and "crude photography of the base aspects of life" represented the dialectical opposite of Turgenev's novels ("Literatura zhiznestroeniia," 34–38).[90] In Chuzhak's account, nearly every feature of Turgenev's metaphysical realism found its direct negation in the base materialism of Reshetnikov, who documented outward social behavior instead of probing the depths of the psyche, wrote using the cold mechanical clichés of the journalist instead of the novelist's idiom of sentiment and feeling, engaged with topics of the day instead of timeless generational myths, and favored fragmentary snapshots of superficial reality over "the concealed totality of life" (as Lukács once characterized the subject of the novel).[91]

Chuzhak's essay built on Roman Jakobson's 1921 "On Realism in Art," which distinguished one current of realism that saw the artwork as an "ideogram" aspiring to "the highest degree of verisimilitude" from a second current of "revolutionary realism" that used non sequiturs, unmotivated incidents, and other "unessential details" to explode the mimetic illusion.[92] But whereas Jakobson considered the latter's negation of the dominant line to be just the returning swing on the pendulum of cultural evolution—for the Formalists, every estrangement of the canon will eventually be automatized and canonized in turn—Chuzhak celebrated the flood of noise in Reshetnikov's journalism as irrecuperable, non-Hegelian positivity. He praised the ungainly thingliness of objects that refused to be made to signify and the obstinacy of facts that would never submit to the reader's demand for intelligibility. Using "literary X-rays of small patches of this earth," this materialist prose shifted "away from the invented 'reflection' of fantastical 'fragments of reality' ('projected through the prism of aesthetics') and toward their most precise handling using authentic pieces of reality, like soil from the plow."[93] These "crude sprouts," which still cling to the base and loamy stuff of the world, sought neither to judge nor to interpret reality.[94] For journalists, factographers, and other degree-zero writers, "objects will be *there* before being *something*; and they will still be there afterwards, hard, unalterable, eternally present, mocking their own 'meaning.'"[95]

Everyone knows which of these two lines triumphed in the 1860s. Unlike Reshetnikov, a writer utterly unknown before the publication of Chuzhak's essay in 1928, Turgenev would be celebrated far and wide as the father of the great Russian novel. Reshetnikov's crude prose fragments never succeeded in becoming a major literary genre. "All of this was utterly formless [*бесформенно*]; all of this destroyed the very foundations of literary canonicity, and the aesthetics of Turgenev realism in particular. But all of this assaulted the cherished canons so violently that it could no longer continue to have a decisive influence on the development of realism" ("Literatura zhiznestroeniia," 37). Reshetnikov's offensive on the imagination was simply too radical to be recovered. Banished from the system of cultural patrimony, his materialist prose would nonetheless have an afterlife in the militant journalism of the *raznochintsy*, the stratum of disenfranchised bureaucrats who published imageless prose in periodicals like *The Contemporary* and who would eventually give rise in the twentieth century to the white-collar knowledge worker. Indeed, Dostoevsky's harsh rebuke of the editor of *The Contemporary* Nikolai Chernyshevsky, whom Chuzhak celebrated as the foremost "*raznochinets* theorist," applies equally to Reshetnikov, and, for that matter, to the factographers who traced their own class lineage back to the *raznochintsy* ("Literatura zhiznestroeniia," 42): "You want to force humanity not to talk in images," Dostoevsky railed against Chernyshevsky. "From the very earliest times, man has always talked in images. Every language is full of images and metaphors. You are attacking the expression of thought in images; you are conspirators against progress, you poor unhappy morons."[96]

Sixty years later, Tret'iakov, Chuzhak, and Pertsov revived the conspiracy against the image. And once again, champions of the novel rallied to its defense. The most brilliant and justifiably acclaimed of these defenses was Georg Lukács's "Reportage or *Gestaltung*?," which took up the cause of the realist novel against the factographers and their German scions such as Ernst Ottwalt. The 1932 essay, which was translated into Russian the following year as "Reportage or Image-Creation [*образотворчество*]?," recast the familiar antagonism between fact and image as a choice between journalism and aesthetic form. Factography combines a theory of "anti-gestalt" with a practice of "non-figuration," Lukács explained there ("Reportage or Portrayal?," 66; translation modified). His choice of terms in the title was notable: like the Russian word for image or figure, *obraz*, the German *Gestalt* is a concept associated with holistic qualities such as integrality, proportion, and conciseness.[97] As Lukács saw it, making work without imagery, as the factographers proposed, abandoned contour and form-giving figuration and, along with these defining features, the closure of aesthetic totality. He considered factography to be a literal disfiguration of art. He argued that this prose denies the reader access to "higher poetic reality" and mires consciousness in the mundane details of empirical reality, a thicket of random notations from which no clear mental synopsis can emerge. Later in the decade, when Lukács resumed his invective against this shapeless prose, he would argue that any attempt to record the present in its nascency would invariably dissolve into "a shimmering chaos" ("Narrate or Describe?," 131; translation modified). For him, factography was surface without structure, ornament without image, detail without totality.

The factographers' understanding of imagery borrowed heavily from Formalist accounts of metaphor, a figure of speech that, for both groups, exemplified all tropological language as such.[98] In a 1924 essay in *Lef*, Tynianov had described metaphor as a form of rhetorical "contagion" that displaces meaning across "threads of association that connect to other words." Metaphor, he wrote, is the "unbinding" of reference that results when "two meanings, two lexical units, two basic tokens, have collided in the word and begin to press up against each other."[99] This collision causes boundaries between the units to blur, giving rise to the trans-fer of meaning that is the lexical root of the word *meta-phor*. As the Formalists saw it, semantic slippage and referential imprecision were not just regrettable side effects of metaphorical language, then, but its very essence. The more extensive the network of metaphorical connections between words, the more "smoothed out" (*сглаженные*) and vague language becomes, and the less suitable it is for designating actual facts. A powerful poetic trope like *sun*, for example, has virtually ceased to have any referential value at all because it is dispersed over such a broad lexical field. Such a word, Tynianov writes, "has abandoned all concretion, although a very emotional and often confusing mass of associations remain tangled up within it" ("Slovar'," 92).

For the Formalists, metaphor exemplified the system of meaning advanced by contemporary schools of structural linguistics, in which signs connect to other signs in a closed matrix of differential value that operates independently of concrete reference. Building on this insight, twentieth-century critics and philosophers have argued that metaphorical language is the origin of the dualist worldview, and even metaphysics as such. The 1929 dictionary entry on "metaphor" in *Documents*, for example, stated: "Not only language but the whole of intellectual life is based on a play of transpositions, a play of symbols, which can be described as metaphorical."[100] Metaphor is not just a rhetorical device, but a "technology of linguistic transport" whose interconnected network of meanings becomes the basis of all abstract thinking as such.[101] Materialists like Chuzhak objected that this transfer operation unfolds automatically on a thought-register cut off from empirical reality, where one poetic association conjures another and another in an interminable chain—an endless series of "likes" without any concrete designations. The inability of metaphor to designate lived experience—its remoteness from the gritty particularity of the world—prompted Heidegger's famous remark about the collusion between metaphor and philosophical dualism: "The idea of 'transposing' and of metaphor is based upon the distinguishing, if not complete separation, of the sensible and the nonsensible as two realms that subsist on their own. The setting up of this partition between the sensible and the nonsensible, between the physical and the nonphysical is a basic trait of what is called metaphysics and which normatively determines Western thinking."[102]

At the other end of the linguistic spectrum from metaphor was the factographers' favorite class of words, technical terminology. Following the phenomenologist Gustav Shpet, Formalists like Tynianov and Grigorii Vinokur contrasted the remorseless referential precision of the term to the semantic slippage of tropological language. Unlike the latter, which presides over a large connotative field and which can be used to invoke many different phenomena, terms trigger no mental associations and have just a single concrete thing that they point to with utmost specificity. Vinokur would associate these opposed word-types with two distinct systems of discourse, poetry and science.[103] Devoid of psychological coloring and etymological resonance, terminology functions much like a proper name (*название*), pointing unambiguously at one referent, and nothing else.[104] The interpretive bandwidth of technical terminology is exceedingly narrow. Terms do not tolerate the equivocations of poetry, nor do they leave the reader wondering about the meaning of the text. As examples of the respective aptitudes of term and metaphor, Tynianov contrasted Marx's famous phrase "Expropriate the expropriators!" (*Экспроприируйте экспроприаторов!*) with Lenin's more idiomatic "Steal what's been stolen!" (*Грабьте награбленное!*). While the latter "leads to several meanings," Marx's original formulation establishes a "narrow field of lexical unity" and resists "lexical convergence" with other words. Because the flagrantly Latinate term *expropriate* does not conjure any associations to the native Russian ear, it proves resistant to connotative contagion ("Slovar'," 89).

Technical terminology became a crucial resource in the factographers' quest for a language that was, in Chuzhak's words, "specific through and through" ("Writer's Handbook," 91). "We who are suffering from an irresponsible mania for images and the excesses of metaphor can already learn a lot from technical literature" ("To Be Continued," 55). The factographers inherited their love of specialist jargon from the *zaumnik* wordsmiths who dreamt of an Adamic bond between sign and thing. As a precedent for his work, Tret'iakov cited Aleksei Kruchenykh, who had famously declared in 1913 that "the worn-out, violated word *lily* is devoid of all expression" and who campaigned to drive such figural language out of poetry.[105] "The word must fit consciousness tightly, like a greased boot" (Kruchenykh, quoted in "From Where," 207). But while Kruchenykh sought to restore a primordial and prelapsarian condition of one-to-one correspondence between sign and thing, the factographers approached the problem of reference from the other end of human history by mobilizing the highly specialized jargons of machine civilization. Even in their critique of metaphor the factographers were industrial enthusiasts and cultural rationalists to the core. Whether in the diverse designations for grain in *The Summons* (1930) or in the detailed geological taxonomies of *Nation A-E* (1932), Tret'iakov loved to use the professional lingo specific to his subject. Detractors and fans alike drew attention to the *termini technici* that the factographers picked up in their various assignments. Linguistic purists and advocates for so-called simplificationism (*опростительство*) denounced their use of foreign words and alien terminologies that they considered un-Russian and incomprehensible, protesting that the average reader would need a dictionary to get through most factographic ocherki. Enthusiasts, on the other hand, celebrated this technical lexicon for finally eliminating ambiguity and arresting the semantic slippage of poetry.

Technical language found hospitable conditions in the practice of Soviet journalism. As Vinokur observed in his seminal study "The Language of Our Newspaper," which appeared in *Lef* in 1924, "the lexicology of the newspaper is *sui generis* a terminology."[106] Indeed, Soviet journalism was widely recognized in the 1920s to be a discourse hostile to mental imagery. One anecdote is exemplary on this point. In April 1929 a certain Solomon Shereshevsky walked into the office of the neuropsychologist Aleksandr Luria complaining that he "struggled against images that kept rising to the surface of his mind." Luria's new patient could not cope with metaphorical language, since these images "tended to jam together, producing still more images." Figures of speech "led [Shereshevsky] astray," made him absent-minded, and cut him off from the world around him. "Poetry was probably the most difficult thing for him to read," Luria observed. In stark contrast, the prompt facts of the newspaper seemed to cut through the tangle of mental associations and speak directly to the body of the reader.[107] The course of treatment for this patient was obvious to Luria: Shereshevsky, who would go on to become "Sh.," one of the most celebrated cases in Soviet psychology, found his calling as a newspaper reporter. If the 1920s were a decade inclined to "fantasectomy," as one historian of Soviet culture put it, the prose of fact would be the best scalpel.[108]

Philosophers too have grouped technical terminology and journalism together at the materialist pole of language. Theodor W. Adorno's essay "On the Use of Foreign Words," which was originally written as a defense of the newspaper, characterized terminology as a current of alterity pulsating "beneath the sphere of culture but without fusing with the body of language." The incomprehensible words and manifestly technical forms of speech used by journalists resist the imperative to signify, proving that "subjectivity cannot simply be dissolved in meaning." These manufactured jargons have no inner mental form, no etymological resonance of past usage. For Adorno, artificial words are less felt by the imagination than experienced by and on the body. They belong to a "pure creaturely language" whose "explosive force" impacts the reader almost physically. In the abstract terminology of the newspaper, rarefied technicism converges with base materialism, triggering a dialectical frenzy in which "*ratio* strikes the stream of language, which gleams painfully in it." Adorno thus compared the organic word and the technical term to two very different, even opposed sources of light, one that was natural, steady, and illuminating and another that was mechanical, fitful, and blinding: "The old organic words are like gas lights in a street where the violet light of an oxyacetylene welding apparatus suddenly flames out."[109] Tellingly, Adorno's simile also suggests two distinct modalities of signification, one representationalist and one operative: like a gently burning streetlamp, the native word conjures a scene out of the surrounding darkness for the mind to contemplate, while the technical word is a tool for construction that wounds the imagination rather than activating it.

Whatever the term gains in material concretion, it forfeits in longevity. Unlike metaphors, terms are not easily retained in thought, and any writing that is based on them will be quickly forgotten. These mnemonic defects were obvious to the opponents of the factographers, who argued that Lef's program for imageless writing essentially led to a literature of amnesia. One article in

RAPP's house journal *On Literary Guard* quoted an example of vivid narration from one of their own authors and then contrasted this excerpt with the technicist prose of the factographers: "The image is not a means of decoration, a fancy ornament; it fulfills the productive function of helping us to see all sides of a given process vividly. Once you have read this description you will remember it forever. But a different kind of description, one that designates using scientific terminology and that offers a dry enumeration of some or other branch of industry, will not be retained in memory for long. It will evaporate without a trace."[110] When Shklovsky finally broke with Tret'iakov in 1931 after a period of increasing disagreement over the dangers of imagelessness, the Formalist in fact cited the ephemerality of his writing as the reason for defecting. "The ocherk? No, that's not a solution. It perishes quickly. It doesn't survive past its own day."[111] (In his own recantation of factography several years later, Tret'iakov would concede: "The shortcoming of my kolkhoz books is that they fade quickly."[112]) Like other factical writers, Tret'iakov rejected the vivid, hallucinatory prose of contemporaries who aspired to enduring monumentality. "The aesthetics [of Gorky] tells him to work toward eternity," Chuzhak wrote ("Literatura zhiznestroeniia," 42).[113] For scions of the League of Time, the last thing writing should be is timeless. Their presentist prose was instead deliberately, even militantly, forgettable.

Thus the prevalence of terms in the daily press and other presentist ephemera. Consumed by the reader and then immediately forgotten, terminology is the lexical corollary to the fleeting temporality of the newspaper. Metaphors may be imprecise, but their tendency to liaise with other words makes them one of the hardiest, most memorable species in the ecosystem of language. Not so the delicate term, which refuses association and is doomed to a short life as a result of its isolation. Punctual and precise but also highly fugitive, technical terminology is unfit for the wear and tear of everyday life. It is "weakly preserved in consciousness," Tynianov observed ("Slovar'," 89). The "hard, artificial, unyielding" terminologies of the newspaper in turn reminded Adorno of a "quickly fading daguerreotype," a chemical facsimile of reality that was paradoxically both petrified and evanescent at once.[114] The term might be the most concrete form of language, but this concreteness is experienced by the reader as its exact opposite, as abstraction devoid of determinate image-content. The technical term has "a 'thingly' concreteness and a lexical non-concreteness" ("Slovar'," 100). Echoing the philosopher Gottlob Frege, who had posited an inverse correlation between reference (*Bedeutung*) and sense (*Sinn*), Tynianov explained that "the most concrete *designation* of the thing—pointing to it—is the least concrete from the perspective of language," and that, conversely, "the most concrete word—the word that is connected with a mass of associations—is the least concrete when it comes to designating a completely defined, concrete object" ("Slovar'," 88).

The popularity of terminology in early Soviet Russia responded to a general hunger for material facts and referential specificity in the transitional phase. "The people of our time are preoccupied with intensive detail—they are a people of the Baroque," wrote Shklovsky (*Hunt for Optimism*, 128). Heralding a new era of accuracy and exactness, political and cultural leaders called for technical punctiliousness at work, conscientiousness in everyday life, and the reorientation of human perception toward the minutiae of experience. Trotsky, an enthusiast of meticulous stenographic recording, published articles like "Attention to Trifles!" and "Alas, We Are Not Accurate Enough!," which warned that "the correct organization of today's economy is unthinkable without precision and accuracy";[115] Gastev enjoined "Enough words about the great. / Attention toward the 'detail' — / to the microscope, / to what is barely perceptible";[116] and shortly after Lenin's death, Mayakovsky reflected on the late leader's love of detail, declaring "An eye toward trifles! — / The command of Il'ich."[117] The new pathos of the trivial and the general attunement to the microscopic in these years marked a sharp reversal from the hyperbole and Manichaeism that characterized the rhetoric of the Civil War period. If the latter was an era of legendary feats and world-historical contrasts, the reconstruction period that followed was oriented instead toward finely tuned gestures and subtle gradations. After the great revolutionary wave had destroyed the capitalist order, Soviet society focused its energies on the careful business of rebuilding, a task that, Pertsov observed, demanded a new sensibility for "precision," "small scales," and "minimalism."[118]

But cultures of precision are fundamentally hostile to the imagination, which requires a degree of vagueness in which to stage its play of associations. "Moscow–Beijing" begins with the Leaguist directive to record everything indiscriminately, but when followed to the letter, this injunction explodes all reasonable proportion, atomizing literature in a cloud-swarm of details: "A note written according to NOT: before putting out a cigarette, it is necessary to moisten it with saliva to avoid a fire," "NOT information: the conductor supplies the linens," and so on ("Moskva–Pekin," 34, 35). Nothing escapes through the fine mesh of the factographer's dragnet. And with the capture of each additional detail, Tret'iakov dims the light of the mind's eye a bit more, until there is nothing left to see. "Not imagery, but precision" (*не образность, а точность*) was the formula of factography ("Writer's Handbook," 86).

Formalists and factographers alike understood the imagination to be an essentially negative faculty. Shklovsky famously defined artmaking as a subtractive process that utilizes "braking," "estrangement," "making difficult," and other apophatic devices. Writing poetry demands not just giving verbal material a formal structure but also withholding crucial details and depriving the reader of information. "The ellipsis—an omission—is the principal trope of poetic discourse, the principal figure of poetry itself. The ellipsis is a principal image"

(*A Hunt for Optimism*, 129). For Shklovsky, the image is not actually a presence but an absence, something taken away from reality. In this regard realism and modernism actually share the same logic. Indeed, seen from this perspective, modernist abstraction would be just a pathological hypertrophism within the basic representationalist system of realism—subtraction taken too far. This was the reason a materialist critic like Carl Einstein rejected both movements, which he considered equally complicit in Western metaphysics. Under modernism, the impulse to reduce and pare away eclipsed all other aspects of artmaking, leading to the world-negating asceticism of movements such as Suprematism. Einstein observed that abstract painters like Malevich were "oriented toward reduction just like the old metaphysicians" and concluded that "such an art could only correspond to an early, negative stage of the revolution." For Einstein, the problem with the "hygienic" paintings of the Suprematists was that this austerity only energized the audience's imagination: by withholding perceptual data, these artworks enjoined the viewer to fill in the gaps, to restore in her mind the missing information that the artist had left out.[119] The more impoverished the painting, the more vigorous the spectator's imagining at the reception end.

By this logic, every aesthetic act consisted of two distinct phases: first, the subtractive moment when the artist removes some quantity *x* from reality and, second, the additive moment when the spectator then restores what was withheld. Early in his career, the theater director Vsevolod Meyerhold thus endorsed using just "one or two bold brush-strokes" instead of "a host of details" so that "the spectator's imagination can supply all that is left unsaid."[120] Gaps and omissions in the production offered footholds where the imagination could get traction. For modernists like Meyerhold, reducing the sensory bandwidth of the performance actively recruited the audience as collaborators in the aesthetic act. This was why he also rejected the use of real-life models and mannequins in his plays, since actual facsimiles of reality would only disable the inner visions of the spectator.[121]

Tret'iakov's assault on the imagination started already in the early 1920s, when the playwright began filling in the gaps at Meyerhold's Proletkul't theater with facts from real life. He used actual harvesters and pigeons in *Earth Rampant* (1923), sprayed irritating ammonia into the air at the Moscow Gas Works where *Gasmasks* was staged (1924), imported authentic ethnographic artifacts for the set of *Roar China!* (1925), and concluded *I Want a Baby* (1926) by inviting the audience on stage to inspect an exhibition of live infants. Reviewers of these productions were perplexed by their strange combination of spare constructivist sets and extreme naturalistic detail.[122] Introducing more and more factual elements into his work, and further limiting the powers of the imagination with each such addition, Tret'iakov finally banished all poetic ellipses with his turn to photography and journalism. He fashioned himself into "a kind of apparatus that absorbs everything," recording each event, encounter, and detail without discrimination or discernment ("Writer's Handbook," 91). Tret'iakov's mechanical auto-correspondence, which transcribed reality directly onto paper with minimal processing by the author, left the reader with nothing to ponder, no missing content to reconstruct or ambiguities to resolve. Like Surrealist *écriture automatique*, this practice yielded prose in which "sound and image, image and sound, interpenetrated with automatic precision and such felicity that no chink was left for the penny-in-the-slot called 'meaning.'"[123] The result, in the words of one scholar of factography, was a literature that "explodes the imagination" (*взрывает воображение*).[124]

Cinematography, photography, and other mechanical inscription technologies provided the models for this precisionistic writing. Shklovsky pointed out that film, for example, is deficient "in the area of allusion, which in literature sustains one's interest in the resolution of mystery. Film does not allow ambivalence."[125] Likewise, Kracauer observed that photography overwhelms consciousness with detail and noise, burying the imagination "as if under a layer of snow." Through its exhaustive "warehousing of nature . . . the flood of photos sweeps away the dams of memory," creating a world "alienated from meaning" that neither demands nor even permits the interpretive exertions of the spectator.[126] For this reason, the defender of the literary imagination Wolfgang Iser would later warn that allowing technical media to fill in the omissions and gaps (*Leerstellen*) in the text would leave nothing for the mind to contribute, no penny for the reader to put into the hermeneutic slot. "In an age of information, images tend to become a transmitting agency which, in bombarding our perception, shrivels our use of the imagination."[127] Iser recognized that the technical media's "aesthetic of precision" (*Präzisionsästhetik*)—to recall Reger's characterization of interwar reportage—was fundamentally irreconcilable with his own "aesthetic of reception" (*Rezeptionsästhetik*).[128] The latter required narrowing the bandwidth of perception to make space for transcendental reflection. But the unabridged recordings of the factographers permitted no such amnesty from reality, no chance to look away. Like the newspaper that "presents life like a sharp photograph" (*Gazeta*, 143), factography turned the imagination of the bourgeoisie inside out, replacing metaphysics with materialism, reflection with reflexes, and quiet contemplation with psychotechnical stimulation.

THE TECHNOLOGICAL FANTASTIC

The campaign to eradicate the imagination marked a striking reorientation in the pathos of the Russian avant-garde. The Futurists had become famous internationally in the 1910s for their visionary defiance of reality and their implacable hostility to life in its current form. Mayakovsky had condemned everyday life (*быт*) as the "stabilizing force of an immutable present, overlaid, as this present is, by a stagnating slime, which stifles life in its tight, hard mold."[129]

And prior to the revolution, at least, the utopian projections of his circle had constituted a progressive historical force, a wellspring of alternate realities that transcended the inert slime of the present and challenged the repressive status quo of tsarist Russia. But the program of the avant-garde changed after the Bolsheviks came to power. The industrial explosion of the reconstruction period and the socialization of the forces of production led to a growing sense that concrete reality was starting to outstrip the creative powers of the Futurists, and that the mundane present, rather than some distant utopia, was now the site of cultural invention and renewal. Everyday life, once inert and stagnant, was becoming a locus of dynamism and change. The faculty of the imagination in turn seemed unable to keep up with, much less anticipate and surpass, actual developments that were unfolding at a breakneck pace in real time. With this reversal of fortune, radical members of the Russian avant-garde abandoned the poetry of subjunctives and the art of counterfactuals and refashioned themselves into journalists, engineers, and photographers.[130] They replaced aesthetic creation with laboratory experimentation and sensory reduction with empirical observation. As Chuzhak wrote, the watchword for the avant-garde after the revolution was no longer "Futurism" but "future-exactism."[131]

Mayakovsky's circle lamented the loss of their utopia. "We were sad to give up the imagination," wrote Nikolai Aseev about Tret'iakov's ascent.[132] But what the Futurists had failed to grasp was that the rationalization of art and the embrace of technical media had not destroyed creativity, but only changed its countenance. Contemporaries observed that the imagination was replaced in these years by fantasy, a creative faculty that inclines consciousness toward reality rather than withdrawing from it. In 1928 Ilya Ehrenburg proclaimed the advent of a new "technological fantastic" that broke decisively with the literary imagination of the previous century. Decades of industrialization had at last succeeded in building a "second world" for humanity, a "conditioned reality" that was no longer ontologically distinguishable from the first reality of given, spontaneous nature.[133] As Ehrenburg explained, the resulting confusion recalled the fantastic novels of the nineteenth century, which had once vexed readers by blurring the boundaries between the supernatural and the natural worlds, artifice and reality.[134] Although the mixing of science and fiction in the new technological fantastic recalled this Romantic precedent, Ehrenburg insisted that the fantastic of his own time was unlike its shadowy predecessor in one crucial regard: previously "fantasy in verses or in painting always ran up against the desperate resistance of the intellect," but the fantastic of industrial civilization was fully illuminated by reason. The hallucinations of the nineteenth-century fantastic had left the pages of the novel and could now be recorded with cameras and calibrated with instruments.[135] According to Adorno, who likewise welcomed the waning of the imagination in the interwar period, the faculty of fantasy was distinguished by "the richness of the detail on which it dwells rather than hurrying past it to the whole."[136] The German philosopher traced the precisionistic, this-worldly creations of modern fantasy back to the materialism of the English empiricists, which he contrasted with the negative pleasures and numinous sublime of Kantian aesthetics. Fantasy, which lacks the latter's vertical thrust, "abides strictly within the material which the sciences present to it," explained Adorno.[137] Whereas the literary imagination once recoiled from reality, the technological fantastic embraced fact and difference. The creative mind no longer had to close its eyes, as the Futurists once did, but could now stare reality directly in the face. As Ehrenburg said of the new fantastic, "humanity has started to dream 'in broad daylight.'"[138]

The epochal transition from the literary imagination to the technological fantastic was the subject of Tret'iakov's 1928 sketch "Through Clouded Glasses." He wrote the ocherk on the flight from Moscow to the town of Mineral'nye Vody, the first leg of the journey to the remote kolkhoz where Tret'iakov would serve intermittently for the next five years. Like the train journey of "Moscow–Beijing," "Through Clouded Glasses" was occasioned by the factographer's encounter with a technology of modern transportation that destabilizes his usual phenomenological framework. The experience of physical dislocation and discomfort caused by his first flight makes Tret'iakov keenly aware of his own body, prompting him to write about things like the visceral distress triggered by an episode of turbulence, the resistance of the air when he sticks his hand out of the window, or the irrational urge he has to throw himself from its portal. In contrast to the realist text, which absents the body of the writer, the factographic sketch is saturated with sensation. "Through Clouded Glasses" registers all of the nausea and fatigue, desire and disquiet, that a writer like Gorky leaves out. But Tret'iakov cannot explain the strange reactions that these stimuli touch off inside his own body. He can only record them. Lacking the knowledge necessary to process these sensations, the factographer confronts *in nuce* the problem that faces all writers in the transitional period: in an epoch of world-historical firsts, everything is too new to make sense of.

Like all methodologically consistent factographic texts, this ocherk is at once both the direct inscription of an event and a metapragmatic reflection on the act of inscribing itself. The injunction to record everything does not stop with the outside world: every rigorous factographer must also include himself in that account. In the case of "Through Clouded Glasses," the flight prompts Tret'iakov to think about his lack of language for capturing these new sensations and his resulting recourse to poetic platitudes. Despite his efforts to find words adequate to this experience, the factographer can only muster old clichés from Russian literature, the "habituated metaphoristics of art." In contrast to the plane's pilot, who discerns a wealth of technical information about things like thrust and wear in the sound of the engine, Tret'iakov hears only a monotonous drone. In lieu of precise knowledge, he has only threadbare figures of speech and hackneyed imagery that veil his perception of the motor. Thus the lament that gives the ocherk its title: "I look at the motor through clouded glasses" (*непротертые очки*, literally: glasses that need to be cleaned) ("Skvoz'," 24, 20). Literary tropes unfurl at a rapid pace: the fallow fields remind Tret'iakov of inkwells, the forests are scattered below him like vegetables in a cook's apron, and the dappled surface of the earth recalls a patchwork quilt. "With every turn of the propeller swells a turn of phrase," he notes in real time. "Through Clouded Glasses" documents Tret'iakov's first flight, but even more dramatically it records the factographer's struggle to free himself from the baggage of literary tradition and its predictable cascade of metaphors. Tret'iakov, whose pen is ineluctably "drawn to the phrase," flees helplessly from image to image like Gorky, unable to break out of the picture gallery of tropes. "Another image," he protests. "My brain shakes off the comparison with disgust" ("Skvoz'," 21).[139]

Before Tret'iakov has even made it to the kolkhoz, it would thus seem that he has already lost his struggle against literature. But the factographer remains convinced that he can still escape the pull of poetic association if only his hand can move fast enough, if only the tempo of his writing can outpace the tropes unspooling in his mind. And after repelling image after image, his fidelity to fact is finally rewarded when, at the apex of the flight, a world free of poetry is at last disclosed. At this moment, the cataract of trope is removed, giving way to a flat, imageless mode of perception. The aprons, quilts, and inkwells are replaced by precise rectilinear shapes. The fields arrange themselves into a sequence of alien ciphers (*шифры*)—most often *О*, *Т*, *Ш* but occasionally also *П* or *Ф*. Without the scum of poetry clouding the view, "the flight unfolds below me an amazing geometry of fields, a geometry of human labor that reticulates the earth and that dyes these parallelograms, rectangles and trapezoids in the colors of different crops" ("Skvoz'," 23). Seen from the "reverse telescope of the flight," humanity now appears like a "species of termite" that builds "structures of geometric regularity, crystals made of clay, straw and wood." Tret'iakov's comparison of imageless vision here to a geometric scheme is significant: as Husserl noted, this branch of observational mathematics directly connects concrete perceptual data to "pure thought construction" without any mediating images or recourse to likeness.[140] The surfaces, angles, and volumes of the shapes below Tret'iakov are both empirical objects and abstract idealities at once. In this geometry of vision, optics and reason coincide. In this way factography plugs the eye directly into the brain, without the mediation of literary figures. "Once the eye has been honed on the present . . . it will dictate to the brain a reflex of rapture for the composite tracts in the fields of the *sovkhoz*" ("Skvoz'," 24).[141]

Tret'iakov's own photography similarly pivots from the figural to the informatic. Like Rodchenko, who used the contingent angles of his handheld camera to undermine the static memory-image, Tret'iakov often photographed from eccentric viewpoints, although his favorite method of image-destruction was to schematize the picture. One photograph from *A Month in the Country* showing the kolkhoz brickworks from above arrays the contents of the picture like geometric features on a map (fig. 1.10). Photographs like these order, organize, and diagram. Their data-rich surfaces invite the viewer to scan, count, compare, and analyze, but never to visualize a scene. Another photograph, which shows minors in a Chinese textile workshop, pushes this tendency to optical patterning even further (fig. 1.11). The horizontal beams of wood and the vertical lines of thread capture the children behind a stark grid, giving the scene a distinctly carceral quality. More importantly, though, this reticulation of space recalls a graphic matrix for representing data. Tret'iakov, a vocal critic of romantic Orientalia, presents the underage Chinese workers as facts and information, not as images.[142] He withholds their faces and refuses to indulge in the aesthetics of empathy or the moralizing of social reformism. Compared with Lewis Hine's portraits of children working in textile mills, which aimed to change labor law but which stopped short of indicting the capitalist labor system as such (fig. 1.12), Tret'iakov's photograph takes a far more radical position. It refuses the dubious pleasures of identification. For the factographer, the revolution was both an affect and a logic, but it was not a sentiment. Like his friend Bertolt Brecht, Tret'iakov, a lawyer by training, came to his communism through rationality, not through humanism. Rejecting the pathos of meliorists like Hine, his photograph of Chinese minors instead recalls William Henry Fox Talbot's "Articles of China" from 1844, which mustered a collection of porcelain objects in a quasi-taxonomical manner that denuded them of all exoticism (fig. 1.13). Tret'iakov's photography speaks not to the leftist imaginary but to communist reason.

Perhaps the most spectacular example of the fantastic convergence of reason and sensation, though, were the festival events held on the tenth anniversary of the revolution. There humanity started to dream in broad daylight, as Ehrenburg put it. Several months before the anniversary Tret'iakov wrote an editorial demanding that organizers of the events utilize newspaper, film, and radio to saturate the urban spaces of Moscow with all variety of information and fact. Each of these "three fundamental media" had a key role to play: the newspaper would serve as a "travel guide" that participants would carry with them through the streets, cross-referencing the information on the page with the landmarks on the march itinerary; chronicle films showing "authentic facts" would be projected onto the architectural surfaces of the city, transforming the buildings into screens for the news; and live radio would continuously apprise the demonstrators of the progress of the event through loudspeakers in the streets. In each of these cases, Tret'iakov proposed to use media less as a means to tell the story of the revolution than as logistical technologies for directing and

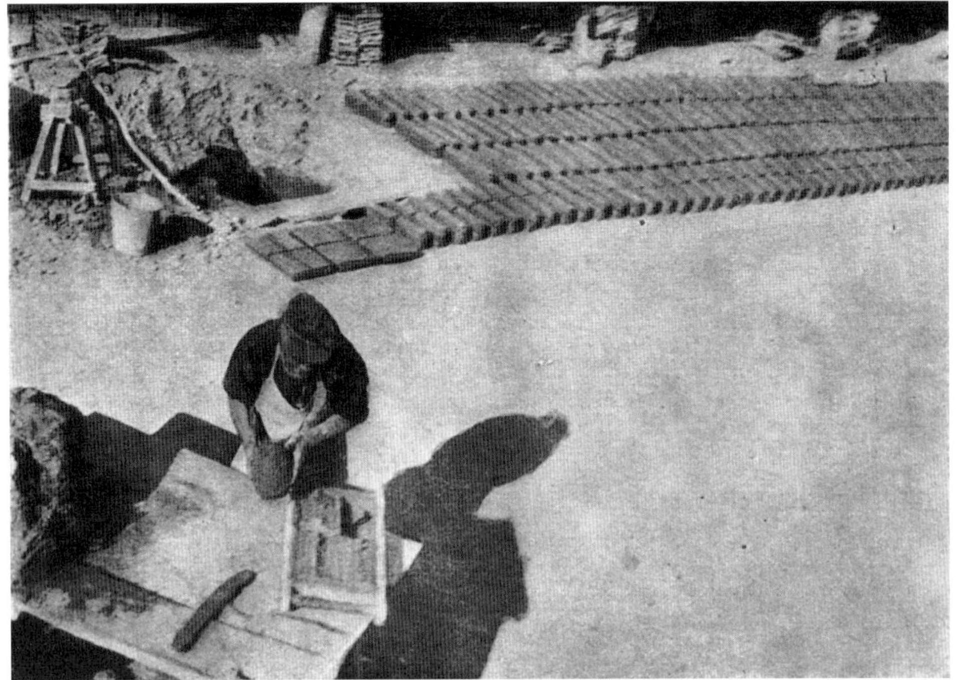

1.10 "The brick works near Communist Lighthouse." From Sergei Tret'iakov, *Mesiats v derevne* (1931), unnumbered plate.

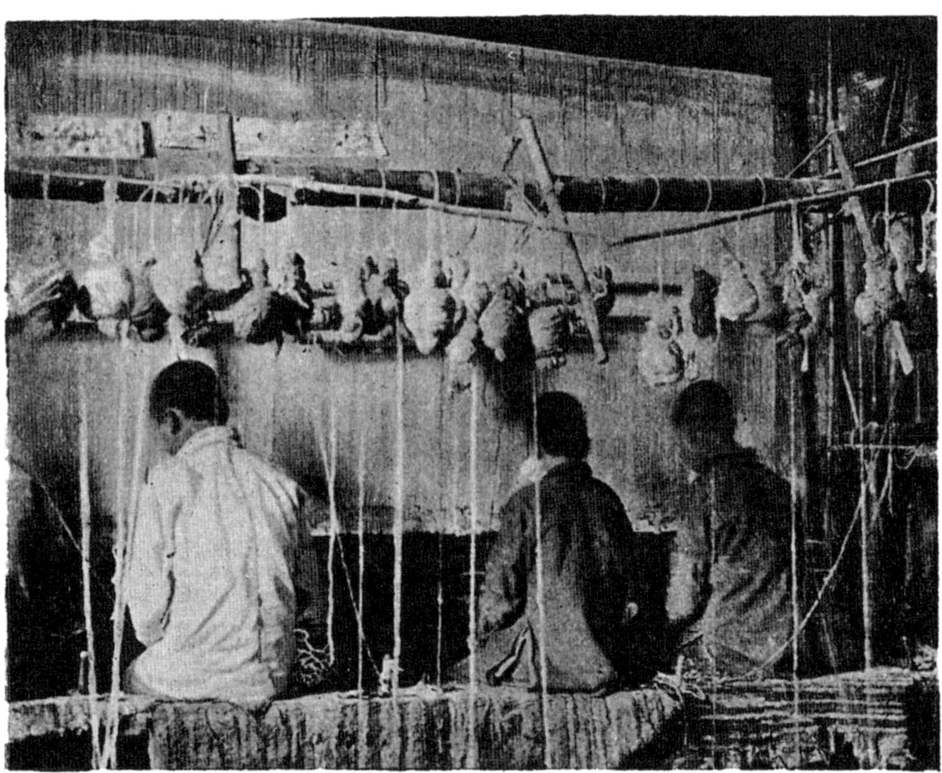

1.11 "Minors in a textile workshop." From Sergei Tret'iakov, *Chzhungo* (1927), 128. Getty Research Institute, Los Angeles (88-B29498).

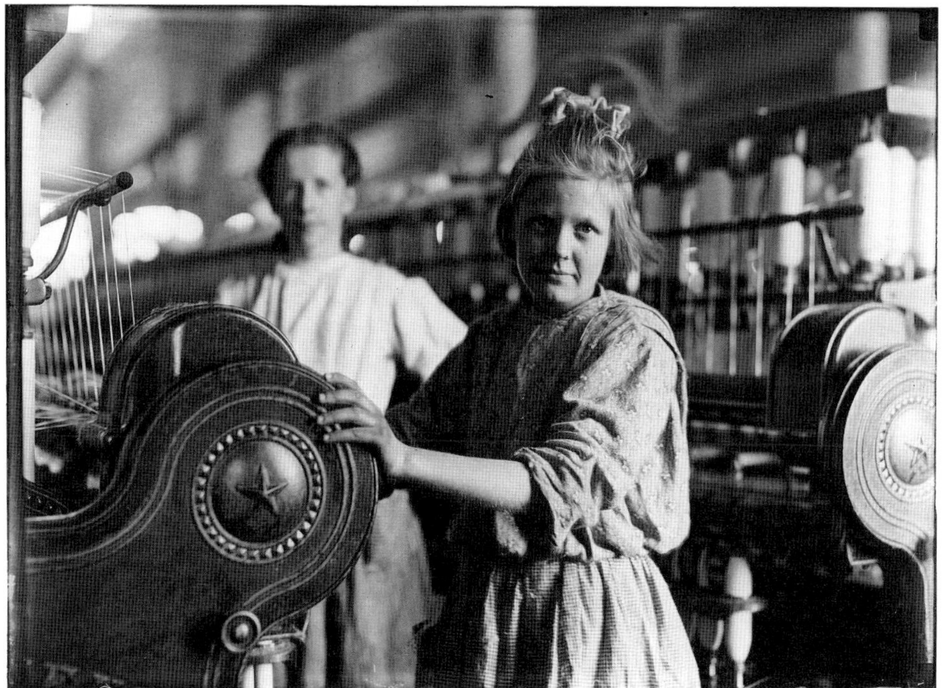

1.12 Lewis W. Hine, "A Typical Spinner," Lancaster Cotton Mills, Lancaster, South Carolina, 1908. National Child Labor Committee Collection, Library of Congress, Prints and Photographs Division (LC-DIG-nclc-05378).

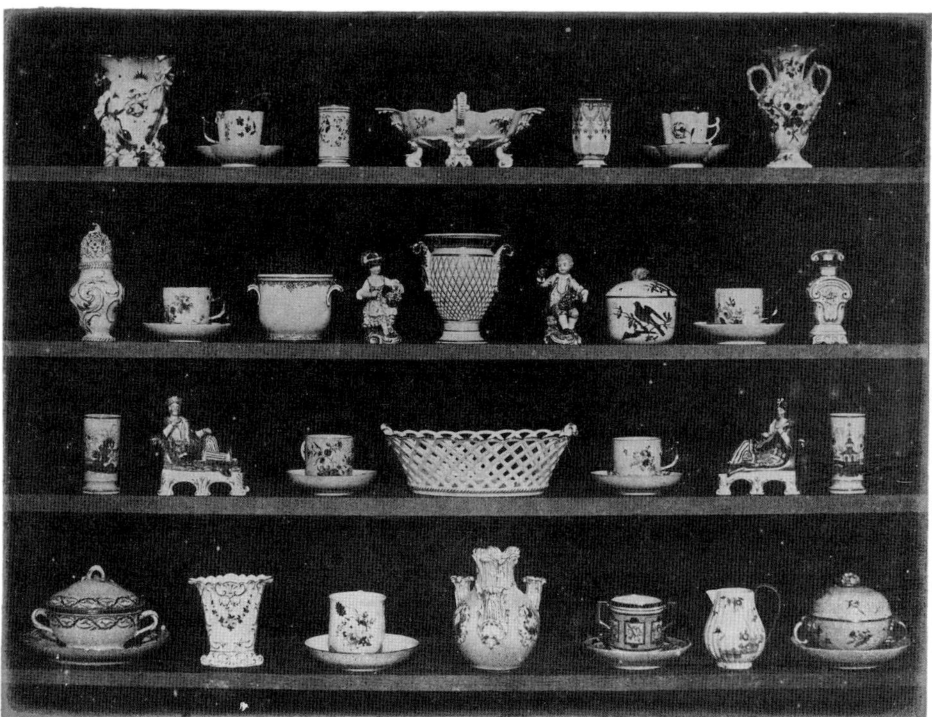

1.13 William Henry Fox Talbot, "Articles of China," 1844. The J. Paul Getty Museum, Los Angeles (84.XO.1369.3). Digital image courtesy of Getty's Open Content Program.

regulating the movement of bodies through the urban space. For the operative producer, communication media transmit signals, not images.

As envisioned by Tret'iakov, the feedback loop established through these media would create a single integrated space in which everyone found themselves at once both inside and outside the festival events—a factographic fantastic where reality and data, sensation and reason, intermingled indistinguishably. "There are no passive spectators on the sidelines," proclaimed Tret'iakov, since "the spectator is himself also a participant" ("Kak desiatiletit'," 37). No asylum would be granted to the transcendental subject on the tenth anniversary of the revolution. Anticipating the geometric revelation of "Through Clouded Glasses," which plugged the eye directly into the brain, Tret'iakov's proposal for the 1927 festivities culminated with the transformation of lived space into an immersive display of graphs, symbols, and ciphers. Instead of hanging decorative drapery on the façades of buildings, for example, he recommended installing "bars of street diagrams" on the urban surfaces. He suggested that every factory along the march route dispense a "carte-de-visite" with facts about itself. He wrote that commodities in store windows should be curated into small informational exhibits—"graphic announcements . . . that are assembled out of the things that fill the vitrines": tins of food stacked to make the columns of a bar graph showing fluctuations in the production of canned goods; fish of different sizes arranged to depict the quantities of catch from the sea; and bottles at the apothecary configured to display changing ratios of imported to domestic aspirin. Tret'iakov insisted that even traditional "aesthetic means" like fireworks, lighting, and music could be repurposed to convey statistics and facts about Soviet life ("Kak desiatiletit'," 36–37). All of these suggestions underscored a key distinction between the October 1927 celebration and the mass festivals of the capitalist West: the latter stimulate the spectator in order to captivate and thrill, but socialist festivals agitate in order to educate and enlighten. For Tret'iakov, the techniques of spectacle society were entirely justifiable, but only if this *Gesamtkunstwerk* served reason, not the imagination.

After the anniversary passed, *Novyi Lef* published a series of reviews and documents about the festival events in the capital city. One picture by the young photojournalist Roman Karmen, "Moscow at Night during October Days" (fig. 1.14), showed a city utterly transformed. Karmen's photograph all but completely erased the familiar visual features of Moscow, dissolving its identifiable landmarks into so many luminous letters, lines, and faceted surfaces. It transformed streetlights into a scheme of points and tracery, crystallized the wet cobblestones into a patterned grid, and reduced the architectural façades on Sovetskaia and Sverdlovskaia Squares to supports for the written word. The depictive function of photography is subordinated almost entirely here to its graphic function. Indeed, if "Moscow at Night" has any precedent, it is found not in the tradition of realist art but in the analytical chronophotography coming out of the Central Institute of Labor (fig. 1.15). These graphisms were data visualizations, mathematical magnitudes, and formulas made flesh. They were diagrams of comportment, geometries of movement, and slices of congealed time. But one thing they were not were images. "These records, if they are to be thought of as representations, are not to be confused with pictures."[143] Karmen, who would go on to become one of the leading documentary filmmakers of his generation, later described "Moscow at Night" as an experiment in time- and motion-capture, a transitional object between his early snapshot photography and his subsequent career in cinema.[144] Karmen's photograph materializes time in the band of headlights that moves from right to left and in the stutter of *X ЛЕТ* ("X Years"), first bright and then dim, that gives the impression of lights flashing on and off. Rendering time as a set of spatial coordinates in this way, "Moscow at Night" translates the living city into so many data points on a two-dimensional diagram.

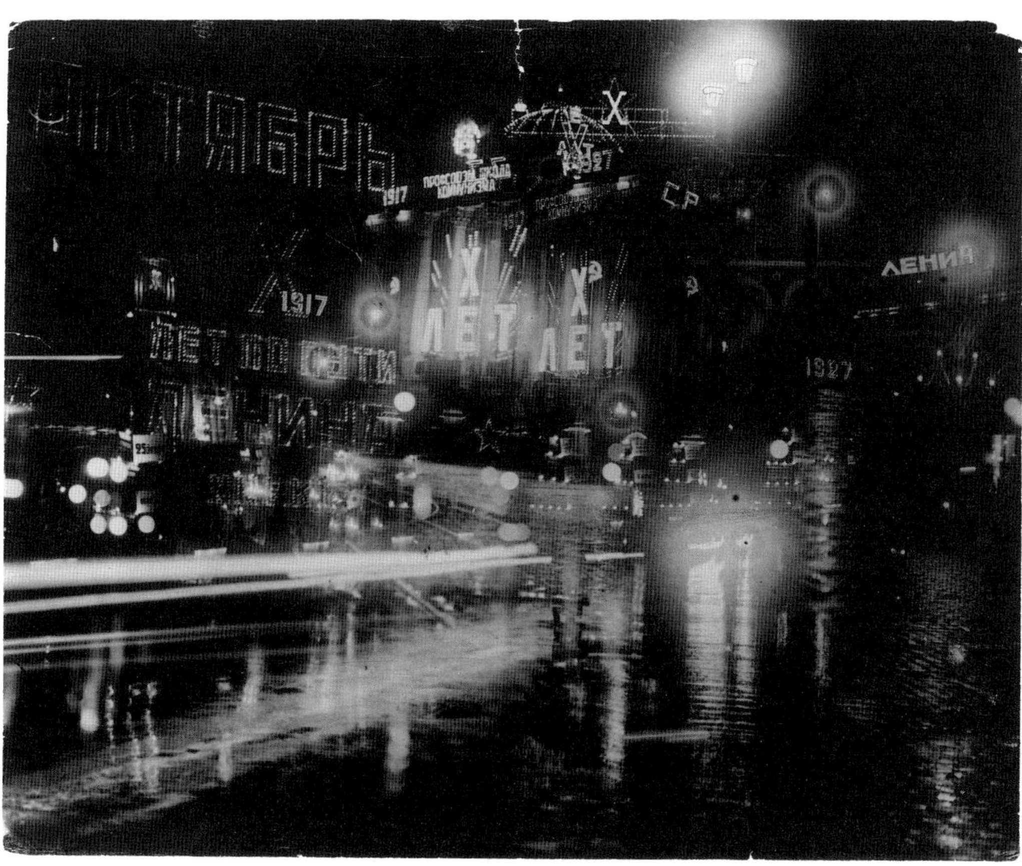

1.14 Roman Karmen, "Moscow at Night during October Days," 1927. Museum of Modern Art, New York (1712.2001). Thomas Walther Collection, Abbott-Levy Collection funds, by exchange. Digital Image © The Museum of Modern Art / Licensed by SCALA / Art Resource, NY.

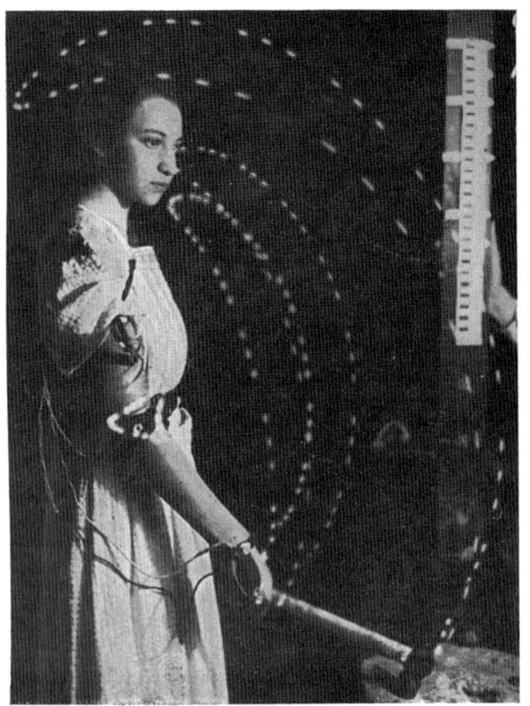
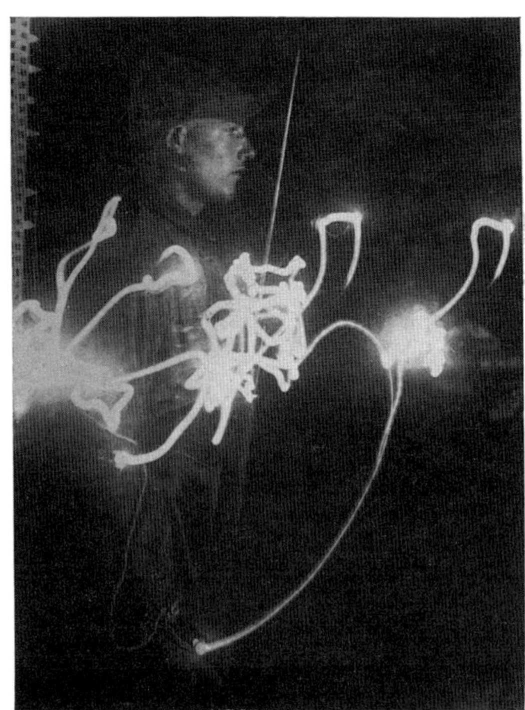

1.15 Motion Study, Central Institute of Labor (Moscow). From René Fölöp-Miller, *Geist und Gesicht des Bolschewismus* (1926), plate 171.

Karmen's photograph was printed in *Novyi Lef* alongside Tret'iakov's enthusiastic review of the anniversary events, "A Newspaper on Poles." The factographer, who had expressed high hopes during the run-up to the festival, was not disappointed when October finally arrived. The conversion of Moscow into a graphic space of reading and accounting turned out even more successfully than he had anticipated. "A Newspaper on Poles" marveled not just at the sheer quantities of text that papered the city that day, but at the particular complexion of this writing. Language had become more factographic. The boisterous, energetic hand-painted letters normally seen at demonstrations had been replaced by uniform typefaces, and the usual bright drawings were now drained of color. Of the thousands of posters and banners that passed in front of Tret'iakov, few rehearsed the standard repertoire of demonstration slogans. Tellingly, he confessed that he was unable to remember most of them. The catchphrases and caricatures typically seen at political rallies had evolved into more complex forms of discourse, mathematical formulas, and informational diagrams. "The demonstration is interested only in semantics," he noted about the new technical orientation of this language. "Heroic-symbolic posters" had given way to banners that took entire paragraphs verbatim from the daily press. "Numbers and statistical tables on poles" delivered "diagrams and accounting numbers" about revolutionary life. Extrapolating from this general trend, Tret'iakov predicted that future demonstrations would see the final triumph of the informatic over the figural, the diagrammatic over the pictorial, and the factographic over the literary. "Taking note of the leading role that the newspaper paragraph and the newspaper caricature are playing in the demonstration, we should point out that the Soviet demonstration placard is undergoing an even greater rationalization of meaning. More and more numbers are appearing next to phrases on the banners. Numbers and formulas are climbing up the poster. Alongside the drawing and the caricature is growing the poster-diagram, in which coloring and volumetric figures correspond closely to the task of statistical information." The anniversary events had realized the technological fantastic on a new scale, creating an interactive arena of information that could be felt and experienced physically by the demonstrators. Words and numbers were no longer confined to the printed page, but became tangible entities whose weight and facture responded to the movements of the marchers and the lineaments of the architecture. "I was struck by a single fact," wrote Tret'iakov: "the extent to which our [physical] designs had been transformed into something verbal (something word-based)."[145] Semantics were inseparable from somatics.

Reading the news in the factographic city demanded that the marchers navigate space with their bodies. One article that was published in *Novyi Lef* with Tret'iakov's "A Newspaper on Poles" described, for example, how demonstrators had to walk around various structures and monuments of Moscow in order to apprehend the phrases written on them.[146] The contents of the newspaper had undergone a radical desublimation, reformatted for kinetic apprehension by the entire body, not just the eyes. For all the standardized typefaces and colorless diagrams, the tenth anniversary turned out to be highly stimulating in this respect. "The fact that these numbers and statistical tables on poles triggered a heightened emotional explosion in the festival masses magnificently confirms LEF's idea that it is possible and imperative to agitate with real and authentic reality rather than with artistic inventions, with authentic proportions and tempos of growth rather than with the inspired monumentalizing distortions of 'creatives.'"

In order to advance the informatization of lived space, Tret'iakov proposed a new Soviet profession: the newspaper reporter who is also a demonstration organizer. Part journalist and part choreographer, this new kind of cultural worker would have a "good sense for the scale of the street and for the reflexes of the flowing masses," and would translate fact and news into rhythm and gesture ("Gazeta na shestakh," 20). Like Eisenstein, who suggested that reciting *Capital* while pacing and rehearsing specific movements would enhance the reader's understanding of complex concepts such as surplus value, Tret'iakov believed that translating information into concrete spatial values and giving it a physiological form would improve its comprehension.[147] Between the lines of the newspaper and on the pages of technical literature he sensed a subcutaneous motion-score for the reader. By tuning into these somatic rhythms, the reporter-organizer would synchronize the affective patterns of the body with abstract magnitudes such as industry's "actual proportions and rate of growth" ("Gazeta na shestakh," 19). The literary imagination might not help anyone understand the principles of political economy. But the psychophysical writing of the factographers—the subject of the next chapter—would encode these concepts directly into the muscles of the readers and program statistics into their nerves.

"I'm nothing!" said Chiklin—and began to think about his head, which alone in his entire body was unable to feel.
—ANDREI PLATONOV, *The Foundation Pit*[1]

2

OVERCOMING THE DELAY

From psychoanalysis to reactology, nearly every school of psychology has defined the mind-body problem in terms of time: consciousness, in its many modalities and periodicities, always lags behind the flesh. Determined to overcome the philosophical dualism of the bourgeoisie, the factographers enlisted lighter, faster forms of art and literature that promised to eliminate this structural delay. They championed the mechanization of artmaking as a means of accelerating consciousness and, in so doing, dissolving the boundary between matter and mind. Drawing from research in psychotechnics and the emerging field of Soviet newspaper studies, this chapter explores some of the sensory modalities, affective states, and even physical movement-scores that were provoked by the rigorously chronometric art of the factographers. As we will see, their prompt method also undermined the dualist system of realist art, which presumed a perceiving subject at a temporal—and thus epistemological—distance from reality. Embedded "operativism," as the factographers called their program of militant monism, would necessarily preclude any aesthetic of reflection.

THE SENSATIONALIST PRESS

Whenever the factographers came under attack, opponents cited their presumption to connect mind and world directly without formal devices or critical translation. Shklovsky pointed to this lack of mediation when he finally broke with Tret'iakov in 1931. "Facts have pinned you down to the subject," he wrote to his friend: "You have lost your chance to make a literary move. You have lost the moment of transformation" (*A Hunt for Optimism*, 74). Having assimilated Bogdanov's empiriocritical method during their Proletkul't years in the early 1920s, Tret'iakov and Chuzhak remained faithful to this phenomenalist system late into the decade, long after the premise of mind-body parallelism had become both a political and a poetological liability. When the movement's omnibus *The Literature of Fact* appeared in 1929, readers picked up on the persistence of Bogdanovite elements in Chuzhak's program for a "literature of life-construction." One reviewer of the book reformulated Chuzhak's famous watchword as "the literature of the *objective transmission* of reality," explaining that

> when the Lefists advance the theory of a literature of *life-construction*—when they declare that a real-life fact which is transmitted objectively by the factographer *is reality itself*—they are in essence assuming an idealist point of view that *equates material existence with consciousness*. At this moment the Lefists lose any notion of the subject-object as a unity, albeit a unity that is contradictory. Through its own productive function, being has consciousness, but to declare being and consciousness to be qualitatively indistinguishable—to be something that is "continuous"—means slipping into the lap of the most "decent," "honest" empiriocriticism, and from there into idealism.[2]

Not unusually for his time, this particular reviewer mistook dualism for dialectics, but his insight that factography marks the site of an epistemological breakdown was still valid. Another review of *The Literature of Fact* concurred: the Lefists "assert that art is identical to reality, which means that consciousness is identical to material existence—that subject equals object."[3] Tret'iakov and Chuzhak refused to differentiate qualitatively between mental life and physical being, and remained pinned to reality as a result.

Invoking the Cartesian terminology popular in those years, contemporaries assigned factography to the realm of physical extensity, the concrete and quantitatively measurable dimension of empirical existence that is typically distinguished from the realm of psychic intensity. They saw factography as an art that spoke to the body, not to the mind. Tret'iakov had already earned renown early in his career for writing some of the most somatically charged verses of his generation. As a Futurist poet he strove to transform the word from a medium of ideas into a physical stimulus, "a part of real life like the blow of a hammer, like a kiss, like a piece of bread."[4] One essay in the prominent Formalist journal *Poetika* titled "On the Motor Impulses of Verse" classified the work of contemporary poets according to their motor quality (*по их моторностю*) and concluded from this survey that the poetry of Tret'iakov, in particular, "organically *demanded* gesture." In contrast to Symbolists such as Akhmatova and Blok, whose visionary, introspective, and image-laden poetry showed a "minimum of motor qualities," Tret'iakov's verses compelled the reader to move about and gesticulate.[5] This conclusion came as little surprise given how much of Tret'iakov's early poetic output consisted of demonstration slogans that were written for marching crowds. In dictating the pace and rhythm of feet, breath, and gesture, these kinetic phrases were meant to contribute to the physical choreography of public assemblies.

Building on the *Poetika* study, Il'ia Dukor's 1928 essay on Tret'iakov applauded the poet for thus transforming "an emotional wave . . . into a booming verbal signal that coordinates movement and doesn't leave any room for 'psychology.' If the signal still lingers behind in consciousness, it is only as a direct demand, as a rhythmic-emotional impulse that is addressed more to physiology than to psychology." For Dukor, the words used by Tret'iakov were not symbols but signals—physical stimuli that had less in common with literary metaphor and the syntax of the imagination than with the bells and flashing lights found in a psychotechnical laboratory. Since these contentless words depicted nothing and triggered no mental associations, they also left no mnemonic traces behind in the mind after the act of reading. If anything endured of these signals past the moment of perception, it was only the physical reaction that had been encoded in the nerves and muscles of the subject. "The word is transformed from a representation, from an image, into a clear, graphic factor. The muscles of the throat appeal directly to the muscles of the hand, almost entirely without the participation of reflexes of association" ("S. Tret'iakov," 48).

Working in the theatrical studio of Proletkul't gave Tret'iakov the opportunity to explore the interface between language and movement more systematically than in his early poetic experiments. Combining the empiriomonist method of Bogdanov with the biomechanical dramaturgy of Meyerhold, Tret'iakov and his collaborator Eisenstein worked out a program for a "theater of attractions" that divided the performance into "a series of pressures on the audience's psyche to be brought about by theatrical means." These productions introduced sensory stimuli (attractions) at precise intervals in the play to provoke, parse, and regulate the emotional responses of the audience. Tret'iakov contrasted the somatic intensity of the Proletkul't events to the "aestheticizing plastic poses" of the Moscow Art Theater, where a static, declamatory language induced "muscular narcosis" in performer and spectator alike.[6] As a workshop for the "direct processing of the audience," Proletkul't theater drilled movement-repertoires and reflexes into the spectator who, at the end of the performance, would then carry this embodied information out onto the street and into all corners of everyday life.

Tret'iakov's Proletkul't scripts emphasized the physiological and psycho-acoustic aspects of language over mental images and naturalistic storytelling. When adapting the texts of other writers like Marcel Martinet's *Night* or Aleksandr Ostrovsky's *Enough Stupidity in Every Wiseman*, Tret'iakov translated the original scripts into what he called "semaphoric speech," a quasi-mechanical form of diction made of discrete units that could be rearranged in a combinatory fashion. This language did not reflect the inner life of the character, but instead created a "vocal mask" for the "speech apparatus" of the actor.[7] Thus, even when he was working with a preexisting script, Tret'iakov would orchestrate a second, subsemantic score within the performance that consisted of signals (semaphores) that were addressed not to the minds of the audience but to their bodies. This strategy, he later explained, was indebted to the trans-sense poets' experiments with verbal facture, which had emphasized material dimensions of the "autotelic word" (*самовитое слово*) that were independent of conceptual meaning and the hermeneutics of sense ("The Theater of Attractions," 25; translation modified).[8]

Despite the superficial impression of clarity, this semaphoric diction provoked emotional responses in Tret'iakov's audiences that were singularly complex and often outright discordant. His efforts to liberate affect from the yoke of literary imagining resulted in plays that subjected the body and the mind of the spectator to two divergent scripts, as it were. Theatergoers felt themselves being pulled in two different directions at once. One reviewer of *Enough Stupidity in Every Wiseman*, for example, complained that the biomechanical alternation between "tense attentiveness" and "discharge of tension" did not map onto the arc of suspense and resolution laid out in Ostrovsky's script.[9] Audiences were so confused viscerally that plot synopses had to be read before each performance so they would understand what was happening on stage.[10] As Tret'iakov and Eisenstein explained, the system of attractions "functions outside of the play's action" ("Montage of Attractions," 78). Indeed, Tret'iakov fully expected spectators to be disoriented, since the stimuli in these plays "provoke audience reflexes that are almost entirely objective [i.e., physiological] and that are connected to motor structures that are difficult and unfamiliar for the spectator." About *Wiseman*, he wrote that "several very effective attractions (for example, the balancing act) are linked to the plot in a completely artificial way, through arbitrary motivations" (fig. 2.1). He boasted that "none of the power of this performance relies on the motivating text" ("The Theater of Attractions," 25). As the chasm between the attractions and the plot expanded over the course of the performance, Tret'iakov's audiences grew uncomfortably aware that the body

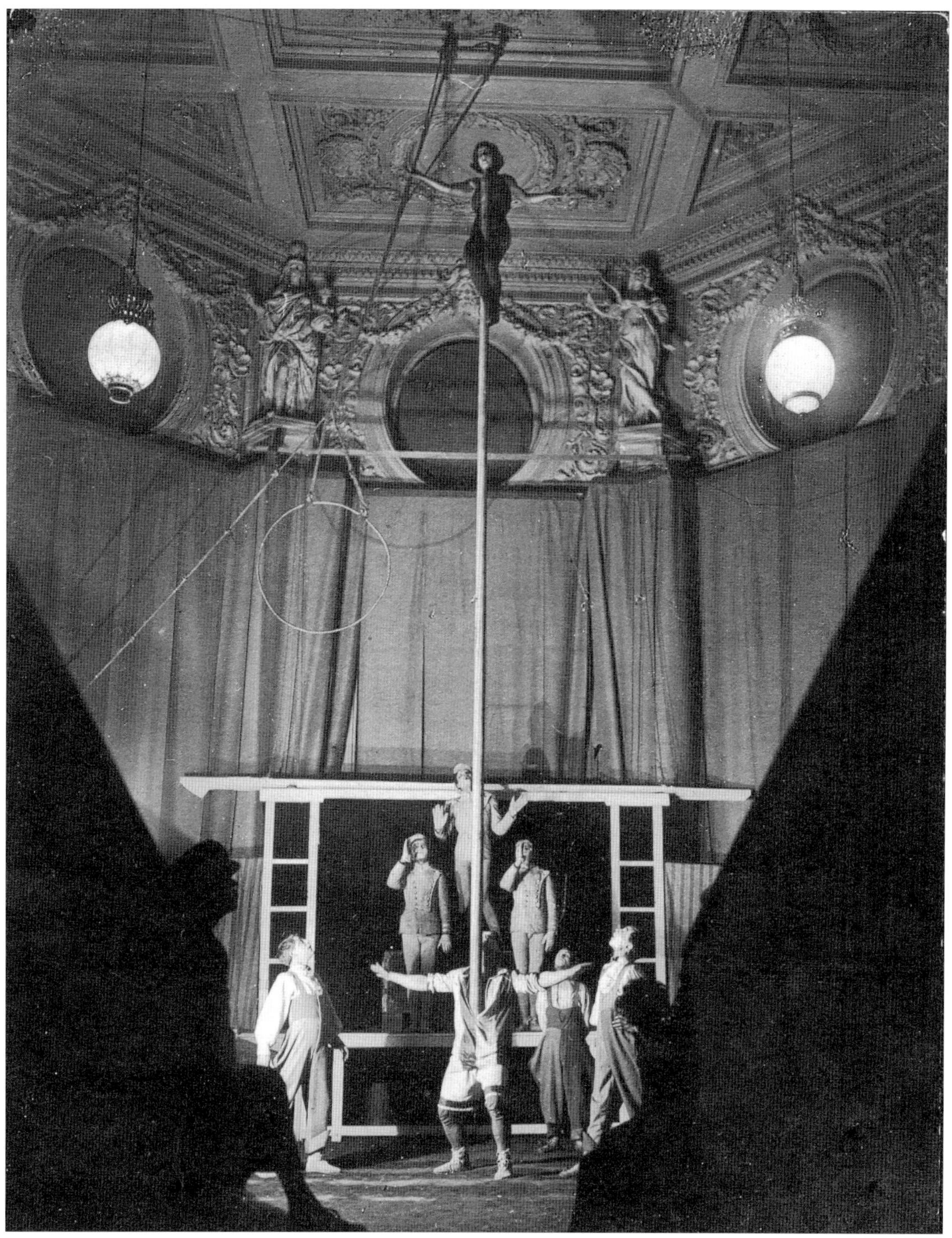

2.1 Attraction no. 7. Sergei Tret'iakov and Sergei Eisenstein, *Enough Stupidity in Every Wiseman*, 1923. Society for Co-operation in Russian & Soviet Studies (SCRSS) / TopFoto.

might have an agenda independent of the will and that consciousness was not always master in its own house. Watching Ostrovsky's play, they sensed a knot of affective resistance tightening within themselves, the obstinate stupidity of a body refusing to submit to the ideas of the wiseman.

But activating the somatic features of movement-arts like march slogans and theater was relatively straightforward compared to literature, a cultural form that is consumed silently in moments of static repose. Nonetheless, here too the monists in Lef saw great potential. Chuzhak's 1924 Proletkul't brochure *"Literature": On the Artistic Politics of the Russian Communist Party* culminated with an injunction for writers to study the convergent discipline of reflexology as a rationalist platform for literary creation. As he explained, all writing entails "exerting some kind of determinate pressure on the emotions of the reader of the work, pushing in some direction, and, ultimately, triggering reflexes of some variety . . . The artist must use scientific means to get a clear idea of (and moreover, should invent) all available devices of stimulation and know exactly what serves which ends. He should master the science of reflexes (discarding any musty vitalism) and allow himself to be guided by it along with the laws of the development of society."[11] Claims like these prompted rival critics like Aleksandr Voronsky to compare Chuzhak to Emmanuil Enchmen, the most notorious reductionist working in the field of Russian behaviorism. In the eyes of Voronsky, who contrasted Lef's program for "art as life-construction" to his own "art as life-cognition," Chuzhak had reduced all of culture to "a unified system of organic movements."[12] It was hard to object to this assessment: for the ultra-rationalist faction within Lef, contemporary artists and writers had much to learn from biology and sociology, but little to gain from psychology, and nothing whatsoever to learn from aesthetics. The factographers preferred to base their work on outwardly demonstrable and empirically quantifiable data from scientific experiments than on vague speculation about "interiority, spontaneity and emotions," Tret'iakov wrote.[13]

Building on Lef's proposal for a reflexological literature, the poet Tikhon Churilin wrote an essay for Chuzhak's 1926 Proletkul't anthology exploring various strategies to transform the mass press into a relay for biomechanical signals. Churilin's contribution called on neurologist-editors to track the circulation of stimuli through the text and to verify the "discharge" of these verbal irritants among its readership. He predicted that, with proper psychotechnical engineering, literary production could become just as rationalized as the industrial workplace. "If the *word* is physiological—the *same movement* that is found in all other kinds of muscular *movement*—then its motor process can be considered, weighed, calculated, like every other *labor process*. Thus we can analyze the word as organizational material according to a scientific system; we can 'measure' it in the same way that thrust is 'measured' by a dynamometer (just with a comparable physical instrument); and we can find the numerical determinant of its dynamic." For Churilin, writers shouldn't bother trying to crack open the black box of the mind or speculating about esoteric matters of literary meaning. The "movement-word" (*движение-слово*) should instead be directed at the nervous system of the reader, whose somatic response could be gauged and calibrated with suitable scientific instruments. Words should be weighed and calculated, their concrete extensional values established through precise empirical analysis. "In the conceptual system of yesterday's literary psychology, the word was a thought that is intuitively manifested in a visual image that reflects life. Today's scientific (reflexological) formula: 'The word is a *movement* that reacts to a determinate *stimulus*, one that is essentially analogous to the movement of a hand or of a leg—the difference between the two being the nervous centers and groups of muscles whose motors are engaged.'" In order to bridge the gap between cognitive and physiological processes, Churilin called for the establishment of a new academic subfield that he christened the Physical Culture of Literature (*Физкультлит*), a "socio-bio-mechanical" discipline that combined reflexology and literary criticism and that approached the written word analytically "like any other kind of muscular movement."[14]

In his Proletkul't years Tret'iakov had emphasized the importance of cultivating what he called "world-sensation" (*мироощущение*), a "sum of the emotional (sensory) judgments" that operated independently of worldview (*мировоззрение*) and world-understanding (*миропонимание*). In his critique of Bogdanov, Lenin defined the root of this Machist concept—sensation (*ощущение*)—as the "direct connection between consciousness and the external world" and "the transformation of the energy of external excitation into a fact of consciousness."[15] Tret'iakov's world-sensation was the phenomenological corollary to the platform of "immediate socialism" promoted by the Proletkul't leadership, who demanded that "the proletariat must now, immediately, create for itself *socialist forms of thought, feeling, and everyday life*, independently of interrelations and combinations of political forces."[16] If the world-understanding of the Bolsheviks was "built upon cognition, upon logical systems" and belonged to the domain of conscious ideation, world-sensation went deeper. The latter flowed "along the lines of sympathies and repulsions" and encompassed primary affective states like joy, fear and, of course, the consummate Soviet affect, enthusiasm. Ideological organization and political decision-making had important roles to play after the revolution, but, for Tret'iakov, "no worldview could be vital if it was not alloyed to a world-sensation, if it had not become the living driving force which determines all actions of the human being, his everyday physiognomy."[17] Without transforming the human senses, without embedding and replicating itself in the immediate conditions of lived habitus, the worldview of communism and the world-understanding of the Party would remain forever virtual, a revolution from above without basis in quotidian experience. Socialism already had its doctrine, but what it needed was to become a reflex,

Tret'iakov demanded: "Together with the scientist, the art worker must become a psychoengineer, a psychoconstructor" ("From Where," 207, 214; translation modified).

There was broad consensus that the mass media, and the newspaper in particular, offered the best means to coordinate the circulation of affect within and between individuals. Proletkul'tists like Churilin celebrated worker-correspondents for transmitting "sociobiological stimuli from their labor-productive environments"[18] and famed neurologist Vladimir Bekhterev conducted research demonstrating that the newspaper could create a "compound subject" (*собирательная личность*) far larger than any other cultural form (he reckoned that theater, by comparison, could innervate a collective of 500 individuals at most).[19] As the previous chapter showed, journalism was regarded to be a uniquely embodied, even athletic, form of writing that synchronized the cadence of the hands and feet with the rhythms of thought. The same psychophysical activity was evident also at the reception end, in readers' responses to the newspaper. Leading theorists in newspaper studies urged editors to learn how to "produce habitual reactions in the frequent reader—'conditioned reflexes' in the realm of the perception of newspaper information."[20] To do this, they had to address physical and environmental variables within their readership. Unlike the mass media of the liberal bourgeois public sphere, which presumed a universal subject unmarked by concrete experience, Soviet papers were tailored to their audiences biologically. In his popular study *The Newspaper*, Kerzhentsev explained that each edition was adapted to the different bodily dispositions and postures of its reader as well as to the changing settings in which news was consumed. According to the founder of the League of Time, morning papers should be scanned hastily while on the commute to work, whereas evening editions, which are typically read at home at the end of the day, could accommodate more leisurely news items and human-interest stories (*Gazeta*, 122). In other words, early editions of the newspaper should be more reflexological, more physically stimulating, while later ones could afford to be more contemplative in the manner of traditional representationalist literature.

Other figures in newspaper studies similarly recommended adjusting the physiognomy of each edition to suit specific reception situations. When determining print features like spacing, format, font size, column width, and illustration type, editors were instructed to consider a variety of environmental factors, such as whether the reader was sitting at a table or walking outside,[21] whether the acoustic setting was distracting or conducive to contemplation,[22] and whether the page was illuminated by streetlight or a lamp at home.[23] Mikhail Gus, one of the rising stars at the State Institute of Journalism, explained that the polygraphic style of print media "is connected as much with the content of the newspaper as it is with its printed form and with the conditions of reading. The splashy, lively, poster-like layouts, the abundant clichés, the enormous headlines are calculated to attract the attention of the reader swiftly and effortlessly, to expedite reading in a streetcar or in the street."[24] Soviet newspapers were optimized to suit diverse physical milieux. Taken to its logical conclusion, this principle led to the seamless incorporation of the newspaper into built space itself. Kerzhentsev proposed projecting "light newspapers" (*световые газеты*) onto the surfaces of buildings in the city, for example. The architect Grigorii Barkhin even designed a building for the daily broadsheet *Izvestiia* whose flat rectangular façade, vertical columns, and bold lettering cast a massive front page over Moscow's Pushkin Square (figs. 2.2, 2.3). The *Izvestiia* building, which was dedicated on the tenth anniversary of the revolution among thousands of "newspapers on poles," was paper architecture rendered in concrete.

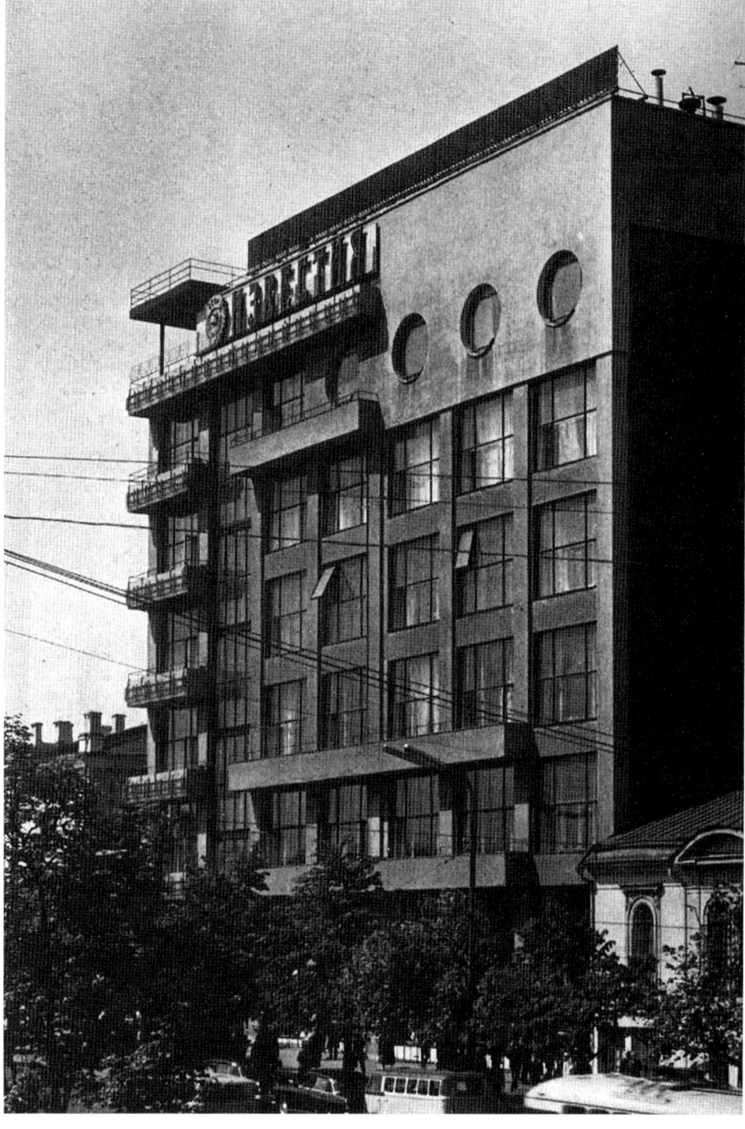

2.2 Grigory Barkhin with Mikhail Barkhin, *Izvestiia* newspaper building, Moscow, 1925–1927. From Selim O. Khan-Magomedov, *Pioneers of Soviet Architecture: The Search for New Solutions in the 1920s and 1930s* (1987), plate 1137.

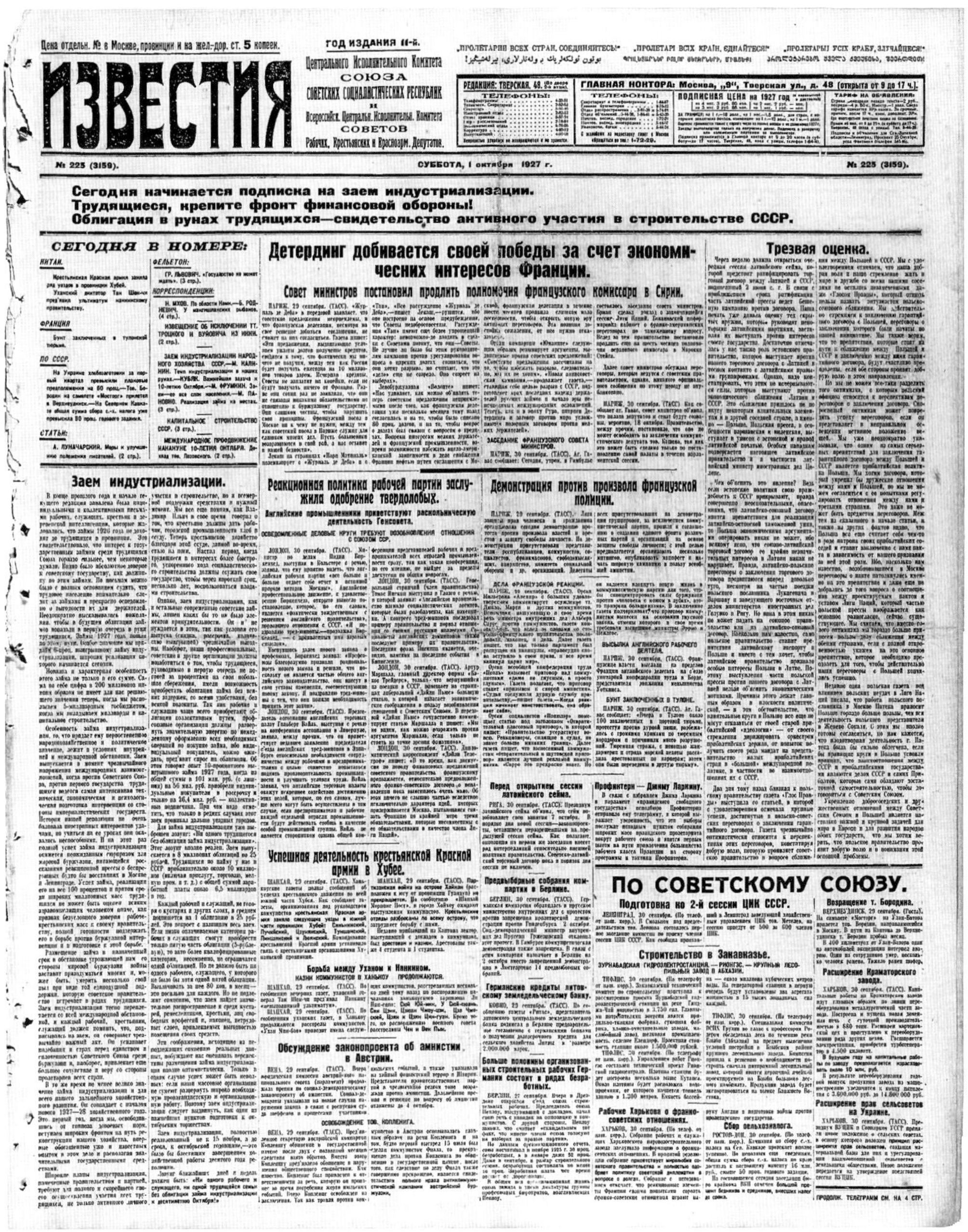
Цена отдельн. № в Москве, провинции и на жел.-дор. ст. 5 копеек.

ГОД ИЗДАНИЯ 11-й.

ИЗВЕСТИЯ

Центрального Исполнительного Комитета СОЮЗА СОВЕТСКИХ СОЦИАЛИСТИЧЕСКИХ РЕСПУБЛИК и Всероссийск. Центральн. Исполнительн. Комитета СОВЕТОВ Рабочих, Крестьянских и Красноарм. Депутатов.

„ПРОЛЕТАРИИ ВСЕХ СТРАН, СОЕДИНЯЙТЕСЬ!"

№ 225 (3159). СУББОТА, 1 октября 1927 г. № 225 (3159).

Сегодня начинается подписка на заем индустриализации.
Трудящиеся, крепите фронт финансовой обороны!
Облигация в руках трудящихся—свидетельство активного участия в строительстве СССР.

СЕГОДНЯ В НОМЕРЕ:

Детердинг добивается своей победы за счет экономических интересов Франции.

Совет министров постановил продлить полномочия французского комиссара в Сирии.

Трезвая оценка.

Заем индустриализации.

Реакционная политика рабочей партии заслужила одобрение твердолобых.

Демонстрация против произвола французской полиции.

Успешная деятельность крестьянской Красной армии в Хубее.

Обсуждение законопроекта об амнистии в Австрии.

По СОВЕТСКОМУ СОЮЗУ.

2.3 Front page of *Izvestiia*, no. 225 (October 1, 1927).

Certainly the most spectacular exploration of newspaper somaticism was the Russian contribution to Pressa, the International Press Exhibition held in Cologne in 1928. Tasked with presenting the Soviet news industry to a world audience, the All-Union Society for Cultural Relations with Other Countries (VOKS) engaged two of its greatest talents in the theory and practice of the media, Gus and the avant-garde designer El Lissitzky. Although the Soviet contribution to the so-called "Olympics of Publishing" faced a variety of material obstacles, which ranged from budgetary constraints to the logistical challenges of transporting works from Moscow, the greatest barrier turned out to be the Russian language itself. As was clear from preliminary discussions in VOKS and from the many opinion pieces about Pressa published in *The Journalist*, the organizers could not count on European visitors being able to engage with an exhibition that consisted almost entirely of texts written in Russian. The Soviet pavilion had to convey the unique characteristics and achievements of their press without actually describing them in words.[25]

In response, Gus and Lissitzky delivered a pure phenomenology of the news. Lissitzky's installation presented journalism as a vector of force absent any determinate message. "The assault of abundant numbers, pictures, and slogans attempts to seize the visitor," wrote one German review. Even the color red, it continued, had been utterly desemanticized, transformed from a symbol of the Soviet state into pure optical stimulation (*Erregung*).[26] Everywhere paper jumped off the wall to engage the visitors, creating a hybrid space of encounter in which sculpture, print, and architecture interpenetrated seamlessly (fig. 2.4). Like Mikhail Plaksin's contribution (fig. 2.5), most of the works made by the brigade of Soviet artists had been shipped flat from Moscow and reassembled in Cologne, where they oscillated restlessly between two and three dimensions. While other national pavilions at Pressa emphasized the pictorial aspects of the print media, Russia dramatized the physical presence of the newspaper to create a "multitudinous, throbbing, intensely living picture."[27] In his introduction to the Soviet catalogue, the Chairman of the State Publishing House explained that their objective had been to "give the printed word a plastic form, that is, to transform a material that is perceived through sound into one that is perceived through vision and touch."[28] If Western metaphysics has its roots in a phonetic paradigm of language that divides abstract content (*pneuma*, spirit) from the concrete vehicle of the signifier, as Jacques Derrida later argued, the team of materialists behind Pressa refused to separate meaning from its graphic instantiation in this way.[29] Visitors commented that the phonetic dimensions of language were foreclosed—literally drowned out—by the incessant "hum of machinery" and the "whirring of motors" that powered the various turbines, transmissions, and presses in the installation.[30] "What a contrast between the English hall and the rooms of Soviet Russia!" declared one review. Indeed, the sensory flood of the Soviet pavilion was the very antithesis of the refuge for silent reading built by capitalist England, which offered a serene setting for metaphysical reflection complete with soothing botanical decors (fig. 2.6).[31]

The enveloping kinetic frenzy and continuous machine murmur of the Soviet installation recalled a busy street corner far more than a study, library, or any other space for quiet contemplation. Lissitzky and Gus sought to rep-

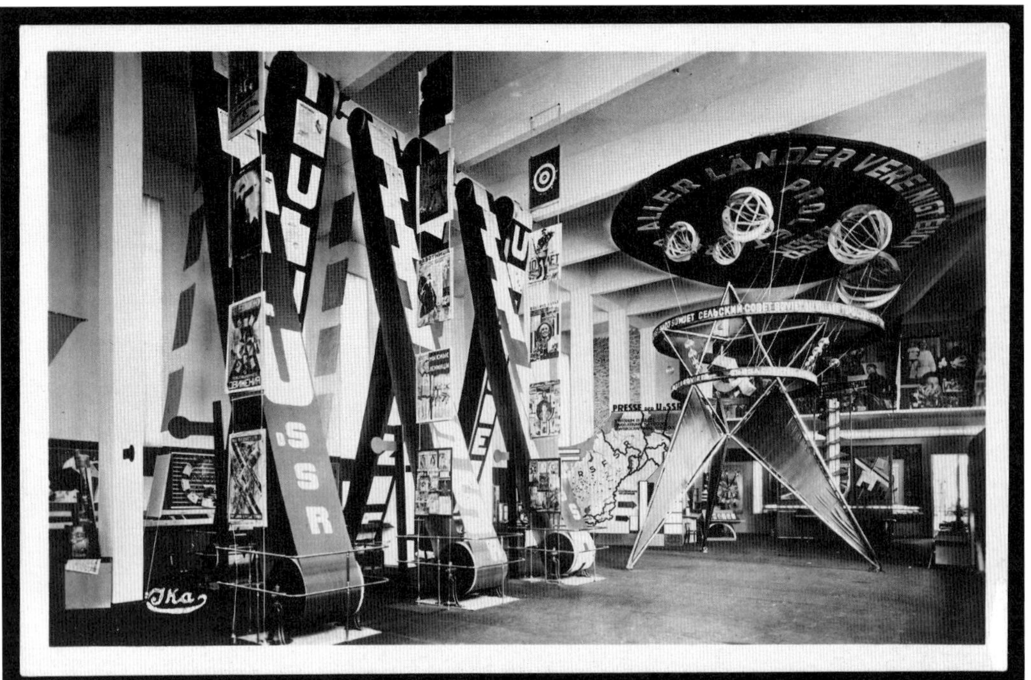

2.4 El Lissitzky, main hall of the Soviet Pavilion, International Press Exhibition Pressa, Cologne, 1928. Getty Research Institute, Los Angeles (950076).

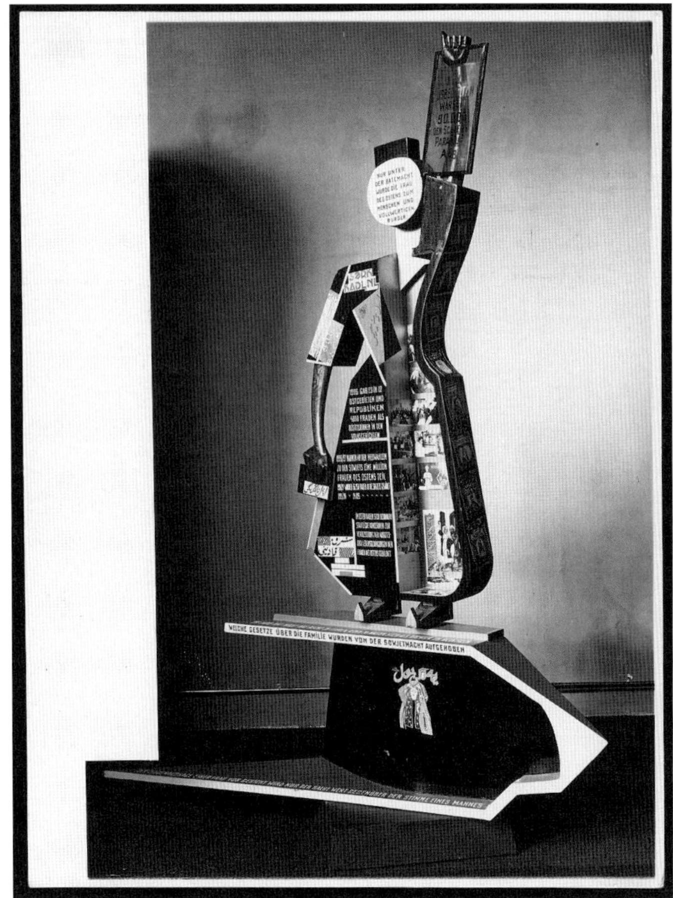

2.5 Mikhail Plaksin, sculpture for the Soviet Pavilion, International Press Exhibition Pressa, Cologne, 1928. Getty Research Institute, Los Angeles (950076).

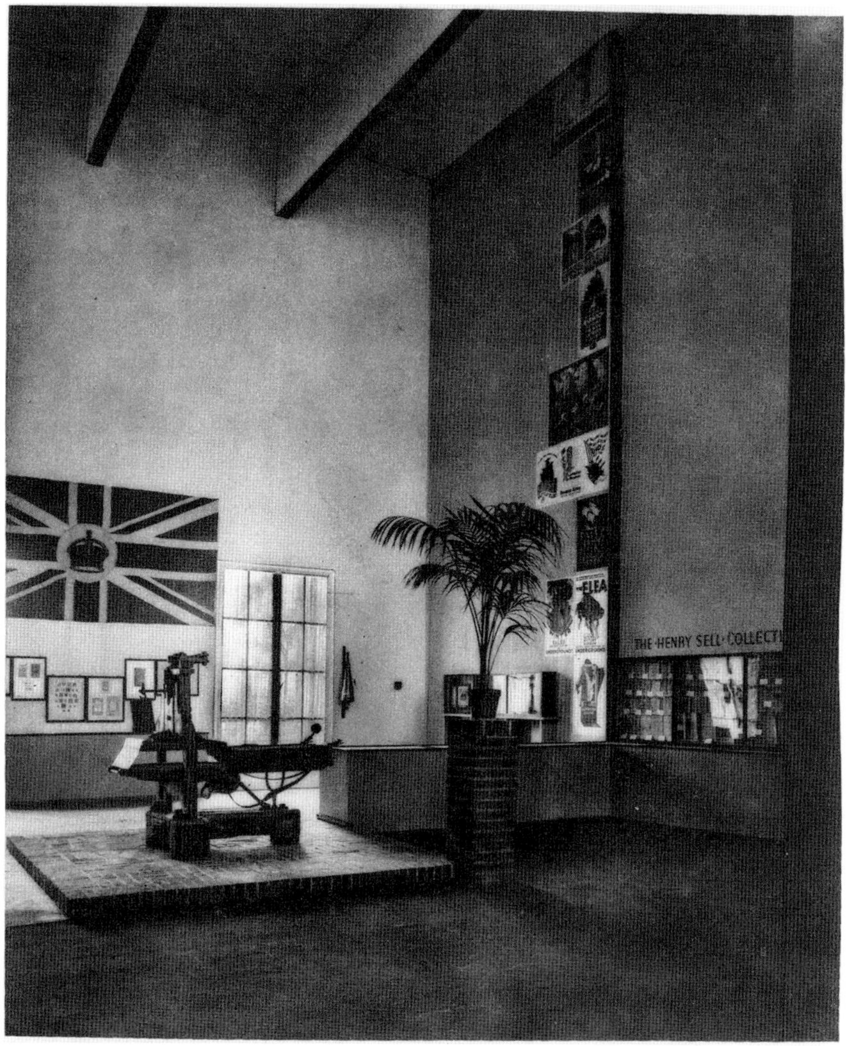

2.6 Installation view, British section, International Press Exhibition Pressa, Cologne, 1928. From *Pressa, Kulturschau am Rhein* (1928), 124.

licate the perceptual conditions under which newspaper information was typically consumed, whether on the wall at the factory, over a neighbor's shoulder on the commute, or at nighttime under the electrical illumination of the streetlight. The installation denied visitors a clear overview of the exhibition, demanding instead that they navigate the space physically in order to decipher the individual works. Lissitzky's concertina-fold photomontage printed at the end of the Soviet catalogue, which stitched together spatially incongruous photos into a continuous optical sprawl, captures well the horror vacui and structural incoherence of the installation. Especially in the main hall, a room that was designed to provide viewers with a sweeping vista of the exhibition contents, Lissitzky took extra measures to break apart the giant space into a warren of smaller part-volumes that refused visitors a clear overview of the artworks. Sergei Senkin's huge fresco on the far wall, made of photographs on a transparent fabric that was suspended in front of a written text, changed its appearance and legibility continuously with the visitor's movement. With every step, the three-dimensional word-image rebus revealed (and concealed) a different aspect of its message: "The education of the masses is the main task of the press in the transitional period from capitalism to communism." Lissitzky further segmented Senkin's photofresco with vertical blinds that impeded the total view of the frieze and compelled visitors to walk the length of the hall if they wanted to see the entire work in each of its discontinuous parts (figs. 2.7, 2.8). By thus undermining the experience of pictorial unity, the massive photomontage overturned the generic presumption of historical panoramas to provide a synoptic overview of events and refused any conception of time as a singular and coherent progression. During the transition from capitalism to communism, the conceit of a monumental history was replaced by a documentary history composed of discrete episodes and blinkered presents.

The most important theoretical influence on the Soviet installation was Nikolai Rubakin, the self-identified "bibliopsychologist" whose research was essential to Gus's understanding of the newspaper.[32] Rubakin had sought to map out the many physiological, affective, and sociological variables that determined subjective responses to the written word, from oculomotor movements and depressive dispositions to class identity. He defined letters on the page as "physical vibrations" that travel from the eyes to the brain and the text, in turn, as "a stimulus for the reader, nothing more."[33] His reflexology of print media posited an inverse correlation between sensation and comprehension, facture and meaning. Thought demanded refracting, or braking, immediate perceptual stimuli; conversely, "the poorer the contents [of the written word], the more excitable it will be."[34] For the bibliopsychologist, the printed word was "something that arouses, and not something that transmits contents or thoughts." Predictably, critics denounced Rubakin's system as a legacy of Bogdanov's empiriomonism and warned that the "negation of the objective content of the word, speech, and the book casts the librarian into the arms of the Machists."[35] But fans of Rubakin such as Gus were thrilled to replace the "spiritualism" of literary hermeneuts for empirical studies of the "mimico-somatic reactions" of the reader.[36]

Rubakin moved beyond purely retinalist accounts of the act of reading, foregrounding the role that the total organism and the physical environment, or medium (*среда*), played in the reception of the word. "The reader is a psychophysical organism that carries into specific conditions of time and place a certain kind of instrument through which it acts on its environment: this source of stimulation is called the book. Because of the long evolutionary process that unfolds over centuries and that embraces both organic and inorganic nature, there

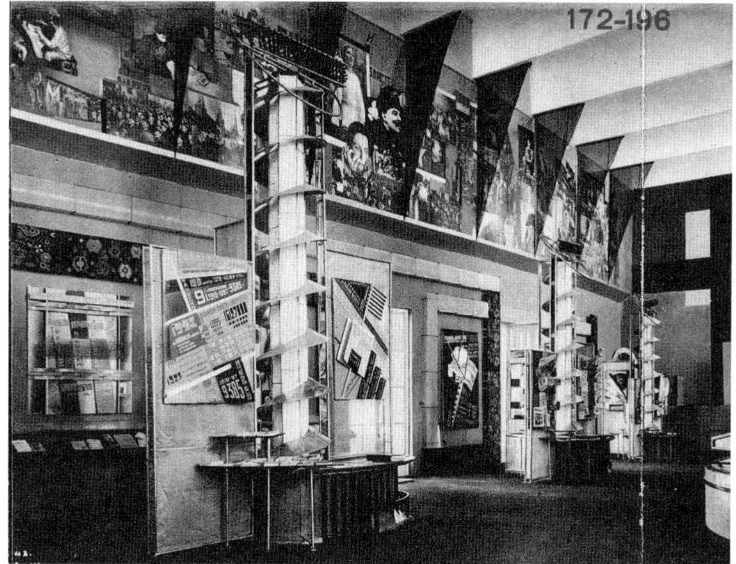

2.7 El Lissitzky and the Committee for the Soviet Pavilion at the International Press Exhibition Pressa, Exhibition Catalogue (1928). Getty Research Institute, Los Angeles (88-B26405).

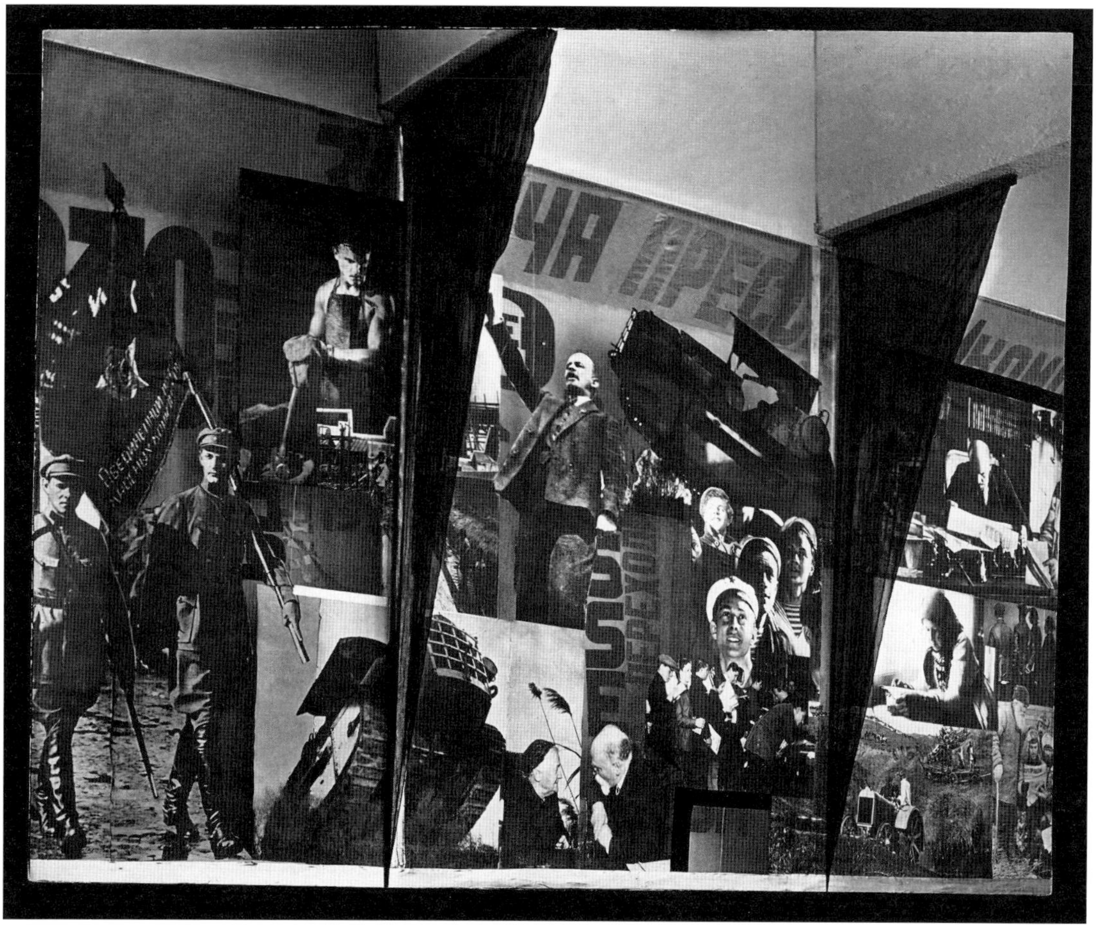

2.8 Sergei Senkin, photofresco for the Soviet Pavilion, International Press Exhibition Pressa, Cologne, 1928. Getty Research Institute, Los Angeles (950076).

always was, is, and will be a close functional dependency between this organism and the environment that gave birth to it."[37] Drawing upon the work of the influential German evolutionary biologist Richard Semon, who had described the human organism as a phonograph-like recording apparatus that registers external excitations as "engrams" in the nervous system of the body, Rubakin approached reading as a complex physiological act that could not be localized in any one organ. He argued that the act of reading triggered certain motor reflexes of the body while inhibiting others; that the movements of the eye over the page could not be isolated from those of the feet and the hands; and that the different physiochemical memory traces that were activated in the course of reading often overlapped, resulting in a synesthetic blur of "sensation-complexes."[38] Ultimately, abstract comprehension and emotional responses to a text could not be predicted solely, or even primarily, from the ideational content of the written word, but were instead a dynamic, embodied negotiation between the organism and its changing environment.

Through Gus, Rubakin's environmental theory of media exerted a profound impact on the Soviet Pressa installation. Movement was essential to grasping its contents. Although the itinerary that was published in the final exhibition catalogue proposed a relatively straightforward route through the installation (fig. 2.9), Lissitzky's original floor plan outlined a much more complex movement-score for visitors (fig. 2.10). Instead of progressing from work to work in a linear fashion, the numeration of the earlier version sets up a series of reversals and switchbacks so that every time spectators were done looking at one work they were then expected to double back in order to approach the next one. For example, the great star and the transmission belts—two highlights of the show—would be passed several times as the visitor walked to the electrified map, then back to the historical overview, then forward again to the display about the Academy of Sciences. Through this continuous zigzag, Lissitzky cut the largest architectural volume of the Soviet pavilion into a number of smaller, local sites of encounter. At the same time, this switchback itinerary also guaranteed that the visitor would first encounter many of the works laterally, in passing rather than head-on. Denied the visual synopsis of a clear frontal approach, the spectator instead became aware of the works slowly and gradually as they emerged beside or even behind him, through partial views at the edges of sight. Here Lissitzky had taken up the suggestion from one article in *The Journalist* that enjoined the Soviet Pressa delegation to exploit the "askance" (*сбоку*) of vision.[39] His installation, which unfolds in the margins of the eye rather than in its foveal center, stimulates optical zones that remain dormant when reading words on a page, above all, the corners of sight that have for centuries been associated with embodied sensation and primal psychic states. One European reviewer marveled at the "bizarre primitivity" of Lissitzky's pavilion, and with good reason:[40] as hunters, trackers, and nomadic peoples have long known, it

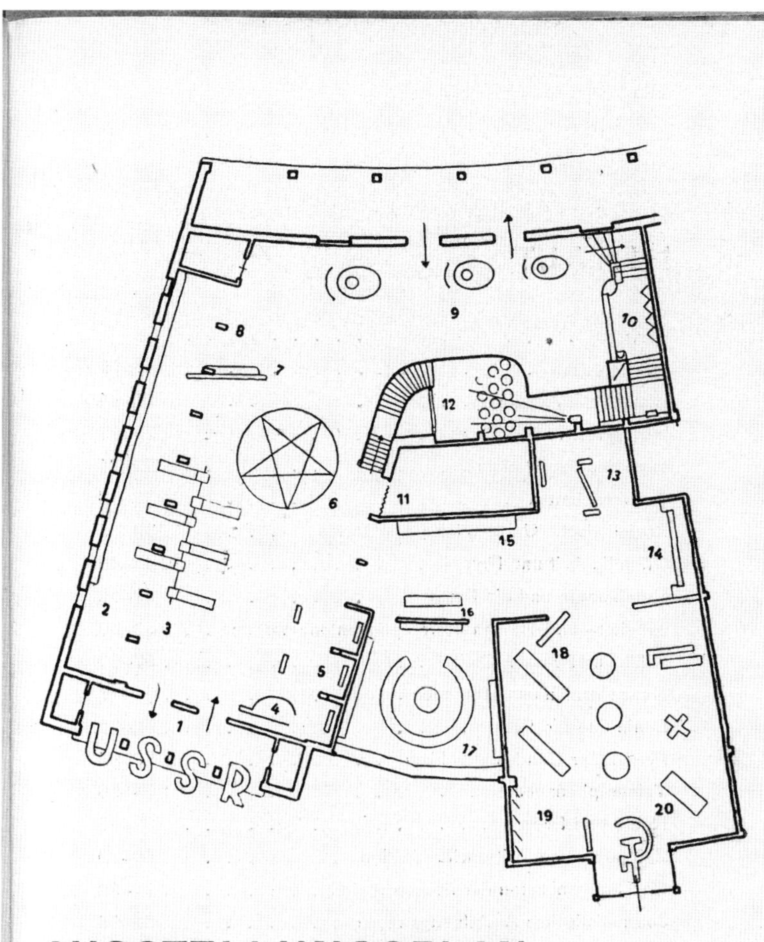

AUSSTELLUNGSPLAN

1 HAUPTEINGANG
2 HISTORISCHE ABTEILUNG
3 TRANSMISSIONEN
4 GEWERKSCHAFTEN
5 SOZ. UMBAU DES DORFES
6 GROSSER STERN
7 LANDKARTE UdSSR
8 AKADEMIE DER WISSENSCHAFTEN
9 BUNDESREPUBLIKEN
10 LENIN ALS JOURNALIST
11 BÜRO UND AUSKUNFT
12 KINO (ESTRADE: BUNDESREPUBLIKEN)
13 GESELLSCHAFTEN
14 WELTKARTE „TASS"
15 POST
16 VERKAUFSSTAND
17 LESERAUM
18 KORRESPONDENTENBEWEGUNG
19 ROTE ARMEE
20 STAATSVERLAG

3

2.9 Visitor itinerary. El Lissitzky and the Committee for the Soviet Pavilion at the International Press Exhibition Pressa, Exhibition Catalogue (1928). Getty Research Institute, Los Angeles (88-B26405). © 2024 Artists Rights Society (ARS), New York.

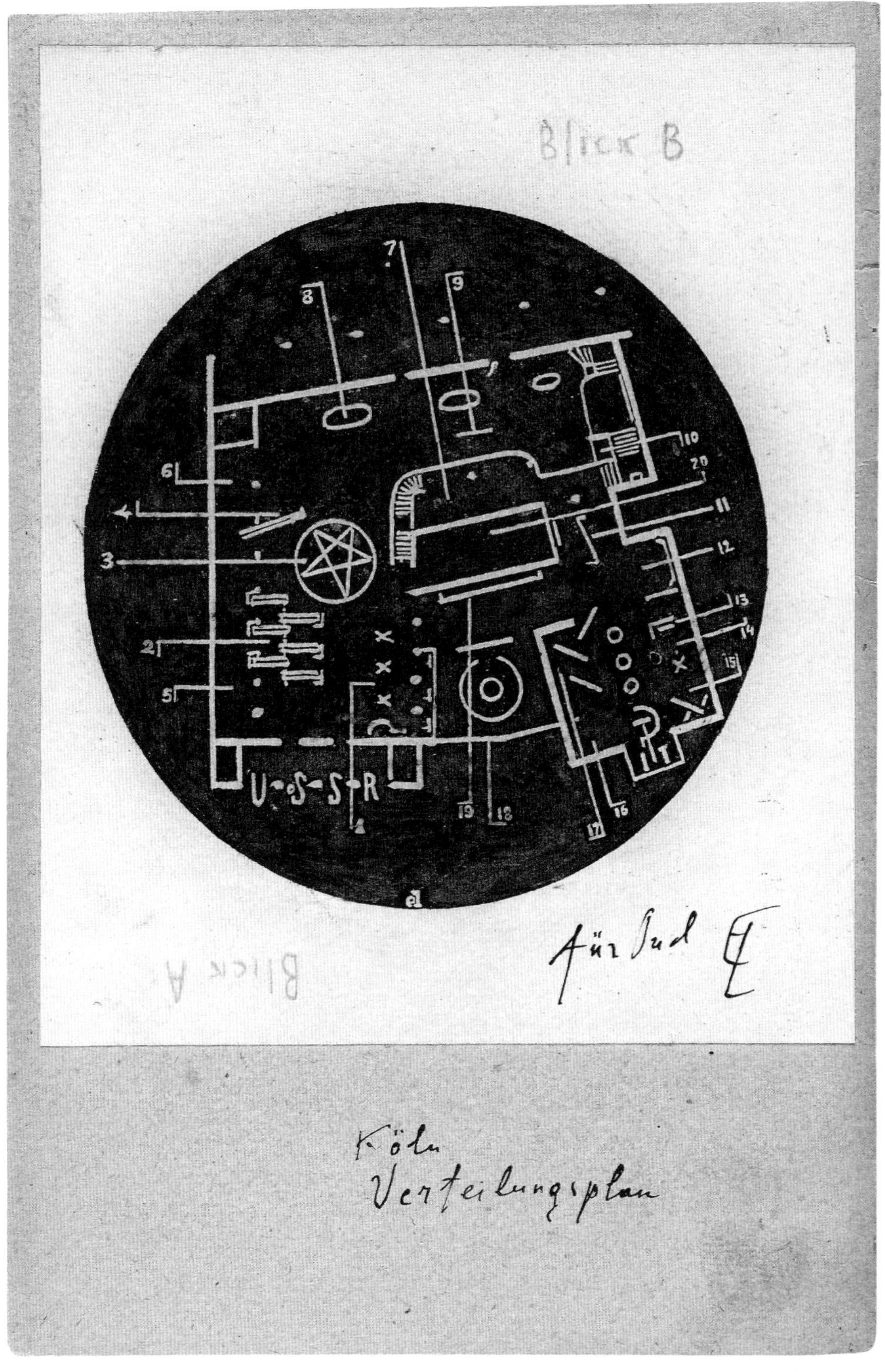

2.10 El Lissitzky, original visitor itinerary for the Soviet Pavilion, International Press Exhibition Pressa, Cologne, 1928. Carnegie Museum of Art, Pittsburgh: Edward N. Haskell Family Acquisition Fund (2006.11). © 2024 Artists Rights Society (ARS), New York. Photograph © 2024 Carnegie Museum of Art, Pittsburgh.

is easier to detect movement by looking away from its source because the peripheral photoreceptors of the eye are more sensitive to motion than the fovea.[41] The edges of vision might be poor at discerning shapes and letters, but then again, making text understandable was not Lissitzky's assignment at Pressa. His contentless phenomenology of the news moved the action away from the valorized retinal centers of the eye that were associated with civilized pastimes like viewing paintings and reading books. By filling the sidelines of vision with "objects with different kinds of physical and optical movement, with a flashing and extinguishing of lights," as Gus's catalogue boasted, Lissitzky simulated the embodied disposition that distinguished the Soviet newspaper from other, more serene print media.[42]

Indeed, notably underrepresented at Pressa were the monumental arts of the book, a print form that was granted generous space in other national pavilions but that was limited in the Soviet sector to a secluded reading room that was tucked behind the merchandise stand (fig. 2.11). The contrast between the boisterous halls exploding with newspaper print and the modest library for the book summed up the Soviet view on these two media: the codex format had little if anything to contribute in the transitional epoch. Members of the avant-garde objected that the book immobilized the reading subject twice over. First, it did not allow the eye to range freely across the page but restricted ocular movement to a plodding unidirectional movement. For Lissitzky, the linearization of writing was inseparable from the phoneticism upon which Western metaphysics was based: "The old book was constructed for the ear, for silent reading, from left to right, from top to bottom."[43] Tret'iakov, who likewise called for "less interiority while reading," was equally critical of the collusion between silent reading and the imagination.[44] For him, the practice of book reading also presumed a second kind of immobilization, that of the absorbed reader sitting in a chair at a moment of repose. The old codex format, and especially its literary apotheosis in the novel, is willfully indifferent to its surrounding environment. Indeed, the success of fiction's reality effects presumes the reader's ability to shut out everything that is happening around her and conjure the world-negating forces of the imagination. Optimal conditions for this feat of transcendence can be found in the *intérieur* of the bourgeois home, the domestic isolation tank that Adorno once called the "prototypical cell of abandoned inwardness."[45] There the subject could take shelter from the pressing events of history and practice the art of sensory deprivation known as silent reading.

Thinkers on both ends of the political spectrum celebrated the newspaper's hostility to the psychic interiority of the bourgeoisie. Ernst Jünger's *The Worker* (1932), a book influenced in countless ways by the total mobilization of the Soviet economy, welcomed modern journalists who had finally outgrown their profession's naïve faith in objectivity and come to see the newspaper as an instrument of psychotechnical stimulation. Public opinion, the pillar of the clas-

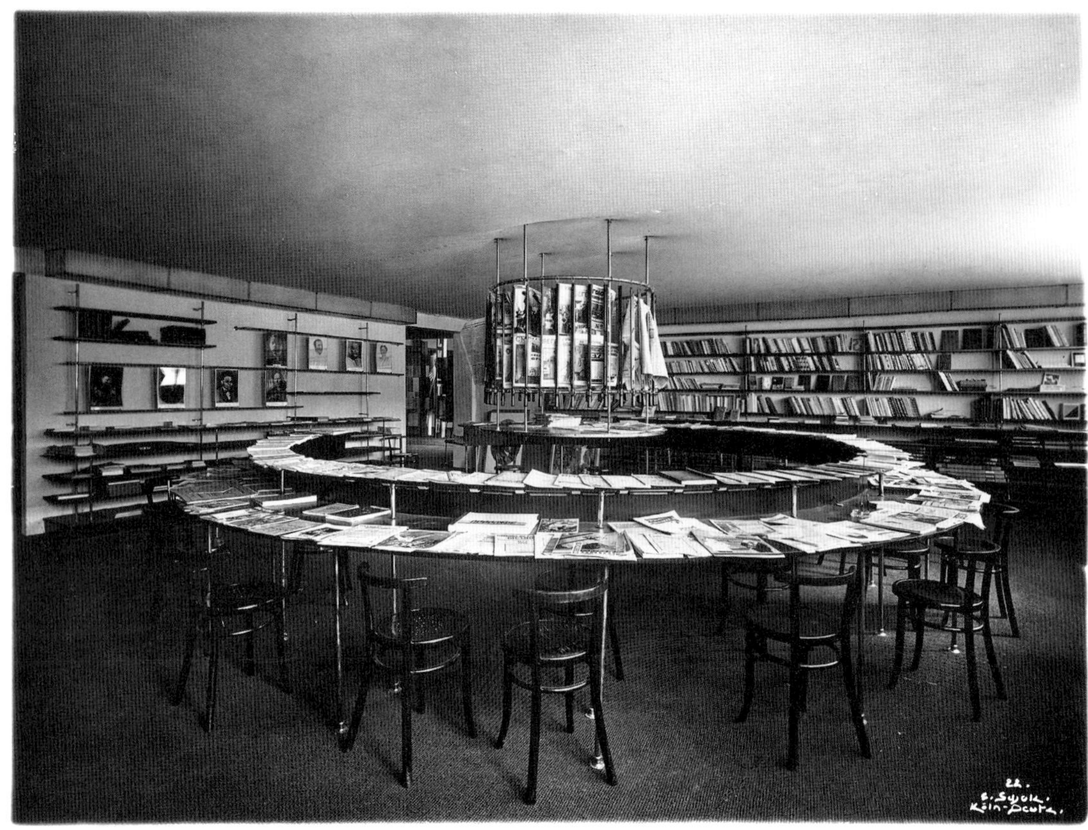

2.11 El Lissitzky, reading room for the Soviet Pavilion, International Press Exhibition Pressa, Cologne, 1928. Getty Research Institute, Los Angeles (950076). © 2024 Artists Rights Society (ARS), New York.

sical liberal public sphere, had been transformed "from an organ of the bourgeois concept of freedom into a magnitude of pure labor," he wrote there. For Jünger, an accelerationist who despised the slowness of parliamentary debate, the punctual language of the newspaper also presented a means to overcome the political standstill of Western democracies. In the modern press, "decisive impact no longer merely shapes opinions or builds majorities, but occurs through action." Reading, an activity that once provided amnesty from life, had come to resemble factory labor, crossing the street, or other activities requiring vigilance and heightened mental presence.

> Reading too no longer resonates with the concept of leisure; rather, it displays the signs of a specialized work-character. This is very clear with the chance to observe the reader, above all on public transport (whose mere use is also an act of work). We detect from this observation an atmosphere at once alert and instinctive, correlated to a news service of the highest precision and speed. We

get the impression here of a world changing as we read, but at the same time this change is constant, like the monotonous changing of light signals rushing past. This is news in a world in which the event is characterized by a presence that strikes every atom with the speed of an electrical current.

For Jünger, industrialization has transformed the newspaper from a forum for civil discourse and the exchange of ideas into an instrument of discipline. The daily broadsheets deliver summons to action, not prompts for reflection. In order to understand the ideological dimensions of the mass press, one must look past its content and instead examine it as a behaviorist would by considering, for example, the sequence of conditioned movements that it provokes. "The gesture with which an individual opens and browses his newspaper is more telling than all the lead articles in the world, and nothing is more informative than a quarter of an hour standing at a traffic junction." For Jünger and other critics of the bourgeoisie, the newspaper was less like a book than a traffic light.[46]

Following the terminology of the Central Institute of Labor, Tret'iakov called the condition of sensory vigilance that was induced by the newspaper *nabliudatel'nost'*, the faculty of observation. This orientation of consciousness toward the present, invoked already in the first paragraph of "Moscow—Beijing," was the specific perceptual mode cultivated in every factographic work. In Gastev's programmatic essay "The New Cultural Orientation," which appeared shortly before Tret'iakov's first ocherk, the Institute's lead theorist ranked *nabliudatel'nost'* as the first and most important of nine "qualifications" that were needed to survive in the modern world ("Novaia kul'turnaia ustanovka," 92–93).[47] There were two reasons for its preeminence. First, observation is the form of perception most suited to industrial environments that are saturated with machines and media. It is the sensory disposition that is native to technical milieux. In his 1924 book *Nabliudatel'nost'*, which appeared in the Institute's *Orga-biblioteka* series with a foreword from Gastev, the perceptual psychologist Nikolai Levitov traced the psychogenetic origins of this modern sensory mode back to the nineteenth-century laboratories in which scientists once had to maintain careful watch over a room full of instruments. Measuring, monitoring, quantifying, and recording their experimental subjects, these researchers oversaw the datafication of life. As historians of science later confirmed, the practice of observation is a technically mediated mode of perception, "a highly contrived and disciplined form of experience that requires training of the body and mind, material props, techniques of description and visualization, networks of communication and transmission, canons of evidence, and specialized forms of reasoning."[48]

Levitov recounted how the practice of observing migrated gradually out of the laboratory setting, expanding first into industrial workplaces that were undergoing automation and then eventually into an urban environment that was becoming increasingly saturated with mechanical sensors.[49] Gastev collectively designated these sensors *pokazateli* ("indicators," "indices"), a word that encompassed the diversity of dials, viewfinders, gauges, and other graphic displays that provide the modern subject with a continuous stream of information about the world around him. Calibrated to "infinitely small units," these sensors gave their users access to crucial dimensions of experience that were situated beyond the range of the natural, organic senses. Micro-time was made visible by the chronometer, force by the dynamometer, pressure by the plethysmograph, and so on. Gastev wrote that "the most important part of the new cultural interface is the ability to use all kinds of sensors for observation like the compass, the watch, the chronometer, binoculars, and all kinds of telescopes." Finding one's way in the industrial lifeworld required technical calibration of the body's spontaneous perceptions, an "education of our sensory organs" in accordance with the mechanical technologies that were becoming increasingly indispensable for modern existence ("Novaia kul'turnaia ustanovka," 92–93).

The second reason for prioritizing observation over other perceptual modes was its promise to attune consciousness to current events and situations that are developing in real time. Gastev defined *nabliudatel'nost'* as the "ability to listen at any given moment, to perceive at any given moment, to be ready at every moment to be distracted [*отвлечься*] from what he or she is doing." This paradoxical readiness-for-distraction gave rise to a diffuse state of bodily alertness (*настороженность*) and a heightened receptivity to changes in the surrounding environment (fig. 2.12). Discussions of *nabliudatel'nost'* at the Central Institute of Labor regularly referenced the examples of hunters, trackers, and the American Boy Scouts, a mass organization that was training the next generation in "a primitive, almost savage form of observation" ("Novaia kul'turnaia ustanovka," 92). The Institute cultivated *nabliudatel'nost'* in its own members by organizing expeditions into the factories and streets of Moscow, where participants were taught to scan their environments for slight indications of movement and variation.[50] Levitov characterized this heightened state of awareness as a "general readiness to receive living impressions and to process them" (*Nabliudatel'nost'*, 16). Observation demanded psychosensory vigilance toward a dispersed field of impressions, a mindset keyed to the askance and to events located on the margins of perception. For this reason, Levitov categorically distinguished observation from both concentration (*интенсивность*) and attention (*внимание*), two modes of experience with which it was too often confused (*Nabliudatel'nost'*, 28). Unlike the latter states that contract consciousness to a point, observation dilates the aperture of perception and primes the mind for interruption.

Gastev and Levidov's theorization of observation anticipated Benjamin's conclusion a few years later that distraction (*Zerstreuung*)—the perceptual condition cultivated by technical media such as cinema—attunes the subject to

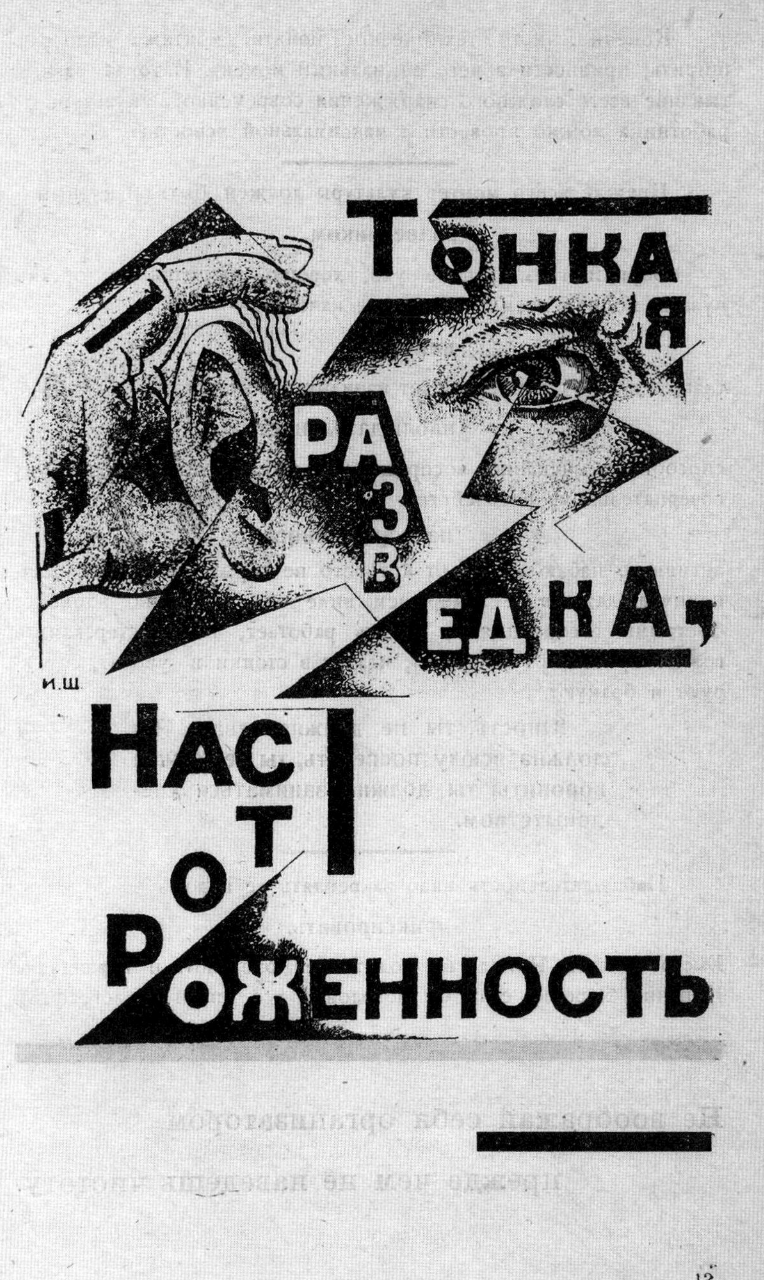

2.12 Iosif Shpinel′, "Sensitive reconnaissance, alertness." From Aleksei Gastev, *Iunost′, idi!* (1923), 7. Cotsen Children's Library, Princeton University, Princeton, NJ.

rapidly changing circumstances and is, consequently, an indispensable sensory disposition for surviving in modernity's fitful temporality of crisis. Much like Benjamin, who associated this "increased presence of mind" (*gesteigerte Geistesgegenwart*) with the tense posture of a gambler who awaits the right moment to risk his fortune,[51] the theorists in the League of Time believed that leading a successful revolution required careful observation of events and a good sense of timing.[52] Through the twin strategies of mental vigilance and chronometric sensitization, the League hoped to align the subjective and objective coordinates of time and bring about a revolutionary conjuncture. An enthusiast of "fierce games of chance," Tret'iakov too emphasized alertness while awaiting the fortuitous moment in which to intervene in history. "Yesterday you had to be able to explode like a bomb, expending all available energy in a single superhuman effort. Today you must know how to meter yourself out sparingly for the thirty years of revolutionary workdays that lie ahead" ("New Leo Tolstoy," 48). In the modern era, when mass-political events no longer follow a continuous line but instead coalesce suddenly at instants of historical rupture, it was essential to know when to stake your assets or when to wait for the next round.

The two aspects of observation outlined by NOT—its suitability to industrial milieux and its intermittent temporality—led Soviet media theorists to promote this perceptual disposition as the ideal for newspaper reading. In his classic 1927 study *Questions of Newspaper Culture*, Iakov Shafir wrote that "by reading newspapers, attention is diverted toward different objects, and this has a positive significance. Reading newspapers is a salubrious means for 'hygiene of the soul.'"[53] Distributing attention across multiple sources of interest, the newspaper loosens the fixed syntax of the imagination and frees thought from the ruts of mental association. In this way, the Soviet newspaper vitalizes the reader and makes him more receptive to events in the world around him. Here Shafir referenced Kant's *Anthropology from a Pragmatic Point of View* (1798), which recommended newspaper reading as a strategy of "mental dietetics" (*Diätetik des Gemüts*) that would teach people "the art of distracting themselves in order to collect their powers." Novels shackle the mind to the "involuntary reproductive power of imagination," but these endless mental "reverberations" can be stopped "by distraction and by applying attention to other objects; for example, reading newspapers."[54] Anticipating Luria's remedy for the journalist Shereshevsky by more than a century, Kant recommended diffuse observation and newspaper reading as cures for the poor soul who was lost in fiction.

Observation resembles the activity of monitoring, a mode of reception that philosopher Stanley Cavell later associated with live news programs on television and radio. Unlike viewing or listening, monitoring does not presume any particular sensory modality. It entails a dispersed and atmospheric way of attending to the world, one that keeps events running continuously in the background of awareness without allowing the mind to become absorbed by them. Watched intermittently and without particular focus, technologies of monitoring articulate time by "dividing and repeating the day in terms of minutes and seconds." Indeed, to reprise a point from the last chapter, what distinguishes the news media are not the images and stories that they supply about reality, but their ability to create and texture time itself. When monitoring, the subject continuously scans the array of events for any variations in the signal that might indicate that history is poised to take a new direction. Experience is shaped and skewed by this "tropism toward the event."[55] In his writings on the time-consciousness of the clock, Heidegger would call this condition *Wachsein*, wakefulness.[56] It was a condition that the editor-in-chief of *The Literary Newspaper* described in a 1924 article from *Time* as a state of restless innervation: "Between one alarm signal and another, between a visitor and a telephone call, on break from a meeting, on the streetcar, during intermission at a play, at the barber—people look through the newspaper, pausing at the more important and sensational items, glancing over the rest of the news, 'flying through' the articles."[57] Newspapers aren't read; they are observed and monitored. They cultivate a population of readers that is permanently on edge, one distinguished by a "constantly renewed willingness to be prepared for surprises, disruptions even."[58] After his visit to Moscow, where he witnessed innumerable time collisions and catastrophes, Benjamin delivered the perfect emblem for the observers in the League of Time, one that read like a precise description of Rodchenko's 1923 watch advertisement for *Time*: the most advanced artists politically—those who had fully grasped "the present orders" of the *Communist Manifesto*—were the ones who "exchange, to a man, the play of human features for the face of an alarm clock that in each minute rings for sixty seconds."[59]

THE TANGLE OF CONSCIOUSNESS

Interest in the psychomotor dimensions of writing and other systems of communication was not unique to the factographers. After his tour of Russia in the mid-1920s, the Austrian journalist René Fülöp-Miller gushed about experiments that he saw with "the mechanization of poetry": "This is in truth the great achievement of revolutionary thought: that the connection between art and conditioned reflexes, between Don Quixote and the excretion of spittle in a dog, has been definitely fixed, and that poetry has been defined as the mechanical combination of sounds and tones according to a chemical formula."[60] At this point renowned international scientists had in fact been investigating the somatic strata of language already for decades, and much of this research was circulating widely in popular thought by the time the Bolsheviks took power. The behaviorists in America had demonstrated how language and thought triggered reflexes in the hands of test subjects, giving rise to involuntary movements that, according to one researcher, "can be brought nearly or quite to the verge of automatic writing."[61] Psychologists in Germany concluded from their experiments on imageless thought that words and concepts could be encoded not just as pictures in the imagination, as the ancient rhetoricians did, but also as physical response patterns in the muscles. Research like this, which compared the mind to a motor rather than a mirror, found fertile ground in Soviet Russia, where psychoneurologists argued that consciousness was nothing more than an assembly of physical reflexes that had been organized into a multidimensional edifice of memory traces and associations. The complex feats of cortical processing that produce phenomena of emotional life may be more elaborate and involuted than the shorter stimulus-response arcs found in the nerves and muscles, but ultimately there was no qualitative difference between the two orders of reflexes. This motor arc extended all the way up to the highest echelons of human culture. The Formalist critics working at the Institute of the Living Word, for example, used laboratory instruments to investigate the complexes of physical sensations and movement-templates found in literary works. For Boris Eikhenbaum, the Formalist most intrigued by psychotechnical methods, literature comprised a score of affective states, "formal emotions," and other "nonindividual, abstract intensities" that were devoid of determinate image-content.[62] The factographers, in turn, discerned profound political potential in this research, which promised to close the rift between physical and mental life under capitalism. For Chuzhak, who demanded abrogating "the law of the division of labor that enslaves the human being, and with it the opposition between mental and physical labor,"[63] and for Tret'iakov, who proclaimed "the convergence of intellectual and physical labor as one of the basic conditions for the realization of socialism,"[64] reflexological methods would finally enable cultural producers to engage with the new Soviet subject as an integrated psychophysical being.

The 1926 publication of "Mental Labor from the Reflexological Point of View" by the renowned psychoneurologist Vladimir Bekhterev was recognized by lead theorists in newspaper studies as an important advance in overcoming the dualism of bourgeois thought.[65] Bekhterev's experiments demonstrated that physical movement, symbolic reasoning, and introspective states were all connected to one another through "mimico-somatic" linkages. To be sure, each of these processes moved at different speeds and possessed its own distinctive morphology, some linear and others recursive, but they all shared the same neural pathways in the body. The analysis of mental workers like scribes and computors, for example, revealed the participation of diverse muscles of the body even in abstract cognitive operations of logic and mathematics, prompting Bekhterev to conclude that physical reflexes extended upward even into those refined acts of intellection that showed no outward motor component. Neuromuscular activity was evident in literature and art as well, where Bekhterev researched aesthetic reflexes at the moments of both production and reception.

Like bookkeeping, programming, or any other labor of the salaried intelligentsia (*служащие*), these cultural forms were just higher-order expressions of the body. Bekhterev's experiments, which appeared in the banner anthology *The Reflexology of Labor*, made it possible at last to connect the physical labor of the industrial proletariat—already well researched in the chronocyclographic laboratories of the Central Institute of Labor—to the cognitive labor of typists, the creative labor of writers, and the perceptual labor of readers.[66] "Mental Labor from the Reflexological Point of View" finally filled the research lacuna that critics like Eikhenbaum pined after: "In an age interested in the study of labor processes, in the scientific organization of labor (NOT!), there is a powerful need for studies about the contexts and conditions of mental labor."[67]

Much of the most brilliant research into the reflexology of culture was conducted in the laboratory of Ukrainian neurologist Zakharii Chuchmarev (1888–1961), a rising star in the field of psychotechnics who published diverse studies in the 1920s on literature, poetry, music, and painting. According to Chuchmarev, who closely followed the work of the Formalists and that of Eikhenbaum in particular, art and literature were "technical instruments for organizing emotions and concrete human behavior in general."[68] Following Spinoza, he proclaimed that "all ideas can be deduced from matter" and argued that any philosophical system that would seek to distinguish categorically between physical reality and its reflection in thought was doomed to fail since "ontology and epistemology," being and knowledge, did not constitute two separate orders of existence. Chuchmarev explained that the privilege that the consciousness enjoys over the body, for example, was just an instance of highly complex matter asserting control over less complex matter.[69] The will is another aspect of physical being, even if its structure is more convoluted and idiosyncratic than the flesh.

The most important study to come out of Chuchmarev's Kharkov lab, "An Attempt at Experimental Artistic Criticism," was published in two parts in 1925–26 in *Soviet Art*, a monthly journal that was edited by Chuzhak and that regularly featured texts by theorists and critics close to Lef. This was evidently the audience that Chuchmarev had in mind, since the introductory remarks to his essay made direct reference to the clash between the Lefists and the champions of "old realist form" such as Iurii Libedinskii (a novelist who would soon become a leading figure in RAPP). "An Attempt at Experimental Artistic Criticism" proposed to adjudicate between avant-gardism and mimeticism experimentally by measuring the ratio of affect to consciousness in specific artworks. This approach, he explained, would allow psychotechnicians to "resolve topics that are also being debated in poetics" and finally settle the dispute between Lef's "life-construction" and the realists' "life-cognition." Like Bekhterev, who claimed that all forms of communication and expression, even the most abstruse, left a material imprint on the body that could be measured using laboratory instruments, Chuchmarev believed that every word—a "verbal stimulant" (*словесный раздражитель*), in his phrasing—had its own empirical "emotional value" that could be established independently of its lexical meaning.[70] As if responding to Churilin, the Proletkul't poet who called for an instrument that could measure the force of the "movement-word" in the same way that a dynamometer measures thrust, Chuchmarev's team used a plethysmograph to record changes in the pulse rate and strength of test subjects as they listened to a sequence of words. His approach combined the laboratory apparatus of Charles Féré, who had used the plethysmograph decades before to gauge affective reactions to color, with the conceptual system of Wilhelm Wundt, who had correlated cardiac response to the six basic emotional experiences of excitement and inhibition, tension and relaxation, and pleasure and displeasure.[71] The basic experimental setup used by Chuchmarev, which could be found in laboratories across Europe and America at the turn of the twentieth century, offered a "practical means of deterritorializing the body" that allowed the researcher to access signals of the autonomic organs independently of the test subject's conscious will.[72]

But Chuchmarev wanted to investigate more than just the somatic strength of words. He also asked participants to reply to each verbal stimulant with a word of their own and then recorded the association. "An Attempt at Experimental Artistic Criticism" included a table showing the four verbal associations of a test subject "M." along with a plethysmogram of the accompanying cardiac events (fig. 2.13). She responded to the first word, *thieves*, with the association *caught*. The interval between the two words was marked by an increase in pulse rate and a decrease in pulse strength—an indication of displeasure, per Wundt. The second word, *chronoscope*, triggered no change in pulse rate but caused M.'s pulse to grow weaker before she responded with the word *microscope* after a pause (signaling inhibition). Most strikingly, though, M. had no response to

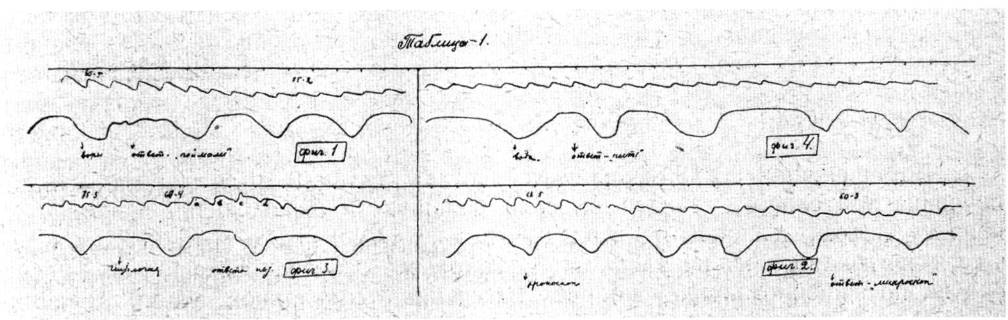

2.13 Plethysmogram showing cardiac events in response to four verbal stimulants: "thieves," "chronoscope," "histology," and "water." From Zakharii Chuchmarev, "An Attempt at Experimental Artistic Criticism," *Sovetskoe iskusstvo*, no. 9 (December 1925): 29.

the third word, *histology*. Like all technical terminology, this anti-metaphor possessed no "inner form" à la Shpet and, according to Chuchmarev, prompted no act of introspection (*интроспекция*). Looking at the plethysmogram for *histology*, Chuchmarev observed that "the record testifies to an intellectual affect (a high degree of feeling) with stimulation predominating" (indicating an experience of pleasure). Finally, M. responded quickly to the fourth word, *water*, with *drink*, but the association was accompanied by no significant changes in either pulse rate or amplitude.[73] Of all four test stimulants, then, *histology* was ideationally the poorest, but affectively the richest.

Chuchmarev recorded a third factor in addition to affective intensity and verbal association: the processing time necessary for each participant to respond. Like other neurologists working in the field of mental chronometrics, he considered longer times to be an indicator of the activity of consciousness. As Wundt had demonstrated in a series of influential reaction-time experiments undertaken in the 1880s, variations in the delay between a perceptual stimulus and the subject's response indicated different processes taking place in the mind. Wundt observed that the time needed for specific mental operations such as apperception, discrimination, association, and selection each remained within a fixed range of values down to the thousandths of a second. The act of introspection might solicit diverse psychological accounts from test subjects, who described the images unfolding in their imagination differently, but the processing rates nevertheless stayed constant across participants. Nervomuscular, sensory, cognitive, and volitional reactions all transpired at different, but reliably consistent, speeds.[74] Discrimination, for example, clocked in at a brisk 132–226 milliseconds, while association required 706–874 milliseconds: this, Wundt surmised, was because acts of association demanded greater reflection than mere discrimination, which was essentially just a sensory reflex without inner experience (*innere Erfahrung*). The general rule was that more elaborate mental tasks resulted in higher latency. Consciousness takes time: it may not be made of different material stuff than the body, but it travels at a markedly slower speed. Based on Wundt's experiments, psychoneurologists working internationally used the delay between stimulus and reaction to analyze and differentiate a variety of mental activities, including, for Chuchmarev, aesthetic response. His "Attempt at Experimental Artistic Criticism" delivered empirical confirmation for one of the avant-garde's foundational insights: art was indeed a braking of perception (*заторможение*), a physiological inhibition that rendered immediate sensation available to conscious reflection and ideological organization. Eisenstein put it this way: if you punch someone who has insulted you in the face, this is an "unmediated reaction," but "if the reaction is delayed and vengeance devised, we have a whole 'work of art.'"[75]

The year after "An Attempt at Experimental Artistic Criticism," Chuchmarev published *Psychophysiological Research into the Labor of Telegraphists*, which pivoted from questions of aesthetic response to issues of language and communication more generally. Inspired by the work of Hugo Münsterberg, the German psychotechnician who used reaction-time experiments to assess the suitability of test subjects for careers ranging from telephone operator to streetcar driver, Chuchmarev promoted his 1927 book as a practical contribution to the growing body of research on professional selection (*профотбор*) coming from the Central Institute of Labor. According to Chuchmarev's criteria, the ideal telegraphist would be capable of converting abstract signals into words and back with minimal encumbrance or delay. He does not pause to consider content or meaning. On this point Chuchmarev echoed the pioneer of communication theory Ralph Hartley, who insisted that research into telegraphic transmission should "ignore the question of interpretation" and instead measure performance "based on physical as contrasted with psychological considerations."[76] Conscious reflection only obstructed the circulation of information. One of the illustrations for *Psychophysiological Research into the Labor of Telegraphists* mapped out the elaborate circuitry of the cortical processors and nervomuscular system that lay between the signal received at the ear and the hand writing down the words (fig. 2.14). Between input and output, Chuchmarev's diagram depicted consciousness as a tangle of lines full of recursions, mnemonic tracery, and other mental ornament.[77] Taking up the same chronometric method that he had developed for the study of literature, his book on telegraphists once again measured the affective intensities and reaction times that accompanied a given stimulus, although this time he expanded the variety of stimuli beyond the spoken word to include other sorts of triggers such as buzzing sounds. Not without a certain humor, he compared responses to the word "shock" (a symbol) against those provoked by an actual electrical shock (a signal). By measuring differences in the reactions to these two kinds of phenomena, one verbal and the other perceptual, Chuchmarev again classified stimuli according to the degree of consciousness that they provoked. The results of these tests, he explained, would complement Gastev's research into the temporal microregimes (*микрорежимы*) of labor.

Psychophysiological Research into the Labor of Telegraphists took on a topic central to the language politics of the 1920s. Telegraphy, like stenography, had become a universal ideal of writing, both high and low. Mayakovsky opened his one factographic poem *Good!* (*Khorosho!*, 1927) with the invocation: "Fly, strophe, as a telegram! / With enflamed lips fall down and drink / from the river named 'Fact.' / This age is buzzing on the chords of the telegraph."[78] Compressing information and accelerating its transmission were regarded as cultural imperatives of the decade. One Proletkul't theorist observed in *Pravda* that "our lexicon is becoming telegraphically sharp and brusque, condensing the content of the word to an immense degree."[79] In the pathbreaking survey from 1929, "The Russian Language and Revolution," celebrated philologist Pavel

— 47 —

Фиг. 1

СХЕМА (упрощенная) НЕРВНЫХ ЦЕНТРОВ и ПРОВОДЯЩИХ ПУТЕЙ РАБОЧЕЙ РЕАКТИВНОЙ ДУГИ КЛОПФЕРИСТА

(СПЛОШНЫЕ ЛИНИИ-КОРКОВЫЕ ЦЕНТРЫ ПО БЕХТЕРЕВУ, ПУНКТИРНЫЕ ЛИНИИ - ЭКСТРАПИРАМИДНАЯ СИСТЕМА ПО Lewy).

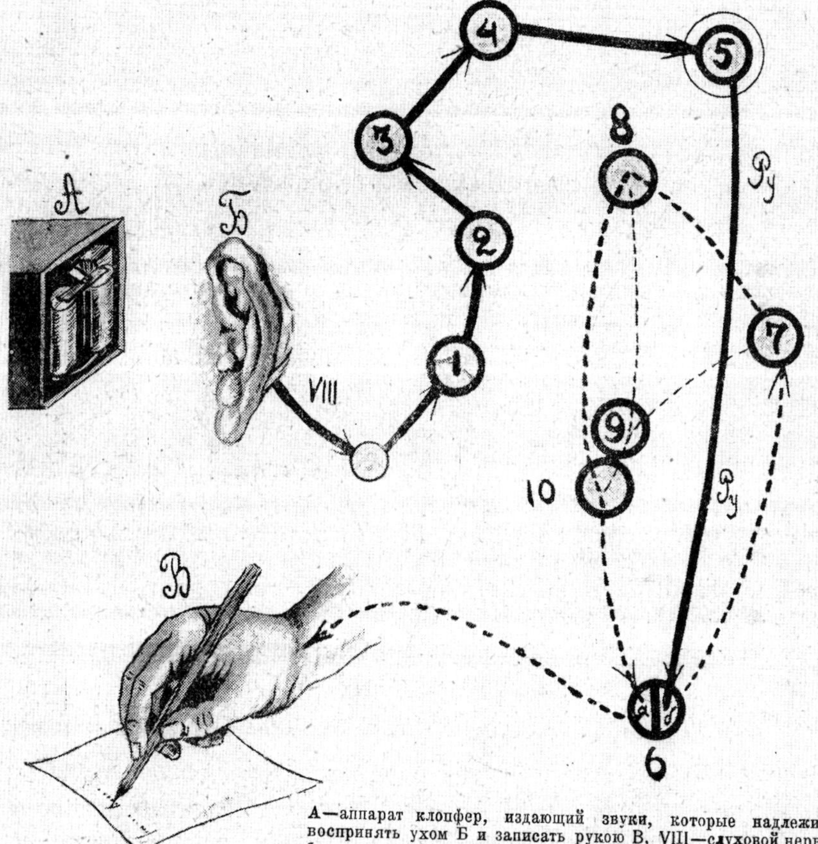

А—аппарат клопфер, издающий звуки, которые надлежит воспринять ухом Б и записать рукою В, VIII—слуховой нерв. 1—внутреннее коленчатое ядро. 2—слуховая область коры (извилины Heschl'я и внутренняя часть 1-ой височной извилины. 3—о'ласть активного сосредоточения (предлобная часть мозга). 4—ассоциационные центры. 5—центр произвольного движения руки (средняя часть передней центральной извилины). Ру—путь к спинному мозгу произвольного двигательного импульса—пирамид ый путь. 6б—вставные клетки спинного мозга (Hinterhornsschaltzelle). 7—малый мозг—аккумулятор нервной двигательной энергии—по Lewy. 8—система полосатого тела—распределитель двигательной энргии. 9—центры тонуса. 10—Nucleus assotiatorius motorius tegmenti, 6а—передние рога спинного мозга.

2.14 "(Simplified) Diagram of the Nerve Centers and Conductive Pathways of the Working Reaction Arcs of a Telegraphist." From Zakharii Chuchmarev and V. A. Lavrova, *Psikhofiziologicheskoe issledovanie truda telegrafistov-klopferistov* (1927), 47.

Chernykh attributed the prevalence of abbreviations and telegraphic syntax to technical modernization and the social changes introduced by October. Everything was faster in the transitional period—art, literature, and music included. "In our days a Beethoven symphony, as a rule, is performed at a faster speed than the one at which it was composed by the author." Building on Wundt's *Ethnic Psychology* (*Völkerpsychologie*), Chernykh proposed a dromological approach to cultural analysis that categorized different peoples and populations according to respective rates of perception and speeds of communication. "The fact of a certain acceleration of the tempo of life in recent times can hardly be in doubt. It would be worth comparing the tempo of life today in the European metropolis with the tempo of life in the typical European countryside . . . in order to confirm the connection between this acceleration and the progress of culture." According to Chernykh, the pervasive experience of acceleration in the industrialized world was intensified even more by recent political crises. "Events like war and revolution contributed a new impulse in the development of the tempo of life," he observed.[80] The historical migration from the countryside to urban centers and the technical evolution from agriculture to the industrial mode of production had triggered a first round of social acceleration, which, in Russia's specific case, had then been further compounded by the Bolshevik Revolution. In the East, consciousness and communication were now moving at an unprecedented speed. As one of the leading industrial rationalists wrote in *Time*, "we have to fit the *maximum number of thoughts*, the maximum content, into a *minimum of words*. We have to study the language of telegrams."[81] Literature would be displaced by telegraphy, a technical form of writing that has abandoned the paradigm of representationalist realism. Telegraphy is "an affective problem, rather than a reality problem," writes media theorist Jonathan Sterne. "Whole modes of being are condensed into the rhythms of telegraph signals, which in turn index the subtle and quick movements of operators' hands."[82]

Accelerating expression was a core directive of Soviet journalism. Experts designated the informational density of newspaper language *napriazhennost'*, a word meaning "tension" and "compression" but also, with reference to the actual hardware of the telegraph, electrical "voltage." The association between journalism and telegraphy was at least in part based on the simple fact that many Soviet newspapers combined short items from the Telegraphic Agency of the Soviet Union (TASS) with contributions from local amateur correspondents.[83] Following Lenin, who had enjoined reporters to stop writing long-winded articles and instead submit brief notes "in telegraphic style" ("Character of Our Newspapers," 96), Trotsky published an essay in *The Journalist* explaining that "a correspondent is evaluated according to a single feature: he is obliged to convey the maximal quantity of facts in the minimal quantity of words. This impacts his style. And the style of telegraphic correspondence is then transferred onto the article as well."[84] In response to these injunctions from the Party leadership, researchers in newspaper studies took up a question central to all modern communication technologies, whether telegraphs, fax machines, or the internet: How to balance the imperative of speed with the need for intelligibility?[85]

None grasped the impact of telegraphy on the grammatical and generic features of writing better than the Formalist Grigorii Vinokur, whose studies of newspaper language in the 1920s would later be heralded as an important predecessor to the pioneering works in information theory of Claude Shannon, Andrei Kolmogorov, and Norbert Wiener.[86] As Vinokur explained in the *Lef* essay "The Language of Our Newspapers," journalism is distinguished from other forms of writing by the priority it grants to "thinking syntactically" (*мыслить синтаксически*) over thinking lexically. "If we divide the resources of language's means of expression into grammar and vocabulary, then we will see that newspaper speech privileges an *orientation toward grammar* over an orientation toward vocabulary." Whereas the exposition of information in most exchanges takes place over time, the newspaper can squeeze even an extended message into a single syntactic unit. "By definition, the telegram's objective is to accommodate the greatest possible quantity of facts within the framework of the most *succinct and compact grammatical scheme possible*."[87] The Russian language, in particular, has more grammatical resources to facilitate this compression than other languages. By using present active participles instead of subordinate clauses, for example, writers can condense an entire series of thoughts into a single segment and in this way achieve the desired degree of "tension." Because of the remarkable syntactic flexibility of Russian, Chuzhak likewise argued that Russian writers are not bound to laws of linear exposition and that, in contrast to their French or German counterparts, they excel "in celerity, in an instantaneity of living perception, in an interconnectedness between impressions so extensive that it captures even the accidental." Exploiting this exceptional capacity for syntactic compression, the Soviet newspaper realized Chuzhak's call for a "style of a fugitive oneness of impressions [that] differs from the old style of 'sequentiality' [*последовательности*]."[88]

The density of Soviet journalism distinguished it from other speech genres like verbal exchanges and storytelling, which demanded longer syntagmatic sequences. Vinokur writes: "*An attentiveness to syntax* is manifested in the systematic distribution of copulative particles and words over an entire segment, and permits an entire series of facts to fit into a *single grammatical chain*. The exposition of these facts in typical *conversational speech*—as well as in all other kinds of written speech besides that of the newspaper—would demand a completely different narrative form made of several independent phrases." The purpose of the newspaper was not to relate stories but to transmit information with maximal efficiency and speed. Whereas plotted prose unfolds diachronically through a series of transformations across the length of the text, the contents of the telegraphic newspaper are instead apprehended by the reader all at once. For this reason, Vinokur called on journalists to eschew linear narrative. News items are not novellas, he insisted: "If we tried to divide up the very text of the [newspaper] telegram in this way, we would thereby deprive the telegram's language of its most basic characteristic, and what we would then be dealing with would no longer be a telegram, but some kind of historical narrative."[89] The extreme grammatical density of the newspaper, which Vinokur called the condition of "saturation" (*насыщенность*), prompted one scholar to observe that Soviet journalism exhibits "a curious syntactical horror vacui."[90] There was no open, unutilized space. For similar reasons, members of the constructivist avant-garde argued that the literary precedents for modern journalism were actually to be found not in narrative prose but in poetry, where the orientation toward grammar and syntax led to the "centripetal organization of the material."[91] Poetry, like journalism, is a dense matrix of differential informational values. It shifts meaning from content and lexicon onto the structural registers of the text—provided the poet doesn't indulge in excessive imagery. "Poems should be made of steel" rather than "wet wood," Tret'iakov wrote: "Write shorter. More concretely. Compress the line."[92]

In the telegraphic language of the newspaper, syntax took priority not just over lexicon but even over semantic clarity. Opponents of Vinokur who were skeptical of his avant-garde sensibilities feared that compression and automation impaired the intelligibility of the text. Indeed, Lef's own Boris Arvatov detected a connection between telegraphy and the notoriously puzzling trans-sense poetry of Futurists Kruchenykh and Khlebnikov.[93] Scholars at the State Institute of Journalism conducted research which confirmed that readers often didn't understand the vocabulary used in the newspaper: one confused reader thought, for example, that a "demonstration farm" (*показательное хозяйство*) like Tret'iakov's own kolkhoz Communist Lighthouse was actually a kind of domestic cupboard for displaying valuable objects.[94] Gus thus stipulated that, for journalists, "there is a single rule: write as short as possible. . . . The maximal compression of form [*сжатость формы*] is needed, *though not to the detriment of intelligibility*."[95]

For Vinokur, privileging grammar over lexicon was essential to fulfilling the newspaper's goal of automating communication. He quoted the famous lines from Goethe's *Faust I* in which Mephistopheles instructs a pupil in the art of writing without thinking: "It's precisely where concepts are lacking / That a word appears at just the right time" ("Denn eben, wo Begriffe fehlen / Da stellt ein Wort zur rechten Zeit sich ein").[96] On the page of the mechanized newspaper, a demonic language seemed to write itself without reflection, thought, or intention. Journalism transmitted "syntactic signals" rather than ideas, Vinokur wrote.[97] Borrowing a concept from his GAKhN colleague Gustav Shpet, Vinokur explained that the words used in the newspaper have no "internal form" (*внутренняя форма*).[98] Later critics would consequently observe that the prompt mechanical writing of the Soviet newspaper undermines the "image-quality" (*образность*) of words and "tries to deprive language of the very ability to represent anything."[99] The telegraphic writing of the newspaper was unencumbered by the processing delays of the imagination, even of consciousness itself.

Soviet scientists attributed the chronometric discrepancy between mind and body to their differing degrees of structural complexity.[100] Echoing Pavlov's influential definition of consciousness as a secondary signal system that was built atop the primary signal system of the senses, Vygotsky defined the mind as "a reflex of reflexes"[101] and Chuchmarev described thought as a "repeated refraction of reflexes."[102] By this logic, consciousness was essentially a system of feedback, just the diversion of the organism's basic reflexes along different, more circuitous neural pathways. According to Gastev, the capacity for recursive self-stimulation was in fact the only thing that distinguished humanity from inorganic constructions: "From the perspective of the contemporary biological sciences that consider the living human machine like any other kind of machine—albeit one with an autoregulator [*автоматом-регулятором*], the brain—there is no qualitative distinction that would necessitate a different organizational approach to the human than the one used for a machine-instrument."[103] As scriptural confirmation, Vygotsky, Chuchmarev, and Gastev all referenced the famous passage in *Capital* where Marx wrote that "what distinguishes the worst architect from the best of bees is that the architect builds the cell in his mind before he constructs it in wax." Unlike simple organisms that merely execute the instincts that are hardwired in their anatomy, humans live in a condition of permanent anticipation and are always out of sync with the present. The highest states of this desynchronization can be found in human culture. "The impossibility of technologically processing data in real time is the possibility of art. Literature, as an art of human beings, is a gift of interception."[104]

This understanding of consciousness as inhibited instinct and delayed sensation was fundamental to the empiriomonists around Bogdanov and, by extension, the factographers. In "The Material of Collective Experience and Organizing Its Forms," which appeared in the watershed anthology of Russian Machism *Essays in the Philosophy of Collectivism*, the economist and revolutionary Vladimir Bazarov approached the hoary cultural opposition between spontaneity (*стихийность*) and consciousness (*сознательность*) through the lens of chronometrics.[105] Following the vitalist Henri Bergson, Bazarov explained that the "biological purpose" of mind was to break apart the continuous stream of organic sensation like a cinematograph and to rearrange these discrete image-cells into higher organizational complexes. Like Marx, Bazarov illustrated the difference between intellect and instinct with an example from entomology:

the wasp operates on its victim with the same precision as a human surgeon, Bazarov wrote, although its actions are not informed by any mental picture or internal representation (*представление*) of its victim's anatomy. The insect possesses no "potential schemes of activity" (*возможные схемы активности*) but operates only in and for the "real act." The virtuality of the imagination and the subjunctives of the *as-if* are alien to wasp-mind, which knows only actuality. From this Bazarov concluded that the difference between thought and reflex is but a factor of time: "Consciousness plays a role only if the organism hesitates, if a given stimulus triggers a condition of vacillation [*колебательное состояние*], a series of emerging and reciprocally neutralizing impulses." Mind was for him a way of not being present in the world. "Consciousness turns out to be a kind of delay [*задержка*], a kind of suspension in the process of interaction between nature and the organism," Bazarov explained.[106] The experiences of interiority and selfhood that form the core of human subjectivity are nothing more than effects of this suspension. As the philosopher of speed Paul Virilio put it some years later, it is not consciousness but duration itself that "thinks, feels, sees."[107]

Soviet researchers like Chuchmarev wanted to establish where various features of language were located on the spectrum between pure consciousness and pure reflex. Like the factographers, Chuchmarev discovered metaphor at the former extreme and technical language at the latter. In contrast to symbolically freighted words like *thieves* and *water*, which both prompted the test subject M. to compose micronarratives—she responded to *water* with *drink* and *thieves* with *caught*—the words *microscope* and *histology* did not impel M. to fabulate. In fact, *histology* did not prompt any mental activity at all, but instead triggered a powerful somatic response. As M. explained afterward, she did not know what the word *histology* meant, although she recognized it from a sign on a door in the Kharkov laboratory: for her, the word functioned purely referentially, as an index rather than a symbol. Whereas *water* set the machinery of memory and imagination in motion, the scientific term *histology* cut through the ornament of consciousness and struck the test subject like an electrical pulse. To explain this response, Chuchmarev drew a comparison with the chronometric word-association experiments of C. G. Jung, who used a set of 100 stimulus-words to diagnose mental complexes (*Komplexe*): for the Swiss psychologist, a particularly slow response to any of these words indicated an emotional node overfreighted with connotation, a master image that tied together an entire network of memories and associations.[108] As Chuchmarev discovered, only the technical term *histology* appeared to be free of all such entanglements. It was a psychical nonentity, a word that pierced the veil of metaphor and dictated a reflex to the brain promptly and directly, as Tret'iakov put it. Like all factographic writing, such technical language is dominated by the sign-class of the index, a signifying operation which, according to Jakobson, has more in common with machine communication than literary symbolism and which belongs properly to the science of cybernetics, not to poetics.[109] Like a buzzer in a behaviorist laboratory, a traffic signal at a crosswalk, or an attraction in a Proletkul't play, the verbal index triggers a sensorimotor response in the subject with no corresponding act of reflection. As Charles Sanders Peirce wrote, the indexical sign has "no cognitive value" and provokes attention, not imagination. The index "takes hold of our eyes, as it were, and forcibly directs them to a particular object." Stimuli like these, which "act upon the hearer's nervous system," are "pure physiological compulsion; nothing else."[110]

As the previous chapter explained, Chuzhak saw a precedent for this materialist language in the "uncannily artless records" of the *raznochintsy*, the social stratum that ran the Russian state administration in the nineteenth century and that birthed the Soviet technical intelligentsia in the twentieth. If there was any prototype for factography, it was not the realist novel but the memoranda, ledgers, and records of managerial knowledge-workers who processed information automatically and mindlessly. Like Chuzhak, Eikhenbaum, the Formalist who saw literature as a category of mental labor, discerned a model for operational writing in the chancery-speak of the *raznochintsy*. The latter's imageless language was for him exemplified by the most famous bureaucrat in Russian literature, the copyist Akaky Bashmachkin from Gogol's *The Overcoat*. As Eikhenbaum demonstrated in his brilliant study from 1918, Gogol's short story did not just mock the unthinking mechanicity of nineteenth-century bureaucratese but actually staged its contentlessness in the prose itself. Below the surface of Gogol's story, Eikhenbaum discerned a second, psychomotor text that was scored for the face, mouth, throat, and hands. He observed how reading *The Overcoat* produced a comic-grotesque play of laughter and sorrow in the body of the reader that did not coincide with the image-content of the narrative. As the reader performs the subsemantic "mimetic-declamatory" script of *The Overcoat*, the imagery of the story gradually begins to fade away, and finally disappears entirely at the moment Gogol uses the word "hemorrhoidal" (*геморроидальным*) to describe Bashmachkin's complexion. This medical term

> is so placed that its phonic structure acquires a special emotional and expressive force, and is perceived as a comic phonic gesture, independent of the meaning . . . In its final form, this sentence is not so much a *description* [*описание*] of Akaky's appearance as a *reproduction* [*воспроизведение*] of it by mimetic means of articulated sound. The words are chosen and placed in a certain order, not in accordance with any principle of character-delineation, but in accordance with the principle of acoustic semantics. The reader's inner eye remains blank. (I can think of nothing more difficult than to make drawings of Gogol's heroes); all that remains of the entire

> sentence in one's memory is the impression of a certain order of sounds, which culminates in a resounding word virtually devoid of logical meaning yet extraordinarily expressive as sheer articulated sound—"hemorrhoidal."[111]

An author celebrated by the Formalists for writing without images (*безобразно*), Gogol replaced the metaphysics of representation with a record of physiological reflexes.[112] Like Tret'iakov's Blinch, Gogol's Bashmachkin cannot be described. The *raznochinets* cannot be envisaged by the reader—nor, for that matter, can he himself envisage: after all, the job of the copyist, like that of the telegraphist, requires processing information as accurately, mechanically, and thus as thoughtlessly as possible. For bureaucrats like Bashmachkin, imagination is a professional liability.

The reaction time of the intelligentsia was a central theme of *I Want a Baby*, Tret'iakov's 1927 romantic comedy about a geneticist's efforts to get pregnant. As the director Igor' Terent'ev explained in his commentary, the play approached its subject matter through the lens of "reflexology" and defined love as the "irradiation of a stimulus": "the condition of being in love has been replaced by a heightened voltage in the brain that is constructive and production-oriented."[113] At the beginning of Tret'iakov's play, the protagonist Milda determines that she is too "circumspect" and that in general her reflexes are too slow, prompting her search for a sperm donor whose genes can counteract her own biological tendency to inertness. As one friend puts it to Milda during a heart-to-heart, "there are geniuses of revolution. There are geniuses of stabilization. You are a genius of stabilization." For Milda, mating with a genius of revolution is the only way to transform her own stabilizing intellect into spontaneous action. Otherwise she risks compounding consciousness with still more consciousness and giving birth to a "pedant who is twice as slow." As Tret'iakov explained in a statement about *I Want a Baby*, the fate of socialism itself hinged on successfully converting intellect into instinct in this way: "Only when thought about the new purposiveness has evolved into habit, when the new consciousness has become a new instinct—only then will we have succeeded in putting human behavior onto new tracks."[114] Through the evolutionary fusion of affect and thought, of working class and intelligentsia, he predicted the emergence of a new hybrid social group that he dubbed the "prole-chintsy," a revolutionary generation that combined the physical prowess of the *prole*tariat with cognitive capacity of the razno*chintsy*.[115]

Tret'iakov had borrowed the distinction between "geniuses of revolution" and "geniuses of stabilization" from the German chemist Wilhelm Ostwald, whose contribution to the popular series *Studies on the Biology of Genius* had differentiated faster "romantic" thinkers from slower "classical" ones. In this book, Ostwald, who had received the Nobel Prize in 1909 for his experiments on catalysis and reaction speed, categorized prominent figures according to the "speed of their mental reactions." According to Ostwald, this novel methodological combination of chemistry and biography reconciled two distinct scales of being, "atomizing psychophysics" and "the psychology of the actual total person." Classifying historical personages according to "the pace of the mental pulse-rate" in this way, Ostwald divided humanity into two fundamental types: on the one hand, "the swift ones" (*die Geschwinden*) who revolutionize and invent, and who live in the present; and, on the other, "the slow ones" (*die Langsamen*) who stabilize and systematize, and who live instead in the past and the future.[116]

Milda recognizes that she belongs squarely in the latter category. Thus, after declining a proposition from her own class conspecific—the desirable but much-too-thoughtful physician Dr. Softer—she decides to choose a sire not on the basis of sentiment or physical attraction, but on the candidate's performance in a test of reflexes. The play's pivotal scene, titled "Selecting a Father," depicts an improvised psychotechnical aptitude test after the model of Münsterberg or Chuchmarev, in which Milda assesses her subjects according to the speed of their reactions. After scrutinizing her various prospects, she finally reaches a decision when she sees the proletarian Iakov navigate street traffic with particular deftness. "The reflexes on that one are good," admires one onlooker, sealing Iakov's fate.[117] In the later film adaptation of Tret'iakov's play, it is again the reflexes of the working-class specimen that win Milda over in the selection scene. Looking on, notebook and stopwatch in hand, she observes approvingly that Iakov took exactly one-tenth of a second to respond to the test stimuli—a reaction time that, according to the psychometrics of Tret'iakov's day, would indicate an act of direct perception that is absent any introspection.[118]

The factographers recognized that reconciling consciousness and spontaneity would require new forms of art and literature that were chronometrically more precise than the bulky and monumental culture of the bourgeoisie. Pertsov, whose factographic opus *The Literature of Tomorrow* likewise drew on Ostwald's studies of reaction time, published an essay in Chuzhak's *Proletkul't Almanac* outlining a number of technical strategies to make writing, in particular, more responsive to time. His article "Word—Optical Image—The Future" opened by contrasting the phonetic language found in the novel to the spatial sign-systems used in diagrams. Each of these two formats engage a different "function of time," Pertsov explained: in the horizontal writing found in the older codex book, signs follow one another consecutively and comprehension unfolds gradually, whereas visual graphics convey information in multiple dimensions almost instantaneously. Although Pertsov celebrated swiftness (*беглость*) in communication, importantly, he did not simply reject all linear writing: denser texts requiring thought and reflection must still be permitted to take time. The problem for Pertsov, rather, was that all kinds of writing, irrespective of purpose or content, continued to be subjected to the same basic rule of linear exposition. Contemporary readers needed to be able to control the tempo of mental labor themselves:

> After the literary work has left the laboratory of the artisan and the typographer, the printed text is like a locomotive in the hands of a reader who doesn't know how to use the controls. Even worse is when the artist-mechanic has not even equipped his engine with a system for controlling it. He has just turned it over to the impulses of the reader "free of rudder, free of sail."
>
> Having already established that words are a function of time, we have to recognize that *controlling the literary work means regulating it in time*. In the current state of affairs, the means for regulating are very weak, if almost nonexistent.

The linearity of traditional literature must be broken up to facilitate the "chrono-regulation of the reader's perception," explained Pertsov. Citing Münsterberg's *Psychology and Industrial Efficiency*, he enjoined scientists to quantify in thousandths of a second every facet of literature, from material aspects like page layout and typography to linguistic features like syntax and lexicon. On the basis of these concrete psychotechnical data, writers could then collaborate with graphic designers to engineer the desired velocity of any given text.[119]

"Word—Optical Image—The Future" ends with special praise for cinema, the seventh art from which the other six could stand to learn. Recent films demonstrated to Pertsov that the cinematograph was above all "an apparatus that is precisely regulated temporally" and an instrument that "allows the full potential to control time."[120] Pertsov's essay did not credit any particular filmmakers with this insight, but the likeliest candidate had to be Dziga Vertov, whose own contribution to the same *Proletkul't Almanac* broke down film genres not according to their content but their duration: newsreels were 10–30 meters (one to 2.5 minutes), cartoons were 10–40 meters (one to three minutes), comedies were 100–200 meters (8.75 to 15 minutes), and detective mysteries were 1500–2000 meters (125 to 162.5 minutes)—values that proved once again that facts were more punctual than fiction. Vertov had been obsessed with chronometrics since the beginning of his career. His first published statement about film culminated in a decidedly Leaguist lament: "The 'psychological' prevents man from being as precise as a stopwatch."[121] This early preoccupation with the delays of consciousness established a program for all of Vertov's subsequent work, prompting countless experiments with spacing, slowing, arresting, accelerating, reversing, interpolating, and otherwise manipulating the dimension of time. For Vertov, who fixed watches to make ends meet during hard times, the cinematograph promised to repair the non-synchronicity of mind and world. One of the most celebrated sequences in his entire oeuvre, the passage in the middle of *Man with a Movie Camera* when all movement suddenly comes to a halt, represents an attempt to modulate the ratio of thought to perception by alternating the speed of film. The sequence starts with a galloping horse that is gradually slowed until frozen mid-stride, at which point Vertov presents a series of static images (fig. 2.15). Like Bazarov and Shklovsky, who compared the human intellect to a cinematograph that divides the continuous flow of time into discrete segments, Vertov arrests the movement of the horse and subjects it to conscious analysis. Choosing to exemplify the powers of reason by filming a horse, of all animals, was of course a nod to the father of moving pictures Eadweard Muybridge, who had once used chronophotography to answer the nagging question of whether there is ever a moment when a running horse has all four feet off the ground (fig. 2.16). The moment of stasis in *Man with a Movie Camera* opens an interval for reflection, an island of consciousness amidst the film's unremitting stream of stimulation and movement. Right on cue, Vertov then introduces the editor Elizaveta Svilova, who is shown working with the footage at the cutting table (fig. 2.17). Scrutinizing the cells of life that have been preserved on film, cutting them apart with scissors, and then arranging these excerpts according to taxonomies on the wall before her, Svilova is the very personification of the dissecting power of intellect. By bringing movement to a standstill, she makes spontaneous experience into an object of knowledge.

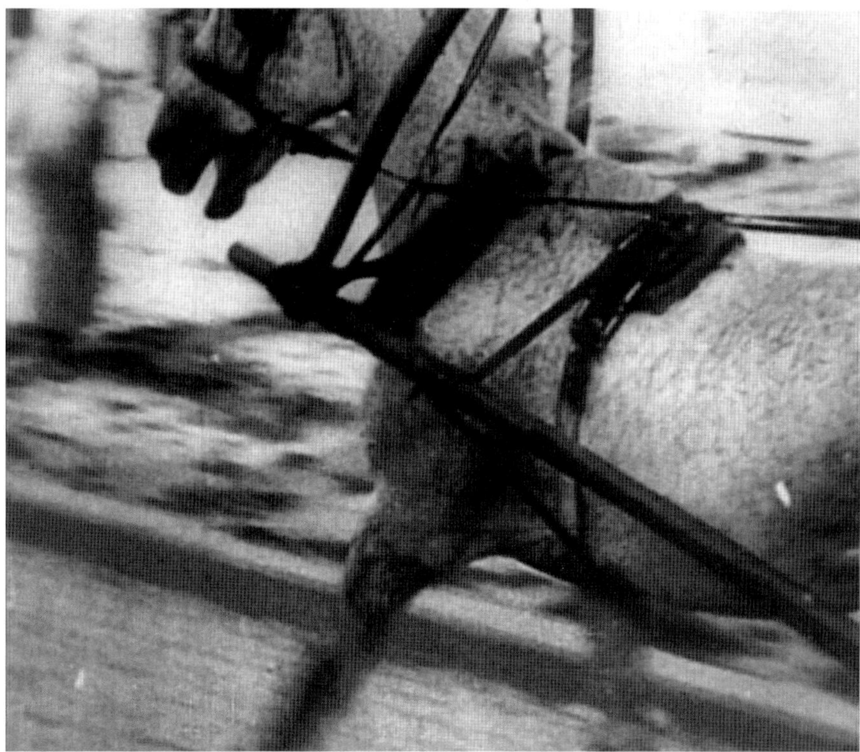

2.15 Horse at a gallop. Frame from *Man with a Movie Camera* (dir. Dziga Vertov, 1929).

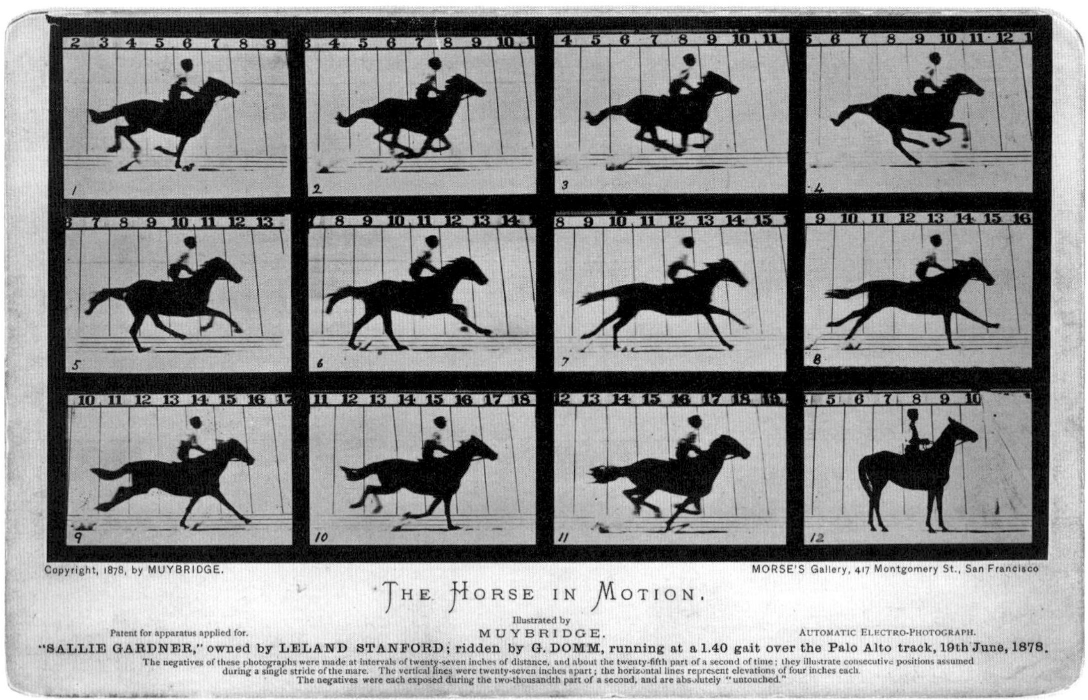

2.16 Horse in motion. Eadweard Muybridge, "Sallie Gardner," owned by Leland Stanford; running at a 1:40 gait over the Palo Alto track, June 19, 1878. Library of Congress Prints and Photographs Division (LC-DIG-ppmsca-06607).

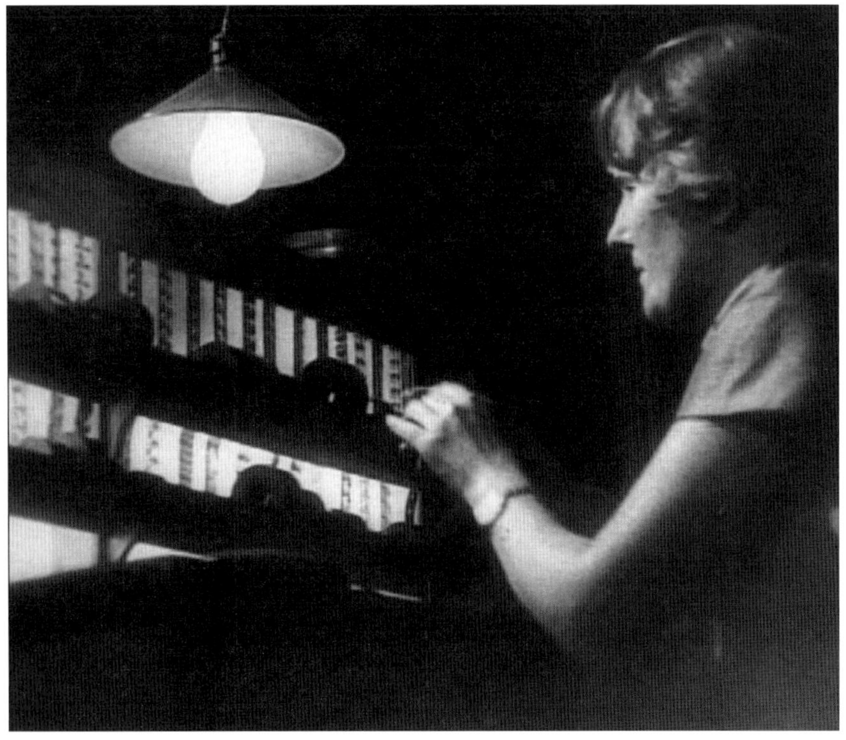

2.17 The cutter Elizaveta Svilova. Frame from *Man with a Movie Camera* (dir. Dziga Vertov, 1929).

The newspaper was recognized as the print form that came closest to matching cinema's precise control of time. Adjusting the topography of the page and the typography of the print made it possible to vary the speed at which information was communicated and thereby calibrate the exact ratio of instinct to intellect in language. In the 1920s psychotechnical experiments conducted by specialists in the field of Reading Hygiene had established that the eye can apprehend a nine-centimeter-wide line of text in a single glance, so that an article of that width could effectively be scanned from top to bottom without any lateral movements of the eye.[122] In this way, the punctual lexicon of the newspaper, which used facts and terminology instead of images and metaphors to reduce cognitive processing time, was matched by a spatial layout that accelerated the movements of the eye over the page. In contrast to traditional phonetic writing, whose sluggish depth-hermeneutic was encoded anatomically in the drag of the reader's eye from left to right, the newspaper took flight in vertical columns that unspooled from top to bottom like strips of film. "The reader should read all the news almost at once," wrote the constructivist designer Laszlo Moholy-Nagy.[123] As important "attempts to enhance the temporal regulation of lit-work," Pertsov cited two recent avant-garde periodicals that had radicalized the lessons of the newspaper: Lissitzky's multidimensional journal *Veshch'–Gegenstand–Objet* (fig. 2.18) and the publications coming out of Pertsov's own former place of employment, the Central Institute of Labor (fig. 2.19), both of which he praised for their extreme chronometric precision.

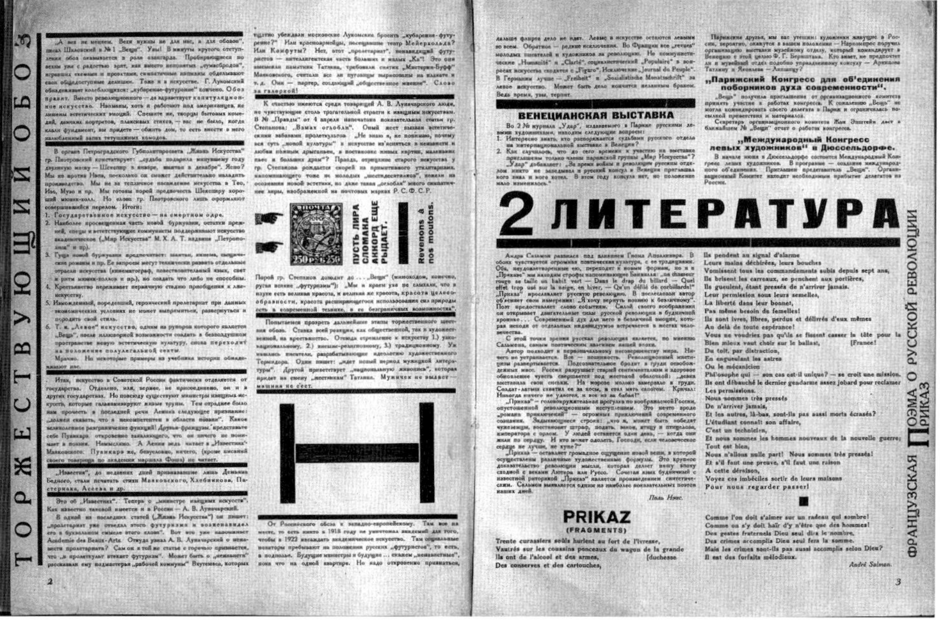
ТОРЖЕСТВУЮЩИЙ ОБОЗ

ПУСТЬ ЛИРА СЛОМАНА КИНОРЕД ЕЩЕ РЫДАЕТ

Revenons à nos moutons.

ВЕНЕЦИАНСКАЯ ВЫСТАВКА

„Парижский Конгресс для об'единения поборников духа современности".

„Международный Конгресс левых художников" в Дюссельдорфе.

2 ЛИТЕРАТУРА

PRIKAZ
(FRAGMENTS)

ФРАНЦУЗСКАЯ ПОЭМА О РУССКОЙ РЕВОЛЮЦИИ ПРИКАЗ

2.18 El Lissitzky and Il'ia Erenburg, *Veshch'–Gegenstand–Objet*, no. 3 (1922): 2–3.

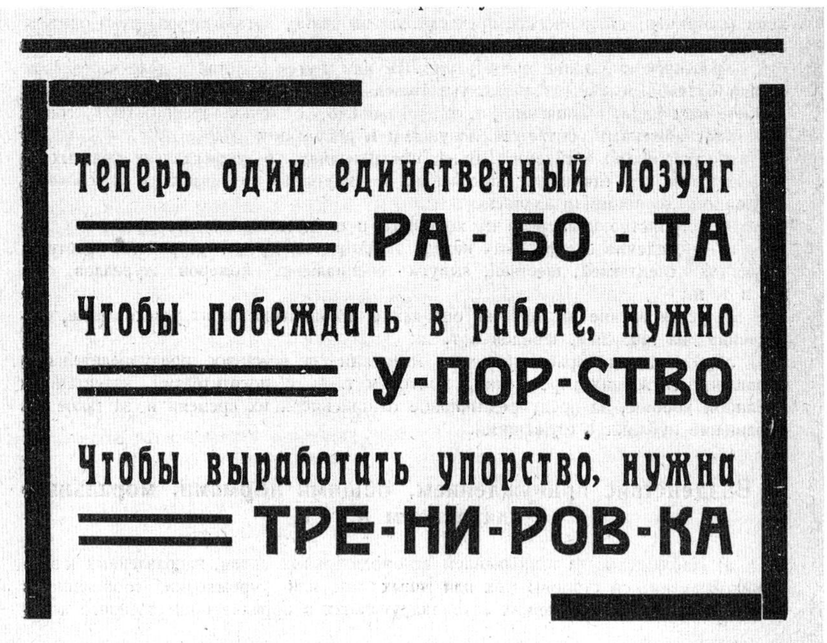

2.19 Slogan, Central Institute of Labor. From *Vremia*, no. 3 (1923): 44. Getty Research Institute, Los Angeles (85-S956).

Russian periodicals developed complex temporal economies based on these principles. For example, each issue of *Proletarian Culture*, which was edited by the Machist Bogdanov and the Leaguist Kerzhentsev, combined two different layouts, one that observed the slow pace of the book and another that emulated the swift newspaper. While feature articles with demanding content were allowed to span the entire page, the sections consisting of correspondence, reports, reviews, and other news items were typically split into two columns. By extending the line and slowing down processing time, a simple fact would become an occasion for reflection, just as, conversely, splitting the page and accelerating apprehension would induce an act of embodied perception.[124] Variations in the length of the line signaled instantly to the reader which texts required thought and which were meant to be taken in all at once. If filmmakers like Vertov articulated the threshold between reflex and consciousness in frames per second, newspaper editors measured it in column widths. Gus's collaborator Vladimir Kuz'michev explained in his book *Agitation and Propaganda in the Press* that reading is "an antagonistic process of 'excitation' and 'inhibition'" and that "the conscious process of coordinating agitation should likewise be a similarly dialectical combination of irritation, inhibition and disinhibition." The newspaper achieved the objective of agitation quite literally through physical irritation just as, conversely, it facilitated political enlightenment by curbing the pace of excitation. Like Pertsov, Kuz'michev advised writers and editors to keep in mind where they hastened reading and where they slowed it down. "Comprehension is the result of a protracted process."[125]

At the other end of the spectrum from the newspaper sat the novel, the psychotechnically most inert and chronometrically most unregulated artifact of bourgeois culture. Factographers rejected novels not just because these fictions distracted readers from the construction of reality but because the sheer quantity of time that they encumbered was a grotesque extravagance. Pertsov's 1927 essay "The Volume of the Work of Art and the Time-Budget of the Russian Worker," which expanded on the arguments of "Word—Optical Image—The Future," reckoned that *War and Peace*, printed at 1,423 pages and with 2,520 letters per page, would require 46 evenings for the average worker to read.[126] If, as Pertsov reasoned, "art's place—or rather, its *time*—is defined by the contemporary worker's budget of time," then there was clearly no place for Tolstoy's tome in the postrevolutionary period.[127] Instead Pertsov recommended that readers buy a pamphlet like *A Sheaf of Orders*, the collection of prompt and imageless prose sketches that his former boss Gastev published as his—or even *the*—last work of literature. Any writer wanting to reconcile mind and body would have to abandon the bulky book for short print ephemera like these. As Benjamin explained in a collection of sketches that he dedicated to Bekhterev's student Asja Lacis, "significant literary effectiveness can come into being only through the strict alternation between action and writing; it must nurture the inconspicuous forms that fit its influence in active communities better than does the pretentious, universal gesture of the book—in leaflets, brochures, articles, and placards. Only this prompt language shows itself actively equal to the moment."[128] The illusionism of the novel was one defect, but for acolytes of fact, these pretentious books were simply too long. The proletariat did not have such resources of time, especially in the compressed era of the transition. Only an unproductive, parasitic leisure class could afford to squander forty-six evenings on a single work. "We have no time, we have no desire, to lie on a couch with a thick novel, experiencing life secondhand," explained one Presentist. "There is no time. We need every hour."[129]

This was the message that Tret'iakov took with him on his European book tour in 1931. "Are the methods and genres used by the classics of any use?" he asked his audiences. "We doubt it. Because reality's forms were so stable and changed only gradually, the writer was able to work on a text for years. The demand that the writer be a polyhistorian created the epic breadth of literature." But the events of 1917 had turned this breadth from a virtue into a liability. As one example, Tret'iakov recounted the case of one unfortunate writer who was still scribbling away at his novel about the Communist Lighthouse three years after visiting the kolkhoz. Hoping finally to wrap up his manuscript, the novelist had recently contacted the farm's council with a request for updates on some outstanding matters. Had they ever acquired a fourth tractor, as they had once planned? Had the chicken stall ever been outfitted with the new equipment? But the novelist's questions were already long out-of-date. Not only had the Communist Lighthouse bought a fourth, fifth, and sixth tractor since his visit, but the tractors of the kolkhoz had subsequently been absorbed into the regional network of Machine-Tractor Stations that collectively had over 700,000 horsepower at its disposal. Meanwhile, poultry production had been abandoned as an inefficient use of kolkhoz resources and relocated to a different farm with better equipment. In both cases, revolutionary reality had overtaken the lumbering pace of the epic. As a literary form, novels turn out to be doubly dilatory, then: not only do they require too much time to read, as Pertsov had pointed out, but they also take too long to write. For Tret'iakov, this delay at the production end disqualified other cultural forms and genres as well. A second anecdote that he recounted told of a painter who went to the collective farm to find a kolkhoznik who sported the customary beard of the peasantry. The artist finally found a suitable sitter, but after several sessions painting the patriarch "according to classical perspective," the model decided to modernize his face by shaving off the beard. The portrait had to be abandoned. The easelist, like the novelist, had fallen victim to time.[130]

If aesthetic production impounds time, Tret'iakov and his colleagues drew the only acceptable conclusion: no art in the transitional period. It was a policy that came to be known as the "belatedness" thesis (*отставание*) of factography. As noted in the introduction to this book, many European audiences questioned the validity of such reasoning outside of Soviet Russia's specific historical conjuncture. To give one prominent example: Johannes Becher, a founding member of the Association of Proletarian-Revolutionary Authors (BPRS, the German counterpart to Lef's archenemy RAPP), heard Tret'iakov talk about his efforts "to overcome the delay [*das Zurückbleiben*]" and ridiculed this "nonsense about 'the end of literature'" along with the basic premise that "there is no time for art."[131] But the value of punctual factographic methods within transitional Russia could not be denied. As Kushner explained in his key statement "The Causes for the Delay," inefficient craft techniques were to blame for the fact that "proletarian literature is lagging behind the pace of socialist construction." In the era of cultural revolution, which enjoined citizens from every background to take up the pen, the problem was not the lack of writers but the way that they worked. "The central causes and deepest roots [of the lag] can be found in the very thing that makes literary labor distinct: in its traditions, the creative practices and methods that have now been adopted by many proletarian writers." According to Kushner, a production-theorist-turned-industrial-ocherkist, proletarian literature faced the same challenge that had arisen on the economic front, where manufacturing was constantly threatening to fall behind the headlong pace of reconstruction. As he saw it, the cultural forces of production needed to be just as up-to-date and modern as the technical ones. If literature and art were to run on time, they would have to abandon great genres like the novel and easel painting. "The unwieldy, immobile, ungainly form . . . turns out for us to cause a disconnect between the work of the author and the revolutionary tempo of our day." The protracted gestation (*вынашивание*) and long-winded world-making of these epic forms only compounded the structural delay that, according to reflexologists, was already endemic to human consciousness. Kushner's essay thus concluded with a call for generic innovation. "We will sweep the useless junk and trash of bourgeois aesthetics out of our house" and replace this clutter with "minor forms" that are mobile, modular, light, and more responsive to the needs of the present.[132] Monumental forms like the novel and easel painting would be succeeded by lesser fact-based practices like the ocherk and the photograph.

THE DARKNESS OF THE LIVED MOMENT

Abolishing the "aesthetic hiatus" (*эстетический перерыв*) between the world and its representation provoked bewilderment in readers and spectators who found themselves unable to draw clear distinctions between real life and the artwork, outside and inside, extension and intension ("From Where," 211; translation modified). At a conference held in early 1934, the year in which the cultural tides turned decisively against factography, the young Formalist Lidiya Ginzburg offered an incisive critique of Tret'iakov's monistic writing. "An image is needed to stand between the material and the reader," insisted Shklovsky's student. "Knowing the material from within [*изнутри*], [Tret'iakov] delivers it from without [*извне*], he delivers it extensionally. And what results is a great confusion that . . . dramatically diminishes the cognitive dimensions of the ocherk."[133] Relaying sensory information to the reader directly and without mediation precluded the possibility of generalizing from these experiences or extrapolating laws from the facts. For Ginzburg, who would specialize in psychological prose during the wartime period, phenomenalist books like *The Summons* atomized the literary text and deterritorialized the consciousness of the reader. Much like Lukács, she saw factography as a technologically updated rendition of Impressionism, the nineteenth-century movement that had abandoned the classical, objectivist model of representation for a subjective psychophysics of embodied sensation. "Apprehending the world only in its details, seeing only its isolated, separate sections: this is where the empiricist theory leads," explained another critic of the literature of fact.[134] The cinema of fact was likewise marred by epistemological breakdown. "Many of our first efforts with the new materials of observation were halting and confused," Grierson wrote about the "unpatterned" factical films he made at the beginning of his career before inventing the great documentary form in the 1930s. "The surfaces were often apparently ugly and the system of their relationships difficult to discern."[135]

According to the inveterate Futurist Mayakovsky, the act of aesthetic creation demands stepping away from the present. Just as art requires a "change in planes" (*перемена плоскости*), poetry too requires a "change in place or time." "As in painting, for example, when sketching an object you must walk back a distance equal to three times its size," so too does the writer need some degree of dislocation to achieve a clear view of his subject matter. For Mayakovsky, it was structurally impossible to write about history at the same time that he was participating in it. This was the error of his factographic colleagues, who had failed to grasp that any account of events made from within the present would by definition "always be incomplete, even incorrect, or, at any rate, one-sided [*однобоко*]." "A break away from the environment in which some or other fact took place—a distance—is necessary." Just as home will appear more vivid from exile and the fog of war will clear up in peacetime, the best poem about "gentle love," Mayakovsky mused, will be the one that is written on the bumpy and crowded No. 7 bus from Lubianskaia Square to Nogin Square.[136] The history of literature is full of devices for distancing the writer from the present in this way. Realist novelists, for example, used the preterite tense to transpose all actions into a consummated past. Futurist poets looked in the opposite direction, so that even when they wrote about their own historical moment, it was always through the planar shift of the future anterior. Mayakovsky's work contains numerous examples of forward flights that retrospect to the present, whether the postapocalyptic scene of "Brooklyn Bridge," where the remains of the city that he visited on his 1925 tour of America are excavated by "a geologist of the centuries," or the Phosphorescent Woman who time-travels from the future back to the current year 1930 in *The Bathhouse*. Even when Mayakovsky wanted to write about contemporary life, the Futurist always kept his distance.

Revoking the distance of the aesthetic led the factographers to develop a platform of media operativism (*оперативизм*). Lukács explained that a factographer "omits the intermediary between fact and practice. . . . He ties 'fact,' i.e. surface appearance not yet understood as conforming to law, to an immediate reality without the necessary mediation with praxis, which is therefore deformed into mere 'practicism.'" Invoking the famous Russian cultural binary, Lukács observed that this program favors spontaneity over consciousness and "restricts the 'functional' significance of literature in the class struggle to the most 'immediate' level" ("Reportage or Portrayal?," 65; translation modified). Tret'iakov would hardly have disagreed with this assessment. Realist literature worked "though ricochet" (*по рикошетом*) while factography was "an instrument for head-on impact, for direct action through writing," he wrote.[137] His program for "immediate practical effectivity" might have scandalized European critics like Becher and Lukács, who wanted writers and journalists to keep reality at arm's length, but the phenomenon of press operativity was a ubiquitous, even banal topic in Soviet Russia ("Writer and the Socialist Village,"

69). Tret'iakov popularized operativism in the West, and he certainly thought through its poetological consequences more rigorously than any of his contemporaries, but he hardly invented the phenomenon. Issues of *The Journalist* were full of articles on the subject, which dismissed the principles of noninterference and journalistic neutrality as ideological vestiges of the liberal public sphere of the bourgeoisie.[138] Soviet newspapers launched campaigns to revive entire industries, correspondents denounced negligent colleagues by name, and periodicals led literacy initiatives. "Not only does the newspaper mirror the present in words, but it also exercises an active influence on this present and transforms it," Tret'iakov wrote about this feedback loop between events and the news.[139] In the era of mass journalism, all corners of life were being continuously recorded, textualized, and transformed by an army of amateur correspondents. Under these circumstances, objectivity—the dubious epistemological dividend of realism's poetics of belatedness—had become an untenable conceit. "What sort of novel, what *War and Peace*, can we contemplate, when every morning we take the newspaper in our hands and turn over another page of that most amazing novel called the present day?" asked Tret'iakov: "We ourselves, the writers and readers, are this novel's characters" ("New Leo Tolstoy," 50).

Tret'iakov witnessed this operative feedback loop firsthand over the six years he spent at the Communist Lighthouse, an assignment documented in scores of ocherki and the three anthologies *The Summons* (1930), *A Month in the Country* (1931), and *One Thousand and One Workdays* (1934). When the factographer returned to his kolkhoz each summer, he would note the changes that had taken place since his last visit and the impact that his writing had had on developments there. Since Tret'iakov was publishing many of the individual sketches in newspapers such as *Pravda*, curious kolkhozniki could read what he had to say about them more or less in real time. They did not hesitate to share their thoughts on his portrayal. The later chapters of *The Summons* contain scenes in which the kolkhozniki praise, or more often, admonish the factographer for the way he had depicted them earlier in the book. "The real-life models are protesting" (*натурщики протестуют*), Shklovsky wrote.[140] Tret'iakov professed his love for books in which characters "explain to the author what he did well, what he did poorly, and what could be improved" ("Der Schriftsteller im Aufbauwerke," 4). Giving feedback to writers and artists was evidently a routine event at the Communist Lighthouse, a so-called demonstration or model farm (*показательное хозяйство*) that attracted cultural workers interested in seeing the industrialization of the countryside firsthand. Visitors who took poetic license were mocked by the kolkhozniki, who made fun of the rhetorical excesses and terminological imprecision of the books that were published about them. When, for example, the farm agronomist read a scene describing how the commune sat "with bated breath" one night listening to him speak, he burst out laughing and recalled that his bored audience had actually fallen asleep the moment he began to lecture on soil.[141] Sometimes, when the stakes were particularly high, the censure of the kolkhozniki grew more hostile. At one point in *The Summons*, the farmers complain about the disastrous consequences of following Kushner's advice to sow flax rather than wheat when he visited shortly before, a decision that caused them to lose an entire tract (*Vyzov*, 61).[142] Operativism posed a direct challenge to objectivity, but it also entailed an ethical imperative. Discovering this changed how Tret'iakov worked. "I no longer just described people, but assumed liability for my characters," he wrote: "Working in this way means that you cannot simply stand on the sidelines and contemplate the object of your labor, but must remain organically connected to it through continuous collaboration."[143]

Operativism also posed significant formal and aesthetic challenges to writers, who found themselves both outside and inside the text at once. "When I am involved with the characters from my works, with readers *in situ*, when I am involved with a living person, it becomes an extremely difficult kind of portrait," Tret'iakov explained. This was because "I enter into the notation with them."[144] Having relinquished the transcendental security of realism, the embedded writer faced a kind of Heisenbergian predicament in which her own acts of observation were constantly inflecting and transforming the subject that she was observing. This entanglement of event and representation means that every operative book is constantly revising itself, mutating *Quixote*-like in the very course of being written. Auto-correspondence, as Chuzhak called factography, should thus be understood in two senses, both as the automation of inscription and as a circular practice of writing to oneself, even of writing oneself into the text. Factographic stenography might reduce writing to a series of mechanical gestures, but the corollary demand for self-reflexivity vastly complicates the text at a structural level. "Operativity does not simplify the task but instead makes it more difficult," Agapov cautioned.[145] The factographer, who is constantly catching glimpses of his own shadow in the text, must find some method for writing in both the first and the third persons simultaneously, as both subject and object of the account. "The writer and the agent should merge into a single character," stipulated Pertsov.[146] From Tret'iakov's *Den Shi-Khua* to Vertov's *Man with a Movie Camera*, all key works of the factographers attempt this impossible feat of double vision. Rigorous adherence to the principle of operativism results in essays that document life at the same time that they reflect on their own madeness, and in films that place the cameraman both behind and in front of the camera.

The formal quandaries of operativism quickly become apparent in *The Summons*. Already in the book's second chapter, which follows upon the auto-correspondence of "Through Clouded Glasses," the architecture of representation has started to buckle and warp. At the outset of the sketch, which is titled "To the Collective Farms!" after a popular slogan of the day, Tret'iakov proclaims that "the most important thing for the ocherkist is his point of observation, i.e., the role that he plays in his own observations" (*Vyzov*, 17). But situating the point of observation within the field of observation itself leads to "a great confusion," as Ginzburg later wrote about *The Summons*. Indeed, the very first sentence in the sketch expresses perplexity about the slogan in its title: "This formula was confusing." The writer's epistemological disorientation is manifested in the text as a positional disturbance, an uncertainty about the boundary between outside and inside: at times Tret'iakov recites the slogan "Writer, *to* the collective farms" (*писатель на колхозы*), but elsewhere the formula reads "Writer, *on* the collective farm" (*писатель на колхозе*). The factographer seems unsure whether he is on the outside looking in or is located within the field of representation. Uncertain of where to draw this line, Tret'iakov's auto-correspondence lapses into the free indirect speech of modernist prose, which blends the writer's voice indistinguishably with those of the characters. Until the appearance of the commune's director Pavel Chebotarev four pages into the sketch, these fragments of language are untethered to any particular figure. Speech circulates without source or ownership. Some of the lines appear at first glance to be dialogue, although there are no quotation marks to differentiate reported speech from the author's own. Tret'iakov himself seems unsure of which phrases are actually his, prompting him to hedge: "My words sound unconvincing even to me" (*Vyzov*, 20). Even the speech that comes out of his own mouth feels alien and clichéd, as if it belongs to someone else. The lack of clear attribution in the sketch leaves the reader wondering which words record speech that Tret'iakov heard on his trip, which are the internal reflections of the factographer, and which ones, finally, belong to the architecture of mimesis itself. Objective fact, subjective commentary, and literary code blend indistinguishably in the operative text.

The Summons confirms the basic tenet of the Russian Machists that consciousness is a "zone of indeterminacy" (*полоса неуверенности*).[147] The closer the mind comes to reality and sensation, the more these experiences elude formalization and cognizance. The blindness of consciousness to the present has of course been an enduring theme of philosophy, starting with the legendary king Oedipus who proved incapable of seeing what was directly in front of him despite—or perhaps because of—his renowned intellect. In psychoanalysis, the culminating achievement in the European sciences of the mind, consciousness became something that was not just structurally distinct from external reality but a barrier that actively works to keep facts outside, a membrane that protects the psychic apparatus from reality's continuous barrage of shocks and stimuli. In a series of essays on presentism in art, the philosopher Ernst Bloch identified the challenges that faced cultural movements like factography, which dared to occupy this zone of indeterminacy and make work within the "darkness of the lived moment" (*Augenblicks-Dunkel*): "In the immediate moment, right within, you cannot even experience something, much less depict it or present it from the right angle (which simultaneously has to be a synoptic one). In general it is like this: all nearness makes matters difficult, and if it is too close, then one is blinded, at least made mute. This is true in a strict sense only for a precise, on-the-spot experience, for the immediate moment that is as a dark 'right-now' lacking all distance to itself" ("On the Present," 120; translation modified).

As an example of this indeterminacy, Bloch cited the legendary autoscopic portrait of the founding empiriocritic himself, Ernst Mach. In "The Self-Regarding Ego" (1886), a drawing that Mach declared an "antimetaphysical picture," the ground of vision bleeds into the contents of the image: "In a frame formed by the ridge of my eyebrow, by my nose, and by my moustache, appears a part of my body, so far as visible, with its environment" (fig. 2.20). At the apex of the visual pyramid at the drawing's center one crucial detail is missing: "My body is seen without a head," boasted Mach.[148] In this decapitated self-portrait, Bloch writes, "the real subject of human existence is not what it has been understood to be, even though it continues to remain much as it appears: its head invisible, its principal idea still unformulated, its center occupied solely by cortical thoughts and sensations rather than by optical relations in which the self encounters its own being. The eye that sees cannot yet see itself; the human who draws the outline of history cannot yet draw his own outline." As Bloch saw it, the Viennese physicist's drawing was undeniably dilettantish, but it was still more radical than the celebrated work of the Surrealists, whose automatic writing and autoscopic experiments aspired to incorporate the body of the writer and artist, but who never actually succeeded in fully canceling "the mirror relation implied by self-portraiture."[149] In the end the Surrealists wound up sublimating cortical sensations as artistic visions and recovering the "grotesque distortions" of the present as marketable writerly style.[150]

Mach's autoscopic portrait offers an apt emblem for factography. As one critic wrote of *The Summons*, "Tret'iakov is helplessly dissolved into the things that surrounded him, or rather: insofar as the vulgar empiricist approach to reality inevitably leads to a destruction of perspective, he dissolved himself into the chaos of things."[151] It was Vertov who realized this neo-Machist practice in cinema. Indeed, as a rule, Vertov did not make pictures; he scorned optical relations. From the beginning of his career, he expressed a pronounced disdain for long shots that affirmed the perspectival scheme of Euclidean space and the visual hierarchy of figure and ground, preferring instead to use close-ups that compressed distance and cut apart the gestalt of his subject into fragmentary part-objects. Vertov's notes for an early *Kino-pravda* reel about the Politburo member Mikhail Kalinin describe a sequence that is full of movement but bereft of imagery: "Kalinin walks past the front of soldiers. He sees faces flashing. A horizontal panorama is unacceptable. The camera should move in parallel with the front of soldiers. A soldier in formation sees Kalinin passing for 1–2

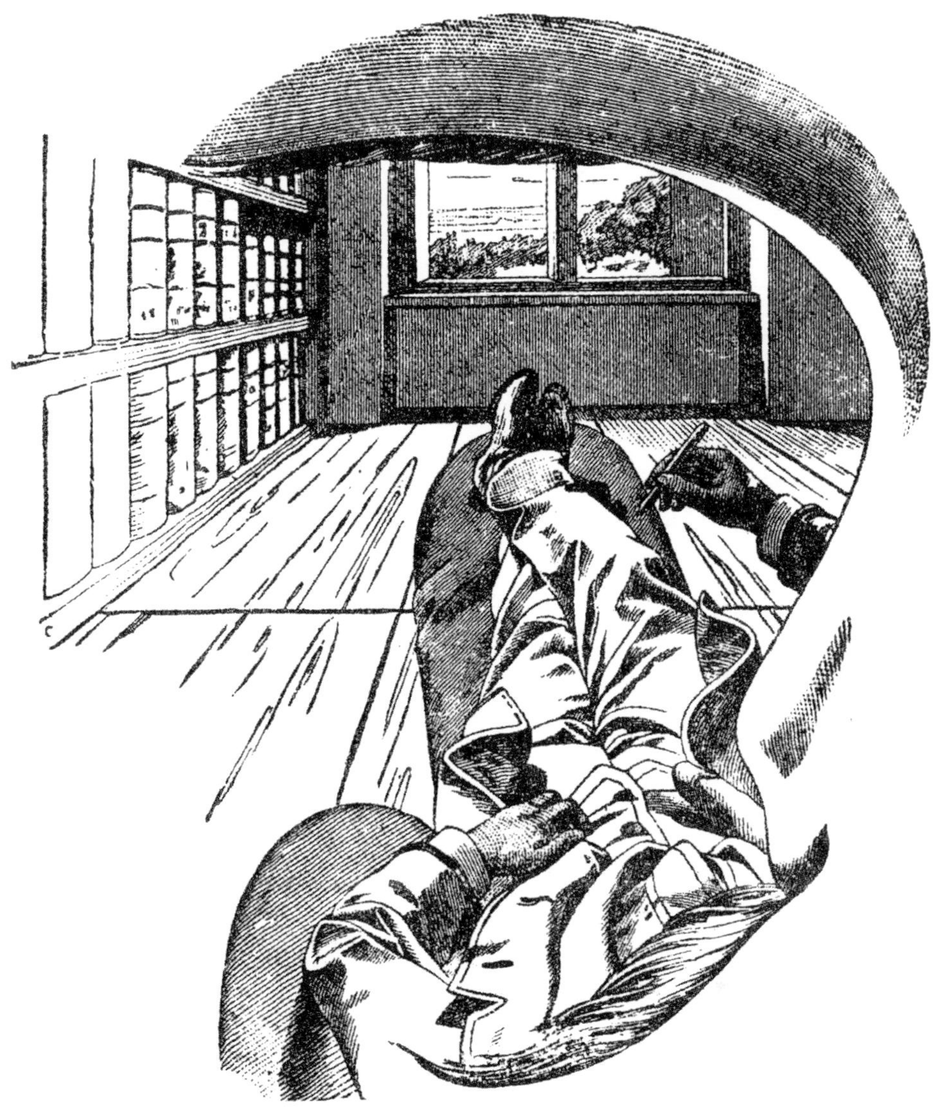

2.20 "The Self-Regarding Ego." Ernst Mach, *Beiträge zur Analyse der Empfindungen* (1886), 14.

seconds. The company watches him the entire time with all of their eyes. The camera should move through the ranks of the soldiers, in parallel with Kalinin's movement. Abusing the horizontal panorama is nauseating."[152] In this sequence, Vertov's camera cuts physically into the space of the picture, first following the formation of soldiers and then the path of Kalinin himself. He often used tracking shots in this way, to trace the contours of his subjects or to echo the vectors of their movement.

Vertov's desire for proximity eventually led him to mount the camera directly to his subjects, typically the machines whose precision and timing he so admired, but also other elements like church bells and buildings. The subject of the film was no longer in front of the lens, no longer an image to look at, but was instead absorbed into the camera apparatus itself to become an agent of vision. Shot characteristics such as elevation and angle were dictated by bodies and objects found on location at the site where he was filming. This vision is not indifferent, distant, or objective, but is instead always contaminated by things: in Deleuze's words, Vertov realizes "an eye in matter, a perception such as it is in matter."[153] In many of these cases, camera movement itself reflects the topography of the local space or the participation of objects that are not directly visible to a spectator: to film the shore of a river, Vertov floats his camera on a boat; to film a mine, he sets it on the conveyer belt that moves the coal; to film a dam, he affixes the camera to a crane; to film a horse, he props it on a neighboring vehicle; to film railway tracks, he mounts it to a locomotive, and so on. In each of these examples, variations of which appear in nearly all of his feature films, the distinctive movements of the camera testify to the presence of something that does not actually appear within the frame of the image but that nonetheless enables the scene as an infrastructural component (boat, conveyer, crane, automobile, train). The logic of camera position and movement does not express pictorial values or optical relations but is instead established by the contents of space itself, by the physical objects that Vertov drafts to serve as coefficients in the act of looking. He expands the gaze to include its own enabling condition and to reflect vision back upon its source. Rather than put the cameraman or the camera within the field of vision, as he did in a more obviously self-reflexive film like *Man with a Movie Camera*, such sequences instead realize the autoscopic injunction of factography on a more profound, technical level. They enact the embeddedness of empiriomonism rather than thematizing it.

According to Tret'iakov, the best camera operator "photographs not just objects, but also his relationship to them."[154] Like Vertov, he thought little of pictorial compositions. Tret'iakov emphasized haptic values over optical ones in his own photographic work and enjoined correspondents to "learn to photograph by guiding their camera not with their eyes but only with their hands."[155] This method yielded images of dubious artistic quality, but their evidentiary value was exceptional. As he saw it, formal flaws in the photograph testified to the presence of the cameraman on the scene. Instances of operator error such as "wavering outlines" and "insufficient exposure" were invaluable "from the perspective of dynamic expressiveness" and preferable to "monumental shots that are sharp down to the last detail but hopelessly static."[156] A well-composed, aesthetically accomplished photograph tells the viewer a lot about conventions of representation, but very little about the historical circumstances in which the photograph was made, and nothing at all about the status of the camera operator at that event. Brik likewise observed that "those photographic shots and experiments which [are] considered unsuccessful by knowledgeable photographers" often turn out, upon closer scrutiny, to be the ones with "the greatest photographic value."[157]

For forensically minded lawyers like Tret'iakov and Brik, blurred vision, aperture errors, and other unintended optical artifacts directly indexed the presence of an otherwise invisible photographer. "Impoverished images and defective media" stake "documentary claims" more insistently than artworks that have polished away the facture of matter and masked the conditions of their own making.[158] When closely scrutinized, these defects can reveal concrete information and details about the context of the event, the operator's behavior, and other factors that lie beyond the frame of the image. Forensic investigator Eyal Weizman thus explains that "cameras record from both their ends: the objects, people, and spaces their lenses capture, as well as the position and movements of the invisible photographer. . . . Rushed and erratic movements might indicate the risk involved in taking some images. A blur is thus the way the photographer gets registered in an image. As such, looking at blurry images is like looking at a scene through a semitransparent glass in which the image of the photographer is superimposed over the thing being photographed."[159] It thrilled Tret'iakov to discover these moments of "defect" (*брак*) in the image. He valued these maculations not as proof of contingency (Surrealist chance operation), assertion of truth-to-material (absolute photography), or a signifier of verisimilitude (reality effect), but as the instant when the maker stumbles into the frame by accident. Like the awkward episodes in *The Summons* when the embedded author glimpses his own shadow, photographic defects were for Tret'iakov the fingerprints that the camera operator had inadvertently left behind on the image. They pinned the factographer to his subject.

The last 15 years have disabused us of the habit of prophecy.
—ILYA EHRENBURG, 1930[1]

3

PARADIGMS OF FACTOGRAPHY

What is the status of knowledge in the zero-hour after the revolution? How does the mind get traction in a society that has disavowed traditional norms, suspended the institutions of authority, and vacated the archive of inherited ideas—a society, in other words, that proclaims all existing concepts to be void? At this moment of theoretical adhocracy, the systems of science, culture, and thought have to be bootstrapped anew. Following Lenin, who rejected philosophical abstractions and instead endorsed the newspaper as a compass for navigating the "concrete situation" of the transitional period, the factographers looked to the mass press to deliver points of cognitive orientation in a reality that was changing from one day to the next. But the provisional concepts found on the pages of the newspaper looked very different from the generalizations of bourgeois philosophy: empirical and observational, but also highly tentative and ephemeral, newspaper consciousness renounced the security of transcendental reflection and the stability of transhistorical categories in favor of embedded materialist thinking. Facts eclipsed laws in the theoretical casuistry of the revolution.

With factography, what you see is what you get. A line from Barthes about news photography offers an apt description of its poetics of the manifest: "The fact, surprised, explodes in all its stubbornness, its literality, in the very obviousness of its obtuse nature."[2] Sketches and photographs made in this positivist mode speak to a reality that is all surface, a world made of things without ideological depth and people without inner life. Factography vexes interpretation with this plain, direct, and, in Chuzhak's phrase, "frighteningly guileless" manner of presentation. The quotidian objects that it documents carry no particular symbolic weight or evident emotional significance. Equally guileless are the characters in these works, who never dissemble or pause to reflect. The factographers avoided speculating about things like internal experience and emotional motivation, preferring instead to focus on the outward physiological reflexes and behavioral patterns that individuals manifest in response to changing social circumstances, configurations of production, and technical milieux.[3] Exchanging the latency of the symbol for the presence of the fact, their work exhausts itself in the simple evidentiary operation of documenting. Factography just points to life and enjoins, *look*. That's it; nothing to decode here.

Vertov's 1926 film *A Sixth Part of the World* exemplifies this artless literality. Amid repeated incantations of an intertitle stating "I see" (*Вижу*), the director puts on display the Soviet Empire's vast resources of raw materials, from fur

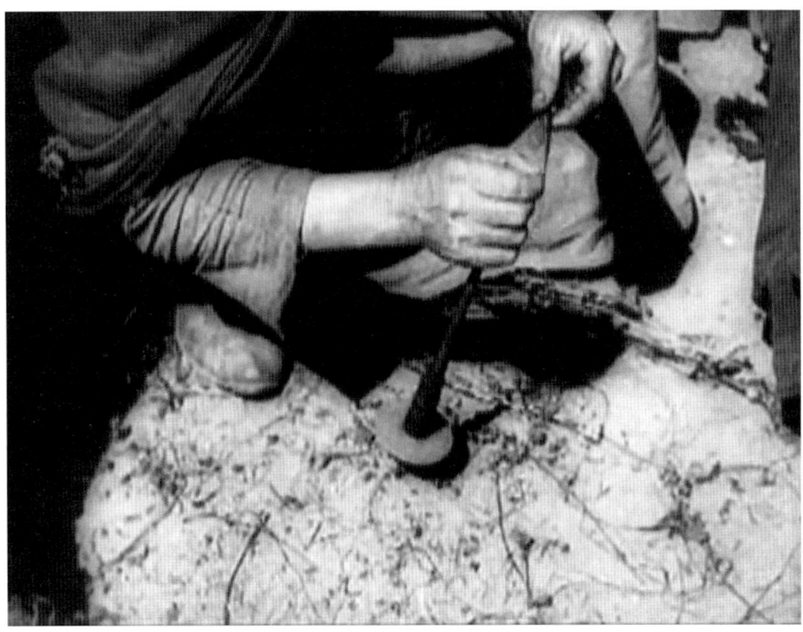

3.1 Close-up of hands at work. Frame from *A Sixth Part of the World* (dir. Dziga Vertov, 1926).

pelts to fruits, as well as its diverse forces of production, from the industrial proletariat to the various national minorities. Commissioned by the State Trade Organization to advertise the Soviet economy to potential international partners and investors, *A Sixth Part* was a kind of shopping catalogue meant to show off the natural abundance and labor capacities of Russia. Even prior to any propagandistic messaging for the new regime, then, the primary purpose of *A Sixth Part* was just to enumerate the material wealth of the Soviet economy. Vertov, a known admirer of Walt Whitman, chose to structure his paean to the manifold as an ode, a poetic genre that, according to Deleuze, approaches reality as a "collection of heterogenous parts: an infinite patchwork, or an endless wall of dry stones (a cemented wall, or the pieces of a puzzle, would reconstitute a totality). The world as a *sampling*: the samples ('specimens') are singularities, remarkable and nontotalizable parts extracted from a series of ordinary parts."[4] Like the ode, *A Sixth Part* conjures a mundane space of limitless expanse, creating a Borgesian map of the world that is as large as physical extension itself. The film tries to encompass a seemingly infinite number of nonvalorized subjects and prosaic phenomena, each one of which Vertov takes singly from reality without making any claim for its typicality or representative status. At the level of device, Vertov realized this Whitmanian poetics of the minor through close-up shots that refused the spectator a synoptic view of the figure. He instructed the cameramen on his team that an astonishing 80 percent of the footage they deliver should consist only of details and busts (figs. 3.1, 3.2).[5] *A Sixth Part of*

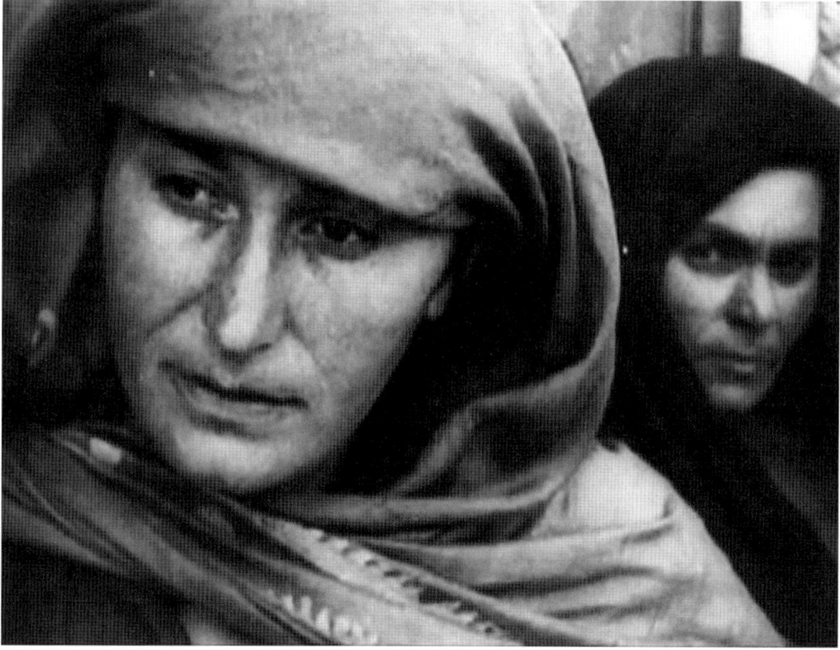

3.2 Close-up of face. Frame from *A Sixth Part of the World* (dir. Dziga Vertov, 1926).

the World would be made of parts not wholes, fragments not totalities, facts not symbols.

Between the film's opening and closing phrases, from "I see" to "All of this is in your hands," Vertov musters a sweeping inventory of the people and things in the Soviet world, addressing these figures directly with vocative intertitles: "You, suckling at your mother's breast" (fig. 3.3), "You, chipper centenarian" (fig. 3.4), "You, child playing with a captured arctic fox," "You, who still drink warm blood," and so on. With each such act of naming, *A Sixth Part of the World* invites the viewer to carefully examine the physiognomies and activities, habiliments and habitus, of the people on the screen in all their rich ethnographic detail. Vertov wanted his audiences to experience above all amazement (*изумление*), the primitive and pre-semantic perceptual state that Aristotle once claimed as the foundation of all higher thought.[6] His materialist approach to filmmaking replaced top-down theorizing with bottom-up observation. Such acts of thick description invite us "to generalize within cases," Clifford Geertz later explained.[7] Presented one by one, with unrelenting specificity, the contents of Vertov's film are offered up without literary metaphors or conceptual abstractions. The words of the intertitles, which are largely redundant with the pictures on the screen, contribute little to the spectator's understanding of what she is looking at. The role of language in *A Sixth Part* is instead purely heraldic. This "naïve device from medieval art," as one contemporary wrote of the film, does not seek to interpret, comment upon, or otherwise illuminate the world that the camera has put on view.[8] In declaiming the world rather than explaining it, Vertov revived the early cinematic technique that Noël Burch called the "primitive mode of representation," a style characterized by stark frontality, semantically poor imagery, and the use of montage editing instead of narrative emplotment.[9] There is no suspense in *A Sixth Part of the World*, just the regular alternation between word and thing, announcing and showing.

For factographers, concepts could not do justice to the material wealth of the new Soviet reality. At its most extreme, this wariness of theoretical abstraction led cultural producers like Vertov to reject all verbal language as such. Having concluded from practical experience that "visual phrases could not be conveyed in words," Vertov turned to works like *Man with a Movie Camera* that were made entirely without either literary plot or intertitles.[10] His distrust of words expressed a prevalent skepticism in his generation toward linguistic models of meaning that seemed to impede concrete reference and even to preclude historical change.[11] The hegemony of verbal signifier over concrete referent reduced life to the reenactment of a script, an eternal performance of what Althusser later called the "always-already" of ideology. But acolytes of fact like Vertov believed to have found a strategy to escape the structural retrospectivism of the sign: ostension, naked acts of showing. *A Sixth Part of the World* put empirical specimens on display without commentary, and pointed at the world

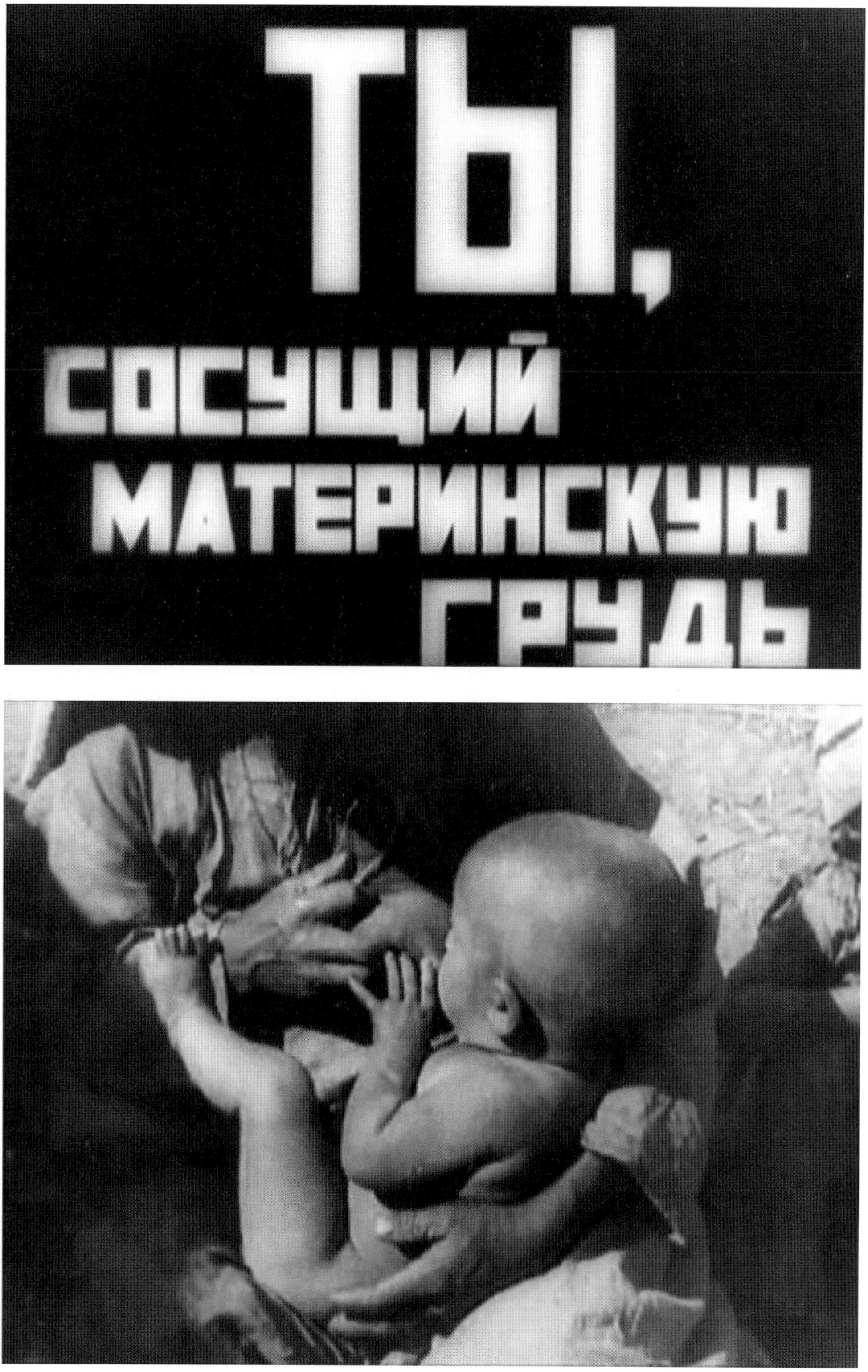

ТЫ,
СОСУЩИЙ
МАТЕРИНСКУЮ
ГРУДЬ

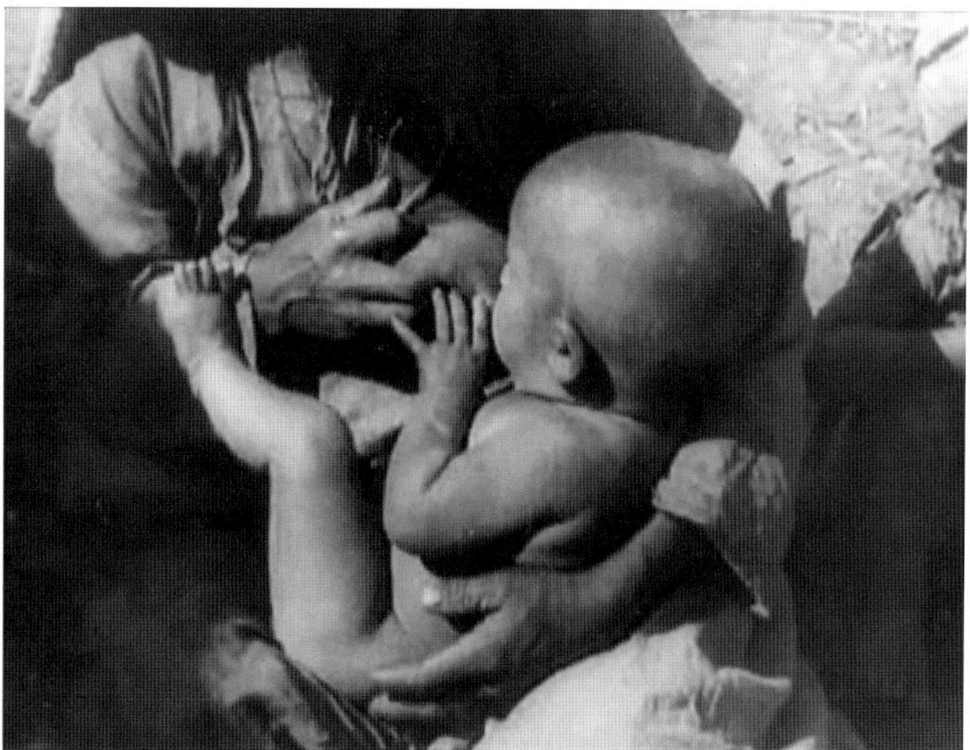

3.3 "You, suckling at your mother's breast." Frame from *A Sixth Part of the World* (dir. Dziga Vertov, 1926).

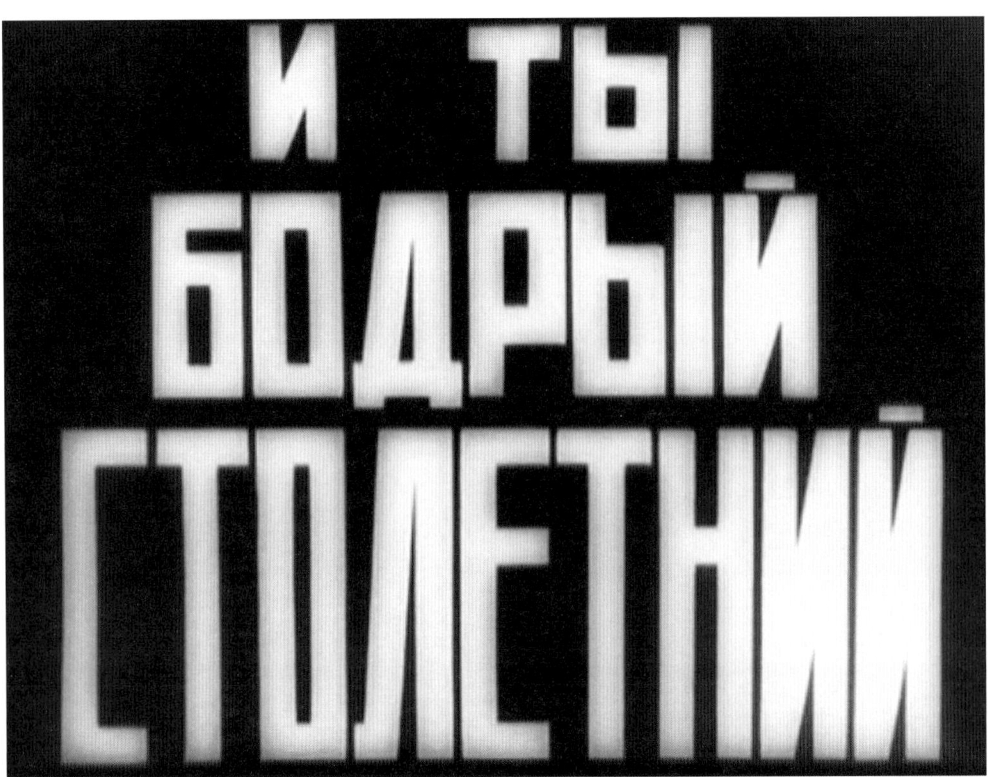

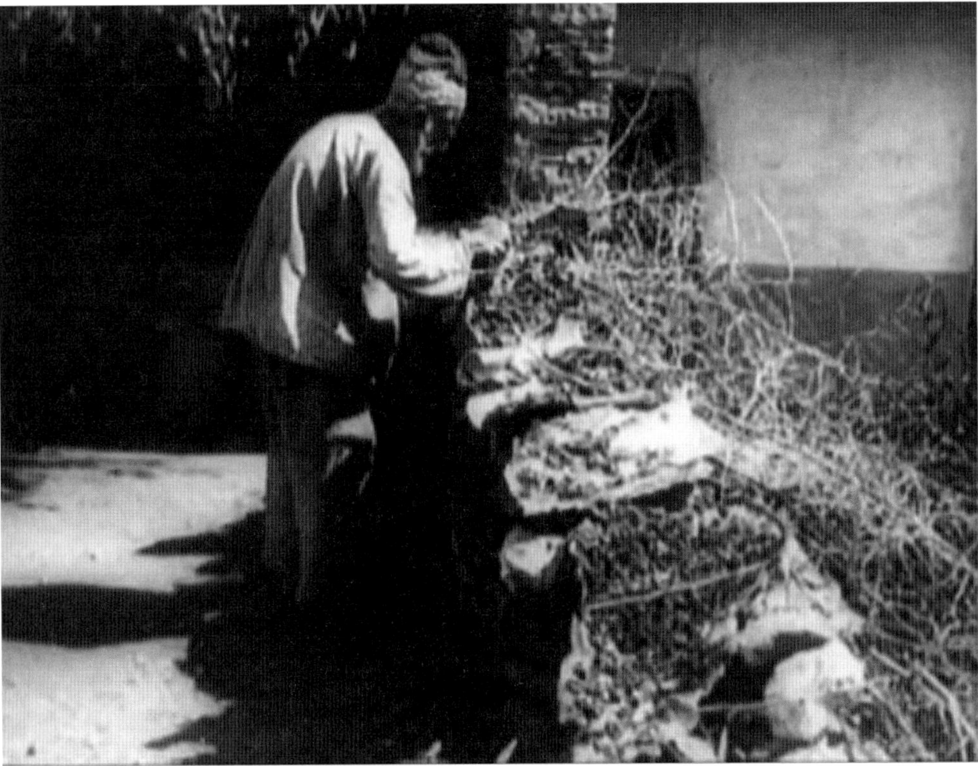

3.4 "You, chipper centenarian." Frame from *A Sixth Part of the World* (dir. Dziga Vertov, 1926).

(*показывать*) without narrating it (*рассказывать*).[12] The Czech theater theorist Ivo Osolsobě would later characterize this strategy of ostension as a "sheer anti-semiotics" that reverses the anteriority of the sign and allows concrete objects to "serve as messages about themselves."[13] Whereas the code predetermines the message in other forms of communication, in the ostensional act, matter precedes its conceptualization. Ostension is a "language of things," a system of "objectual messages."[14]

The factographers believed that the only way to advance toward communism was to silence the chatter of philosophers and listen to Soviet reality itself. "We just have to get them to tell us about themselves," Tret'iakov pined about the new things that had come into existence since October.[15] After the revolution had razed the old taxonomies and concepts, the factographers took it upon themselves to rebuild the archive of human knowledge piece by piece. Proclaiming "a mental orientation toward the fact," Tret'iakov followed this mandate with relentless precision: "Local topic. Local progress. Local misdeed. Identified by first name and patronymic. Dated. Addressed."[16] Producers who deviated from the policy of rigorous referentiality were censured for losing sight of the facts on the ground. That had been a misstep that Vertov made with the symbol-laden *Stride, Soviet!* (1926), for example, but one that the filmmaker corrected in his next project *A Sixth Part of the World*.[17] As Jakobson observed, metonymy, not metaphor, is the rhetorical operation proper to factical film.[18] So too did Tret'iakov proclaim the unwavering specificity of factographic prose in *Den Shi-Khua*: "We demand precise knowledge. Political essays and schema deliver an algebra of events in China. Names are washed away, people gather into the amoebae of classes, and the eye of the algebraist follows the movement and voraciousness of these amoebae, which are expressed in numbers. We demand that the numbers have names."[19] Chuzhak likewise insisted that the new literature shouldn't just rehearse the same old inherited concepts: "*Concretize literature completely*. Nothing 'in general.' Down with incorporeality, nonobjectivity, abstraction. All objects will be called with their proper names and classified scientifically. This is the only way that we can cognize [*познавать*] and construct life" ("A Writer's Handbook," 88). By identifying and cataloguing everyone and everything in this manner, from the suckling infant to the chipper centenarian, the factographers would work their way through the new reality, discovering its laws and logics inductively, case by case. Marx and Engels had once celebrated the nominalism of early philosophy as "the first form of materialism," an inaugural effort to extrapolate knowledge directly from things themselves.[20] Centuries later, after the great metaphysical detour of Idealism, the factographers returned to the zero-hour of philosophy and began once again to observe and name the things around them. "We have to leave behind speculation and grope our way forward," wrote Chuzhak ("A Writer's Handbook," 92).

Critics protested that a cultural practice which recognized only facts but not laws would never be able to transcend the mundane details and contingencies of its own historical moment. At the height of factography's influence, novelist Joseph Roth quipped that "current Russian literature is in fact, with few exceptions, a collection of material for cultural historians."[21] For Roth, the great museum of Soviet specimens that was being curated by the factographers would be of interest only to some archival researcher in the future. Many found the primitive accumulations of fact tedious, lacking in both exceptionality and suspense. One contemporary complained of the "monotony" and "emotional boredom" of *A Sixth Part*'s endless "enumeration." Showing every Soviet person and thing one after the other was an interminable task, and one whose cognitive gains remained questionable.[22] Indeed, the random drift of facts struck many as literally mindless.[23] The empiriocritical method of the factographers seemed to disorganize and derange the very categories of thought. One review of *The Literature of Fact* concluded that the group's program to concretize literature would necessarily "exclude one of the most important forms of human thought, without which any cognition of reality is impossible, namely, *abstraction*."[24] For such critics, the nominalism of fact seemed to be inimical to higher consciousness itself, and the state of amazement induced by these works perilously close to stupefaction.

In defense of their program, the factographers invoked the authority of Lenin himself, whose canonical 1918 *Pravda* article "The Character of Our Newspapers" had proclaimed that "the chief task of the press" during the transition from capitalism to communism was "to educate people through living, concrete examples and specimens taken from all spheres of life" ("Character of Our Newspapers," 98).[25] The priority that Lenin's article gave to strategies of ostension during the transitional period marked a striking change from his previous stance. Whereas the theoretical program of Marxism had dictated Party strategy prior to 1917, after the revolution their political work had to be grounded in the detailed study of the new social relations, technical inventions, protocols of communication, and other actualities of revolutionary life that were arising spontaneously everywhere. This Cambrian explosion of new, proto-communist forms of being exceeded old philosophical dogmatisms and abstract points of orientation. "We have to admit that there has been a radical modification in our whole outlook on socialism," Lenin conceded in 1923. "Our rule must be: as little philosophizing and as few acrobatics as possible."[26] He now urged a factographic approach, enjoining people to "note every new fact . . . in telegraphic style" ("The Character of Our Newspapers," 98). There was a logic behind this change of tactic. As Lenin saw it, theory is more advanced and radical than everyday reality only during phases of political stagnation: with the shift into the transitional phase after the revolution, it was instead empirical fact and positivist method, not any abstract conceptual system, that became the engine of political progress. In his 1917 "Assessment of the Present Situation," a text prized by Chuzhak, Lenin had stipulated that "a Marxist must take cognisance of real life, of the true facts of *reality*, and not cling to a theory of yesterday, which, like all theories, at best only outlines the main and the general, only *comes near* to embracing life in all its complexity."[27] The revolutionaries had reached the turning point in history when the virtual ceded priority to the actual: "In appraising a given moment, a Marxist must proceed *not* from what is possible, but from what is real" ("Assessment of the Present Situation," 45, 46). The "concrete situation," as Lenin designated the period after 1917, in turn assigned a different, if diminished role to the Bolshevik Party, which Lenin now envisioned less as a political vanguard leading the disorganized masses than as a research unit for verifying and synthesizing the data coming out of the great Soviet experiment. He demanded "less political ballyhoo. Less scholastic reasoning. Closer to life. More attention to the way in which the workers and peasants are actually building the new in their everyday work, and more tests to determine how much of the new is communistic." The revolutionary theories and utopian rhetoric that once fueled the movement would now be replaced by factographic documentation and the diligent analysis of this observational data.

Lenin's endorsement of revolutionary positivism, which signaled a dramatic reversal after his attack on the Russian Machists in *Materialism and Empiriocriticism* of 1908, reflected a growing conviction that the coming communist society could not be built using old conceptual instruments. Having toppled the monarchy and defeated the Whites, the Bolsheviks had cleared the ground for something else, but they did not know yet what. Partial and fragmentary views of the new society could be glimpsed, although its full contours were still concealed. Paradoxically, getting to that society required abandoning suppositions about the future and instead scrutinizing the socialist facts that were cropping up spontaneously in the present. Drawing up blueprints for the society to come only restricted the creative powers of the revolution. "To speak of an end is to think of a pre-existing model which has only to be realized," cautioned Bergson: "It is to suppose, therefore, that all is given, and that the future can be read in the present."[28] Along similar lines, Lenin reasoned that laying out the pathway to communism beforehand and leaping over the churn of the transitional period would foreclose the emergence of truly new social formations. It is the very nature of the revolutionary swerve—Lenin's "abrupt turn in history"—that it cannot be scheduled in advance and that its plural effects can never be predicted in their full scope. "An event that can be anticipated and therefore apprehended or comprehended, an event without absolute encounter, is that an event in the full sense of the word? One must not see it coming. If one anticipates what is coming, which is then outlined horizontally on a horizon, there is no pure event."[29] For Lenin, there was no Plan. Instead he counseled patience and inaugurated the New Economic Policy, a historico-philosophical hiatus in which new forms of socialist existence could emerge slowly and unprompted. As is well known, this strategy was criticized by those Bolsheviks who venerated "unusually bold theoretical constructions," in Lenin's words.[30] To these "frightfully revolutionary" comrades, Lenin quoted the distinguished presentist Mephistopheles: "Theory, my friend, is grey, but green is the eternal tree of life" ("Assessment of the Moment," 45).[31]

One of the most famous examples of extemporaneous, lived socialism, heralded by Lenin and the factographers alike, was the first subbotnik that took place in Moscow on May 10, 1919 (fig. 3.5). What happened on that Saturday, when workers gathered voluntarily and uncompensated to repair the Moscow-Kazan Railway, exceeded all frameworks of rational prediction and economic calculus. Work time was cut in half and productivity increased nearly threefold. Freed from the measure of the commodity value-form, the emancipated work of the participants resembled an act of improvised creation, something more like artmaking than reified labor. Firsthand accounts marveled at how instruments seemed to come to life in the hands of their users and at the way that inert matter appeared to collaborate with the workers instead of resisting their touch. Music playing in the background gave the scene a holiday atmosphere. Indeed, as the word itself suggests, the subbotnik—the Russian word for sabbath—stands outside of the linear time of the workweek and belongs instead to the sacred time of the religious festival, a vertical interruption in the horizontal course of chronological history. In his canonical essay on the first subbotnik, "A Great Beginning," Lenin characterized this unplanned outburst of labor as an exception (*исключение*). The sabbath is "a temporal fencing off in time and space," a "'time out' from the secular flow" that constitutes a "form of resistance to state and market power."[32] According to the historian Stephen E. Hanson, the 1919 subbotnik thus anticipated the fitful temporality that would soon be theorized in the nonlinear organizational science of Bogdanov and formalized institutionally by the League of Time.[33] In this respect, the spontaneous exception of the subbotnik epitomized the messianic time of the revolution itself, a miracle (*чудес*) that had broken definitively with historical sequence.

The May 1919 subbotnik was not merely an economic phenomenon. That aspect was in fact secondary. More than just a novel form of production or a higher order of labor discipline, what appeared on that day was a new approach to collaborating with things and a concrete outline for new social relations. The first subbotnik overturned traditional conceptions of work, creativity, and connectedness in a single stroke. It changed Lenin's feelings about cooperativism, for example, and seems to have prompted him to reconcile with Kropotkin a few days later. As the first manifestation in human history of "work in a revolutionary way," the subbotnik also constituted "the creation of a new social bond" and "one of the cells of the new socialist society," Lenin wrote. The subbotnik was

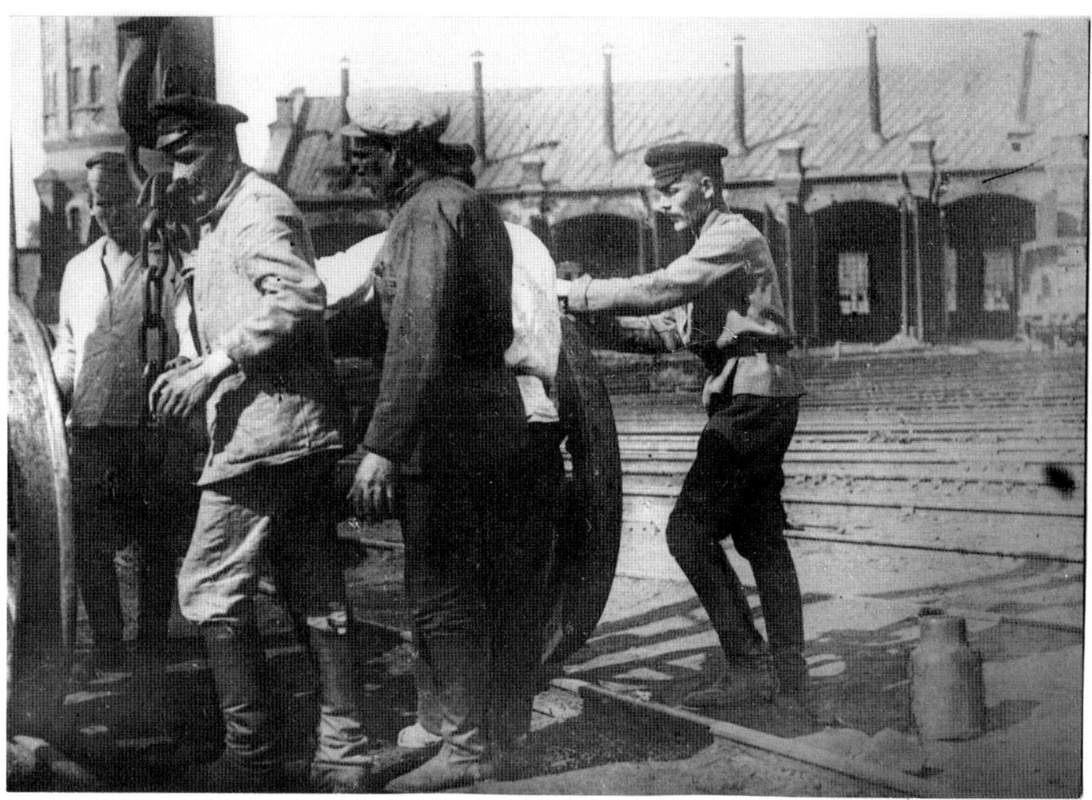

3.5 Unknown photographer, Communist subbotnik at the station, Orenburg, 1919. Collection of Multimedia Art Museum, Moscow.

the "*actual* beginning of *communism*": it emancipated women from the slavery of petty housework, infected people with the revolutionary affect par excellence, enthusiasm, and created "real values of immediate worth." Lenin highlighted the way that the event seemed to expand the ambit of concern (*забота*) beyond the confines of the bourgeois family.[34] Echoing Nietzsche's exhortation to replace "neighbor love" with "love of the farthest," Lenin explained that "communism begins when the rank-and-file workers display an enthusiastic concern to . . . husband every pood of grain, coal, iron and other products, which do not accrue to the workers personally or to their 'close' kith and kin [*ближние*], but to their 'distant' kith and kin [*дальние*], i.e., to society as a whole, to tens and hundreds of millions of people united first in one socialist state, and then in a union of Soviet republics"[35] ("Great Beginning," 412, 423, 427). The subbotnik uncoupled labor from the state (an institution doomed to wither away, per Lenin), but more importantly, it proposed new emotions and epistemologies, new ways of relating and creating. "In the transition to communism, the critical stake of struggle is the possibility of dissociating politics from the state by associating (or fusing) politics with labor, *praxis* with *poiesis*," comments Balibar.[36]

For this reason, Lenin declared May 10, 1919, to be a date more decisive in the history of humanity than any of the battles in World War I.

Tret'iakov too heralded this visitation from the communist future. He believed that the forms of shock work that were manifested in the subbotnik—the "form of truly free labor that is emerging for the first time in the history of mankind"—offered a tantalizing, albeit still fugitive, glimpse of the society to come. Like others, Tret'iakov noted the strange Leaguist temporality of the subbotnik, which broke with the linear logic of capitalist accumulation. "It seems as if time has come to a standstill," he marveled. As an advocate for communist world-sensation, Tret'iakov was particularly interested in the affective composition of these brigades, which seemed to suffuse everyday labor processes with the passion of amateurism (*Liebhaberei*, *Lieblingsarbeit*). To him, the shock worker resembled a lover of art who produces out of pleasure rather than out of necessity and who sees no distinction between work and creativity. The brigades broke down the distinction between labor and leisure that structured all of life under capitalism. Much like Lenin, who claimed that the subbotnik expanded the radius of concern so that people now cared for "every pood of grain, coal, iron and other products," Tret'iakov heralded these acts of communist labor for demonstrating in practice something previously unthinkable: "How people can love their products."[37] The challenge that now faced engineers of world-sensation like Tret'iakov was how to institutionalize the improvised subbotnik by integrating this intermittent psychic "symptom," as he called it, into a more encompassing libidinal economy. Echoing Lenin's own call for "verifying and testing [the subbotnik], corroborating it by experience, and making it more durable," Tret'iakov explained that "this symptom must be welcomed and scrupulously studied."[38] Making this proto-communist apparition more durable would require embedding it in the habits, reflexes, and sensations of the population so that it might take root as instinct and begin to regenerate and renew itself as spontaneous affect.

To aleatoric materialists like Lenin and Tret'iakov, the first subbotnik perfectly illustrated how the New makes its way into history: it begins with an unforeseen swerve that is then stabilized, rehearsed, and reproduced. Lenin wrote that participants in the 1919 subbotnik "*first* demonstrated *by deeds* that they are capable of working like *Communists* and then adopted the name of 'communist subbotniks' for their undertaking" ("Great Beginning," 432). For him, communism first had to be evidenced as an empirical fact before it could be designated, classified, and conceptualized. If concepts precede facts in nonrevolutionary conjunctures—to reprise an earlier point—during the transitional period facts begin to outpace concepts and demonstration precedes naming. Like Lenin, theorists of ostension have emphasized the primitive strategy of showing as a means of communicating in periods of epistemic shortfall. Pointing to a concrete example establishes "a non-verbal symbol for which we have no corresponding word or description"—at least not yet.[39] When inherited concepts prove inadequate, presenting facts directly and indexically—rather than circumscribing them discursively—shapes the material stuff of reality into a placeholder, a makeshift sign, for an idea yet to come. For this reason, educational theorists since Augustine have proposed pointing as a strategy of instruction when learners do not know the word for a new thing.

The degree to which techniques of ostension expanded beyond explicitly pedagogical scenarios to become a master strategy of communication after the revolution shows how all of Soviet society had become a vast school in those years, an enormous institute for discovering, implementing, and testing communist life-forms in situ.[40] Acts of showing became an indispensable resource during the transitional phase. They were the cognitive vector of the New. Althusser later explained that Lenin's "concrete situation" "consists exclusively of singular, unique objects, each with its own specific name and singular properties. 'Here and now,' which, ultimately, cannot be named, but only pointed to, because words themselves are abstractions—we would have to be able to speak without words, that is, to show. This indicates the primacy of the gesture over the word, of the material trace over the sign" (*Philosophy of the Encounter*, 265). Having toppled the bourgeoisie's temples of knowledge, the Bolsheviks now needed to reorganize the encyclopedias around proletarian lemmas, restructure the universities into polytechnical disciplines that combined mental and manual learning, and socialize the sciences to reflect the new reality of collective experience. Following Lenin's command to "educate people through living, concrete examples," the mass media were turned into a showcase in which every person and thing, every technical invention and act of collaboration, seemed to express some unusual new feature of revolutionary existence. In the words of one reporter, "everything was new, everything was for the first time. The first factories, the first collective farms, the first collective kitchens. . . . Just information in and of itself was interesting."[41] Every day Soviet citizens encountered things that as yet had no designation, not to speak of a corresponding concept. So-called demonstration farms (*показательные хозяйства*) like Tret'iakov's Communist Lighthouse were not just advertisements for the success of agricultural industrialization but also small-scale maquettes for testing socialist propositions in real life under controlled conditions. The "staging of subbotniki reflects the new, future system of the socialized economy in miniature," Kerzhentsev wrote.[42] From collective farms to subbotniki, from agit-trials to factory prototypes, Soviet reality was full of demonstrational phenomena which proved that while the communist future could not yet be conceptualized, it could nonetheless be pointed at.

Documentation became a key strategy for establishing tentative footholds for thought during this zero-hour of knowledge. Invoking the origins of this word in the Latin *docēre*, "to teach," Lisa Gitelman writes that "documenting is an epistemic practice: the kind of knowing that is all wrapped up with showing, and showing wrapped up with knowing."[43] As a didactic tool, the document enables learning not through deductive reason, which only reproduces the same structures of thought over and over, but by referencing and extrapolating from concrete examples. Lenin explained that reconstructing knowledge in the transitional period entailed showing specific instances of Soviet being one by one: "Model production, model communist subbotniks, model care and conscientiousness in procuring and distributing every pood of grain, model catering establishments, model cleanliness in a specific workers' house, on a specific block, should all receive ten times more attention and care from our press" ("A Great Beginning," 430; translation modified). Having initiated this process of collective learning, Lenin also placed an embargo on speculative thinking. The revolution had reduced theory to the statement "this is how it is" and philosophy to "the observation of a facticity," Althusser wrote about "Assessment of the Present Situation." In this historical hiatus, a moment uniquely hospitable to the monistic worldview, "*there is nothing left to say about . . . the problem of knowledge*, and of its dual correlative, the knowing subject and the known object" (*Philosophy of the Encounter*, 177).[44] Echoing the famous phrase of Ludwig Wittgenstein, Althusser thus noted that the world of the transitional period comprised, simply, "everything that is the case" (*alles, was der Fall ist*). Language cannot illuminate reality in moments of philosophical exception, which demand instead a combination of silence and showing, *Schweigen* and *Zeigen*.[45] Orienting consciousness in Lenin's "concrete situation" required thinking in and through singularities.[46]

This particularism put the factographers at odds with the proletarian realists who favored typological abstractions. In his "Conversation with Writer-Shockworkers," Gorky had disqualified documenting as a creative method because of its referential explicitness. "Comrades, you shouldn't write about one specific person. . . . This is how newspapers work. But in an ocherk, you should make the hero into a type rather than making a direct portrait of Ivanov, Nikolaev, or Petuchov. . . . Take twenty outstanding workers and paste together a single outstanding one out of them. In this way he will be more successful because he will be clearer and more vivid."[47] Gorky advocated the good gestalt of the novel over the formless precisionism of the newspaper. Faithful as ever to Gorky's model of realism, the authors of RAPP made generality the foundation of their practice. Supposing "I want to write a story whose theme would be the history of a factory," mused one: "To do this I study the history of any three typical factories and then, on the basis of the material that I've collected, I write the history of a factory."[48] Deriding Lef's primitive poetics of documenting as "aconceptual photographing" (*безыдейное фотографирование*), RAPP demanded that writers enhance the ideal-typical features of their characters to give readers a set of stable and familiar signposts in unfamiliar times.[49] But the factographers argued that these generalities erased what was specific about the emergent communist forms of the transitional period. Blurring out the features of twenty individual faces like Francis Galton to make "some kind of synthetic 21st face" or combining the histories of three existent factories into "a story about a fourth nonexistent factory" only distanced readers from reality at the very moment in history when proximity, detail, and precision were most needed. The writer must grow "closer to the fact" ("Blizhe k faktu," 32).

The factographers insisted that their method was not per se aconceptual. Their concepts just looked different. Aleksandr Kurs, the leader of the Presentists and a vocal admirer of Tret'iakov's work, explained that their practice "rejects invention because the epoch of socialist construction is rich in the kinds of facts that no poet would ever be capable of inventing. . . . The literature of fact doesn't 'create' the heroes of our times by means of cryptic generalization, in the cryptic subsoil of the subconscious, but takes them directly from life, together with their name, patronymic and surname, with their address and places of work and service." The transitional period had dramatically diminished the métier of the revolutionary artist, who was no longer asked to conjure lofty visions of a communist future, but, turning her gaze earthward, was instead enjoined to scan the soil of everyday life searching for "feeble shoots . . . of the New" (*слабыми ростками . . . нового*), as Lenin put it ("A Great Beginning," 426). Kurs insisted that factical writers did indeed utilize conceptual thought in their work, although the concepts that they mobilized were materialist through and through. The abstract laws of socialist reality revealed themselves immanently through matter itself, expressed in patterns and regularities that had not yet been around long enough to be theorized systematically. "Our very life itself—which possesses sensitive 'organs of cognition' such as the Party, trade unions, and the press—makes generalizations such as chubarovism, eseninism, koren'kovism [*чубаровщина, есенинщина, кореньковщина*]."[50] Unlike the composite Galtonian abstractions of the RAPP novel, all the "generalizations" cited by Kurs here had unambiguous historical referents: *chubarovism* referred to a crime that took place on August 22, 1926, off Chubarov Lane in Leningrad; *eseninism* to the moral decline in rural society that was identified with the 1925 death of the poet Sergei Esenin; and *koren'kovism* to the dangers that private life posed to women, which came to the fore in the 1926 trial against a komsomolets named Koren'kov who drove his wife to suicide. Each of these three concepts originated in a specific event or phenomenon, a concrete fact from the news that was felt to express some general law of existence during the transitional period. For those working in the factographic mode, even abstract ideas must be as referentially precise as an alley in Leningrad or the proper name of a komsomolets.

Kurs's factographic concepts were formed using the Russian suffix *shchina* ("–ism," or "–ness"), a morpheme that, when added to a proper name, extrapolates a general characteristic, historical trend, or social pattern from a specific instance. *Shchina* transforms an individual specimen into the representative of a species: it makes a wife into woman as such (*жена* into *женщина*), a specific town into a geographical district (*Полтава* into *Полтавщина*), or a concrete act of communication into the community that is constituted through this exchange (*общение* into *община*).[51] This morpheme creates what philosophers call a paradigm, a knowledge-structure that "entails a movement that goes from singularity to singularity and, without ever leaving singularity, transforms every singular case into an exemplar of a general rule that can never be stated a priori."[52] As Pertsov explained, "the *shchina* of the newspaper" drives thinking inductively, from the bottom up rather than from the top down: "By selecting facts that appear as generalities, the ocherkist preserves the fact in its singularity, in its concreteness."[53] Factographic concepts were just as specific, but also just as ephemeral, as the daily newspaper from which they were taken. In a talk delivered at a VAPP conference in 1928, Tret'iakov boasted that *shchina* gave them conceptual traction on transient historical phenomena, helping them to think in and through concrete instances without recourse to the eternal and static typologies of the novel. "Have you observed a curious phenomenon in the practice of newspapers, journals, and political publishing—its capture of '*isms*' [*уловление 'щин'*]: koren'kovism, golovanovism, voronskiism, mayakovskiism? Instead of fiction's method of studying ten individuals and building from them, in advance, an eleventh person made of paper—one who has been invented, irresponsibly invented—journalism has a method for finding the kinds of concrete figures in reality who characterize a given group and can become generalizations. No writer who uses the methods of the novel could ever keep pace with the '*ism*' of the newspaper."[54] As Tret'iakov explained to his (doubtless unsympathetic) audience of RAPP novelists, the *shchina* is faster and more up-to-date than realist fiction. Lifted directly from the pages of the daily press, the paradigms of factography are more responsive to contemporary developments than the transgenerational, mythical archetypes of the novel. Like the technical term that the factographers deployed against metaphor, the *shchina* of the newspaper mobilizes the metonymic properties of language to ground thought in material reality. And also like the technical term, the ephemeral paradigm vanishes along with the reality to which it corresponds. Through ostensive pointing, "organs of cognition" like the newspaper create an "ad hoc concept" directly from life that is better able to speak to the revolutionary present than monumental arts like the novel and easel painting.[55] Little wonder that there was a massive uptick in the use of this "extremely productive" morpheme during the transitional period, as Afanasii Selishchev observed in his 1928 *Language of the Revolutionary Epoch*: exemplification through the *shchina* of fact was the best means to actualize and update concepts at a time when the rules of reality were changing from one day to the next.[56]

A LITERATURE OF BECOMING

Immediately after the revolution, the self-described "zealous Kantian" Mikhail Bakhtin began to struggle with the way that recent historical events were contaminating the a prioris of Idealist thought.[57] Previously, philosophical categories and concrete experience had maintained a safe distance from one another: "The closer one moves to theoretical unity (constancy in respect to contents or recurrent identicalness), the poorer and more universal is the actual uniqueness," while, conversely, "the further individual uniqueness moves away from theoretical unity, the more concrete and full it becomes." But the revolution seemed to have removed the cordon sanitaire separating universality from singularity, and, along with it, the statute of transcendental consciousness. Lenin himself put it well in 1917: "Events have moved [theory] from the realm of formulas into the realm of reality, clothed it with flesh and bone, concretized it and *thereby* modified it" ("Assessment of the Present Situation," 45). History had given material contours to speculative philosophy and, by incarnating its abstract postulates, had inflected and transformed these concepts factually. The revolution engendered a situated and contingent form of knowing that Bakhtin designated "participative thinking" (*участное мышление*). Bakhtin recognized that the "fatal theoreticism" of philosophy was a poor guide for thought in the space of the transition,[58] and, while the now-faltering Kantian was hardly ready to convert to Marxism, he nonetheless conceded that historical materialism, not Idealism, offered the most viable method by which "a striving and action-performing consciousness can actually orient itself in the world."[59]

The strategy of participative thinking that Bakhtin christened a "philosophy of the answerable act" anticipated many basic tenets of Tret'iakov's media operativism. Both abandoned the transcendental subject's position on the sidelines of events, both embraced an ethics of feedback that they called answerability (*ответственность*), and both utilized the contingent givens of the historical present as a tentative scaffold for thought. Like Tret'iakov, Bakhtin explained that the embedded mind navigates the transitional space of the "ongoing event" not by following rules of abstract logic but by identifying exemplary phenomena that generate their own concepts quasi-spontaneously. After the revolution, opaque and mundane facts of existence had become transparent to consciousness, momentarily illuminated by the light of Ideas. "The ongoing event can be clear and distinct, in all its constituent moments, to a participant in the act or deed he himself performs. Does this mean that he understands it logically? That is, that what is clear to him are only the universal moments and relations transcribed in the form of concepts? Not at all: he sees clearly *these* individuals, unique persons whom he loves, *this* sky and *this* earth and *these* trees."[60] Experience became intelligible, thinkable to Bakhtin, but only from within the historically unique horizon of the present moment: Vitebsk, 1919. Althusser would later describe conjunctures as axial moments of "encounter between concepts and things" in which the "singular *case* is at the same time *universal*,"[61] moments when "'practical' approaches and theoretical 'constructions'" converge.[62] For philosophers like Bakhtin, the revolution was not just a political paroxysm but a knowledge-event as well.

Bakhtin noted how acts of participative thinking were accompanied by a curious temporal flicker, the oscillation between present and future, actual and virtual, that philosophers of deontic logic call a "modal collapse."[63] The wall that Kant had once built between *Sein* and *Seinsollen* began to fall apart, leading to the "methodological indiscrimination of what is given and what is set as a task, of what *is* and what *ought* to be" (*данного и заданного, бытия и долженствования*).[64] This indiscrimination permeates the work of the factographers, whose operative method, as we saw in the previous chapter, records objective phenomena at the same time as it inflects and transforms them, pushing them into the future. Echoing the language of deontic logic, Agapov once defined the constitutive "property of the documentarian" as the "coupling of the existent with the ought-to-exist" (*сопряжение сущего с должным*).[65] Factographers like him were drawn to the anomalies of socialist reality that were concrete and tangible but philosophically unconsummated, as Bakhtin would say. Tret'iakov sought out events like the subbotniki, places like the Communist Lighthouse, and people like Den Shi-Khua, all revolutionary phenomena that were factually existent, although they had not yet achieved a resolved, stable state. Tret'iakov had a favorite anecdote about this temporal collapse: he once met a member of a youth delegation from Ufa who boasted about their marvelous factory that employs 20,000 workers—even though the enterprise had not yet actually been completed. As Tret'iakov explained, girls like this were everyday dialecticians who "speak in the future tense and in the imperative mood, but without cutting themselves off from the present tense; they perceive their dream as a reality, but without becoming sleepwalkers."[66] For him, the rapidly changing world of the transitional period demanded that people grasp both modalities of existence at the same time. They must learn to inhabit "not *byt* in its inertia and dependence on an established pattern of things, but *bytie*—a dialectically perceived reality that finds itself in a process of uninterrupted becoming [*в процессе непрерывного становления*], reality understood as the advancement toward the commune" ("From Where," 213). As Bloch put it, "Marxist reality means: reality plus the future within it."[67]

The challenge of reconciling the *byt* of being with the *bytie* of becoming led the factographers to develop a practice that they called the "demonstration genre."[68] Tret'iakov discussed this approach at a 1927 Lef roundtable on cinema, where he outlined three different approaches to filmmaking according to their manner of using source material. First, and predictably, he dismissed outright the familiar target of the factographers, the scripted film that uses professional actors in a fictional story. He was more sympathetic to the second strategy, the chronicle film that shoots material *in flagrante* (*флагрантный материал*) and captures current events that are still "ablaze" in the present. Finally, he proposed a third strategy that transcended these two extremes of subjectivism and objectivism and proved that "the very opposition between fiction and nonfiction film is an infelicitous formulation":

> I film a woodcutter at work; I bring him to a tree that I've selected and ask him to chop it down while I film. His work is being done to order, but I have set in motion his professional habits and therefore the deformation involved is minimal. This is a precise description of the way that work with the actor-model [*натурщик*] proceeds: a person is selected as material whose concrete qualities, habits and reflex actions correspond to the image required on the screen. This is how Eisenstein works, by choosing people with the appropriate faces, habits and movements. This structure undoubtedly shows a certain orientation toward performance, of course, but to a far lesser degree than working with professional actors. The "free," subjective element introduced by the actor is here replaced by the authentic action of a correctly selected reflex. ("Lef and Film," 76, 74; translation modified)

According to Tret'iakov, the practice of showing "model" people and things represents a third poetological mode distinct from either creative invention (played film) or passive recording (chronicle film). Here, the performance of the woodcutter is staged, but the gestures that he executes are taken from his real-life repertory of reflexes, not acted but reenacted in the profilmic space established by the camera.[69] This approach anticipates what Rancière later designated the "ostensive image," a variety of post-abstract art that the philosopher, like Tret'iakov, distinguished from two other categories of imagery: the metaphorical image, which provokes "the operation of interpretation," and the naked image, which arrests "the rhetoric of exegesis." The ostensive image provokes none of the mental associations of the metaphorical image, but nor does it inhibit thought, like the naked image. It crafts excerpts of real life into signs of themselves, giving rise to a semiotic tautology in which "presence opens out into presentation of presence." This particular tautology is not a dead end, however, but a springboard, a means for thought to bootstrap itself on the basis of sensuous experience. Like the factographic *shchina*, Rancière's ostensive image points to a segment of reality and enjoins the spectator *look!* (*voici!*) so that "the flesh of material presence [is] raised, in its very immediacy, to the rank of absolute Idea."[70] In the deontic space of the demonstration genre, actuality intermingles with virtuality and brings new concepts into the world.

The play between actuality and virtuality was a key dynamic in *Gasmasks*, Tret'iakov's melodrama about a recent incident in a Uralic gasworks that he and

Eisenstein staged in the Moscow Gas Factory using real props (fig. 3.6). Some angered reviewers found the use of scripted elements in the play inconsistent with Lef's outspoken campaigns against "representationalism."[71] According to these critics, the setting, props, and other features of the Moscow Gas Factory—down to the real-life workers who trundled across the stage on the way to their morning shift—were ultimately gimmicks designed to enhance the mimeticism of a traditional fictional play. To them, the "facts" of *Gasmasks* were reality effects, just of a higher order. In response, Tret'iakov conceded that some aspects of the play were indeed staged, but he insisted that the unique dramaturgy implemented in the production was wholly consistent with the anti-reflectionist platform of the productivist avant-garde:

> It might seem illogical for me to be protesting against passive reflections of life at the same time that I am recording life in this play. But the fact remains: the play's thoroughly agitational tendency and its great effort to move directly from the representation of human *types* to the construction of *standards* (patterned models) at the current transitional moment nevertheless permit me to consider this play a pivot that eliminates the pure representation of life and that begins to move toward a theatrical construction of the standard person [*стандарт-человека*] and the standard environment [*стандарт-быта*].[72]

As Tret'iakov saw it, the critics who denounced *Gasmasks* for lapsing into naturalism had failed to grasp its operative play between depiction and production, passive and active, *is* and *ought*. To be sure, *Gasmasks* took people and objects directly from life in a quasi-documentary fashion, but these carefully selected "standard" entities, as he called them, also advanced socialist construction by pointing to the future.

The "standard" would become a key device in Tret'iakov's work in the 1920s. With this word, he had in mind neither the mathematical average of a group nor an ideal type for audiences to emulate, but a basic unit for comparing and appraising behaviors and phenomena, like the gold standard or a standard meter.[73] The standards, or "model patterns," that he presented in a play like *Gasmasks* were instruments of measurement not mimicry, of reference not resemblance. The platinum rod that is kept in Sèvres, France, does not represent the idea of a meter so much as it enables this idea by instantiating it, as Peirce once noted.[74] The standard object is at once both a concrete unit and an abstract concept, a paradigm that "defines the intelligibility of the group of which it is a part and which, at the same time, it constitutes."[75] So too did the standard people of *Gasmasks* or *I Want a Baby* (another play that Tret'iakov designated an "exhibition of standards"[76]) provide points of reference with which to evaluate a variety of behaviors according to their revolutionary qualities. Model

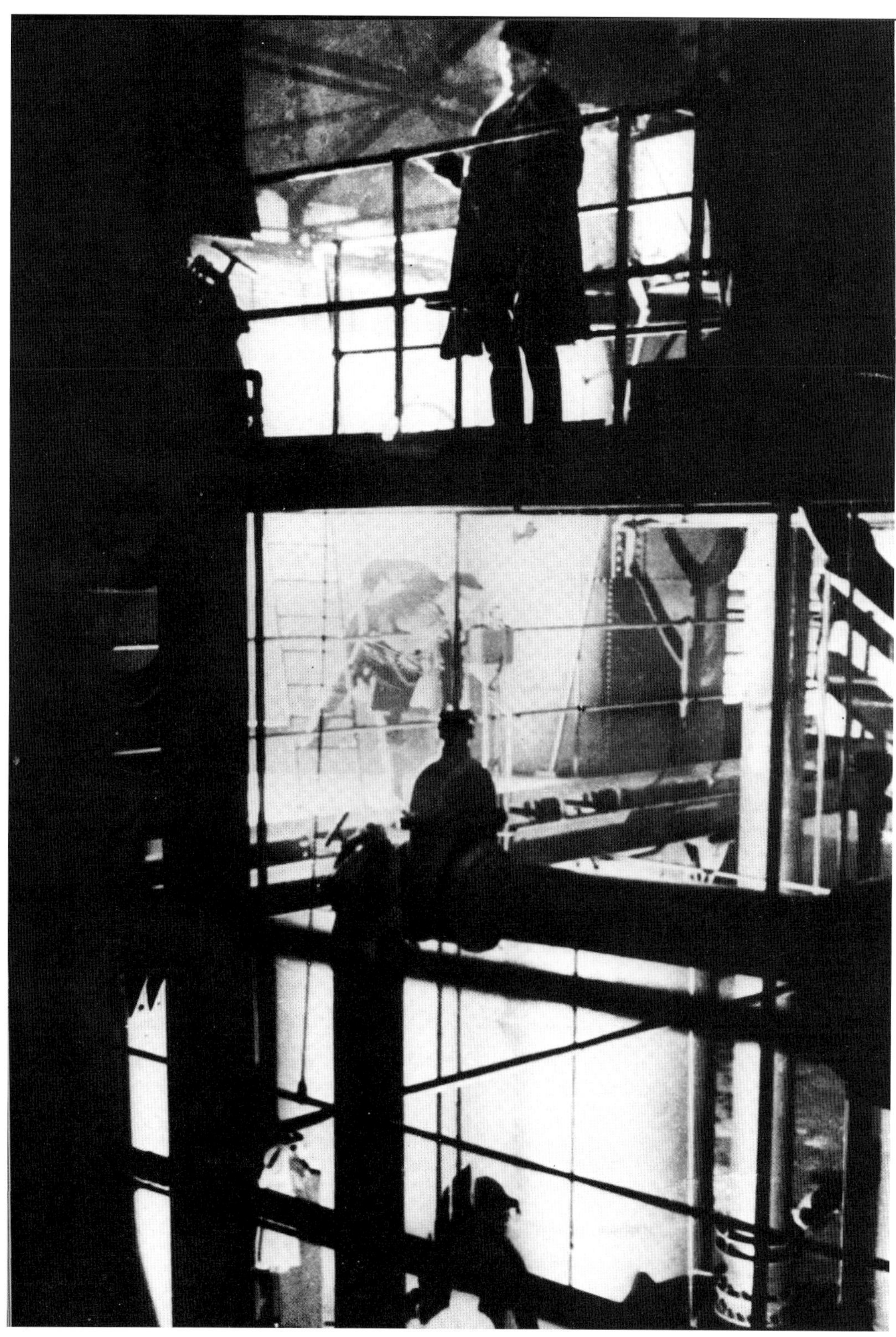

3.6 Sergei Eisenstein and Sergei Tret'iakov, *Gasmasks*, as staged at the Moscow Gas Factory (1924).

patterns like these were not didactic propaganda but analytic levers, or "pivots," that helped audiences to test, classify, and systematize reality at a time when the old categories of thought were no longer valid but the new ones were not yet in place.

Tret'iakov's experiments with demonstrational genres were heavily indebted to the thinking of Chuzhak, who had started to grapple with the aporia of art-making in times of epistemic rupture already long before the revolution. Unique among members of Lef, the philosophical formation of the elder Bolshevik was well suited to address the challenges that the institutions of knowledge and culture would face after 1917. Combining the emergentism of Vladimir Solov'ev with the functionalism of Bogdanov's organizational theory, Chuzhak arrived at a position similar to Engels, who famously claimed that "the world is not to be grasped as a complex of ready-made things, but as a complex of processes, in which apparently stable things no less than their images in our heads, its concepts, undergo uninterrupted change of becoming and passing."[77] Chuzhak's writings from the first decade of the century engaged the question of how to achieve theoretical certainty in the face of this continuous "fluidity of forms" (*текучесть форм*), a problem that became even more urgent during the transitional period that demanded tactical and time-based strategies of thought.[78] Art's vocation under these new circumstances was not to reflect reality passively but to establish "models for tomorrow" (*модели на завтра*), in Chuzhak's famous phrase.

Glimpses of the communist future could be seen everywhere after the revolution, although the forms that this future assumed in the present were still dialectically unresolved and ideologically equivocal.[79] Communism was no fait accompli after the October Revolution, but nor did it lie in an impossibly remote future. As Bogdanov observed, "socialism is to be understood not as the outcome of a victorious battle, as a radical break," but as "a question of method."[80] Communism was a Foucauldian heterotopia that was wholly concrete but still axiomatically unconsummated, an "effectively enacted utopia" that was fleetingly revealed in the sudden outbursts of unregulated creativity among subbotniki or in the acts of collective care that exploded the confines of the nuclear family.[81] "Proletarian culture not only *will be*, but already *is*," insisted Chuzhak.[82] Or, as Arvatov put it in a polemic against the utopians of the day, "the future is that which has started today" (*будущее есть начатое сегодняшнее*).[83] In order to hasten progress toward that future, Chuzhak endorsed a number of demonstrational devices, not just *shchina* of the press but also Tret'iakov's display of standards. A play like *Gasmasks*, he wrote, develops "a practice that searches for a bridge to the construction of models for tomorrow, while recognizing that pure reflectionism is completely useless. And Tret'iakov's play is valuable as a device. What distinguishes it is the fact that the author has taken a fleeting fragment of reality and . . . instead of narrating 'what happens next' through to the end [*доказывает*], he *demonstrates* [*показывает*] *how it was*. . . . The search for the necessary *standard* is the vital task of the art of Lef."[84] What people needed most in these years were not stable theoretical platforms but dynamic bridges for thought, practical ways of concatenating the empirical phenomena of socialist reality into tentative conceptual systems. As Chuzhak observed, creating these bridges required artists and writers to abandon old devices of narration that linked phenomena together in a closed chain of inevitability and instead pursue acts of demonstration, which were less conclusive but also more faithful to reality. During their moment of accelerated history, when every frozen philosophical posture was immediately shattered by current events, the display of standards was the only way to keep up.

The contradictions of artmaking in the face of history's continuous "fluidity of forms" is a theme that spans all three of Chuzhak's major theoretical treatises, "Toward a Marxist Aesthetics" (1916), "Under the Sign of Life-Construction" (1923), and "The Literature of Life-Construction" (1928). At the moment of its initial appearance, every new cultural phenomenon contains its own negation within it, he explained in the first essay. For this reason, "the true goal of art seen in the light of dialectics" must always be to heighten this conflict, never to resolve or leap over it. Foregrounding the "antagonistic nature" of "that which is" (*то, что есть*) and "that which will be" (*то, что будет*), Chuzhak argued that art's task is "to reveal the shoots of the forthcoming that are ripening in visible reality; to reveal the new reality hiding in the depths of contemporary life; to cast off the dying forms that are still prevailing for the moment."[85] Practically, this means that artists should exacerbate the struggle between the old and the new, the dying and the ripening, rather than console the spectator with irenic visions of a communistic future. "Under the Sign of Life-Construction" thus explains that the point of art is not to offer images of utopia, but to disclose the virtual within the actually given:

> If some kind of material given lies at the foundation of all forms of activity, including artistic activity (dialectical materialism), but this given is *already* "something *transitional*," i.e., contains within itself "not only an affirmative understanding of what is in existence, but also an understanding of its *negation*," then it should be obvious that the task of art is not to record everyday life in isolation (as many who call themselves Marxists continue to do to this day), but to realize that *antithesis* which is *imaginary* but which is based on the study of reality—an antithesis whose discovery serves the interests of the *coming* day: its task is *to present every synthesized ("realized") form "in its movement," i.e., under the sign of the new and of the new procedures that matter is eternally renewing and developing from the inside.*[86]

This remarkable sentence performs Chuzhak's argument about art through its very syntax. In it, a cascade of words qualifies and negates the grammatical subject of the sentence as it tumbles toward the period at the end, transforming this subject gradually until it is barely even recognizable, no longer identical with itself. Chuzhak demanded that all revolutionary art similarly submit to the dynamics of historical change through techniques that both posit and negate reality in a single gesture. Here as elsewhere, Chuzhak's writing realizes this dialectical metamorphosis through an excess of present active participles, grammatical constructions that processualize the object that they qualify. *Forthcoming*, *ripening*, *hiding*, *dying*, *prevailing*: instead of describing what the object is, qualifiers like these show how the object works, how it becomes what it is through operation and use. For functionalists like Chuzhak, art should likewise express activity rather than ontology, tendency rather than being.

The dialectical view of artmaking that Chuzhak developed in his early essays would eventually lead to factography, the subject of the essay "The Literature of Life-Construction." In contrast to the authors of RAPP and the painters of AKhRR, who created images of a socialist future that were harmonious but fundamentally lifeless, the factographers refused to mitigate the conflicts they saw around them. This dialectical "literature of becoming" (*литература становления*), as Chuzhak called factography, would instead delve into "the fundamental contradictions of the material itself."[87] One admirer of the literature of fact took aim at the proletarian realists for their overhasty utopianism: "It takes no skill to rhapsodize about a building that has just been finished. It is much harder to observe the construction site when it is still covered in scaffolding, when rubble, brick, and sand are scattered around it in disarray, when it is just beginning to seethe with rough, preliminary work."[88] For the factographers, the visions of RAPP and AKhRR were premature, considering that the house of communism was still covered with dust and boards. Worse still, in visualizing the future the proletarian realists turned a blind eye to the conflict of the present, halting the forward momentum of the revolution before the goal had been reached. "Contradiction is the driving force of every movement forward," observed Kuz'michev: "Where there is no contradiction, there is stagnation."[89]

The transitional period had given birth to a variety of both positive and negative phenomena, each of which required scrutiny and testing in equal measure. Lenin derided pollyannaish newspapers that were filled with "fables, boasting, intellectual promises ('things are moving,' 'the plan has been drawn up,' 'we are getting under way,' 'we now vouch for,' 'there is undoubted improvement,' and other charlatan phrases)." Recognizing the achievements of the revolution was important, of course, but the press also needed to consider the downsides of the new life, the "disorder, disintegration, dirt, hooliganism and parasitism" ("The Character of Our Newspapers," 97). In the midst of so much historical change, it was impossible to predict exactly which features of transitional society would one day prove themselves to have been progressive and which ones reactionary. Dialecticians like Lenin and Chuzhak understood that any advances toward communism invariably also entailed provisional phases of negation. Even something as innovative and promising as the subbotnik might not continue to exist in the future, or at least not its current manifestation. "We cannot vouch that precisely the 'communist subbotniks' will play a particularly important role," wrote Lenin: "But that is not the point" ("A Great Beginning," 425). Phenomena like the subbotnik marked a great beginning to the socialist experiment, but nothing guaranteed that they would still be there at the end of this experiment as well.

Not only did the factographers refuse to ignore the conflicts of their own epoch, but they actively reveled in these antagonisms. Chuzhak foregrounded "forms that are realized in the contradictions of the flux of life."[90] In 1927 Pertsov boasted that "we now have slated a series of films and dramaturgical productions, for which the following formula has been drawn up: *pose problems, but don't resolve them*."[91] Like Chuzhak, Pertsov derided the positive heroes of the realist novel for their "absolute, non-dialectical quality" and for a "transhistorical, moralizing hue" that ignored the reality of transitional society.[92] What was needed, he insisted, was "not a moral of the story, but the kind of 'fable' that pours oil onto the fire of the struggle for the new everyday life."[93] Through films like Eisenstein's *The Old and the New*, in which past and future clashed and sparked dazzlingly, or through standard-plays like *I Want a Baby*, which represented "not a program, but a problem,"[94] the accelerationists in Lef stoked the conflicts around them in order to fuel the engines of progress and hasten the evolution of communism. Ivan Matsa, the art critic who had pleaded in *Time* to collectivize the Now (*сейчас*), likewise cautioned against glossing over the antagonisms of the present: the artist must find "moments in the individual phenomena of this reality that drive this reality forward; he must find the leading moments of contradiction, emphasize and display them, thus revealing the dialectics of the historical process within these individual, sporadic phenomena."[95] Like the factographers, Matsa believed the best subjects for art were the people and things that exemplified this antagonism, those explosive phenomena that mixed together past and future, negative and positive, with particular volatility. There should be no meliorist idealizations or happily-ever-afters in the transitional period. Art must instead pour oil on the fire.

Tret'iakov, like Lenin, was impatient with the whitewashing of reality and the self-congratulatory tone of their press. He criticized the "positive fantasy image of conditions in the Soviet Union" that was presented in Max Al'pert and Arkadii Shaikhet's popular photo-essay "A Day in the Life of a Moscow Working-Class Family" ("From the Photo-Series," 76) and jokingly proposed launching a journal named *Our Defects*—a periodical that, he mused, would be much more voluminous than Gorky's *Our Achievements*.[96] In Tret'iakov's view, celebrating successes while concealing mistakes slowed progress because it stifled the process of collective learning. He compared transitional society to a scientific laboratory that will produce more dead ends than successes, and he enjoined his contemporaries to be more tolerant and patient when these failures (*неудачи*) did arise. In this one respect, at least, his comrades could actually stand to learn from the West, where research and development programs simply took for granted that every new invention would be preceded by 100 unsuccessful attempts ("Ferz' ili peshka," 50). The goal was not to fail less but to fail better. This was another lesson that Tret'iakov had taken from Lenin, whose essay on the subbotnik counseled comrades to follow the example of Hideyo Noguchi, the Japanese bacteriologist who conducted 605 experiments before finally discovering the mechanism of syphilis in his 606th. Indeed, according to Lenin, Noguchi had it easy: "Those who want to solve a more difficult problem, namely, to vanquish capitalism, must have the perseverance to try hundreds and thousands of new methods" ("A Great Beginning," 426). Penetrating to the mutable dialectical core of revolutionary life meant showing and learning from the failures, lapses, and conflicts that came up along the way. Heroes and saboteurs, feats of labor and negligent physicians, achievements and defects: each new proto-communistic thing, behavior, and trait must be documented, magnified, and subject to rigorous examination in the press.

The *shchiny*, or paradigms, of the newspaper thus became a decisive instrument for "people who advance reality" (*продвигатели действительности*).[97] Whether these paradigms were good or bad per se was less important than their ability to express some new feature, behavior, or experience that was characteristic of Soviet life. In this regard, the ostension of the factographers differed fundamentally from that of the proletarian realists, who approached demonstration as affirmation and advertisement. RAPP's poetics of the "positive type" (*положительный тип*) proposed role models for readers to emulate and the "positive aesthetic" (*положительная эстетика*) of *Our Achievements* broadcast the accomplishments of the revolution while downplaying its shortcomings. Just like the factographers, the proletarian realists confronted the incompatible temporalities of "what is" and "what ought to be," although in the end their works always wound up siding with the latter's ideal-typical vision of a perfect communist society: according to Katerina Clark, the socialist novel "emasculated" the present by subordinating the open, unfinished temporality of the transitional period to the closed scheme of the epic.[98] In contrast, the *shchina* of the factographers was anything but hagiographic or resolved. (Indeed, this suffix is commonly added to negative phenomena and is for this reason often translated not as *-ism* but as *-itis*, as if naming a disease.) For the factographers, the purpose of showing Soviet life was not to influence the reader or to promote state successes but to scrutinize some new aspect of reality in order to discover the structural condition that gave rise to this "symptom." Invoking Bukharin's slogan that "contradiction is the power that moves things," the opening column of the factographic journal *The Present* announced that the highest form of cultural work was to put these antagonisms on display: "We want to show [*показать*] you and your age in all of its contradictions and complexity."[99] The positive aesthetics of RAPP were of no help, explained one of the editors: "Our reality is complex. The old and the new intertwine in it. The recent, decisive struggles between the old and the new take place in it. It is difficult to observe, difficult to sort out, difficult to approach phenomena dialectically, describing them, explaining their essence. It is much easier to sit at home, to reduce everything that is struggling to something harmonious, to invent both people and plots."[100] For Presentists, Lefists, and other factographers, concealing conflict under a veil of amity only inhibited the arrival of the communist future that was being synthesized, tested, and modified in the laboratory of socialism.

INDETERMINATE YET NONARBITRARY

The positivistic methods of the factographers only further compounded the experience of contradiction. Although the living specimens that they documented and put on display left nothing to the imagination, readers and spectators hardly felt confident about the exact meaning and significance of these phenomena. To the contrary, these sketches and photographs were all the more obscure and enigmatic precisely because of their referential explicitness. The founder of modern hermeneutics, Wilhelm Dilthey, once characterized the fact as "something behind which one cannot go" (*etwas unhintergehbares*) and a sheer positivity that is "never exhausted by thought."[101] A transitional world that is made of facts has only a recto side, no verso. Tret'iakov illustrated the plight of cultural analysis under these conditions with an anecdote about an argument he witnessed while working in the Soviet mining industry:

> There were small black flags on the map, four of them in the shape of a square. One geologist claimed that two veins of coal were located here (the flags marked places where coal had surfaced), and that the veins ran in parallel from south to north. The other geologist also claimed that there were two veins here, but that they ran from east to west.
>
> The whole dispute was about which flags should be paired together. The experts mobilized their experience and intuition to correctly connect the points that were marked by flags.
>
> No less than the geologist, the writer has to know how to connect points by determining which things or human behaviors the general line of the epoch cuts through.[102]

The perplexity of this case results not from a lack of information but from a surfeit, a signifying excess that corroborates the incompatible proposals of both scientists. Based on the factual outcroppings visible on the surface of the earth, the vein of coal might run either from south to north or from east to west. At some point in the future it will become clear which of the two options turned out to have been correct, but for the moment both variants are equally possible, even though they are logically inconsistent.

According to Tret'iakov, establishing the bearing of history based on empirical facts presents a similar challenge. Like the geologist arranging his flags on a map, the factographer organizes his documents into montage constellations in the hope of discerning the patterns that structure the general line of their era. On their own, however, these samples are fundamentally multivalent, and, like the flags on the map, can be mobilized in mutually contradictory construals of reality. "Art lies on the surface of reality in readymade form," Platonov wrote about his era, but the meaning and significance of these trouvailles could not be established with certainty at the current moment. For factographers, the subterranean vector of the general line will one day be obvious, but only in retrospect, when the fog of the present has been dispelled and the conditions of historical necessity revealed. Pertsov explained: "At the present moment the new everyday life presents us with a task that still permits multiple solutions. In the future it will become clear just which one—or perhaps two or three—turned out to be correct, and in which direction the course of development ran."[103] In the meanwhile, though, one had to find a way to navigate within equivocal circumstances, amidst a reality of things and acts that sustain too many interpretations, always keeping open the possibility that any one of the divergent scenarios might turn out in the end to have been correct.

Lidiya Ginzburg later characterized this hermeneutic condition as "the indeterminacy, yet nonarbitrariness of living facts." As she demonstrated in her defining studies of memoires, essays, and other "human documents" (*человеческие документы*), the quality of oversignifying that distinguishes factical prose turns out to be far more baffling than undersignifying, which, as we saw in the first chapter, is the basis for the aesthetic imagination.[104] Ginzburg's teacher Shklovsky had arrived at the same conclusion some time before, when he sat down to write the preface to his 1923 collection of essays *Knight's Move* and struggled to summarize the diverse contents of the volume. For once, the problem was not the inconsistency of his own thought—a real danger for such a notoriously idiosyncratic writer as Shklovsky—but the dynamic culture of the transitional period itself, which could not be encompassed by a single method or reduced to a common tendency:

> Some say—in Russia people are dying in the street; in Russia people are eating, or are capable of eating, human flesh . . .
>
> Others say—in Russia the universities are functioning; in Russia the

theaters are full.

You choose for yourself what to believe.

But why choose? It's all true.

—In Russia there is something else.

—In Russia everything is so contradictory that we have all become witty [*остроумны*] in spite of our own will and desire.[105]

In these lines, Shklovsky tries to distill some common themes about the era based on the empirical facts of experience, only to discover that the facts point in very different directions and sustain too many interpretations. How does one summarize the culture of a country that, on the one hand, had devolved into a grim landscape populated by cannibals, but that was, at the same time, politically the most advanced civilization on earth? Was this hell or paradise? Were they headed backward or forward? "It's all true," replied Shklovsky. Arriving in reconstruction Moscow a few years later, Benjamin would likewise conclude about "the fact of 'Soviet Russia'" that "the only real guarantee of a correct understanding is to have chosen your position before you came."[106] For Benjamin, the view from the ground in Moscow invariably just ends up confirming whatever interpretative framework or worldview the visitor had brought along to begin with. The facts themselves decide nothing. This indeterminacy is evident already in the tone of Tret'iakov's first factographic sketch, "Moscow—Beijing," which is by turns ironic, affirmative, analytic, and constative. At revolutionary moments, contradiction and wittiness become inevitable features of all speech, observes Shklovsky: whatever a speaker might have intended to say, she always ends up saying "something else" at the same time, an additional statement that expresses a second, equally valid construal of reality. Writers like Tret'iakov and Shklovsky could not escape the fundamental amphibology of fact. Even when they insisted on clarity, they still end up meaning too much.

According to semiotician Yuri Lotman, cultural forms take on a particularly broad interpretive bandwidth at historical moments of *vzryv*, or "explosion." Drawing upon chemist Ilya Prigozhin's research on dissipative systems, Lotman described this interval as a state of maximal structural complexity that is situated "between the past and the future and is as if ripped out of time": "The state of explosion is characterized by the moment of equalization of all oppositions. That which is different appears to be the same. This renders possible unexpected leaps into completely different, unpredictable organizational structures." Despite a certain resemblance to the mechanism of sublation, Lotman insisted that *vzryv* must not be confused with the Hegelian concept since the explosion is not a more advanced, temporally subsequent stage of development, but a hiatus in which facts jump erratically from one potential state to another. For Lotman, whose conceptualization of *vzryv* is, following

Prigozhin, chemical and catalytic rather than historico-philosophical, the sudden reconfiguration of cultural facts at this instant resembles mechanical processes in nature that precipitate instantaneously, such as the recombination of elements in a molecule or the phase shift from liquid to gaseous states. *Vzryv* does not obey the laws of linear progression. The rules of succession and patrimony that normally dictate the descent of art forms over time are suspended in this juncture so that the entirety of cultural history seems to contract to a single point, a pivot upon which past and future now oscillate as two symmetrical projections.[107] The interval of explosion constitutes the moment of greatest possible generativity and inventiveness. "*Vzryv* is not just the point of formation of new possibilities, but the moment of the creation of another reality, a leap and a re-comprehension of memory." The cultural critic experiences this instant as a kind of information overload, when facts appear to point in different directions at once and when any one interpretation of an artwork becomes just as probable as any other (*Nepredskazuemye mekhanizmy kul'tury*, 50). The moment of *vzryv* overflows with an excess of meaning that provokes a "double reading of one and the same cultural fact."[108] Lotman thus compared *vzryv* with the coalescence (*слитность*) of meaning in dreams: the "complex and contradictory semiotic tangle [*клубка*]" of dream-phenomena, which are "capable of being filled up with diverse interpretations," generates a "reserve of semiotic uncertainty, a space which must, of necessity, become filled with meaning."[109]

Lotman's *vzryv* bears an unmistakable if unacknowledged resemblance to overdetermination, the concept that Althusser used to describe the hermeneutics of the revolutionary conjuncture. If, for Althusser, the determinants of events in nonrevolutionary times remain dispersed across a diffuse web of factors and interactions, and if the causes of history remain obscure in these periods as a result, in revolutionary moments events instead appear to have too many causes and reagents, as it were, and will confirm any number of incompatible explanations. They are subjected to the mechanism of condensation (*Verdichtung*) that Freud outlined in his work on dreams.[110] This moment is a "junction, con-junction, congealed (albeit shifting) encounter, since it has already taken place, and refers in its turn to the infinite number of its prior causes" (*Philosophy of the Encounter*, 193). The meaning of phenomena at this moment is not obscure but obtuse. Writing about Bakhtin's Vitebsk, the deontic crucible that fused the *is* with the *ought*, art historian T. J. Clark confirmed: "It is precisely the undecidability that counts. It is because War Communism was both chaos and rationality, both apocalypse and utopia . . . that it gave rise to the modernism we are looking at. Proletarian rule, says [Lev] Kritsman, 'exudes a monistic wholeness unknown to capitalism, giving a foretaste of the future amid the chaos of the present.'"[111] In the coalescence of Lotman's *vzryv*—a word that means both "explosion" and "implosion," both dispersal and compression—the cultural historian encounters a simultaneity of antitheses, the collapse of opposites into a single semantically overcoded and hermeneutically inexhaustible fact. Under these circumstances, semioticians must take particular care not to confuse "'does not exist' with 'could not exist,'" Lotman writes, since the factual and the virtual, the *is* and the *ought*, have become indistinguishable. "The events that were realized and those that were not realized at a moment of explosion are variants, and could easily be substituted for one another" (*Nepredskazuemye mekhanizmy kul'tury*, 163).[112]

Eisenstein's *The Old and the New* radiates the semantic surplus of *vzryv*. The story behind the 1929 film—the only properly factographic work in Eisenstein's oeuvre—was typical for projects trying to keep up with the revolutionary present: although the director originally began the film in 1926, rapid developments in the countryside forced him to re-shoot and re-edit the scenes continuously over the next three years, thwarting his attempts to bring the project to a conclusion. Eisenstein never actually succeeded, but he released the film anyway. One reviewer consequently observed that "three years is much too long a time in the history of our Soviet Union. . . . Life has overtaken the film."[113] Originally titled *The General Line*, Eisenstein renamed the final work to reflect the compressed historical space in which elements of the old and the new overlapped and recombined in perplexing and often explosive ways. In the film's most arresting moments, Russia's archaic past and its technoscientific future congeal against the backdrop of the contemporary Soviet countryside. One dream sequence, for example, shows dairy cows wandering among the Corbusier-inspired constructivist architecture of Andrei Burov (fig. 3.7). Even more overdetermined is the pivotal scene with a cream separator that Eisenstein unspools into a series of increasingly complex semantic associations: first the separator's centrifuge is transformed into a spinning roulette wheel; the cream issuing from the spout splashes into a bucket, then inexplicably begins to decant over the hood of a tractor; finally, the sluice of white liquid is inverted in the upward jets of a fountain, and then echoed in the sweeping current of a hydroelectric dam (fig. 3.8). Fortune, fecundity, festiveness, force—the meanings and connotations proliferate. Invoking Freud's concept of semantic *Verdichtung*, the culminating intertitle of the separator sequence confirms "It condensed!!!" (*Сгустело!!!*) (fig. 3.9). As with everything else in *The Old and the New*, the separator, which Eisenstein compared to Arthur's grail, points in two directions at once: both forward, to an industrial future of technical rationality, and backward, to a prehistorical past of legend and myth.

The film concludes with another reconjugation of old and new. A tongue-in-cheek reference to the closing sequence in Chaplin's *A Woman of Paris* (1923), the final scene of Eisenstein's film depicts the encounter on a rural road between a male peasant lounging in his loose tunic in a horse-drawn cart and a female tractor driver decked out in the streamlined livery of a modern pi-

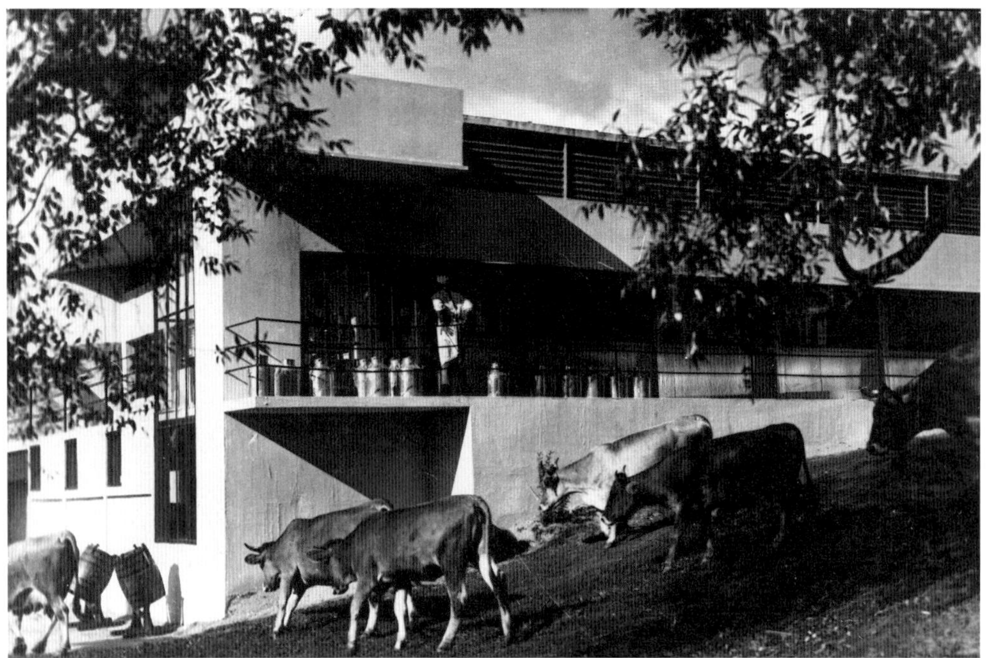

3.7 Andrei Burov, Model sovkhoz. Still from *The Old and the New* (dir. Sergei M. Eisenstein, 1929). ullsteinbild / TopFoto.

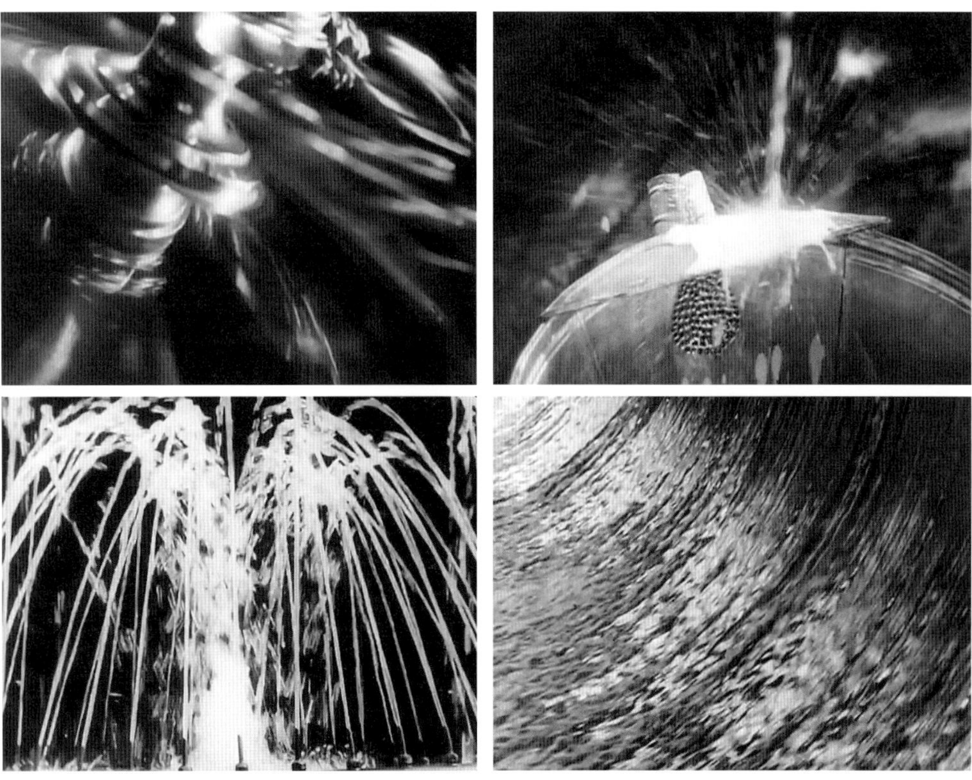

3.8 Metamorphoses of the cream separator. Frames from *The Old and the New* (dir. Sergei Eisenstein, 1929).

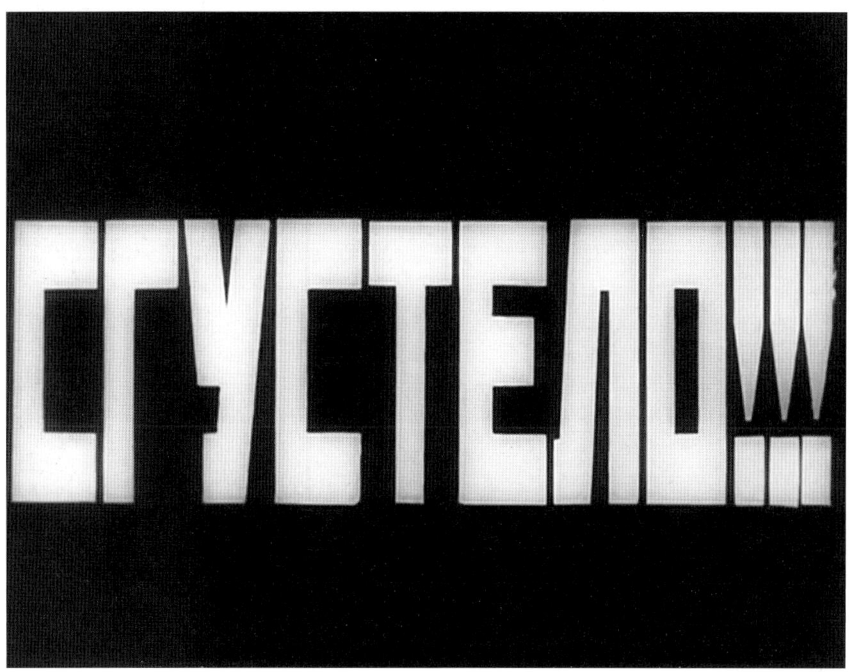

3.9 "It condensed!!!" Frame from *The Old and the New* (dir. Sergei Eisenstein, 1929).

lot (fig. 3.10). Once a *traktorist* himself, the peasant fails at first to recognize the *traktoristka* before him, but then suddenly sees that she is none other than the shy farmgirl he once flirted with, Marfa Lapkina. Following the Bolshevik strategy for *smychka* (conjoining) of countryside and city, the peasant and the machinist have traded places, consummating the chiastic exchange of properties between the old and the new. Importantly, though, the ending of Eisenstein's film does not replace the peasantry with the proletariat, as the Marxist teleology of history would have it, but instead conjoins the two together without sublation. Eisenstein's *smychka* leads to fusion, not supersession. At this moment of mutual anagnorisis, *The Old and the New* recapitulates other moments in the film in which Lapkina—a real-life model performer (*натурщица*) like Tret'iakov's woodcutter—is shown in widely divergent psychic states that range from despair and arousal to ecstasy and rage (fig. 3.11). The purpose of this flashback is not to recapitulate the entelechial development of the character but, just the opposite, to underscore the diverse potential states that Lapkina continues to carry inside of her, each one of which can be reactivated as needed. Like Zalkind's "cold bomb" who can be either tranquil or explosive as circumstances require, the revolutionary persona achieves unity through condensation rather than synthesis. Eisenstein would thus later identify Lapkina as the "embryonic" prototype of all figures to appear in his following films: like a tangle of undifferentiated cells that subsequently individuate through mitosis, Lapkina carries within her a number of characters in a potential state.[114] This kind of overcoding was a favorite device of the actor who inspired the final scene, Chaplin. According to Lotman, Chaplin's performances suggest a "pattern of behavior that represents simultaneously the mixture of two opposing patterns and a unified, organic pattern of behavior." As the famous tramp character, which oscillates between extremes of dignified elegance and abject shabbiness, "Charlie is, in effect, two people."[115] The peasant-*traktoristka* Marfa Lapkina too contains multitudes.

When in 1915 Heinrich Wölfflin surveyed the stylistic evolution of European painting over the previous two centuries, the art historian came to the notorious conclusion that "not everything is possible at all times."[116] Two years later developments in the east would prove him wrong. There, for a short time at least, everything became possible. A glance at the diversity of early Soviet culture indeed reveals an astonishingly rapid turnover of formal strategies, with artists like Rodchenko moving decisively from cubo-futurism to laboratory constructivism to production art to factography in just a few years. Rather than proceeding through a linear progression, as is characteristic of nonrevolutionary moments, all of the devices and techniques that were available to the writer and artist flourished simultaneously at this moment of explosion. The laws of

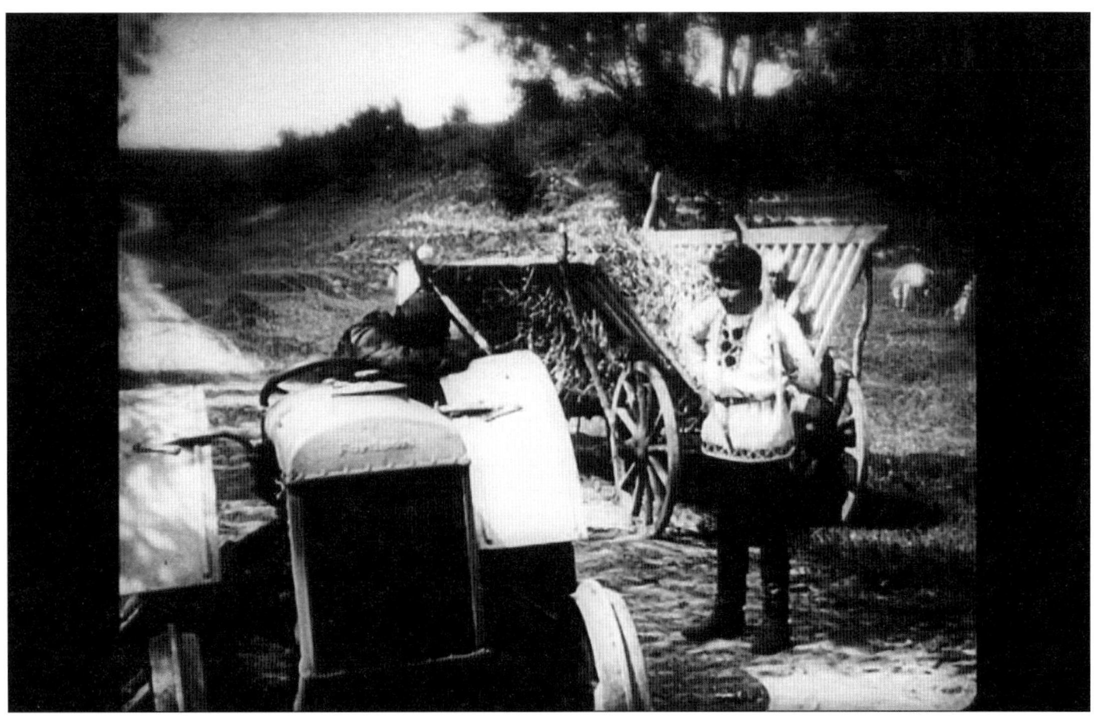

3.10 The *smychka* (conjoining) of peasant and proletarian. Frame from *The Old and the New* (dir. Sergei Eisenstein, 1929).

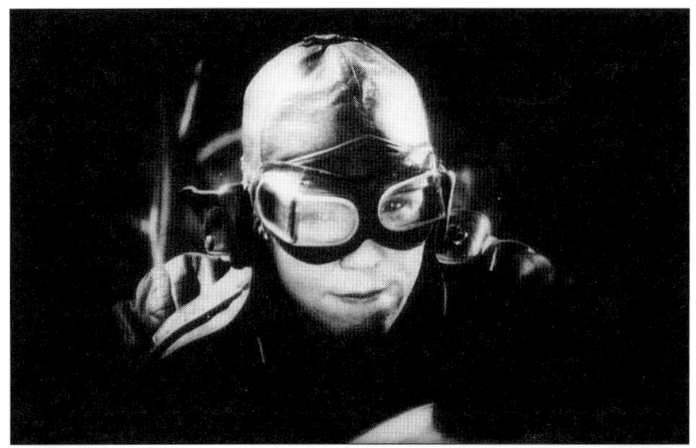

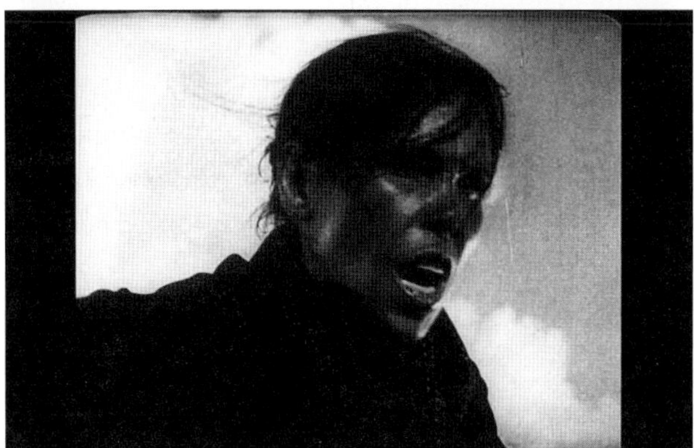

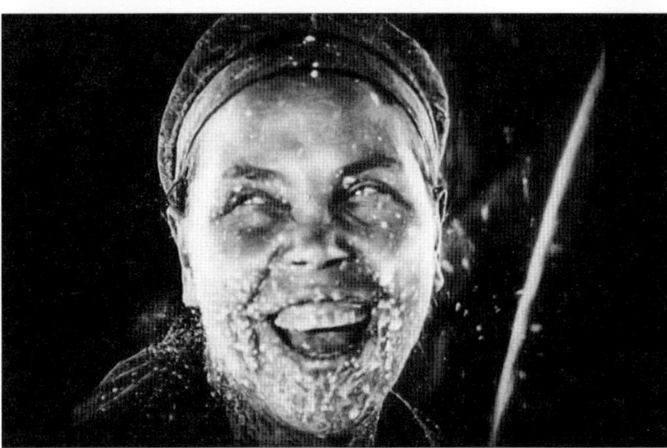

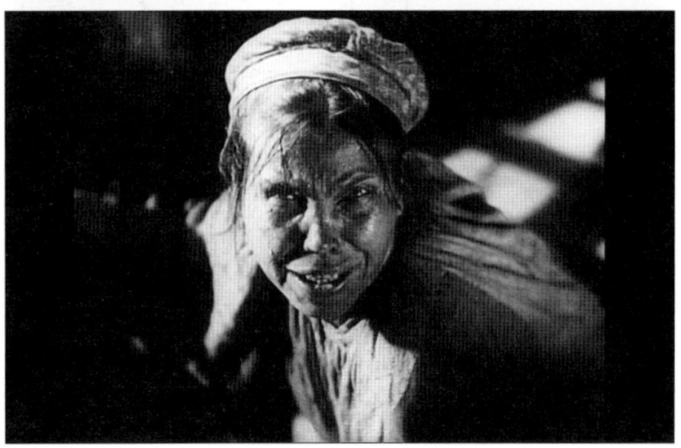

3.11 The emotional states of Marfa Lapkina. Frames from *The Old and the New* (dir. Sergei Eisenstein, 1929).

historical sequence seemed not to apply to Soviet Russia, where diachrony had given way to synchrony. In an article written at the outbreak of World War I, Lenin quoted a letter in which Marx proposed to approach history "not in the vulgar sense it is understood in by the 'evolutionists,' who see only slow changes, but dialectically: '. . . in developments of such magnitude twenty years are no more than a day . . . though later on there may come days in which twenty years are embodied.'"[117] These days at last arrived in 1917. Before October, history had moved forward at a glacial speed, outpaced by the frightfully revolutionary theories of the Bolsheviks and the counterfactual utopianism of the Futurists. But the transitional period condensed entire decades of economic and cultural development into mere days. The factographers saw this acceleration everywhere they looked, whether in the countryside, where Tret'iakov witnessed "days that count as years" (*Vyzov*, 207), or in Moscow, where developments confirmed that "our century equals a millennium in earlier times" ("From the Photo-Series," 73).

Those living in the interval of *vzryv* called this condition "diapason" (*диапазон*), as if all notes on a musical instrument were sounding at once. In a 1930 survey of Russian literature, Ehrenburg wrote that this outburst produced "some excellent writers and, even more importantly, created new literary forms. This is astonishing. This can probably be explained by the fact that history itself has now taken on the attitude of people: it too is in a hurry. A single generation has been saddled with all of the tasks. Whenever fathers destroy, it follows that children will rebuild and grandchildren will then admire. But right now nobody wants to wait. . . . Now we have to create at the same time that we enjoy what we have created."[118] Ehrenburg is quick to point out that the diapason is not a particularly harmonious experience. Certain developments he mocks, others he praises, still others simply confound him. And although Ehrenburg cannot see the aesthetic merit in all of this work, he still admires the sheer fecundity of his own historical moment. He marvels at a generation that was destroying the old world and building a new one at the same time that it was also—like Tret'iakov's youth from Ufa—admiring the results of this construction. The revolutionary *vzryv* at last fulfilled the demand of Faust, a Bolshevik favorite: "Show me the fruit which rots before we pluck it, / And trees, which every day renew their green!"[119] Successive stages of emergence and decline, flowering and decay, had converged in clear violation of the laws that dictated the transmission of aesthetic styles from fathers to children.

Ehrenburg was ambivalent about most writers of his day, but his 1930 essay did identify one development on the periphery of Russian literature that pointed the way forward: the worker-correspondence sections of the Soviet newspaper. Mass factography—not poetry, and certainly not the proletarian novel—was for him the most promising new phenomenon of Soviet culture. To be sure, this tentative practice had not yet matured into a major literary form, but Ehrenburg challenged anyone to deny its profound significance: "This is of course literature, more precisely, a fatuous hydrocephalus, the embryonic form of a new literary genre."[120] Factography might not make for good reading right now, but one day this anomalous and oddly proportioned child would grow up to become the first communist literature.

The "peripheral" begins to bloom everywhere.
—GEORG LUKÁCS[1]

4

THE FATAL QUESTION

The factographers hated the predictability of bourgeois artworks, even modernist ones. Once you identified the aesthetic formula at play, the artwork held no surprises. Worst of all was the device of plot: the dramatic schemes used in narrative film, photo-essays, and literature imposed a formal closure on the material that the factographers considered fundamentally inimical to the open-ended and adventitious nature of life after the revolution. Plot reduced all events to a foregone conclusion and consigned all heroes to a predictable fate. And yet, as the factographers also discovered, they could not simply renounce the structuring power of narrative, lest the artwork dissolve into an incoherent and formless heap of pointillistic detail. In order to solve this problem, they turned once again to contemporaneous research in the field of newspaper studies, where editors and journalists of the daily press were experimenting with mathematical systems of composition that were precisely calibrated and rationally structured but also aleatoric, additive, and open to future change. Rigorously patterned yet still plotless, the unpredictable artworks that the factographers made using these methods mobilized the energies of fortune against the closure of fate.

REALIA OF TIME

Whatever the medium in which they worked, acolytes of fact always questioned the use of narrative plot. They demanded that filmmakers replace dramatic scripts with montage constellations and that writers replace epic storytelling with static inventories. Erik Reger aptly characterized reportage as a "vivisection of time" since it arrested the flow of events and sliced history into a series of frozen cross-sections.[2] The Soviet factographers even considered the great ontological divide between illusion and reality, over which philosophers have racked their brains for centuries, to be a distraction from the more fundamental distinction between plotted and nonplotted art. For them, the battle between fiction and truth was just a smaller episode in the war between the played (*игровой*) and the unplayed (*неигровой*). "What makes Dziga Vertov's choice of cinematic form so valuable is not that he uses random, real people, but that he shifts the compositional structure away from the plot form to the pure juxtaposition of facts," wrote Shklovsky.[3] Being "closer to the fact," Brik also demanded, meant renouncing narrative and developing plotless (*бессюжетные*) and storyless (*бесфабульные*) devices that did not subordinate real-life events to readymade literary constructions and the false causalities of psychologistic thinking.

The factographers argued that plot preserved older cultural values and social codes that were unsuitable for revolutionary life. Like one-point perspective in painting, which entails a broad complex of presumptions about science (the topography of Euclidean space), society (the commoditization of relations), phenomenology (an immobilized spectator), and epistemology (contemplation of the world at a remove), plot is a symbolic form that condenses an entire worldview. The novel specifically—to cite the most consistent target of the factographers—expresses a "rationalistic system whose flowering corresponds to the assumption of power by the middle class."[4] In the novel Tret'iakov discerned a literary-generic corollary to the bourgeoisie's ideology of individualism and Idealism's philosophy of the transcendental ego. "The hero is what holds the novel's universe together. The whole world is perceived through him. The whole world is, furthermore, essentially just a collection of details that belong to him." By constellating all events in the story around a single character and filtering out anything that does not conform to the personal interests and narrative destiny of this heroic figure, the novelist limits and distorts the purview of experience. "The leading hero devours and subjectivizes all reality."[5] As Tret'iakov saw it, the technique of emplotment was incapable of depicting the complexity of collective life in a postrevolutionary society whose multi-nodal agential systems could not be scaled down to a quaint story about the fate and struggles of just one person. If "plot schemata conform closely to the everyday reality to which they give form," as Shklovsky observed, the novel's entelechial scheme of *bildung*, which exemplified the ideals of the eighteenth- and nineteenth-century bourgeoisie, clearly had no place in the new epoch.[6] "Only with difficulty can the traditional psychological novel be acclimated to the Soviet environment, since its formulas for the fabula are not suitable for processing new material," wrote the Formalist. "Simply put: the form doesn't suit the climate."[7] Shklovsky did not lack for *bons mots* about the post-narrative condition: "The novel still exists, although it exists like the light from an extinguished star";[8] or "Plot-oriented prose still exists and will continue to exist, but it has been consigned to the attic" (*Third Factory*, 4); or "Plot devices are lying at my door like the copper spring of a burned-up couch. Dilapidated devices, not worth fixing" (*Third Factory*, 53).

The factographers pilloried peers foolish enough to believe these devices could still be salvaged. Aspiring to become the "red Tolstoys" of the revolution, the proletarian realists of RAPP, for example, studied and emulated the great novelists of the previous century. To the factographers, this program of "learning from the classics" reduced contemporary experience to the same essential character functions, arenas of human agency, and psychologistic schemes of causation that had defined bourgeois literature. By just refurbishing the same old heroes, settings, and plots with a new revolutionary appearance, the proletarian realists were smuggling ideological contraband into Soviet culture. "The fundamental crime of VAPP [the predecessor to RAPP] is that it has directly and uncritically transposed into our environment the formal constructions of artworks that were created in a different class-environment that was feudal and capitalist," explained Tret'iakov.[9] The aristocracy and the bourgeoisie might have been overthrown in 1917, but their values and worldviews had in fact survived the revolution, preserved in the formal conventions of the novel. It did not suffice simply to replace bourgeois heroes with proletarian ones, or to swap out the domestic interior of the family novel for the industrial milieu of the production novel, as RAPP seemed to think. A more profound overhaul at the level of formal construction was needed. As the young Formalist Vladimir Trenin observed in *The Literature of Fact*, the RAPPists failed to grasp the historical dialectic of aesthetic devices. Their "fetishism of classical forms is profoundly mistaken because *we value a form not because of its specific importance in the old literature, but because of its social function*. At a different time and in different conditions the exact same form will fulfill different—and even sometimes diametrically opposed—functions."[10] The ideological valence of a given literary device is not fixed for all time, but evolves in continuous exchange with developments in social and political life. The ethos of individualism and the striving for character that distinguished narratives of *bildung*, for example, had challenged the feudal estate system and stoked revolutionary fervor in the eighteenth century, but the *bildung*-plot lost its progressive quality after 1848, when the collective superseded the individual as the engine of world history. The gradual reversal of the novel's sociological function was then confirmed by the events of 1917, which left no doubt that the bourgeoisie's ideology of individual self-determination was no longer a revolutionary force.

The factographers made a sport of showing how proletarian novelists, for all of their ambition to depict the new revolutionary life, were actually just rehashing the characters, plots, and idioms of bygone literature. Trenin published a review of *The Rout* by celebrated RAPP author Alexander Fadeev that revealed the storyline to be filched from Tolstoy's *War and Peace*.[11] Petr Neznamov argued that the syntax, lexicon, and plot of Sergei Semenov's *Natal'ia Tarpova* were all stolen from Dostoevsky, and that the devices of *Whetstones* by Fedor Panferov, another leading RAPP writer, were taken from Turgenev and Gogol'.[12] Chuzhak too joined in the melee, mocking the proletarian realists for recycling the storylines of Pushkin.[13] Vladimir Bakhmet'ev's popular novel *The Crime of Martyn* was so closely modeled on *Lord Jim* that Shklovsky couldn't even bring himself to denounce it as plagiarism, since, he explained, the novel was effectively just one extended quotation of Conrad.[14] Reaching even further back into the epic tradition, Brik pointed out that the protagonist of Fedor Gladkov's *Cement* looked a lot like Achilles, Roland, and Muromets, but not like anyone Soviet.[15] The proletarian realists promised a new revolutionary literature, but they delivered the infantile gratifications of the ever-same.

The paucity of suitable plotlines after October, and indeed, the bankruptcy of the very premise of plot itself, was obvious to experts and non-specialists alike. Lef member Teodor Grits observed that "the story is now ceasing to be a literary fact" and that plot is now "perceived even by the inexperienced reader as a cliché." Under these circumstances, plotted prose could hope to survive the death of the bourgeois subject only by embracing its new status as historical quotation. If plot were to live on after the revolution, it was only by parodying itself. In a review of Sergei Malashkin's 1927 novel *Two Wars and Two Peaces*, Grits thus explained that plot could earn a place in Soviet literature, but only if it is reborn as a second-order literary device: not *War and Peace*, then, but *Two Wars and Two Peaces*.[16] Factographic films like *Glass Eye* (1928, dir. Lili Brik and Vitalii Zhemchuzhnyi) did something similar, combining original documentary footage with deconstructive citations of Hollywood story genres like slapstick, romance, and adventure. Works like these used self-reflexivity to neutralize the ideological threat posed by the bourgeois plot. "The more we utilize an old form in a blatantly parodic manner, the less danger there is of infection by its function" ("A Writer's Handbook," 94).

The factographers' approach to plot was heavily influenced by the recent output of the Formalists, whose focus had pivoted in the 1920s from verse to narrative prose. At the very moment that seminal studies such as Shklovsky's *Theory of Prose* (1925) and Tomashevsky's *Theory of Literature* (1925) were identifying the systems of narrative construction, the factographers went about eradicating these devices from film and literature. The Formalists uncovered the same stories in a variety of divergent historical contexts and cultures, and concluded from this discovery that the number of available plotlines was in fact quite restricted. Surveying the extensive tradition of oral storytelling, Vladimir Propp, for example, identified thirty-one "functions," or basic narrative operations, that could be found in all Russian folktales. Shklovsky deduced an equally limited repertoire of motif-situations from the comparative literary ethnographies of Aleksandr Veselovsky.[17] And the advent of modernity had not expanded this stock of plots to any significant degree. Today's reader or viewer continues to encounter the same old cache of stories whenever she picks up a novel or walks into a movie theater. "The quantity of plot schemes is extremely restricted," complained Brik: "As a consequence the spectator who goes to the cinema regularly stores several plot templates in his consciousness, which he sees repeated in every new film."[18] Tret'iakov argued that this rehearsal of the same narrative formulas over and over cloaked new features of contemporary life under a blanket of sameness and identity. "It is possible to play out one and the same story either 'against the background' of a tobacco industry, or 'against the background' of a silicate factory, or in the setting of a naval steamer, or in an everyday pastoral environment. The material is violated; transformed into 'background,' the real and everyday setting of production is distorted, adjusted to fit the formula of the story."[19] This was a standard lament of the factographers: novelists and scenarists distort (*искажать*), violate (*насиловать*), and neutralize (*нейтрализовать*) reality by depriving it of concrete detail and glossing over the unique, factual features that make it distinctive and singular.[20]

The factographers might have all agreed on the need to get rid of prerevolutionary plots, but they never reached a consensus about what should come next. Some were reluctant to abandon plot construction as such and explored less restrictive, more capacious forms of narration that, they hoped, could accommodate more contemporary material than the psychological novel or Hollywood drama. "The first task of the day consists in taking out of circulation the plot schemes that are not capable of satisfying the cultural demands of the viewer," proclaimed Brik, who proposed ethnographic genres as an alternative model for authors and scenarists.[21] Shklovsky called for the "denovelization" of the material (*разроманирование материала*) and endorsed the segmented construction of the adventure story and the picaresque as better suited to their own disjointed reality. But hardcore factographers like Tret'iakov and Chuzhak demanded more radical measures. They rejected the very premise of a "revolutionary plot" outright, since all emplotment was, for them, perforce counterrevolutionary. For Tret'iakov, the "craving" of scenarists to write stories was inherently "detrimental and reactionary—chase them out of filmmaking" ("Industry Production Screenplay," 134). Tret'iakov and Chuzhak, whose thought had been profoundly shaped by the Russian Machists, followed those empiriocritics who rejected explanation through linear causation (*причинность*) as hopelessly anthropocentric, and who had argued that all matter, from atomic particles to human consciousness, was instead organized into logical patterns of correspondence (*совпадение*). Only by renouncing plot completely could writers and filmmakers capture the complex networks of collective agency found in revolutionary society and begin to understand the nonhuman, natural processes of reality that did not conform to psychologistic thinking.

The militant anti-plot faction within Lef promoted montage as the best replacement for narrative. Building upon the aesthetic experiments of the Constructivists, the factographers repurposed the formal operation of cutting and pasting to noetic ends. For Tret'iakov and Chuzhak, montage was not just a way of making art but an entire syntax of thought, a singularly materialist method for investigating the world and extrapolating its structural laws. According to Chuzhak, works made using montage assembly were more faithful to the heterogeneity of the world because they preserved the concrete factual details of matter rather than blurring the differences between phenomena through false continuity. "Members of Lef cultivate photomontage (tentatively) because they see in it a bridge from 'nonobjectivity' to 'matter,' from 'cognition' to 'construction,' from 'generalization' that is illusionistic and symbolic to 'particularism' that is concrete and real."[22] Chuzhak dubbed this method "facto-montage."[23] In other contexts, this procedure of materialist thought-assembly was known as "documentation." In a 1923 essay on the sociology of knowledge, Karl Mannheim thus distinguished the "documentary world-picture" from two others: the "expressive world-picture," which was the realm of conscious effort and intention, and the "representational world-picture," which was the realm of form and content. Mannheim did not consider "documentary" to be an artistic genre à la John Grierson, but instead saw a mode of cognition, a strategy for organizing reality into intelligible ensembles without subordinating it to subjective will or masking its details under the veil of metaphor:

> The search for documentary meaning, for an identical, homologous pattern underlying a vast variety of totally different realizations of meaning, belongs to a class apart that should not be confused with either addition, or synthesis, or the mere abstraction of a common property shared by a number of objects. It is something apart because the coalescence of different objects as well as the existence of something identical pervading an entire range of differences is specific to the realm of meaning and intention and must be kept uncontaminated by metaphors which have been derived at least in part from the working of spatial and manipulatory imagination.[24]

For Mannheim, the documentary method that flourished in the 1920s offered a way to make sense of the world that did not rely either on the associationist syntax of the imagination (poetry) or on abstract theoretical concepts (philosophy). As the semiotician Viacheslav Ivanov later explained, the ubiquity of montage in the interwar period reflected a pervasive shift toward documentary discontinuity in the knowledge-architectures of the time. "Regarding the analogues of montage in the sciences, it should be pointed out that the 1920s saw the beginning of the triumph of the principle of discretization in a diverse variety of sciences and the beginning of the 'montage' of entire sciences—the creation of new sciences on the basis of 'montage suturing.'"[25]

Like other Marxists in the empiriocritical tradition, the factographers believed that ideology was less a matter of explicit political messaging than an itinerary or movement of thought, a specific manner of assembling sensations and their corresponding concepts into a coherent totality of experience. Systems of knowledge and belief diverged under capitalism and socialism not because these societies were based upon different facts, but because each organized the same facts differently. Eisenstein, who emerged from the same Proletkul't school of Machism as Tret'iakov and who had thought more about montage-cognition than any other member of his generation, argued that the ideological value of a given fact was dictated not by its semantic content but by its position in a larger constellation of facts. "Content—the act of containing—is an *organizational principle*. The principle of the organization of thinking is in actual fact the 'content' of a work. . . . Nobody believes that the content of a newspaper consists of a report about the Kellogg Pact, a scandal from the Gazette de France or an account of an everyday event like a drunken husband murdering his wife with a hammer on waste ground. The *content* of a newspaper is the principle by which the *contents* of the paper are organized and processed, with the aim of processing the reader from a class-based standpoint." Faced with the question of how capitalists and socialists could share the same world but still inhabit different realities, Eisenstein gives a thoroughly Bogdanovite answer: the distinction lies in their respective organization. The facts may be identical, but they produce divergent political effects based on the way they are assembled. From this perspective, the ideological battle for socialism will be won not by revealing the truth about the facts, but by putting these facts into the right order. "Herein lies the gulf that separates the content of a proletarian newspaper from the content of a bourgeois newspaper even though their factual contents are the same."[26]

Of the many proposals that were advanced for the new plotless prose of fact, it was the ocherk, or sketch, that eventually won out. Combining the occasionalism of essay-writing and the empiricism of the scientific article with the actuality of newspaper journalism, this nonfiction prose form became one of the most pervasive types of literary production in the Soviet Union by the end of the 1920s. While Tret'iakov and his Lef colleagues did not invent the ocherk, whose origins lay in the sketches of the *raznochinets* intelligentsia in the 1840s, the factographers were widely recognized for single-handedly resuscitating this subliterary genre and for imbuing it with an "essentially new quality" that resonated with the culture of the reconstruction period.[27] Tret'iakov tirelessly promoted ocherkizm as a strategy of writing that hewed closer to sensation and experience than any genre of narrative fiction. Equally important for him was the fact that this minor form required little skill or training in the craft of writing, making it a perfect vehicle for literary *massovost'* ("mass quality") during the Cultural Revolution (1928–31). Tret'iakov's campaign evidently resonated widely, considering the popularity that this once-marginal form came to enjoy by the end of the 1920s. The year 1929 alone saw the founding of two prominent journals dedicated to ocherki, *The Literary Newspaper* and *Our Achievements*; the establishment of a standing body to promote the genre called the Production Council of Ocherkists (led by editors of the recently shuttered *Novyi Lef* such as Chuzhak, Kushner, Pertsov, and Tret'iakov);[28] and the inauguration of permanent ocherk exhibitions in Moscow that featured texts and photos by Tret'iakov, who was already widely recognized as a master of the new form.[29]

The meteoric ascent and institutionalization of the ocherk was enabled by three of its formal features. First, ocherki are swift. Taken from the verb *ochertit'* ("to draw a line around"), the ocherk simply circumscribes its object indexically, nothing more.[30] It does not reflect on such abstract things as meaning, essence, character, or any metaphysical value, but instead just records the superficial features of its subject matter quickly, mechanically, and impressionistically. The syntax of the ocherk is compressed and stenographic. Often no more than a single page in length, ocherki enjoyed a celerity unique among literary forms. All other aspects of the genre would indeed be secondary to the defining criteria of speed and punctuality: "The superiority of the ocherk consists only in the fact that it is faster getting to places other genres are not able to make it. The ocherk is a certain kind of light cavalry unit."[31] Unlike lumbering cultural forms like the novel and painting that always arrive on the scene too late, the ocherk could grapple with the facts of revolutionary society that arose on short notice. The ocherk was "the leading scout of literature," and the ocherkist, in turn, a "reconnaissance agent" and a "writer on wheels."[32] For authors who bemoaned the delays of literature, the ocherk alone seemed capable of overcoming the lag of consciousness and engaging operatively with the present.

Second, ocherki are small, modular, and eminently suitable for montage assembly. They typically appear alongside other ocherki in newspapers, journals, anthologies, reference works, and other textual meta-ensembles. Ocherki move in swarms. Indeed, examining a single ocherk on its own reveals little about the distinctive features of the genre, which instead requires studying the aggregate properties and formatting protocols that allow these texts to coalesce into larger collections. Every ocherk invokes the prospect of a composite literature, a kind of molar writing that is constituted from numerous distinct particles. In this respect, the ocherk proves to be the perfect literary corollary to the modern fact, as described by Lorraine Daston: "The typical fact was . . . a discrete event, cleanly severed from those preceding and following it, an atom of experience. Although facts could be strung together in narrations, like pearls on a chain, they could ideally also be unstrung and recombined into quite different narratives, without losing their well-bounded, small-radius, rounded self-sufficiency."[33] The ideological significance of an individual ocherk taken on its own remains ambiguous. But, like the mineral outcroppings that Tret'iakov's geologists marked out on the map, these short, impressionistic reports could be compiled and arranged to illuminate the laws at work below the surface of reality. Through skilled editorial assembly, masses of ocherki could help to reveal the general line at a time of historical transition.

Third, and finally, the ocherk is plotless. The authoritative *Literary Encyclopedia* states that the ocherk captures "static situations that do not serve as a starting point for movement."[34] Like a photographic snapshot, the sketch is a record of a moment, and not even a decisive one. The ocherk lacks dramatic peripeteia or the drive to conclude. Inspired by the psychologically flat and strictly chronometric time of the League, the ocherkist divides subjective experience into a series of interchangeable instants that are prompt, non-cumulative, and, as Tret'iakov would say, "infinitely thin." The reversible, qualitatively uninflected micro-time of the ocherk casts off the chains of inevitability that link episodes together into longer narrative sequences. Hence, too, the open-ended structure of ocherk collections themselves, which can always be rearranged and supplemented at a later date. These collections are best characterized not as works but as projects, for they presume an additive writing that is forever in process and a knowledge that is tentative and incomplete.

The popularity of ocherki in the 1920s reflected a pervasive sense that the telic closure of narrative genres like the novel was, on some profound structural level, antithetical to the ongoing and unconsummated nature of existence during the transitional period. In his essay "The Decomposition of Plot," Brik protested against the false continuity that storytelling imposed on its material: "Every plot construction necessarily does violence by selecting from its material only that which serves the development of the plot; whatever it selects is distorted to those ends [*в тех же целях*]. By selecting and distorting in this way, a unity of plot is created—what we commonly call the totality [*цельность*] of the work. And this totality is achieved by suppressing the individual traits of the material being treated."[35] Since antiquity, philosophers and fabulists had considered the thrust toward resolution to be one of the most important, if not constitutive, features of narrative form. Here Brik identified this quality as *tsel'nost'*, a word that conveys both gestalt closure and striving for a goal, both totality and teleology. Plot creates an integral whole by fusing a set of discontinuous episodes into an Aristotelian "unity of action" (*единство действия*), but in the process suppresses the unique features that make each of these individual episodes pluripotent, singular, and originary in itself. Within the closed world of the plot, every action is read symptomatically and in reverse, as it were, from a future point when the action-sequence has been completed. Barthes called this expectation of a formal closure to come the "proairetic" economy of narrative (*proairesis* being "the human faculty of deliberating in advance the result of an action"). Because the causal chains of narrative demand a mode of reception which reads events backward from the result of the depicted action, these events will never be experienced by the reader as indeterminate or unresolved. The proairetic projection "commits the very future of the story," writes Barthes, so that every deed, even in the present of its unfolding, is effectively already concluded.[36] The reader makes "an interested determination based upon a form of privileged knowledge, ex post facto applied to a process that is supposed to be open-ended."[37] Narrative sequence thus enacts a mode of reading that forecloses the possibility that events could be ever experienced in their nascency, as unfinished moments not yet assigned to a particular future. These acts are never truly contingent, undecided, or alive, but are instead always measured against an anticipated outcome. The result is a paradox that defines the modern novel as a genre: on the one hand, the novel is propelled by the powerful diegetic drive that philosophers like Bakhtin associated with an open horizon of futurity, but on the other, this forward thrust always presumes a final state of resolution and closure. For all of its celebrated dynamism, the novel secretly strives toward stasis and equilibrium. It obeys the logic of the "already-written, already-read, already-done."[38]

Tret'iakov insisted that factical prose and cinema, by contrast, should never seek "to reach plot equilibrium toward the end."[39] Factography must never arrive at a resting state. The refusal of dramatic resolution was especially glaring in a book like *The Summons* (1930), which many reviews criticized for its abrupt and precipitous ending. One praised Tret'iakov's writing for its exceptional energy and tension, but complained that "the voltage drops off sharply toward the end": it seemed that "the author didn't make it" to the book's last page.[40] Because Tret'iakov did not elevate any particular episode in the story over the others, the structure of the book displayed "an arbitrary quality," wrote another reviewer.[41] It was an arbitrariness that was reflected in the rigorously chronometric, qualitatively bereft time of the book's three sections: *1928 (July)*, *1929 (October)*, and *1930 (January)*. Like "Moscow–Beijing," *The Summons* concludes not with an ending but with a static snapshot, this time a "Bulletin about the combine The Summons on May 12" that lists a series of facts, percentages, and other quantitative data from a single day in 1930. Tret'iakov would seem to be more interested in counting and bookkeeping than in storytelling. The next installment in the kolkhoz series, *A Month in the Country (June–July 1930)* (1931), extended this sequence of discrete instants.

Tret'iakov then named the final book in the kolkhoz series *One Thousand and One Days of Labor* (1934) after the famous collection of Arabic folktales, a reference that reflected the enumerative principle and episodic structure of all of his ocherki.

The open structure of Tret'iakov's kolkhoz books was well suited to their subject matter. The agricultural mode of production generates a time that is ongoing and unfinished. Between sowing and reaping, reaping and sowing, the metabolism of life and labor at the Communist Lighthouse is formatted by generational cycles, seasonal rhythms, and meteorological patterns that lay outside the linear logic of accumulation which structures the industrial-capitalist mode of production. In his classical study *Capitalism and Agriculture*, the Russian economist Sergei Bulgakov channeled Bergson, explaining that farm labor undermines the very premise of teleological thinking: "Each epoch furnishes new facts and new forces of historical evolution—the creative power of history never runs dry. Therefore, any prognosis with regard to the future, which is based on the results of the present, must necessarily be in error. . . . The veil of the future is impenetrable."[42] Nowhere are the unforeseeability of the future and the creative potential of the present more pronounced than in the village, which must always reckon with the uncontrolled spontaneity of nature. Tret'iakov's kolkhozniki are constantly caught off-guard, subjected to abrupt turns in history that "threw off all of their calculations" (*Vyzov*, 316). "It's a lottery," Chebotarev tells him: "You can't guess what will happen" (*Vyzov*, 48). Each individual moment in *The Summons* affords its own opportunities and risks, and each, in turn, bifurcates into its own distinct and divergent future. Life in Tret'iakov's countryside is a game of chance, his peasantry a race of gamblers. For books published in the era of Five-Year Plans, Tret'iakov's kolkhoz collections in fact turn out to be willfully, even dangerously skeptical of the idea of centralized planning and its presumption to control the future. Tret'iakov openly criticizes the Party for its ignorance of the periphery (he points out that *Pravda* is always getting facts about the Communist Lighthouse wrong), and chastises Moscow officials for oversights like sending tractors to the farm without also sending the spark plugs to go with them. For all of its resources and vaunted providence, the Party proves incapable of penetrating the veil of the future.

The syntactically enumerative, narratively inconclusive, and psychologically uninflected structure of Tret'iakov's kolkhoz sketches revived the tradition of the medieval annal, a form of historiography that hewed closely to symbolically impoverished registers of everyday life. Agapov pointed out that factography evinced a "much stronger connection to the *realia* of time" than plotted forms like the novel, which aspired to elevate mundane events into *realoria* that were spiritually perfected and teleologically illuminated.[43] A book like *The Summons*, which concludes with a stark list of data about the kolkhoz from a single day, renounced the vertical dimension of existence in favor of purely additive recordkeeping. These serial notations may have looked back to the *realia* of the medieval annal but, far more importantly for the factographers, they looked forward to the machine-logic of modern technical systems. As Wolfgang Ernst notes, "early medieval forms of registering events (in the annalistic tradition as opposed to chronicles and historiography proper) convey a way of experiencing reality in terms of not continuous but discrete time, thus closer to state-based automata with discrete writing or reading of symbols on an endless memory tape."[44] The austere, annalistic inscription of events in *The Summons* follows the same quantitative clock-time that was being promoted by the machine fanatics in the League in the 1920s.[45] "Not one assignment without a time limit, not one task without measuring," Gastev had stipulated.[46]

Tret'iakov compared factography to a conveyer belt that moves materials forward according to a precise timetable ("Biography of the Object," 61). Ticking like a metronome, the mechanical time of this writing taps into the deep phenomenological rhythms that structure and enable all variety of collective endeavor. According to Bogdanov, the inorganic time of the clock "co-ordinates and regulates *all* our social and labour life, daily communications, and spatial and temporal relationships of human action."[47] Factography submits to the temporality of these punctual rhythms, which media theorist John Durham Peters has distinguished categorically from the linear, cumulative time of the calendar: "Calendars deal in what the Greeks called *khronos*, time as duration or span; clocks deal in *kairos*, time as moment or point. Calendars are chronic; clocks are acute. As a rule, clocks indicate the immediate moment, but lack memory or foresight. Curious automata, strange little personae with their 'faces' and 'hands,' clocks say the same thing over and over again, and yet the information they provide is always fresh. They tell you where the 'now' falls in the day."[48] The acute temporality of *The Summons* is that of an alarm clock that rings continuously, a Now-time in perpetuity. Calendars help people to plan ahead, but also to delay; clocks, on the other hand, irritate and goad their users, fueling "the need to take action" on a profound bodily register.[49] The clock's insistent deictic gesturing toward the present came to dominate life in the transitional period, even to the point of absorbing the old linear calendar into its presentist logic. Robert Bird has observed the striking proliferation of tear-off calendars after October, a format of timekeeping that presumes a today unconnected to yesterday and tomorrow, and one that recognizes only two coordinates, the old and the new. Like the newspaper, the tear-off calendar exists for twenty-four hours, just two cycles of the clock. Its flat temporality challenged "a more complicated accounting of time, measured in statistics of production, construction, and participation under the terms of the Five-Year Plans." Whereas the Plans understood the present moment as "a relative position in an abstract scheme [rather] than a material locus in real space-time," the clock-time of the League and of the factographers supercharged every day with kairotic potential.[50] As Peters puts it, "clocks raise the [Leninist] question 'What is to be done?' in a more intense way than do calendars."[51]

Each of these two time-critical technologies had its literary counterpart, ocherk and novel. The latter presumes an eventual cessation of time, a proairetic point at the conclusion of the story from which all actions will make sense. The novelist, to recall Chuzhak's phrase, is "the most 'plan-oriented' writer of our day." This is why Lukács insisted that novels cannot be written in the present tense but are instead always ex post facto reconstructions. Given the "necessary distance in narration, which permits the selection of the essential after the action," the meaning of the events in a novel "could be revealed only in retrospect" ("Narrate or Describe?," 129). The timeworn distinction between description (*ekphrasis*) and narration (*diegesis*), which Lukács aligns generically with reportage and the novel, ultimately boils down to two basic temporal orientations: "Description contemporizes everything. Narration recounts the past. One describes what one sees, and the spatial 'present' confers a temporal 'present' on men and objects" ("Narrate or Describe?," 130). For Lukács, present-day experience precludes the certainty of objective knowledge. In order to "cognize" (*познавать*) reality, as Chuzhak would put it, the unfolding narrative must first come to an end. Lukács thus explained about Tolstoy's metapoetically titled story "After the Ball": "It is clear that all the nuances of the events at the ball could be revealed only in retrospect from the gauntlet scene. The 'contemporary' observer, who could not view the ball from this perspective or retrospectively at all, would have had to see and describe other, insignificant and superficial details" ("Narrate or Describe?," 129). In narrating events with one specific end in mind, the novelist inevitably attends to those details that belong to this projection while discarding those that would lead to other potential teloi. In so doing, she recuperates random incidents as actions that are necessary and purposive. By contrast, the ocherkist leaves these incidents unresolved and unredeemed, resulting in a kaleidoscopic array of details that must be counted and enumerated mechanically one by one. In the present tense of factography, "the 'peripheral' begins to bloom everywhere," concludes Lukács.

Lukács's account of description and narration reprises, in a narratological mode, the same law of consciousness that was explored earlier in this book: experience can become an object of thought only after it is over. As Lukács puts it, "the involved complexity of patterns of life is clarified only at the conclusion." For "the epic poet who narrates a single life or an assemblage of lives retrospectively makes the essential aspects selected by life clear and understandable. . . . The use of the past tense in the epic is thus a basic technique prescribed by reality for achieving artistic order and organization" ("Narrate or Describe?," 133, 127–28). Critics of factical cinema echoed the claim that events become knowable and representable only at the conclusion of their indeterminate becoming.

One of Vertov's detractors wrote, for example, that a "film on a contemporary theme . . . can be produced only at some distance in time only retrospectively, from those elements which have already been shaped in life into definite, clear, crystallized forms, assimilated and digested by consciousness."[52] Details that might appear random or accidental in plotted works are just a ruse, since nothing actually escapes the closed economy of the narrative. The system of plot transforms the noise of positivity into a reality effect of a higher order, a sign that denotes accident but that is not in fact accidental. For there is no true randomness in the finite universe of the novel. "The author in his omniscience knows the special significance of each petty detail for the final solution and for the final revelation of character since he introduces only details that contribute to his goals" ("Narrate or Describe?," 127–28).

This incessant striving toward closure and finality prompted Tynianov to remark that narrative prose "lives by the immense power of inertia." In a 1924 survey of the literary scene titled "The Interval," he explained that novels are driven by a desire for equilibrium and, for this reason, "inevitably end . . . with the death of the protagonist."[53] For all of its diverse varieties of drama, every novel shares the same bleak conclusion: the demise of its commissioning hero. The reader's anticipation of this death casts a shadow of fatefulness over the individual episodes in the story, all of which points to a single outcome. In his 1928 essay "The End of the Novel," Osip Mandelstam argued that this element of predestination defined the genre as such: "The novel may be distinguished from the novella, the chronicle, memoirs, or any other prose genre by the fact that it is a closed compositional narrative, extensive but complete in itself, having to do with the fate [*судьба*] of one person or a group of persons."[54] The proairetic desire that binds the attention of the reader can be satisfied only at the end, when the main character is consigned to her destiny and the sequence of actions is concluded. Through this act of systemic closure, the novel transforms randomness into repetition, movement into inertia, and chaos into equilibrium. This is why the novel, despite its debt to biographical genres, has so often been associated with death and stasis rather than life. "What draws the reader to a novel is the hope of warming his shivering life with a death he reads about."[55] The novel's hostility to change and open-ended becoming prompted critic Peter Brooks to associate the machinery of plot with Freud's death drive, since both long for a state of cessation, both desire an end to desire.[56] As Chuzhak put it, the novel cultivates a "taste for 'the deceased.'" From the first page, the reader senses that the story is already complete and that the end of the hero's life is in the offing. "With its doctrines of predetermination and doom," the novel looks upon "the human from a fatalistic perspective [*в роковом разрезе*]," wrote Tret'iakov ("Biography of the Object," 59). It affords its reader the grim satisfaction of watching a slow and protracted descent toward an all-too-predictable demise.

Not so factography, which abandoned the novel's morbid romance with death to make space for abrupt turns in history. Tret'iakov's efforts to divert fate produced striking results in a book like *Den Shi-Khua* (1930), which sought, against the odds, to divorce the eponymous hero from his narrative destiny.[57] Based upon a series of interviews that the factographer conducted in Moscow with a radicalized student from Beijing, *Den Shi-Khua* ends suddenly when his leading man disappears while still in the middle of recounting his life, leaving Tret'iakov to speculate about Den's fate and, by metonymic extension, the fate of the Chinese Revolution itself. Even more disconcertingly, after Den's abrupt departure, the book is effectively unwritten when his acquaintance Tin Iuin-Pin then turns up in Moscow and informs Tret'iakov that much of Den's life-story had been fabricated. Tin insists that Den had never been interested in political activism and, worse still, that he was a great lover of art, wrote fiction passionately, and was an accomplished ballroom dancer. Thus, after some four hundred pages recounting the young Den's rebellion against tradition, his father's support of Sun Yat-Sen, his study of Marx and Kropotkin, and his induction into the mores of revolutionary life, Tin's testimony at the end of the book turns this account on its head in one stroke. Rather than end with "the final revelation of character," as Lukács said of the novel, *Den Shi-Khua* instead ends with the final concealment of character.[58]

Tret'iakov is unfazed by the sudden scrambling of destiny, an eventuality that every good factographer expects anyway. The conflict between the testimonies of Den and Tin remains insoluble, but, then again, revealing the truth of Den's character had never been Tret'iakov's objective. For Presentists who deny that the past determines the future, whether a hero's life-story is real or invented turns out to be irrelevant, since today's petty-bourgeois aesthete might still become tomorrow's revolutionary. Faced with the two irreconcilable accounts, Tret'iakov cannot bring his book to a close, even at a structural level. Instead he keeps supplementing *Den Shi-Khua*, first with another collection of letters, then with a "Postscript" written two years after Den's disappearance, then with still more remarks under the heading "P.S." Here, as elsewhere, the anti-narrative, purely additive logic of factography gives rise to an interminable text. Every book "should end with the words *to be continued*," Tret'iakov observes (*Den Shi-Khua*, 4). Tret'iakov further noted that maintaining this structural openness posed a particular challenge to the biographer. "Even if it is possible on these grounds to distribute all of the material into neat compartments, this is possible only after the last line of the necrologue. And until the necrologue has been written, a person represents constant movement and you can never rule out the possibility that the very same configuration of personal traits which at one moment may seem dominant and decisive will turn out in the next stage to be a complex that is onerous, inhibiting, and incorrect."[59] For Tret'iakov, traditional biographical methods were ill suited for revolutionary times, when human character constantly changes to suit historical circumstances.[60] Each discrete moment and each new life-context demanded a different persona. When Benjamin visited Moscow, for example, he was struck by the way that city and inhabitants alike were subjected to continuous *remont* (reconstruction), whether the porter who was leaving his post in the hotel lobby for a job at the Kremlin or the director of the Theater of the Revolution, Matvei Zalka, who had previously served as a general in the Red Army.[61] In the transitional period, biographies that began on one particular path rarely concluded on it as well. According to Tret'iakov, only the necrologist—a storyteller authorized by death—is able to plot out a biography with certainty. But for the factographer who writes about lives that are still unfolding such as Den's, every "configuration of personality traits" is only tentative. "One minute you're basing your work on one sociobiological type, and the next minute this type is declared unsuitable and antirevolutionary" ("New Leo Tolstoy," 48). As a result, there will always be more revisions to make and more postscripts to add.

Under these circumstances, knowledge of the past turns out to be no more certain or stable than knowledge of the future. Each time that historical events redirect the destiny of Den, they also rearrange his memories, bringing minor episodes and details to the fore that were previously glossed over but that now, in light of new developments, prove to have been decisive in leading him to the current moment. Present events are constantly infecting the past in *Den Shi-Khua*, reaching back like Tin's testimony to revise what we know about Den. This is evident even at the level of grammar, through verb tenses that scumble the distinction between the past of historical events and the present in which they are recounted to Tret'iakov. Many of Den's deepest childhood memories are related in the present tense and imperfective aspect as if they were taking place right now. Other scenes lack verbs entirely and, like the final paragraph of "Moscow–Beijing," float untethered in time without clear indication of where exactly they fall in the sequence of events. These passages often begin simply with the word "now" (*сейчас*), a deictic indicator that oscillates ambiguously between the time of Den's past and the winter of 1927 when he recalls his life to the factographer. With each such "now," the reader is reminded that "*Den Shi-Khua* was made by two people," as Tret'iakov put it, and that their perspectives will not ever fully coincide.[62] Hence the decision to designate *Den Shi-Khua* a "bio-interview" rather than a mere "biography": Den's story is not his own but a collaboration, the product of a complex negotiation between two parallax views, one interior to historical events and one exterior to it. In his introduction to a later edition, Pertsov thus directed readers to pay special attention to the shifts in the writing between the first and the third person, to those moments when the vantage of Den's *I* abuts, often discordantly, against Tret'iakov's *he*.[63] For Pertsov, these grammatical frictions constituted one of the most important formal innovations of *Den Shi-Khua* and distinguished the bio-interview from genres like the novel and the memoire. If the deep mnemonic sedimentation of the Proustian *roman pur* creates a "pure interiority" that "acknowledges no exteriority," as Benjamin put it, then Tret'iakov's bio-interview follows the opposite program, an anti-*Remembrance* that repeatedly interjects the third person and asserts the power of the present over the past.[64] In contrast to the novelist who is in search of lost time, the factographer is always "in search of the present time" (*в поисках настоящего времени*), Agapov wrote.[65]

Defenders of the novel were irked by the incursions of the present into the past. Even in those passages of *Den Shi-Khua* that were written in the preterite tense they sensed the creeping hand of the present reaching back to meddle with historical memory. As one example, Lukács flagged the scene in which Den recalls listening to his father agitating when he was five years old. The speech that is recounted in the book offers a remarkably precise and detailed analysis of the political crossroads at which the Chinese revolutionaries found themselves in 1907. And yet, as Lukács points out, in order for the scene to be temporally consistent with the rest of the text, it would have to be filtered through the perspective of a young boy who, one assumes, would have only a limited grasp of the concepts of political economy. The complex speech is clearly that of an adult, present-day Den. According to Lukács, much more is at stake in this lapse than just the permeability of organic memory. For him, this corruption of the past is a symptom of the general tendency in factography to subordinate all moments in time to the standpoint and interests of the present ("Reportage or Portrayal?," 61). Indeed, Tret'iakov takes an approach in *Den Shi-Khua* that is not just anti-narrative but explicitly anti-historicist. As he explains in the book's introduction, the technique of the bio-interview is instead structural or topographical in nature: Den "presented the magnificent subsoil of his memory to me appreciatively. I dug around in it like a miner, probing it, blasting it apart, shearing it off, sifting and elutriating it" (*Den Shi-Khua*, 3). Tret'iakov's method is that of an archaeologist who views time not as a linear continuum but as a spatial constellation. Sorting through the past, he brings these different memory-artifacts into contact with one another and then fuses them together in the crucible of the present. The mechanical clock-time of the factographer, which recognizes only the Now, presumes "the total simultaneity of all that was previously historically non-simultaneous."[66] To the novelist, time appears as a one-way arrow, its contents irrecoverably lost to the past, but Tret'iakov keeps all moments in time at the disposal of the present.

Den represented what Tret'iakov called a "casus" (*казус*).[67] Distinct from the everyday Russian word for "case" or "incident" (*случай*), this juridical term designates a certain kind of legal quandary that defies resolution. According to the linguist André Jolles, who wrote extensively on the subject during the interwar period, the specificity of the casus "lies in the fact that it asks the question, but cannot give the answer; that it imposes the duty of judgment upon us, but does not itself contain the judgment—what becomes manifest in it is the act of weighing, but not the result of the weighing."[68] As an example of one such call to judgment, Jolles cited a recent news item about a pickpocket's lover who profited from a crime for which she was not directly responsible. For Jolles, this particular casus exposed the inadequacy of a legal system that could recognize categorical distinctions between right and wrong but not qualitative gradations of moral conscience. (Here, the pickpocket's lover may not be legally culpable, but she still shares in his guilt.) Depending on one's vantage, "the crime can mean two very different things," Jolles writes. News items like these, which "point not to a law but rather to a hole in the law," suggest that the very foundation of legality "has been weighed and found wanting, that the standard of the law is here an inadequate measure of value." In this way, the casus invokes "a morality with mobile judgments of value" (*Simple Forms*, 158).

Transitional culture had great use for such a morality. As Tret'iakov no doubt recognized from his time studying law during the crisis years of the First World War, the casus was a particularly valuable resource for societies in which changing norms of behavior were constantly coming into conflict with institutional authority. The only way to navigate dynamic circumstances like these was to become a "clever and crafty casuist," he wrote.[69] Having once flourished in the particularist, detail-oriented culture of the baroque, the art of casuistry had disappeared with the Enlightenment's turn to categorical thinking, but, as we saw in the previous chapter, October had rekindled the need for a science of the singular.[70] This historical phase confirmed Wittgenstein's formula *Die Welt ist alles, was der Fall ist*: "The world is everything that 'falls,' everything that 'comes about,' 'everything that is the *case*'—by case, let us understand *casus*: *at once occurrence and chance*, that which comes about in the mode of the unforeseeable, and yet of being" (*Philosophy of the Encounter*, 190). Tret'iakov observed that Soviet society had entered a phase "when social maneuvering must be maximally flexible [*гибкость . . . предельна*] and when directives change in response to the day's events. Today, almost from the moment you go on the attack, you are already running for cover" ("New Leo Tolstoy," 48). Chuzhak too wrote of the "maximal suppleness" (*максимальная гибкость*) that culture and morality must exhibit in the transitional period ("K metodologii kul'tury," 39). The factographer's role under these circumstances was not to deliver tidy solutions to the problems of the day, as was the practice of the proletarian realists, but to confront the reader with facts about changing norms, moral conflicts, and other holes in the law.

With its endless stream of unconcluded and inconclusive incidents, the newspaper was a rich source of casuistic thinking. Less so narrative literature, which was inclined toward closure and judgment. Jolles thus distinguished the casus from a comparable short prose form like the novella, whose plotted construction drives toward resolution, and with this settlement, brings the investigation to a close. Along similar lines, Tret'iakov differentiated the "fabulist" who "presents a novella" from the factographer who presents "an assortment of cases."[71] The narrative ambiguity of factography arrests the forward movement of the story in order to submit its episodes to investigation and scrutiny. The casus strives to "keep the matter open."[72] Den Shi-Khua, for example, might be either a revolutionary or an aesthete, depending on whose testimony you believe. But the point for Tret'iakov was not to pronounce a judgment. How the story ended was ultimately irrelevant, since Den's "configuration of personality traits" might always change yet again. There would always be further postscripts to add. Indeed, for all of his interest in forensic methods of detection and analysis, Tret'iakov actually cared little about the final outcome of this process. More important than knowing the right answer was being able to pose the right question and having the right method to work through the problem.

But renouncing plot, as the factographers proposed, created a host of formal challenges for writers and scenarists. Without the binding force of the storyline, the factographic work falls apart into a series of discrete incidents. Critics were swift to point to this danger. "Rejecting plot-construction as 'fiction,' as something that seems inevitably to distort 'the reality of facts,' the Lefists wound up in a dead end, because it is easy to 'reject' something in theory—but what about in practice?"[73] For Mikhail Luzgin, secretary of the Leningrad division of RAPP, the purely annalistic enumerations of the factographers were no solution to this problem: "The material follows a kind of drift; here events are presented in the same sequence in which they appeared to the itinerant author."[74] The prominent journalist Mikhail Kol'tsov likewise warned authors against the additive logic of factography, which he compared to sausage links (*колбасы*) that followed one upon the other in endless seriation.[75] The factographers themselves were hardly unaware of these challenges. "The question has arisen today about what should replace the plot in factual prose," announced Shklovsky ("K tekhnike vne-siuzhetnoi prozy," 224–25). He saw promise in the ostensive strategy of *A Sixth Part of the World* but ultimately concluded that "the example of Dziga Vertov demonstrates that the total negation of the plot solves nothing." The Formalist didn't see how it would be possible to disavow plot without also abandoning aesthetic construction as such and dissolving the artwork into a heap of disconnected parts that were, in principle, infinite in number. Indeed, Shklovsky's chief concern was that plotless works went on forever, in violation of all sense of proportion and measure. For him, waxing on "a planetary scale" in Vertov's odic manner was the "childhood illness of works that are beyond plot."[76]

In the West, too, critics worried about the planetary scale of factical prose and film. Weimar novelist Hermann Broch traced its formlessness to the mindless infinity of the daily newspaper:

> If [reportage] were actually going to succeed at the task of capturing the world, the entire world, just as it is—that is, without selecting anything in particular—then it would not only become just as never-ending as the world itself, as never-ending as the wicked endlessness of the newspaper that mirrors the world; not only would it have to string together fact upon fact in an eternal iteration, but it would not even be able to draw connections between the punctual facts. There are certain psychotics whose monstrous obsession with facts compels them to record and register all events, although they cannot link them together: you find resonances of this in the mind of most newspaper readers or Americans who travel around the world and return home with a collection of data from a guidebook. Something similar would be the ultimate result of any truly rigorous reportage.

Following the empiriocritical method, factical writing atomizes the contents of the mind into a cloud-chaos of data and sensations, leading Broch to conclude that "if reportage were actually consistent, it would, for its part, necessarily lead directly to insanity."[77] Thomas Mann voiced similar concerns when he compared the journalist's ambition "to narrate life as it once narrated itself" to an attempt "to drink up the entire ocean." Any positivistic program for remainderless recording would devolve into a "madness of precision," he wrote.[78] For novelists like Broch and Mann, then, the torrent of facts that streamed through the newspaper didn't just erode plot, it deterritorialized consciousness. The literature of fact birthed a generation of psychotics.

The lapse into aimless drift was what alarmed Grierson about the cinema of fact as well. He cautioned that the chronicle film "has gone dithering on, mistaking the phenomenon for the thing in itself, and ignoring everything that gave it the trouble of conscience and penetration and thought."[79] It offered no insights or access to a higher reality. A film like Vertov's *Enthusiasm* (1931) was for Grierson "completely un-Bolshevik," since it failed to penetrate the veil of appearances and even contradicted the very premise of linear progress that underwrote the policies of the Five-Year Plan. "If the film is any guide, they will be doing in year five the job they already did in year two; they will repeat themselves endlessly." To be sure, Grierson could not help but admire the affective intensity of Vertov's first sound film, which roused its audiences with complex montage syncopations, arresting visual effects, acousmatic sound modulations, and other striking technical inventions. But it failed to displace these "excitements" forward, to discharge these forces by directing them toward a determinate goal. "It all leads nowhere, but it certainly leads furiously." The Soviet film of fact stimulates the spectator through modern psychotechnical means, but instead of then channeling this affective frenzy into a purposive narrative, Vertov leaves the energies of his spectator unbound and without destination. For Grierson, *Enthusiasm* did not reflect a nation that was moving decisively into the future. "Whatever the band of buglers at its head, a film must march somewhere. This film is all bugling and marching and marching and bugling."[80] The film of fact invoked motion without movement and accumulation without summation, an overheated state of enthusiasm with no object of satisfaction or prospect of release in sight.

A QUANTUM OF CHANGE

The Janus face of sensory overload is boredom. As we know from Georg Simmel, the unremitting stimulation of modern life, its kaleidoscopic barrage of impressions, eventually wears out the nerves, inducing a blasé attitude and a general intellectualism of spirit. The factographers were keenly aware of this dialectic in their own work, which oscillated continuously between amazement and monotony, innervation and enervation. They pummeled the nervous system of spectators and readers with the attractions of fact, but refused to sublimate the energies thus conjured through figurative cathexis or narrative resolution. Without the imagination to regulate, direct, and give form to these affects, frustrated audiences grew indifferent. Brik acknowledged that "it's very boring and very uninteresting to collect facts, to delve into these facts, to connect them," and that, by contrast, "it creates a much bigger splash and is much easier to write a stagey story in which everything happens like in an opera or theater" ("Blizhe k faktu," 34). But rather than submit to the intoxications of plot, the factographers tarried in the tedium. "There is no need to fear taking 'uninteresting' moments as subjects for exposition," Chuzhak counseled budding ocherkists: "Nothing in nature is uninteresting." Only by investigating overlooked aspects of mundane life could the factographer hope to discover what Chuzhak called "natural plottedness" (*натуральная сюжетность*), a system of internal correspondences that demonstrated how matter is "plotted from within." "The secret of hidden plottedness does not lie in the flight from 'uninteresting' topics, but in just the opposite: fearlessly diving to the bottom of the 'uninteresting,' the 'simple,' the 'quotidian'—until you reveal the quotidian process (be it the process of working, of striking, of repairing trousers . . . whatever you can think of) in its inner being—in its technics!" ("Writer's Handbook," 90). Uncovering the obscure connections between these prosaic processes was the task of the discipline that Chuzhak called *bytologiia*, a "science of the everyday" that probed the routines, habits, and reflexes of mundane being in order to find the nerves that were still alive below "the callus formed on culture" ("K metodologii kul'tury," 48–54).

Restoring sensation to everyday life required reconditioning audiences who preferred tales of adventure to treatises on trouser repair. Training these readers would be difficult, but if there was one thing that the unlikely popularity of a dry journalistic genre like the ocherk had indicated, it was that the postrevolutionary generation was finally beginning to develop a taste for this kind of detail work. Factical prose and film found hospitable conditions in the practical and distinctly sober disposition of reconstruction Russia. If "it is possible to wage revolutionary struggle sitting in the office instead of the underground, sitting at a desk rather than standing at the barricades," as Brik insisted in "Against Romanticism," then factography was the perfect literature for this new class of white-collar revolutionaries.[81] One review of *103 Days in the West* described Kushner's ocherk collection as a "hot dry wind of a textbook"—a characterization meant as the highest compliment.[82] Tret'iakov celebrated the "pathos of the accountant," a state of arousal achieved not through dramatic catharsis but through analytical pastimes like problem-solving, forensic inquiry, and remainderless bookkeeping ("From Where," 214).[83] If factography had gained a reputation for being tedious, this was only because consumers of bourgeois culture wanted everything handed to them already processed and packaged. Tret'iakov attributed "the mistrust of educational films that people consider 'boring,'" for example, to the fact that these films "force lazy minds to work when they don't feel like it, whereas they can watch the fiction film without any difficulty."[84] For audiences accustomed to having the same old storylines spoon-fed to them (like "manna," griped Chuzhak), factography was coarse fare. Getting through it was hard work. The experience of tedium reflected readers' inability, or simply their unwillingness, to make use of the factographic text and set it in motion. "The reduction of reading to consumption is obviously responsible for the 'boredom' many feel in the presence of the modern ('unreadable') text, the avantgarde film or painting: to be bored means one cannot produce the text, play it, release it, *make it go*."[85] For a productivist like Tret'iakov, the most important books of the reconstruction period were the tedious ones that asked the reader to operationalize the text and that transformed her from a passive consumer of information into its active producer.

This hermeneutic labor demanded a different mode of reception than plotted genres. Instead of focusing the audience's attention like the novel, the Hollywood film, or other hot media, cool media like the ocherk and the newsreel called for vigilant but diffuse alertness. Readers and spectators learned to scan the text or work in search of any small changes or developments that could subsequently prove to be significant or dispositive. In this way, factography proved "in both theory and practice that even the tiniest fact of everyday life can be assessed with regard to its revolutionary quality," wrote Brik.[86] A literary precedent for this condition of heightened receptivity could be found in the nineteenth-century detection genres that required readers to be on the lookout for clues to solve the mystery of the crime. In his 1924 study *Observation*, discussed in chapter two, the psychologist Nikolai Levitov celebrated Sherlock Holmes as the most accomplished master of this perceptual activity. Conan Doyle's legendary creation—"the most perfect reasoning and observing machine that the world has seen"—was a consummate factographer whose every insight was "founded upon the observation of trifles."[87] Holmes always turns up the crucial clue somewhere other than where everyone expected to find it. This disparity between anticipation and resolution is in fact the entire structural conceit of detection genres, in which the storyline points in one direction but the truth of the matter is to be found in another. The tales of Poe, for example, are littered with evidence that leads nowhere and regularly conclude with endings that have no connection to preceding events. Full of plot detours and desultory discoursing, Conan Doyle's own stories are equally inefficient acts of storytelling. This observational prose is hardly suspenseful: it stimulates the reader's attention but does not bind it. It was precisely this resistance to the narrative momentum of fiction that prompted the critic Marjorie Nicolson to describe detective prose in 1929 as an "escape not from life, but from literature."[88] Revealing, against all expectations, how a trifling, unnoticed detail had ultimately determined the course of events, the observational genre demonstrates that even the tiniest fact could turn out to be historically decisive.

It was the same with newspaper readers who were expected to scan articles like detectives in search of clues. Theorists in newspaper studies encouraged vigilant attention to the facts while stipulating that readers should not become too fixated on the final outcome of these developments. Gus cautioned editors against big splashy stories, which risked overshadowing the abundance of lesser facts sent in by worker-correspondents: "'Uninteresting—just a trifle,' say the experts who edit the paper. 'The worker-correspondent: what did he see? An extremely limited tiny fragment of reality. It's a tiny floating particle and it's even written small.'" But "the real art [of organizing a newspaper] consists in being able to maintain the interest in details, to shape them into a picture, to generalize them correctly, neither exaggerating nor diminishing them. We have to be able to understand individual details, since powerful things will sometimes develop from them as if from an egg."[89] According to Gus, the newspaper demands active but equanimous attention and an ability to draw connections between trivial but potentially revolutionary developments that are still in their nascency. The micro-notations of worker-correspondents offer insight into things to come, provided they are configured correctly.

Media activist and public-sphere theorist Alexander Kluge later explained that creating a proletarian lifeworld requires abandoning totalizing narratives that subordinate all events to a master plot (what he called "dramaturgical incest") and cultivating more inclusive modes of reception instead. Every successful counter-public sphere is built upon an "economy of combined trivials."[90] One critic aligned with the factographers, Mikhail Bekker, thus insisted that the constellation of facts and details in a text should never succumb to the gravity of the psychological plot. Just because a gun appears in an ocherk does not mean that it must then be fired, he explained. "In a story, facts are never presented in isolation from one another. There, the fact is put in the service of the human; it is overgrown by an invisible fabric, a setting, a psychology. But the ocherkist often presents facts in a manner 'irrespective of the individual' that presents these facts as concrete magnitudes." In this regard, factography epitomized Lenin's adage that "facts are an obstinate thing": its trivials could not be assimilated to thought, but neither could they simply be ignored. In the ocherk, facts assert an existence beyond human interest and details refuse to express an underlying meaning.

The autonomization of fact in deplotted prose proved challenging to readers. "Because of this dynamic, people read an ocherk with less interest than a story that is composed in accordance with all the rules of a plotted intrigue," Bekker observed.[91] Factography, as we saw above, was haunted by the proliferation of unmotivated detail. This, for Chuzhak, was the essential formal quandary that their work faced: "Now that we've destroyed the prose story, what will hold together works that are beyond plot? This is hardly a trivial question. And not only because we have to put something equally 'captivating' in the place of the plotted prose that we struggle against, but also because the plot has until now been the most effective ligature for prose literature. Like verse without rhyme, prose falls to pieces without plot" ("A Writer's Handbook," 89). The factographers refused to assume the novel's "fatalistic perspective" (*роковой разрез*), as Tret'iakov put it, but suspending the hero's march toward death also disabled the drive of narrative desire, leaving the writer with no means to capture the reader. Chuzhak called this factography's *rokovoi vopros*, a phrase that meant both the "pivotal" or "fate*ful* question" as well as the "fat*al* question" or the "question of fate." How, he asked, could they orient their work not toward death and closure, but toward life and change? Was there any alternative to the form-giving power of the preterite? How could ocherkists hold the attention of the reader while remaining faithful to the material heterogeneity of reality? In sum, how could they write stories without fate?

Theorists in newspaper studies were struggling with the same questions of textual economy. In January 1928 Aleksandr Kurs published "Information (Reportage)," a groundbreaking essay in *The Journalist* that proposed a formula unique for its time: "Informational value equals the degree of non-recurrence of a phenomenon that distinguishes the phenomenon in a recurring series." According to the leading Presentist, information was not the semantic message or abstract idea that was contained in a given statement, but was instead a precise, even mathematically calculable relationship of a given fact to time. Information was not a static thing, but a variable that was in constant flux, a magnitude that changed from one moment to the next. "Informational value is a concept that is relative, fluid, fluctuating, dialectical." Kurs defined information science, in turn, as a method for plotting probabilities and measuring deviation over time. Convinced that information science constituted a distinct field of knowledge separate from politics and literature, Kurs campaigned to establish a separate curriculum for information at the State Institute of Journalism (GIZh) that would be independent of other courses on topics like propaganda and style. As envisioned by Kurs, this curriculum would teach newspaper workers "to select from the millions of facts those that are distinguished by the highest degree of informational value and to seek in every given fact those aspects of nonrecurrence that give the fact social significance." From his perspective, the essence of information was purely differential. "In a newspaper, the fact becomes news when it is possible to find that particular quality which distinguishes it from other facts in the same series." The series itself contains no information—no news—since it possesses no unique, non-recurrent qualities, only sameness: in such cases "the informational value equals zero" ("Informatsiia" [Part II], 45, 43). Kurs concluded that improbable events have a higher informational value than probable ones. The letter *k*, for example, contains more information in the English language than in Russian, where it occurs four times as often, just as rainfall contains more information in Tashkent than it does in London, where it rains all the time. For the Presentist, informational value was nothing other than the degree of an event's swerve, expressed in communication-theoretical terms. It was the yaw of history as it deviated from its predicted course.

Kurs observed that facts possess maximal informational value when they are first reported and that this value declines in subsequent iterations as the facts recede into the background series from which other, novel information may then in turn emerge. With time all information becomes a nonevent. As Kurs saw it, information was less like a concept than a sensation that is registered by the reader not semantically but somatically, as an irritating deviation within an established and familiar rhythm. In this respect, his theory of information transposed Russian Formalism's phenomenological dialectic of estrangement and familiarization into the context of daily journalism: like the first encounter with an artwork, news is most striking at the moment of initial impact but then quickly loses this force.[92] Informational value is momentary and ephemeral, an expression of "timeliness, actuality, and urgency" ("Informatsiia" [Part II], 47). For theorists like Kerzhentsev, the essential power of the newspaper, its most defining feature, lay in this very fugacity: "Although the newspaper only lives for one day—indeed, just for a few hours—and although the lines of the newspaper are read all in all just once and never reread, there is no printed word whose impact on the reader is stronger than the material of the newspaper" (*Gazeta*, 6). Like Kerzhentsev, Kurs too believed that the lifespan of the fact could be measured in mere hours. Information "provides interest to the reader only insofar as he learns it first from the newspaper, specifically on a given day and even at a given hour. Already within a couple of hours such information is no longer needed by anyone and will not be read by anyone" ("Informatsiia" [Part I], 43).

Soviet historians of communication science have suggested that Kurs's 1928 essay represented the first attempt to establish a general theory of information in Russia, with implications far beyond the practice of journalism.[93] The Presentist's insight that information is a time-dependent variable and a process rather than an idea anticipated later developments in Western cybernetics by decades, in particular anthropologist Gregory Bateson's influential claim that "the technical term 'information' may be succinctly defined as any difference which makes a difference in some later event."[94] According to this definition, "the most important characteristic of the information/non-information code is its relationship to time. Information cannot be repeated; as soon as it becomes an event, it becomes non-information. A news item run twice might still have its meaning, but it loses its information value."[95] For Soviet theorists of the newspaper, Kurs's definition of information as a time-based code had revealed something fundamental about human knowledge: that the contents of mind are always inflected by time. Ideas are not just historically contingent, but temporally, even chronometrically, contingent as well. Thoughts are perishable. More important for the Presentists than the question of whether a given idea was true or false was whether the idea was new or old, fast or slow, timely or untimely. The Presentist Boris Reznikov identified this timeliness as the "cognitive function" (*познавательная функция*) of newspaper information:

> the newspaper is not just an agitator, propagandist and organizer, but also a means for the cognition of objective reality. These cognitive functions of the newspaper are carried out by means of information. The newspaper extracts information: this means that it continuously registers emergent events. . . . By means of information the newspaper updates the reader about an objective social process that is continuous and developing. Every day, every hour, every minute, social relations are generating a countless quantity of facts, combinations, and phenomena. Through information the newspaper updates the reader of them and helps to orient him in this seeming chaos of phenomena.[96]

In contrast to philosophers who believed in the immutability of their concepts, factographers like Kurs argued that the properties of these ideas, their "informational value," changed from one day to the next. In the circumstances of the transitional period, understanding reality was less a matter of formal logic and definitional reasoning than of synchronizing mind with world.

The publication of "Information" triggered a firestorm of debate on the pages of *The Journalist*. Critics attacked Kurs's emphasis on novelty over messaging, an approach that reminded them of the sensationalism of the American press. As they saw it, the Presentist wanted only to surprise readers, not to enlighten or educate them. Kurs's definition of information as a quantum of difference did not adequately address the ideational content of the news, not to speak of its ideological dimensions. Opponents blocked his efforts to establish an independent curriculum for information science at GIZh, denouncing this initiative as excessively "formalistic." In response, Kurs argued that repudiating information was effectively a rejection of historical change itself. If he was guilty of "Americanism," then the information skeptics were guilty of "Germanism," an epithet used in newspaper studies to describe an excessive reliance on static concepts and abstract logic. For these Idealists of the news, all events unfolded according to a higher plan. They advocated a version of history in which every event could be foreseen, a chiliastic state that had banned all contingency, fortune, and creative drift. In effect, they denied the very thing that made the news new. In a reply to their critic Vladimir Kuz'michev, the Presentist Reznikov asked: "Are there 'elements of the new' [*элементы новости*, thus also: 'elements of news'] within the fact, i.e., within objective reality? Comrade Kuz'michev says no. But in that case how does an event acquire 'newness'?"[97] Information skeptics presumed a world without innovation or difference, one in which newspaper headlines for years to come could all be written out today. As Reznikov put it, these apostles of the Plan attempt "to encompass the unencompassable" (*объять необъятное*): "For how is it possible to anticipate and predetermine all of the subjects of newspaper information beforehand?"[98]

As the ethos of planning took root and the punctual temporality of the transitional period gave way to a linear conception of time, the information skeptics in GIZh gained the upper hand. The Soviet newspaper eventually ceased to be a conduit of news and became instead a site of ritual incantation, a discursive machine that was distinguished by a "hypertrophy of the code" and the "prayer-wheel like reproducibility" of readymade ideological formulas.[99] But for a brief period in the late 1920s, Kurs's concept of information held sway over contemporaries, not just institutional figures such as Nikolai Pal'gunov, the director of the state news agency TASS, but also members of the avant-garde.[100] It was taken up by the Lefists who were publishing in *The Journalist* at the time of the information debates and who came to admire Kurs's own periodical *The Present*—which launched the same month as the publication of "Information"—as the most advanced factographic organ after *Novyi Lef*.[101] Lef's enthusiasm was reciprocated: Kurs acknowledged his debt to the factographers in various public fora; he published Kushner, Pertsov, and Tret'iakov in his journals *The Present* and *The Pressman* (*Газетчик*); and he invited Shklovsky to speak to the Presentists about the death of the novel during a stopover in Novosibirsk.[102] Kurs had actually started warming up to Lef a few years earlier during his time as film critic and scenarist, when he was editing the journals *Screen* and *Cinema*, writing scripts for films like Kuleshov's *The Female Journalist*, and publishing essays on Eisenstein and Vertov. Indeed, it was the encounter with the latter's cinema of fact, specifically, that seems to have prompted Kurs's initial reflections on the temporality of information. His 1927 review of *A Sixth Part of the World*, for example, was first to foreground the play between redundancy and novelty that would become the basis for his definition of information the following year. There Kurs praised Vertov for replacing plot with the verse method of alternating between repetition and variation. At the same time, the factographer worried that the transfer hadn't been a clean one and that *A Sixth Part* had imported not just the construction of poetry but its lyrical mood as well.[103]

Emerging from this close dialogue with Lef, Kurs's theory of information delivered the most compelling answer to the fatal question of what would succeed plot as the structuring principle of factography. His definition of information-value as a degree of non-recurrence within an identical series offered a method to array facts that was both materially immanent and mathematically rigorous. Renouncing both the teleologism of the plot and the associationism of metaphor, each of which banned contingency from the artwork,

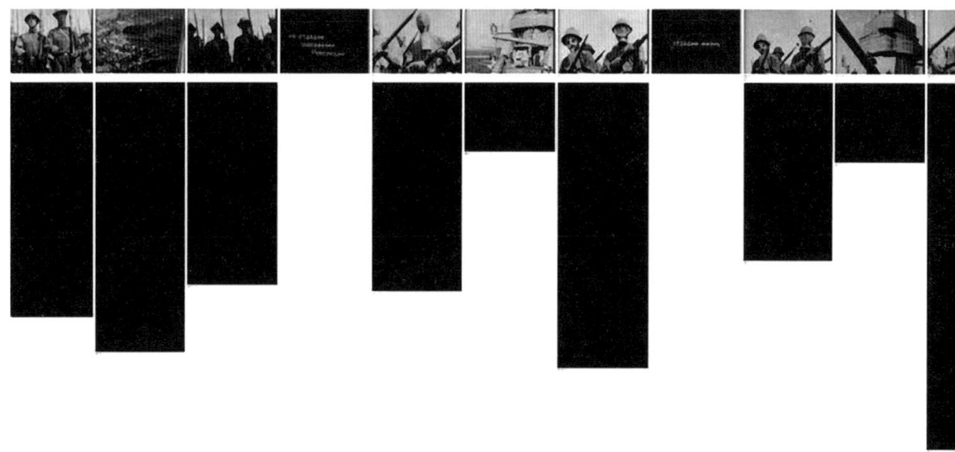

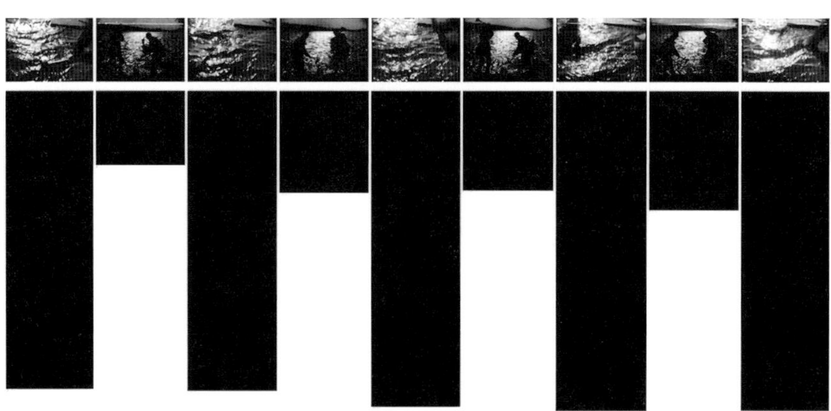

Lef embraced Kurs's method for orienting consciousness within a turbulent and still-unfolding space of historical transition. Echoes of his theory could be heard, for example, in Pertsov's factographic manual *The Writer in Production*, which observed that "the ocherkist captures the fact in its non-recurrence [*в его неповторимости*], in its concreteness."[104] Meanwhile, Vertov purged his work of residual lyricisms and proclaimed his new method to be a "'higher mathematics' of facts." His next project after the publication of "Information," *The Eleventh Year* (1928), would then be edited according to mathematically calculable formal variables such as motion-intensity, shot length, and luminosity, rather than the symbolic or narrative content of the footage (figs. 4.1, 4.2).[105] And just a few months after the launch of the factographic monthly *The Present*, Tret'iakov himself described journalism in distinctly Kursian terms, explaining that reporters must "introduce calculation" into their writing and then modulate this "algebraic" structure with "the accuracy of a cadastral draftsman" ("Our Cinema," 39–40). For someone who insisted that

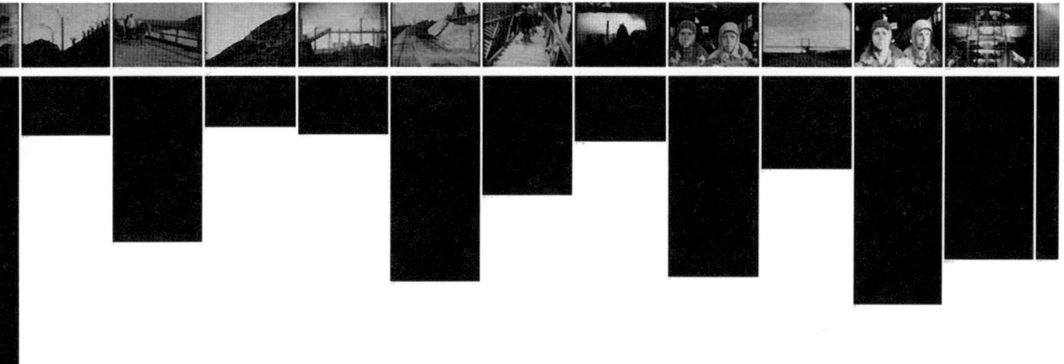

4.1 Lev Manovich, data visualization of movement intensities in a sequence from *The Eleventh Year* (dir. Dziga Vertov, 1928). © Lev Manovich. Courtesy of Lev Manovich and Adelheid Heftberger.

4.2 Lev Manovich, data visualization of light values in a sequence from *The Eleventh Year* (dir. Dziga Vertov, 1928). © Lev Manovich. Courtesy of Lev Manovich.

writers learn "how to work with numbers like they work with images,"[106] and who admitted an obsession with techniques of double-entry bookkeeping and punch-card systems (*Vyzov*, 47), Kurs's information theory would be the perfect means to rationalize literature.

That the factographer-in-chief would take up Kursian informational mathematics so enthusiastically is unsurprising, since Tret'iakov's early poetry already showed his obvious talent for manipulating the tension between repetition and deviation. His 1923 slogan "Everyday Life and the Club," just seven words in length, is a perfect example:

Быт глуп,	Everyday life is dumb,
Быт спит.	Everyday life is asleep.
Рабклуб,	Workers' club,
Бей быт.	Strike everyday life.

The four lines, each consisting of two syllables, are vertically stacked like a newspaper column. In a commentary to this poem, which he considered one of his best, Tret'iakov boasted that "the end is precise and tense. The quantity of words is minimal. Monosyllabic words provide a strong rhythm, compactness. The construction based on the sounds 'б-т-п,' which are plosives, gives the poem a consistent acoustic uniformity and planarity. The economy of material is extreme."[107] This taut, rhythmic construction establishes the frame for a play of informational variation. For example, the pseudo-homonymy that connects the noun *byt* ("everyday life") and the infinitive of *bei* (*bit'*, "to strike") slates the clutter of quotidian existence for destruction. Meanwhile, the stress pattern of the slogan, which consistently falls on the first syllable of each line, anticipates the club's ultimate triumph over everyday life (*byt*): whereas the latter occupies the first syllable in the first two lines, in the fourth line *byt* has been shifted to the second, unstressed syllable as if, through the intervention of the workers' club in the third line, everyday life has been displaced, discharged, vanquished. Il'ia Dukor explained that this same strategy of time-based variation could be found in any number of Tret'iakov's poems. "Tret'iakov uses the system of semantic 'repetitions' very widely. . . . In any particular poem of his you can find dozens of instances where the fact, ceasing to be immutable, is modified and varied, and becomes 'multifaceted' [*многопланным*]." The semantic meaning of a given fact might remain constant throughout the poem, but its specific inflection—its informational value—changes in each instance based on its position within the fixed series. For Tret'iakov it was not enough just to depict the novel facts of Soviet life: the novelty of these facts also had to be enacted in the subsemantic patterns of the text itself through a system of rhythm and deviations, regularity and swerves. As Dukor explained, this rigorously mathematical construction "leaves no space for 'psychology'" ("S. Tret'iakov," 48).

IMPROBABLE ART

The first revolutionary generation was drawn to intermittent mechanical media that reflected the experience of historical discontinuity at an individual level. "Every day cuts us up into ten activities," Tynianov observed in 1924. "This is why we go to the cinema."[108] Indeed, the technology of cinema in particular seemed to provide a perfect cultural expression for the disjointed lives depicted on the chronocards of the League. In contrast to Hollywood directors who emphasized continuity editing and unity of plot, Soviet filmmakers and critics foregrounded cinema's unique capacity to discretize experience. Following Bergson, they regarded film to be a fundamentally static medium.[109] "Movies" may claim to depict movement, but on an unconscious level the spectator always remains aware that she is watching a sequence of frozen instants. "As everyone knows, a movie reel consists of a series of snapshots succeeding one another with such speed that the human eye merges them; a series of immobile elements creates the illusion of motion," explained Shklovsky. For him, cinema was "a child of the discontinuous world" ("Literature and Cinematography," 30).[110] The discontinuity that was inherent to film technology found stylistic corollaries in the Soviet schools of acting and editing that emphasized rupture and collision. Eisenstein developed a dramaturgy of "transitionless acting" (*беспереходная игра*) and the Eccentrists emulated Charlie Chaplin, whose fitful acting divided movement "into a number of passages . . . like a dotted line." These stuttered performances, which seemed to have been cut into pieces and then spliced back together, represented the self-reflexive "laying bare of the purely cinematographic essence" ("Literature and Cinematography," 66–67; translation modified). At the editing table, too, Eisenstein and others like Lev Kuleshov pioneered montage syntax as the most influential alternative to Hollywood's narrative code. For Eisenstein, who returned repeatedly to the motif of the blade in his essays and who chided critics never to "forget the scissors," cinema provided the ultimate tool for cutting life apart and arranging it anew.

For the factographers, cinema was just a technically more elaborate version of still photography. "A movie is 1,600 meters of photographs," wrote Tret'iakov.[111] He was a fan of Rodchenko's essay "Against the Synthetic Portrait, For the Snapshot," which endorsed photography of "0.001 of a moment" and criticized synthetic images that blurred together a "sum total of moments." According to Rodchenko, the turn to the fractional time of high-speed photography expressed a pervasive change in the infrastructure of knowledge after the revolution, which came increasingly to rely on nonlinear media that were more responsive to the needs of the present generation. With the loss of "eternal truths," the archive of science and culture that was previously hoarded in the bulky codex book was now being redistributed among collections of discrete and mobile documents. "Now people do not live by encyclopedias but by newspapers, magazines, card catalogues, prospectuses, and directories," Rodchenko explained.[112] Vertov's films are full of related attempts to break apart durational time and parse continuous movement into a series of nonlinear segments. From the earliest moments of his career, he saw the camera as an epistemological instrument for "the research of complex movements and their decomposition into an alphabet."[113] This analytic impulse produced some of the most arresting moments in his oeuvre, such as the horse frozen mid-stride in *Man with a Movie Camera*. According to Grierson, *Man with a Movie Camera* is in fact "not a film at all: it is a snap-shot album."[114]

The drive for discontinuity prompted the factographers to discretize literature as well. As Gastev had explained, cultural rationalization demanded that all writing "should be restricted in measure, whether the measure of time or that of space" ("Novaia kul'turnaia ustanovka," 94). Tret'iakov advised fledgling ocherkists to stick closely to their own observations, to curtail philosophical speculation, but, above all, never to submit more than three pages.[115] And Kushner told writers to limit their purview to "a strictly bounded segment of time" (*твердый ограниченный отрезок времени*), since "every broad artistic generalization today would turn out to be a dumb fiction, a groundless fantasy."[116] As a model for this time-bound and punctual prose, the factographers once again cited the model of newspaper journalism. In his multi-edition manual *The Newspaper*, Kerzhentsev had praised correspondents' "ability to condense the text" and enjoined them to write as succinctly as possible, since "the laconic style—compressed and short phrases—correspond best of all to the tasks of the newspaper" (*Gazeta*, 40). Items submitted to the newspaper should be maximally compact, modular, and thus amenable to different constellations by the editor responsible for arranging the facts on the page. Correspondents should "write every distinct note on a separate piece of paper whenever possible" (*Gazeta*, 39). Tellingly, when researchers in newspaper studies once surveyed Soviet readers about whether novels should be published serially in the newspaper, many of the negative replies that they received protested against the specific temporality of the novel, whose vast timescale they considered irreconcilable with the promptness of the daily press.[117] Respondents objected that novels didn't belong in the newspaper not because they were works of fiction—as one would expect—but because these tales simply went on for too long. The newspaper was no place for lengthy narrative syntagma. Newspaper readers instead expected to find a mosaic of discrete facts that were connected to one another not through causality but through nonlinear correspondence. Such was the vision put forth in Lenin's 1918 essay "On the Character of Our Newspapers," which proposed to break the newspaper apart into hundreds of short reports just 10–20 lines in length. Each tiny cell of the newspaper, only a dozen lines long, would present a different incident or detail from life, another deracinated fact written "in telegraphic style." Instead of publishing wordy articles that were 200 to 400 lines long and full of speculative "ballyhoo," editors should create a finely meshed grid that captured "every new fact" of the transitional period ("Character of Our Newspapers," 96). In this way, the Soviet paper would replace the hackneyed repertoire of historical meta-narratives with a plurality of local micro-events.

As a technical basis for this modular writing, correspondents were directed to take up the favorite format of the League: the index card. *Time* promoted the card system not just for chronometric life-logging but also for journalism, personal correspondence, bookkeeping, and all variety of information management (fig. 4.3). Leaguists praised the index card as a technique of data processing with unlimited potential. For Kerzhentsev, there was no archive of human knowledge

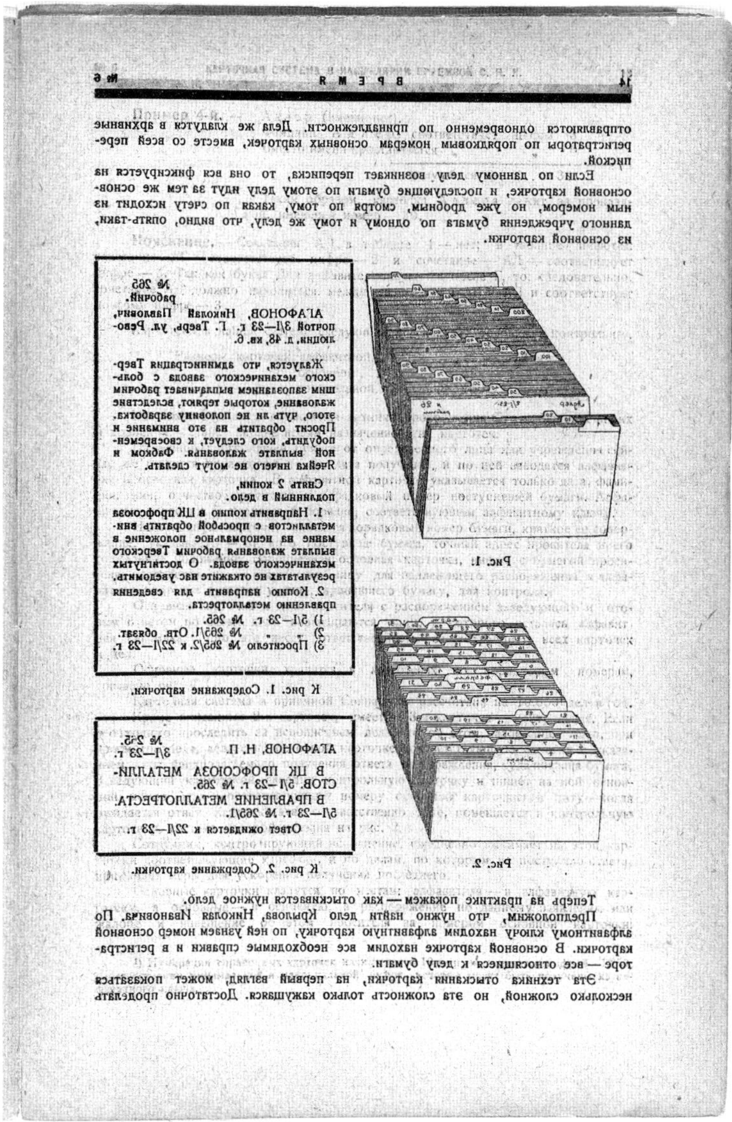

4.3 D. S., "Card System in the Office of the Admissions Council of People's Commissars," *Vremia*, no. 6 (1924): 14. Getty Research Institute, Los Angeles (85-S956).

nor, for that matter, any form of communication or symbolic operation that would not benefit from rationalization through the card system. The founder of the League "is crazy about index cards," wrote one article in *The Journalist*: "If comrade Kerzhentsev had his way, he would cover all of Russia with index cards in an instant."[118] Kerzhentsev promoted one particular combination of index card and decimal classification as a universal system for use in both economic and cultural sectors, but the pages of *Time* were full of heated debates about which exact format was fastest and most efficient. Despite differences of opinion, however, all members of the League agreed on one thing: "The versatility,

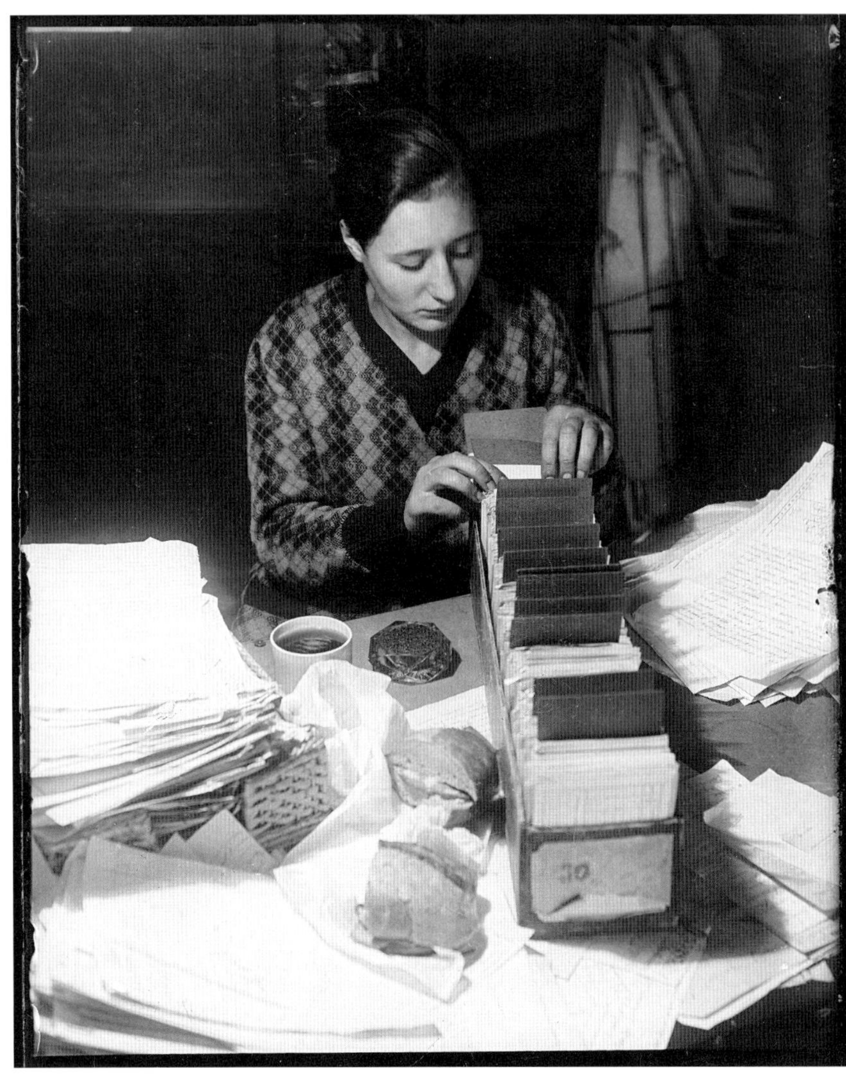

4.4 Aleksander Rodchenko, card index cabinet at the editorial office of *Gudok* (The Whistle), 1928. Rodchenko-Stepanova Archive, Moscow. © 2024 Estate of Alexander Rodchenko / UPRAVIS, Moscow / Artists Rights Society (ARS), NY.

elasticity, and portability of the card make it possible to combine, extract, and parse all problems that need to be resolved in any given enterprise."[119]

As leaders in the field of cultural rationalization, the factographers embraced the card system as an important step forward in the modernization of knowledge. "Lef endorses the card index system of recordkeeping," declared the editorial board of *Novyi Lef*.[120] One 1928 photograph by Rodchenko contrasted a disciplined lineup of index cards with the mess of papers and food found on a desktop in the editorial office of the newspaper *The Whistle* (fig. 4.4). When Rodchenko printed another photograph showing a heap of files on the cover of *Novyi Lef*, his commentary in the issue heaped scorn on the anarchy of loose papers: "A corner in an office archive: a folder with filed papers—dusty, gets torn, gets lost, takes forever to find" (fig. 4.5). Even worse than the loose papers,

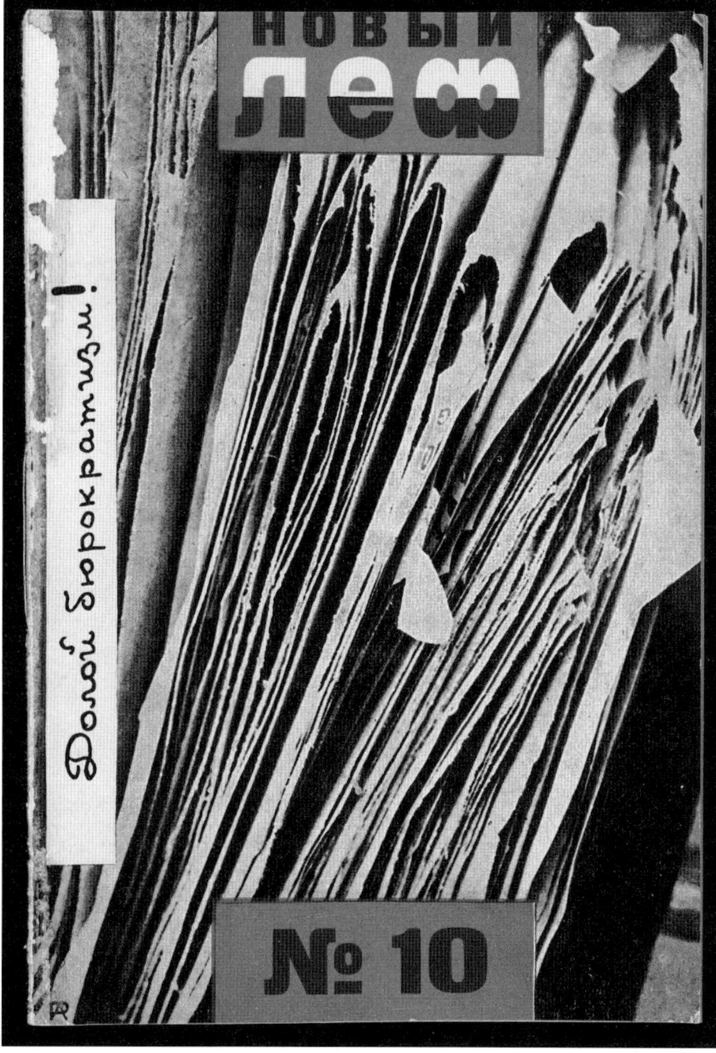

4.5 Aleksander Rodchenko, cover of *Novyi Lef*, no. 10 (1927). Marquand Library, Princeton University, Princeton, NJ. © 2024 Estate of Alexander Rodchenko / UPRAVIS, Moscow / Artists Rights Society (ARS), NY.

though, were the bound books that froze information in a fixed sequence for all eternity. The codex format, which led to overstructuration and stasis, posed the exact opposite danger as the chaos of files. Lissitzky complained that "the book glacier is growing year by year. The book is becoming the most monumental work of art."[121] Scientists, scholars, and cultural workers of the revolution were making all sorts of new discoveries, and yet the products of these momentous labors were less accessible than ever, inhumed in bulky, inflexible formats like the encyclopedia. But here too there was hope: "Rationalization is replacing the book with the card file."[122] Having blasted open the knowledge-prison of the bourgeoisie and liberated information from its linear syntactic chains, the factographers explored new methods of data management that were more responsive to the changing exigencies of the moment than the book.

The documentary revolution led Lef to the card file, which alone was capable of revising, updating, and rearranging the archives of knowledge on the fly. None understood this better than the Belgian bibliographer and philosopher of documentology Paul Otlet. Otlet, whose *Organization of Scientific Labor* Gastev had translated in 1925, predicted that the knowledge worker of the future will learn "to detach what the book amalgamates, to reduce all that is complex to its elements and to devote a page to each." Further: "No more binding or, if it continues to exist, it will become movable, that is to say, at any moment the cards held fast by a pin or a connecting rod or any other method of conjunction can be released. New cards can then be intercalated, replacing old ones, and a new arrangement made."[123] As Otlet explained, the card system allows users to modify search rubrics in response to the values, concepts, and keywords of an evolving society, and, in this way, dynamizes both the contents and the organization of information itself. "The repertories will be kept up to date by continuous additions and intercalations. In reality, they form books all of whose parts are indefinitely extensible and whose order can be re-arranged in any way thought desirable."[124]

Otlet pointed out that the structural openness of the card system also required its exact opposite—closure and punctuality—at the level of the individual informational unit. Only rigorous application of what he called the "monographic principle," which stipulated that documents be clearly delimited and maximally succinct, would at last unleash the infinite potential of human thought. Books that went on for too long, trying to encompass the entire world between their covers, just held up the revolution in knowledge. This was true not just for encyclopedias and reference works but for literature as well. Otlet, a close follower of developments in the Soviet literary scene in the 1920s, called the novel "a detestable genre because it allows people not to conclude."[125] The factographers could not have put it better themselves. "We are outgrowing the epoch of the story and the novel, and entering the era of the ocherk and the monograph," confirmed Tret'iakov ("To Be Continued," 55). For the cultural rationalists in Lef, who railed against the "bulky, sedentary, and unwieldy form of the novel" and who denounced writers who aspired to be "polyhistorians" ("The Writer and the Socialist Village," 65), the combination of closed datum and open architecture offered the best system for understanding developments whose outcomes were still unknown and biographies that were still unconsummated. Just as Vertov advocated the montage of facts as the basis for a "continuous editing process," Lissitzky proposed that the works of living writers be printed on individual cards so that "every new poem he writes can easily be added."[126] Plotted movies and *oeuvres complètes* were fine for the bourgeoisie. But it was cards, monographs, snapshots, and other discontinuous documents that would compose the data architecture of Soviet Russia, where newly established state institutions like the Office of International Bibliography promised, indeed demanded, endless addition and reordering, an information revolution in perpetuity.[127]

The monographic system set the archives of knowledge in motion, but it also transformed the structure of thought itself. According to paleoanthropologist André Leroi-Gourhan, the invention of the index card marked a radical break in the cognitive evolution of our species. For millennia humankind had supplemented the inborn powers of the brain through writing, which extended the reach of communication backward into the past and forward to future generations, and yet traditional written media like the tablet, papyrus, and codex left the basic linear structure of consciousness intact. Only the card system established a technical basis for nonsyntactic information processing that broke, once and for all, with organic memory. In 1926 Benjamin aptly characterized the index card as a form of "three-dimensional writing" because it overturned the two-dimensional a priori of all preceding systems of inscription ("One Way Street," 456). With the card system, thought becomes spatial and constellational for the first time. The card catalogue introduced "the ability—not present in the human brain—of correlating every recollection with all others," observed Leroi-Gourhan. As the paleoanthropologist saw it, this step constituted the final stage in the brain's migration outward into the surrounding technical milieu and its definitive reformatting in accordance with the discrete time of the machine. The invention of the electronic computer—despite its hype as the great atomizer of knowledge—only automated and accelerated basic nonlinear processing operations that had already been established by the index system.[128] It was the card catalogue that first released the mind from the sequential a priori of all preceding thought.

The factographers likewise foregrounded the noetic dimensions of cultural technologies. They understood the device of plot, for example, as a primitive technique for organizing experience into patterns that could be readily memorized and communicated. "It's no accident that plot has existed for millennia for it allows us to process the material with a higher degree of intensity," explained Shklovsky in a review of Tret'iakov. "Like dance, the plotted work can be produced using less space than walking."[129] As the Formalist saw it, plotlines were effectively a set of compression algorithms that helped transfer data more efficiently and "intensively." "Because of the fact that it selects and shapes, the plot plays a deformational role. . . . But we cannot simply repudiate the plot, or the storyline based on the closed construction of the hero's fate. The hero plays the role of the godson in a photograph or of wood chips floating on a flowing river: it simplifies the mechanism for focusing attention. In cinematography, for example, we know that the plotted film uses material more intensively than the chronicle film. Of course, we could also say just the opposite: that plot squeezes out the material" ("K tekhnike vne-siuzhetnoi prozy," 224–25). By distinguishing hero from staffage and action from accident, plots give a familiar and intuitive shape to abstract information, but this process of focalization also results in a loss of fidelity.

For millennia plot was the only compression algorithm available. Indeed, narrative concatenation was long recognized as the earliest and most elementary pre-technical means for storing information—the "quintessential form of customary knowledge."[130] Storytelling was "the only possible form for the transmission of knowledge in society," explained Bogdanov. "When a father passed on to his children his experiential knowledge about the changing location of the sun in its annual cycle, this primitive lesson in astronomy inevitably took the form of a tale about the adventures of a man, powerful and kind, who struggled with hostile forces that at certain times submit to him, and at other times defeat him and inflict wounds that weaken him, etc."[131] Translated thus into a series of myths, even complex theoretical discourses and scientific learning could be passed from one generation to the next. But, as Bogdanov pointed out, encoding abstract information into narrative syntagma also imposed a distinctly human countenance on all of its contents: taxonomies of objects were depicted as families of people; astronomical clock-time was adjusted to patterns of generational succession; and processes of nature were psychologized as dramatic conflicts.

The primitive "Ptolemaic system" of storytelling was perpetuated in the modern epoch by the novel, which tries to fit a vast cosmos of knowledge into a biographical framework ("The Biography of the Object," 59). Striving to be the "summa of an entire era," a book like *War and Peace* touched upon everything from technologies of artillery warfare to the sociology of the Russian nobility, bundling all of its sundry observations together in an epic about Bezukhov, Bolkonsky, and Rostova ("New Leo Tolstoy," 47). For all of their attacks on the contemporary novel, the factographers respected its nineteenth-century predecessor as an important cultural archive—they just considered these *grand recits* too ungainly, too glacial and immobile, for their own time. Better, faster, and less cumbersome techniques for managing information had become available.

The great "canvas" of the novel could now be cut into smaller pieces and its hoardings of knowledge redistributed among a host of lesser monographs that were more modest in scope, but for this reason also more responsive and precise. If the "teacher of life" Tolstoy once had to braid together documentation of the Battle of Borodino in 1812 with quasi-ethnographic studies of the courtship rituals of the aristocracy, these distinct sets of facts could at last be disentangled and vetted by relevant specialists in ballistics and anthropology. "It won't be long until the writer has no more function as a 'teacher,'" wrote Tret'iakov. "Moving into the same place where this last teacher of life recently showed his face are the man of science and technology, the engineer, the organizer of matter and society" ("New Leo Tolstoy," 47, 48). Exhausted and outclassed, the novelist should yield his place to the collective of experts that examines life with the "scientifically precise eye of the geographer, the meteorologist, the entomologist, the zoologist, the ethnographer, the reflexologist, the characterologist—and only rarely with the eye of the writer of fiction."[132]

The turn to ocherki and monographs reflected a wariness of totalizing accounts that were prone to epistemological overreach and error. Echoing the language of the factographers and Otlet, Barthes later described the novel as a "vast, extended canvas painted with illusions, fallacies, made-up things, the 'false' if we want to call it that." For Barthes, the novel's mistake is to presume to connect events and details that are in fact separate and distinct. "In its grand and extended continuity, [the novel] can't sustain the 'truth' (of the moment)" (*Preparation of the Novel*, 108). Put differently: the novel is false not because it is fiction, not because it is invented, but because of its sheer scope. Like the Soviet newspaper readers who rejected the novel because it went on for too long, Barthes attributed the falseness of the novel to its protracted narrative sequence. Also like the factographers, he believed the converse to be true: lesser, journalistic genres that are "of the moment" hew more closely to life, although their fidelity to reality comes at the cost of continuity and comprehensibility.

Barthes, a lifelong user of index cards, characterized the factical notation as an "anecdotal pulsation" that causes the story to "tilt" like a pinball machine that suddenly seizes up (*Preparation of the Novel*, 78). Fitfulness was also a distinguishing feature of factography. This practice "strives for ruptures instead of following developments," Kracauer wrote after hearing Tret'iakov speak in 1931.[133] Factography is full of aborted starts, ekphrastic proliferations, and other violations against efficient storytelling. Decades later Kracauer would revisit this insight in *Theory of Film*, where he proposed an unlikely resemblance between the cinema of fact and the musical, of all genres. "Musicals reflect the dialectic relation between the story film and the non-story film without ever trying to resolve it," he explained there. Like the musical, genres of fact show a natural proclivity for scintillating ornamentalism. In the 1930s, the decade that transformed factography into documentary art, books like James Agee's *Let*

Us Now Praise Famous Men would elevate this tendency into an aesthetic first principle, yielding epic prose that consisted almost exclusively of interruptions, digressions, details, and narrative openings without closure. But the original factographers were more disciplined. Building on the work of Kurs, they always presumed a basic structure, or regularity, as the measure against which the deviations of reality could be perceived. Like dance numbers in a film, the attractions of fact jostle against the formal construction of the work, generating a friction and a fascination that innervates the spectator or reader. Factical works "decompose" the storyline "with their glitter," "corroding the intrigue from within."[134]

Lukács likewise described factography as a "shimmering chaos" that exploded the economism of the plot. As an example of the decompositional force of fact, he cited a diary excerpt that appears suddenly in the middle of Gladkov's 1932 novel *Energy*, without any evident connection to the rest of the story. Like all swerves of fact, this one appears unannounced. The outcropping of life-documents belongs to a character who "does not play a significant role in the plot either before or after. As far as the plot is concerned, knowledge of the diary is unnecessary for the reader. It remains a mere 'document'—just the description of a state—and does not at any moment take the diary's author beyond the level of the episodic" ("Narrate or Describe?," 239). To be sure, Gladkov's novel belongs, like Agee's, to those attempts in the 1930s to transform the experimental methods of factography into a literary device, but this later formalization only confirms that everyone already knew and recognized factography to be a literature of static states, not of developments.

Indeed, whenever Tret'iakov's writing began to pitch toward a determinate end, he would arrest this momentum by introducing extraneous detail. He used photographic documentation, for example, to push against the diegetic current of the accompanying words. Only rarely do the photos in his books connect to the people or events that are being described in the surrounding text. Captions do little to clarify this relationship. One photograph of a peasant woman atop a tractor appears in a chapter of *The Summons* that features no discussions of tractors; another that purports to depict a group of kolkhozniki entering the Party shows up in a chapter containing no such episode. These pictures are not linked to the text in any obvious way, but instead just float there indifferently, as planes of extrinsic information. For Tret'iakov, who praised "those photo-ocherki in which the photo does not just illustrate [the text] but instead expresses a certain subject by means of a picture,"[135] the document should remain unexplained and insititious, a mute material expression of its subject. As one scholar of factography put it, the document is always an alien (*иностранец*) in the text.[136]

For this reason, Tret'iakov seldom identifies the people who appear in his photos, despite his usual adamance about referential specificity. The photographs are not sutured into the text. Instead, he forces the reader to pause and scrutinize them for some indication of relevance. Upon finishing *The Summons*, for example, the reader cannot be certain whether she has glimpsed Chebotarev or Martovitskii among the many group portraits, nor does the reader of *Den Shi-Khua* know if he ever saw the face of the eponymous hero. When the book designer John Heartfield put Den on the dust jacket of the German translation (fig. 4.6), it was just a lucky guess: Tret'iakov had supplied his German publishers with abundant photo-documentation for use in the book but had not named any of the people in these pictures.[137] Tret'iakov's snapshots were meant to show physiognomies not identities, lineaments not characters. In the rare instances that some relationship between the photograph and the text is suggested, the connection remains tenuous and obscure. One photograph in *Den Shi-Khua* laconically captioned "A horse is shoed" appears in the middle of a conversation between Den's father and Sau-Pu that has nothing to do with horses (fig. 4.7). Only later is there a scene that mentions in passing a clatter of hooves that announces the return of Den's father from Teian. It is a trivial detail that the reader would doubtless have overlooked had it not been for the photograph of the horse being shoed several pages before. But now, in retrospect, the photo-document becomes a kind of clue, albeit one whose exact significance is still unclear. Unlocking the mysteries of the factographic text will require diligent study.

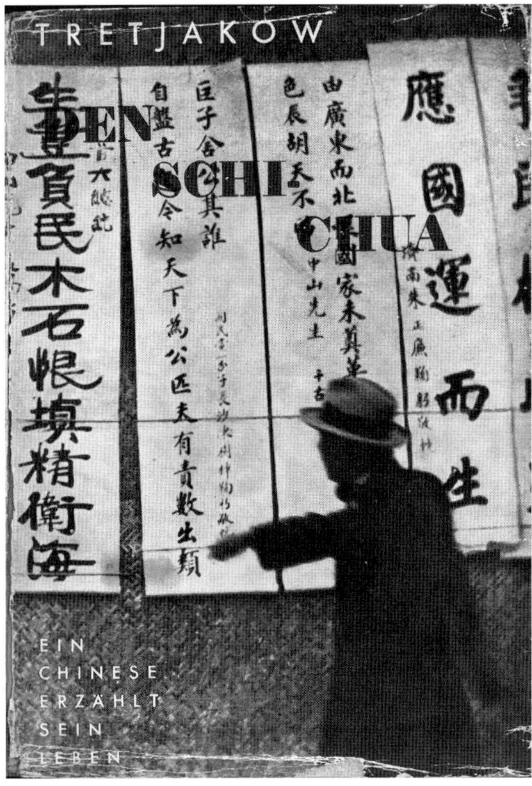

4.6 John Heartfield, cover of Sergej Tretjakow, *Den Schi-Chua: Ein junger Chinese erzählt sein Leben* (1932). Getty Research Institute, Los Angeles (91-B35308). © The Heartfield Community of Heirs / Artists Rights Society (ARS), New York / VG Bild-Kunst, Bonn.

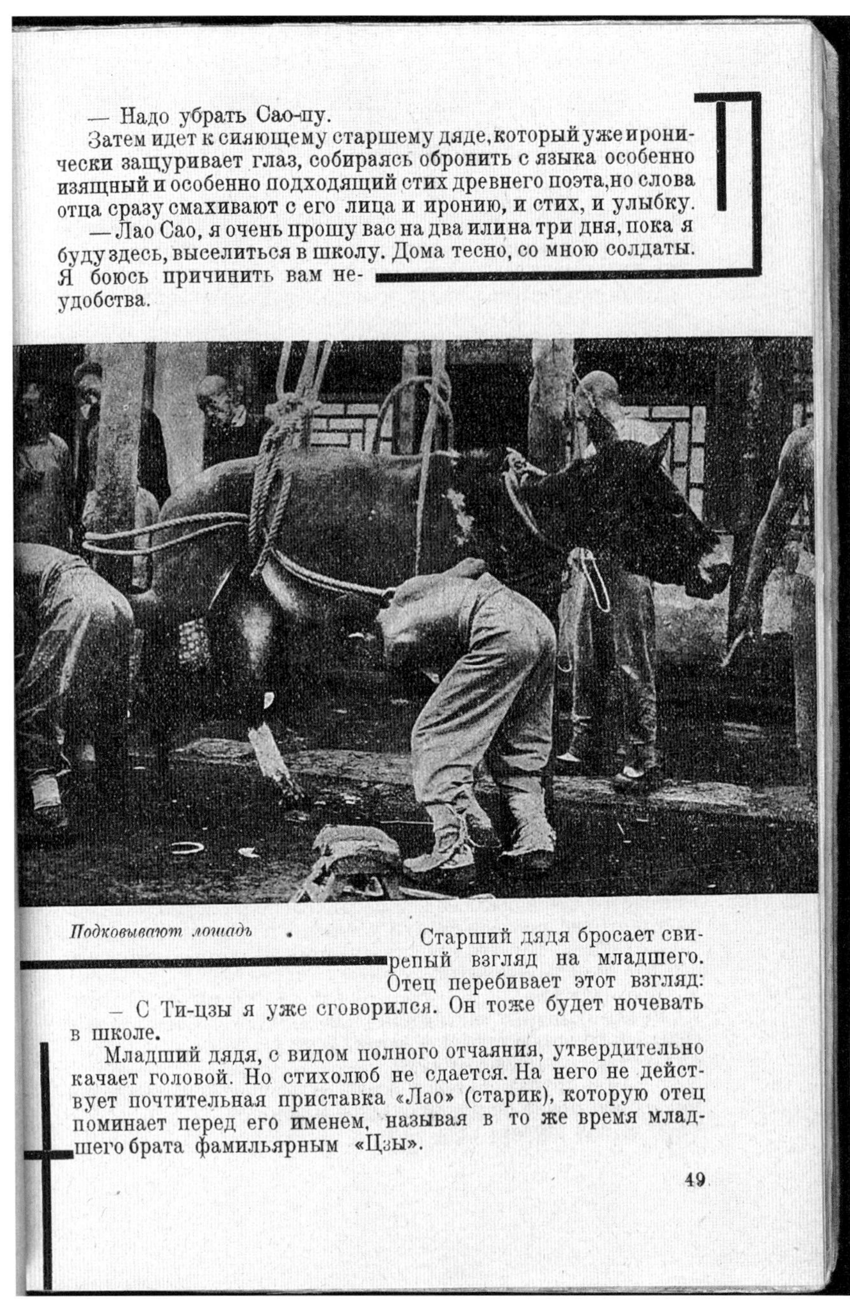

— Надо убрать Сао-пу.

Затем идет к сияющему старшему дяде, который уже иронически защуривает глаз, собираясь обронить с языка особенно изящный и особенно подходящий стих древнего поэта, но слова отца сразу смахивают с его лица и иронию, и стих, и улыбку.

— Лао Сао, я очень прошу вас на два или на три дня, пока я буду здесь, выселиться в школу. Дома тесно, со мною солдаты. Я боюсь причинить вам неудобства.

Подковывают лошадь

Старший дядя бросает свирепый взгляд на младшего. Отец перебивает этот взгляд:

— С Ти-цзы я уже сговорился. Он тоже будет ночевать в школе.

Младший дядя, с видом полного отчаяния, утвердительно качает головой. Но стихолюб не сдается. На него не действует почтительная приставка «Лао» (старик), которую отец поминает перед его именем, называя в то же время младшего брата фамильярным «Цзы».

49

4.7 "A horse is shoed." Sergei Tret'iakov, *Den Shi-khua: Bio-interv'iu* (1930), 49. Getty Research Institute, Los Angeles (88-B29495).

Tret'iakov expects his reader to work like a detective, actively collecting and weighing evidence to reconstruct the course of events. When accounts diverge, the reader must consider different documents in order to adjudicate the competing claims for truth. In his commentary to the famous photo-essay "A Day in the Life of a Moscow Working-Class Family" (1931), for example, Tret'iakov's forensic scrutiny uncovers discrepancies between the photographs and the narrative that they purport to illustrate. Close examination reveals that some of the photos directly contradict assertions made in the text: Tret'iakov points out that no Moscow streetcar could be that empty at the time of the morning commute that is described in the story (fig. 4.8), nor do the receipts correspond to the goods that the mother is alleged to have bought that day (fig. 4.9). If ambiguous photographs subverted the flow of books like *The Summons* and *Den Shi-Khua*, this resistance becomes even more pronounced in "A Day in the Life," where photographs now openly challenge the idealized fable about Soviet life that the writers have tried to impose on their material. Documents are an obstinate thing.

Tret'iakov introduced the intermittent temporality of fact even into highly plotted dramatic forms like agitprop theater. *Roar China!* (1925), for example, a play widely regarded as the most successful example of the factographic program on stage, baffles attempts to reconstruct the clear sequence of historical events that took place in Wanhsien in June 1924. The nine scenes of the play, which Tret'iakov broke apart into a "linked structure" (*звеньевое построение*), do not follow upon each other in a strictly linear fashion. The connections

6 У самого дома Филипповых недавно проложена новая трамвайная линия,—маршруты 11 и 42.

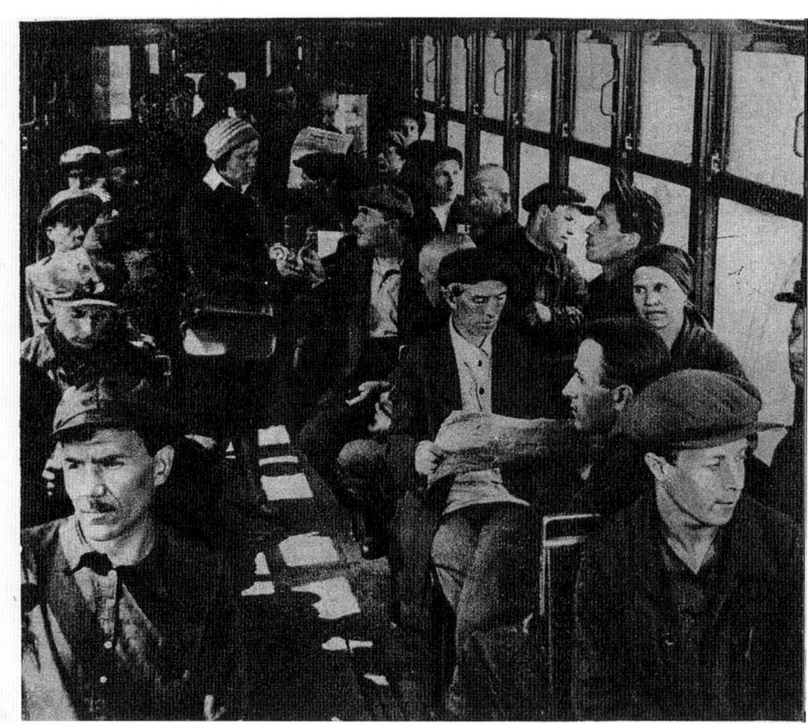

4.8 The commute to work. Maks Al'pert and Arkadii Shaikhet, "A Day in the Life of a Moscow Working-Class Family," *Proletarskoe foto*, no. 4 (1931): 23. Getty Research Institute, Los Angeles (85-S956).

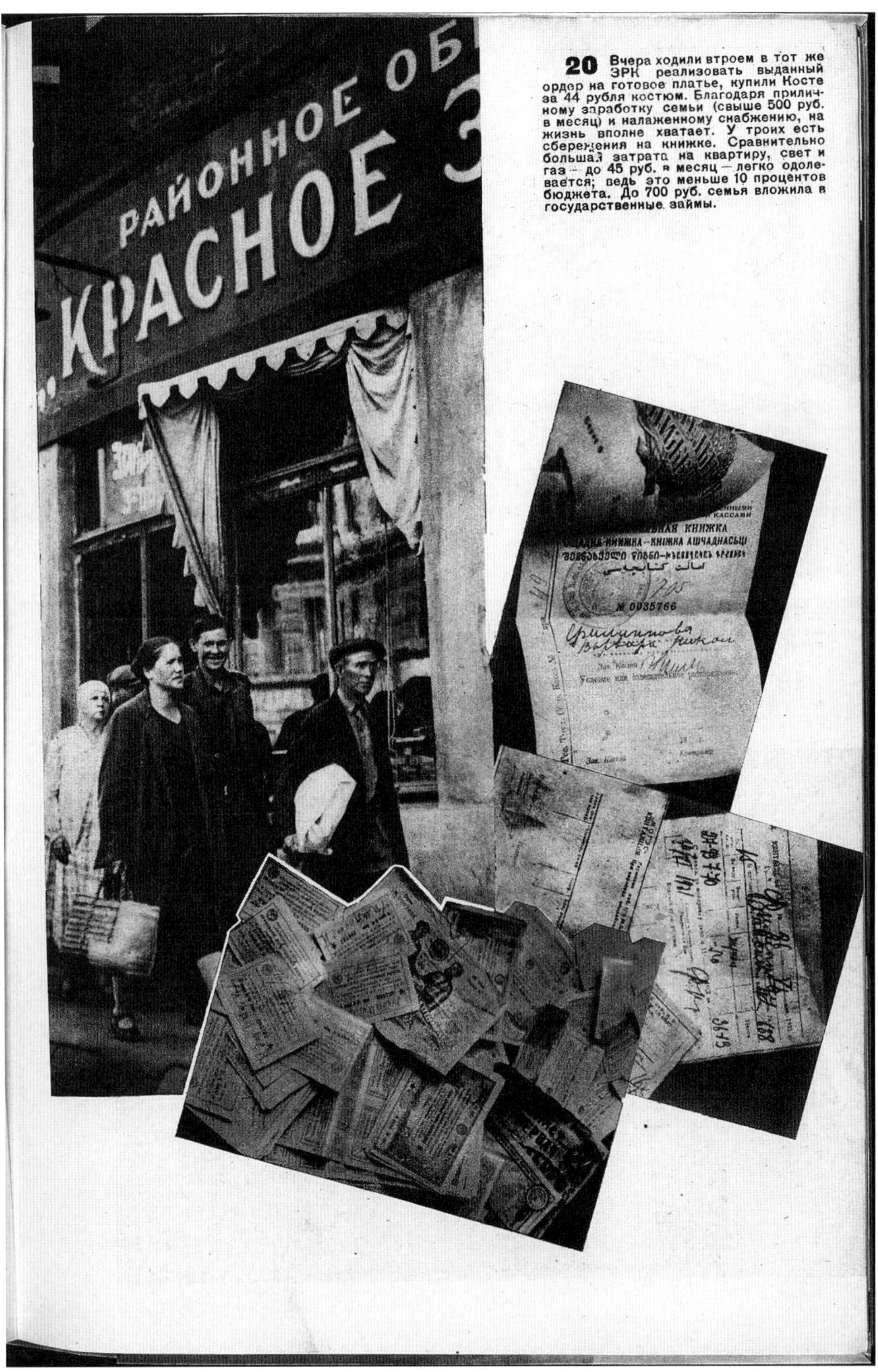

20 Вчера ходили втроем в тот же ЗРК реализовать выданный ордер на готовое платье, купили Косте за 44 рубля костюм. Благодаря приличному заработку семьи (свыше 500 руб. в месяц) и налаженному снабжению, на жизнь вполне хватает. У троих есть сбережения на книжке. Сравнительно большая затрата на квартиру, свет и газ — до 45 руб. в месяц — легко одолевается; ведь это меньше 10 процентов бюджета. До 700 руб. семья вложила в государственные займы.

4.9 Shopping receipts. Maks Al'pert and Arkadii Shaikhet, "A Day in the Life of a Moscow Working-Class Family," *Proletarskoe foto*, no. 4 (1931): 31. Getty Research Institute, Los Angeles (85-S956).

between the episodes are analytical rather than causal in nature. The event that sets the drama in motion—the drowning of an American businessman in the Yangtze River off Wanhsien actually takes place twice on stage, witnessed first from the British gunship HMS *Cockchafer* and then a second time from the Chinese shore. This doubling of the play's commissioning event sets up a tension between the two accounts of what happened from the outset. History divagates and multiplies along a number of possible paths, generating a complex, involuted temporal structure that is redundant at some moments and incomplete at others. The plot is perforated by numerous ellipses, such as a glass that is shattered at the end of the second "link" and then returns at the beginning of the fourth.[138] One review of the 1926 production of *Roar China!* in Moscow complained about the capriciousness of time in the play, which oscillated willfully between melodramatic action and eventless tedium. The reviewer noted, for example, how fifteen minutes passed at one stretch with nothing happening except the actors carrying one hundred parcels of tea one by one across a stage filled with authentic artifacts imported from China.[139] Interludes like these did nothing to move the story forward. Like the photographs in *Den Shi-Khua*, these ethnographic facts did not serve as naturalistic reality effects but, to the contrary, arrested the activity of imagining and provoked scrutiny of the behaviors and objects on stage. Facts like these enjoined the audience to observe, inspect, and count. Only through close forensic examination could the audience hope to determine how "a small fact that is easy to forget" (as Tret'iakov described the 1924 drowning) could have metastasized two years later into the major geopolitical event known as the Wanhsien incident.[140]

As a model of intermittent factographic prose, Chuzhak praised the 1923 book *Chapaev*, the eyewitness account of a Red Army officer who had served under the eponymous commander during the Civil War.[141] "Working on the basis of facts such as documents and historical records," the writer Dmitry Furmanov had succeeded in creating a work free of all "life-corrupting psychologism," Chuzhak observed approvingly. And yet what appealed to the factographer just as much as Furmanov's fidelity to documentary sources was the way that the novice writer had incorporated these facts in the text. He praised Furmanov's use of interruption, in particular, as a "specific, masterly device" that jolted the reader out of her fiction-induced stupor: the points of "hesitation" (or "oscillation": *колебание*) in the book function "like a dissonant note in a symphony that awakens the reader from his hibernation and forces him to live and to think" ("Literatura zhiznestroeniia," 58). For materialists like Chuzhak who rejected all reflectionist art and literature, reality could not be directly represented in the work, although it still could be conveyed, even performed, through subsemantic arrhythmias, dissonant notes, and other swerves of difference that interrupt a predictable series. Take the three letters from eyewitnesses in *Chapaev*: what is striking is not the inclusion of these documents, which are a familiar component of literary reportage, but where Furmanov has placed this cache of archival material in the course of the book—immediately after a pivotal battle scene. Right at the moment when the action begins to crest, Furmanov arrests the forward thrust of the story with a dossier of extradiegetic documents that causes the story to "tilt," as Barthes would say. Members of RAPP who wanted to claim Furmanov's wildly popular book as a model of proletarian realism were chagrined by the documentary hiatus that remained stubbornly disconnected from the events that preceded and followed it. These critics applauded *Chapaev* but complained about its inelegant construction, which they described as an uneasy generic combination of novel and ocherk.[142] Hoping that Furmanov would rewrite his book as a proper novel, they tried to push him onto "the path of cleaning up and smoothing out his allegedly disheveled works," Chuzhak noted. But the writer would not be brought to heel: "There is no need to describe one action after another" or remain beholden to the "precise sequence" (*точная последовательность*) of events, Furmanov insisted.[143] Causality and continuity, the compositional laws of the novelist, were not his concern.

Chuzhak explained in "The Literature of Life-Construction" that the fitful pacing of *Chapaev*, part-ocherk and part-novel, instantiates the centuries-long cultural struggle between truth and verisimilitude, *pravda* and *pravdopodobie*. Tellingly, the latter Russian word, like the German *Wahrscheinlichkeit*, designates not just a likeness of life but also a mathematical probability. Indeed, for Chuzhak, an artwork's mimetic authority—its successful semblance of truth (*подобие правды*)—depends on the likelihood of the events that it depicts. The realist artwork is so convincing precisely because its contents seem plausible and, indeed, are entirely foreseeable. Seen from this perspective, the factographers' critique of realist aesthetics turns out to be inseparable from a critique of its predictability. For them, truth, unlike verisimilitude, always exceeds the powers of foresight. Shklovsky thus argued that the familiar critical binary of realism and abstraction just distracted from the more fundamental distinction between probability and improbability. "There's no such thing as nonobjective [*беспредметном*] art," he explained. "There's only motivated art or unmotivated art."[144] The question for factographers was not whether a work was figurative or nonobjective, or even whether it was fallacious or veridical. The question was whether it was likely or unlikely.

The realist novel, for so many readers the crowning achievement of literary verisimilitude, had indeed demonstrated its predictability again and again. On this point, Pertsov quoted English journalist Arnold Bennett, author of a self-help book about punctuality titled *How to Live on 24 Hours a Day*, who insisted that a competent critic needn't bother reading an entire novel to know how it ends: "The majority of novels—and this applies only to novels—hold no surprises for the professional reviewer. He can predict it like a maritime calendar predicts astronomical phenomena."[145] Events in the novel are over, already-read, before they ever get underway. There are no miracles or swerves in the novel, only the faithful and fatalistic execution of a preprogrammed sequence. As recent histories of the genre have pointed out, the novel's ascent in the eighteenth century in fact coincided with the emergence of probabilistic modeling that was designed to tame factors of chance that were multiplying exponentially after the breakdown of the static feudal order.[146] Which is to say: at the same time that Europe was entering an age of risk and political upheaval, the novel stepped in to contain the explosion of contingency and deliver certainty about the future. For the factographers, such an instrument of prognostication had no place in their own transitional society. The novel only inhibited the creative energies of the revolution and, indeed, foreclosed the possibility of historical change. What cultural producers needed was a fierce game of chance, Tret'iakov wrote, but realist prose and art instead engaged them in a round of solitaire (*пасьянс*) in which the entire course of play was already prescribed from the outset. Only facts could randomize this closed, deterministic system. It is "through notations, through documents, through the newspaper article" and other such swerves of fact that "truth defeats verisimilitude" and reality breaks with prediction ("Literatura zhiznestroeniia," 58). With each such deviation from the projected course of events, the factographers renewed the revolution's pledge to take history in a different direction.

Literature is outgrowing literature.
—TRET'IAKOV[1]

Afterword

CONTACT STRATUM

Two months before the fateful All-Union Congress of Soviet Writers in August 1934 that enshrined Socialist Realism as aesthetic doctrine, Gorky's journal *Our Achievements* summoned the pioneers of the ocherk to Moscow to review the past decade's work. Although the factographers had parted ways several years prior, all original members of the group came to the June conference, where they were now joined by prominent journalists such as Mikhail Kol'tsov, young Formalists like Lidiya Ginzburg, and a new generation of ocherk writers such as Boris Agapov. Presiding over the All-Union Conference of the Artistic Ocherk was Tret'iakov, the former doyen of factography, who delivered the opening and closing keynotes for the event. The participation of the erstwhile Lefist was celebrated by some, although others expressed concern that his presence might trigger an outbreak of avant-garde "recidivism" among contemporary ocherkists. But there was little chance of that happening. Already two years before—an eternity, by the standards of the transitional period—Tret'iakov had abandoned the most radical tenets of factography and accepted the return to monumental literature as inevitable.[2]

Still, the factographic deviation had to be denounced ritually at the conference. And, as was so often the case in the great cultural palinode of 1930s Russia, the most insightful and unforgiving critics of the movement were also the ones who had once been the driving forces behind it. Apostates like Shklovsky again foregrounded the defects of plotlessness in Tret'iakov's writing, while Pertsov spoke about the epistemological calamity that resulted from renouncing poetic imagery. A few months later Tret'iakov summarized the objections in a letter to his friend Brecht: "The extensional subject has yielded priority to the intensional. Reportage literature is searching for great forms and lyricism is penetrating into the epic. One-sided intellectualism (technicism) is being vehemently attacked by the precept of emotion. They are calling for emotional complexity. Literature demands not just a cross section of the flux of life (reportage, naturalism, bourgeois realism) but an incision along the length of time (i.e., into the future, through historical dialectics)."[3] One by one, Tret'iakov's letter to Brecht inverts nearly every feature of factography that has been explored in this book: physical extension and empirical measure are now replaced by psychic intension and the imagination; the minor form is replaced by monumentalism; precision and technicism are replaced by subjectivism and associative complexity; and embodied affect is replaced by lyrical emotion. As Tret'iakov also explains here, refashioning the ocherk into a great art demanded abandoning the mechanical micro-time of the League. Henceforth, synchronic cross-sections and static snapshots would yield to the sweeping longitudinal scale of the epic. Supported ideologically by a Five-Year Plan that was now in its second iteration, luminous images of the future had dispelled the cloud-chaos that had enshrouded life in the transitional period. There was no need for presentist ephemera in Stalin's chiliastic fantasy of eternal socialism.

The positions laid out at the June conference underscored the distance between the militantly minor, anti-art practice that Tret'iakov had first put on the map in the mid-1920s and the great "artistic ocherk" that was now being touted in 1934. The intervening years had seen a bitter struggle over the soul of the ocherk. Despite denouncing factography, members of RAPP had been unable to resist the appeal of the ocherk and began to co-opt the popular form as soon as Lef disbanded in 1929.[4] That this deskilled mass practice was fundamentally inimical to RAPP's campaigns for literary quality and writerly qualification—that it even caused an outbreak of Lefism within its own organization, the Proletkul'tist revival known as Litfront—did not deter the group's leadership, who were determined to bend the ocherk to their purposes. RAPP was officially disbanded in April 1932, but the consequences of their efforts to reshape the ocherk were enduring. By the time of the June 1934 conference, the monumental literature now being heralded as the "artistic ocherk" bore little resemblance to the stark mechanical stenography from which it derived. This avowedly minor literary form had been thoroughly transformed since its heyday in the early years of the Cultural Revolution, when activists like Tret'iakov had wielded the ocherk against fiction, professionalization, and "easelist" literature.

The purpose of the June 1934 conference was to demonstrate once and for all that the ocherk, which still gave off a whiff of amateurism, was actually an artistic form on par with other major genres. Just as poets and novelists were convening preparatory conferences in the months running up to the August Congress, the ocherkists of *Our Achievements* organized their own event to hone their pitch for the ocherk as great Soviet literature. In order to make that case, though, participants at the conference first had to reach a consensus about what exactly it was that they did. They needed to situate the ocherk historically, analyze it formally, classify it generically, and, if possible, preserve it archivally. On all four counts they failed spectacularly. Despite public announcements that discussions were operating "at a high theoretical level," reports from the conference published in *Literary Newspaper* a week later showed that the participants had made little progress in defining the ocherk.[5] There was no agreement about what the so-called ocherk of the great style (*очерк большого стиля*) was, or could be. The special issue of *Our Achievements* containing the papers from the June conference came out in August—just in time for the All-Union Congress—but the contributions did little to secure the ocherk's place in the canon of literary forms. Few speakers mentioned the ocherk in their talks at the August Congress. After that, the disappearance of the ocherk from Soviet letters only picked up speed. In 1936 *Our Achievements* ceased publication, and by the end of the decade there was almost no trace of this practice that had once boomed during the Cultural Revolution but that clearly lost its purchase in the era of Socialist Realism.

June 1934 was actually not the first time that the ocherk had eluded efforts at canonization. Attempts to classify the ocherk at a conference that March had been similarly inconclusive. The brief on the earlier occasion, expressed in the military idiom of the day, had been to organize the ocherkists into distinct "brigades," working groups that could develop some rules for this evasive form. But the participants at the March conference were never able to reach an agreement on the basic criteria for such a classification. Some proposed to group ocherki according to the format of the publication in which they appeared, whether in newspapers, journals, or anthologies, while others insisted that they be classified according to generic models like portraiture or essayism, and still others suggested that formal devices like plot be considered the distinguishing feature. Each participant at the March conference seemed to have a different opinion about what exactly ocherki shared in common and what, in turn, distinguished the ocherk from other literary forms. On a practical level, the efforts to systematize returned repeatedly to the task of creating a bibliography of exemplary ocherki. Several participants at the March conference complained about the lack of such a resource, which Shklovsky then flagged as a major methodological obstacle in June: "The scholarly work of classifying ocherki, of dividing them up according to genre, of clarifying their distinctive features hasn't been carried out. Even a bibliography hasn't been put together, that is, we don't have the rudiments for the most basic scholarly work on the ocherk."[6] Efforts to archive and canonize the ocherk turned in an endless circle: without a set of clear formal criteria it was impossible to put together a bibliography, but without a bibliography in place it was impossible to extrapolate the specific features of the ocherk.

Eventually a tentative consensus was reached that ocherki should be categorized according to their subject matter. Although in practice this meant having no categories at all, since there were effectively an infinite number of topics that the ocherkist could explore in the new Soviet reality. According to Tret'iakov, making "thematic division" the "general principle for the formation of a brigade" caused the varieties of ocherki to proliferate: "We have the kolkhoz-ocherk, the scientific-technical ocherk, the industrial ocherk, the ocherk that follows the history of factories and plants, the regional ocherk, the travel ocherk," and so on.[7] Others at the conference would expand Tret'iakov's catalogue to include the Siberian ocherk, the ocherk of everyday life, the foreign ocherk, the war ocherk, the Tatar ocherk, the portrait ocherk, the physiological ocherk, the border ocherk, the problem ocherk, the production ocherk, all the way down to the arctic ocherk and Uzbek ocherk. The types of ocherki refracted into an infinite number of improvised and adventitious subgenres, as if every act of documenting generated its own particular species of literature. In trying to classify these works, the ocherkists thus confronted a question later posed by the taxonomist of knowledge Michel Foucault: "Is a science of the individual possible and legitimate?"[8]

Tret'iakov strove to capture the specific features of each of his subjects in the lexicon, syntax, and phenomenological rhythms of his own writing and thereby to make language into a direct material "expression" of reality, as he put it. This metonymic approach can be seen already in his first collection of factographic sketches "Moscow–Beijing," a "travel film" whose thirty discontinuous, chronometrically discrete episodes echoed the inorganic, mechanical movement of the train itself. According to the critic Maria Gal', Tret'iakov's subsequent sketches all followed this principle of expressive parallelism, each time with suitably different formal results. His travelogue about the remote mountain regions of Georgia, *Svanetia* (1928), for example, "is scaled from ledge to ledge, upon stumbling phrases and clumpy paragraphs." By contrast, Tret'iakov's account of an aero-skiff race across the northern tundra *At Full Throttle* (1929) "is read in one go. The tempo drives it forward. The ocherk has the rhythm of a motor and the melody of a propeller."[9] Rather than impose literary form onto his subject matter from without, Tret'iakov strove to collaborate with his material, to coax it into generating its own likeness. The result was a language inseparable from its referent, one that delivered reality to the reader without the interference of imagery, psychology, even literary form. Ocherki like these "bring the reader right up against the object being surveyed. . . . Such language is not forcibly separated from the 'place' where it is spoken and is not torn off at the dotted line like a check; it exists in its environment and in its element."[10]

Fusing language and referent in this way meant that every object would necessitate its own unique strategy of writing. For Tret'iakov, it was as if every citizen that he interviewed or protest that he attended, every field or factory that he prospected, generated its own particular genre. The Orphean factographer had to reinvent the categories of literature with each new assignment. "Tret'iakov is the sole writer among us who works in every genre," concluded Gal'. "Tret'iakov's style is multiple. Each book sounds a different tonality, is written by a different hand."[11] Having campaigned tirelessly against the fetish of aesthetic canonicity since his Futurist years, Tret'iakov believed that the formal and generic features of literature must be created provisionally in response to the task at hand. Operative writing cannot just recycle the same methods over and over. Against the professional writers who forced their material to fit into the procrustean bed of aesthetic convention, Tret'iakov insisted that "style arises out of social practice. Genres are created as the new life compels us to apply literary weapons in new ways." To writers struggling with how best to approach a commission, he counseled "less writerly arrogance" and "more consideration of reality and its demands" ("The Writer and Socialist Village," 68). Even when faced with the generic imperatives of Socialist Realism several years later, Tret'iakov continued to reject normative poetics, explaining that "style comes about only at the end: it cannot be imposed on anyone or expounded in a program."[12]

It was this quest for an aesthetic revolution in perpetuity that led the factographers to the ocherk, a genre that, paradoxically, defied the very conditions of genericity. Ever since the heyday of the Soviet ocherk at the end of the 1920s, this positivist, deskilled form of minor writing has eluded clear definition. Agapov, for example, called the ocherk a "green fruit" because it never fully ripens into mature art but remains instead forever in process—a "literature of becoming," in Chuzhak's phrase.[13] In a similar vein, Shklovsky positioned the ocherk as the very antithesis of aesthetic form, as "amnesty from construction."[14] Despite their concerted attempts, even the canonizers in RAPP failed to circumscribe the ocherk after Lef's dissolution. The dividends of their efforts were modest at best: "The ocherk is a transitional genre and, as such, is distinguished by a great versatility that allows it to accommodate internally separate components that it adapts qualitatively according to its assignment," proposed one member of the group.[15] Another wrote, more ambivalently, "nowhere will we find a fully developed poetics of the ocherk, a definition of its specificity as a unique genre."[16] Indeed, the organizational failures of the ocherk brigades in 1934 were already foreseen in the keynote lecture that Mikhail Luzgin delivered at RAPP's conference in January 1931: "We do not have and will never have firm and static markers of the genre established once and for all that would make it possible for us to survey the entirety of ocherk literature in all of its diversity."[17] Scholars of the ocherk in fact never managed to come up with a clear set of generic markers, either in the 1930s or since. Even in the 1960s, when the ocherk made a dazzling comeback during the second documentary wave, one expert would still write that, "as a formal entity, the ocherk remains largely undefined."[18] Again and again, attempts to encompass the ocherk conceptually always led to the same conclusion: "Theory is in arrears" (*теория в долгу*).[19]

In his opening keynote to the June 1934 congress, Tret'iakov put a positive spin on the negative identity of the ocherk, praising this writing for its remarkable plasticity and metamorphism. "I don't want to use the word 'genre' here, even though I can't find a different word. The ocherk is not a genre. The ocherk is a great movement. You have dozens of diverse genres there: it is what is called a 'contact stratum' in geology."[20] As usual, Tret'iakov had chosen his terminology with care: a "contact stratum," as he knew from his recent study of petrology for *Nation A-E*, is a specific kind of mineral formation that, upon encountering another rock and being subjected to the latter's pressures, temperatures, and contours, assumes the appearance of its neighbor. Like this xenolith, the ocherk possesses no inherent traits of its own but acquires features and qualities metonymically, through direct contact with reality. "'Documentarity' presents us not with a phenomenon of genre, i.e., with a conventional literary form, but with a method for transmitting living experience," Pertsov had written in 1931.[21] Enveloping its object like magma, the ocherk took on the character of every entity it encountered.

According to the conservative German philosopher Oswald Spengler, Soviet culture of the 1920s was full of these formless entities. His *Decline of the West*, a book widely read in Russia, lamented the inauthentic "pseudomorphs" that arose from the direct, unmediated encounter between art and life there. Just like Tret'iakov, he compared the phenomena of revolutionary culture to "distorted forms, crystals whose inner structure contradicts their external shape, stones of one kind presenting the appearance of stones of another kind." Squeezed into the confined space of the present and molded to conform to new sociopolitical structures, the molten energies of life were "not free to [crystallize] in their own special forms." The shape and function of the resulting cultural works did not express any true, transhistorical essence. Spengler thus concluded in 1922 that contemporary Russian culture constituted "the last dishonouring of the metaphysical by the social, and *ipso facto* a new form of the Pseudomorphosis."[22]

The ocherk exemplified the pseudomorphic culture of the transitional period. For materialists like Tret'iakov, who dishonored the metaphysical with every line that he wrote, this geological "contact stratum" was the perfect means to drag literature back into history and reforge it under the heat and pressure of revolutionary life. When Tret'iakov's June 1934 talk appeared two months later in *Our Achievements* under the title "The Evolution of Genre" (now minus the prefatory remarks about geology), the revised text described the ocherk as the final phase in a centuries-long evolution of literary forms that now concluded with the supersession of all generic boundaries. There was no longer any distinction between tragedy and epic or even between poetry and prose. Much like the proletariat, the class whose political triumph abolishes the category of class as such, the ocherk destroys the categories of writing. Soviet writers were now confronting the "breakup of literature," Chuzhak wrote ("Literatura zhiznestroeniia," 62). Indeed, it was the assault on the cultural canon—not the pretense to record reality objectively—that some European observers found to be factography's most radical aspect. Benjamin described Tret'iakov's program as "the scene of a literary confusion" and a crucible for "a mighty recasting of literary forms, a melting down in which many of the opposites in which we have been used to think may lose their force." Echoing Spengler's phrase about the dishonoring of metaphysics, Benjamin celebrated the Soviet newspaper as "the scene of the limitless debasement of the word" ("Author as Producer," 772). Lukács had a similar assessment, although the cultural traditionalist was less enthusiastic about the upshot of this debasement. Attacking reportage as "a pseudo-art with respect to form," he denounced this practice of direct sensory transcription for its "one-sided exaggeration of content." No fan of the avant-garde, Lukács feared that the methods of positivist documentation had initiated an interminable "experiment in form" ("Reportage or Portrayal?," 51, 49).

Russian observers were struck by this cultural pseudomorphism as well. And, while some advocated the restoration of traditional genres like the psychological novel, others like the Formalists celebrated the mighty recasting of culture. In essays like "Waiting for Literature" and "In Search of Genre," Eikhenbaum argued that the breakup of literature had been well underway even before the revolution, evidenced by the feverish succession of schools—the many *isms* of aesthetic modernism—initiated already at the end of the nineteenth century. By the mid-1920s the sense for genre had disappeared entirely, giving rise to a contemporary "middle style," as Eikhenbaum called it, that blurred the boundary separating high literature from everyday speech and the poetic function of language from its communicative function.[23] Under the present historical conditions, reviving old forms would only delay the reckoning at hand. For Eikhenbaum, the way forward instead led through those fact-based practices where literature "takes root in everyday existence": "the feuilleton, the ocherk, the humoresque, the memoire, the biography, the anecdote, and finally, the letter."[24] It was in mass factography, above all, that literary codes came into direct contact with history and were renovated, updated, and transformed. "The ocherk is located at the point of contact between artistic literature and the newspaper," explained Tret'iakov.[25] The literature of fact was "a place where we find not just a 'stockpile of materials'—a warehouse of raw matter and of readymade components—but also sources of new literary forms, new constructions, a new stylistics."[26] Similar claims were made about the cinema of fact, where the montage of documentary footage likewise replenished the resources of a medium in the throes of an identity crisis. Aleksandr Belenson's influential study *Cinema Today* (1925) thus argued that Vertov's *Kino-Eye* offered a perfect illustration of the theses of Eikhenbaum's "In Search of Genre."[27]

Eikhenbaum credited his insight about the centrality of fact-based practices at the current moment to his colleague Iurii Tynianov, whose signal 1924 *Lef* essay "The Literary Fact" had explored the metabolism between cultural forms and their historical environment. The formal features of literature are not fixed for all time, and genre is continuously "displacing itself" (*смещается*), Tynianov famously wrote there. As he saw it, art was the product of a restless process of recoding taking place at the point of contact between high culture and the profane everyday. Tynianov's essay essentially described the cultural logic of the readymade, a procedure by which writers and artists take anonymous trouvailles from everyday life and imbue these found objects with aesthetic value, elevating them into major features of the cultural landscape. Invoking the evolutionary model of Darwin, Tynianov explained that the organism of literature must be constantly renewed and regenerated through interaction with other organisms in the ecosystem of language.[28] When one set of literary devices becomes inflexible and automatized, when an inherited genre no longer reflects the reality of lived experience, writers abandon the old form and begin prospecting the margins of culture for extra-aesthetic linguistic material to inject into the stagnating gene pool of literature. As an example of this evolutionary transfer-operation, Tynianov cites the decline of the lyrical ode in the eighteenth century and the accompanying turn to minor forms of writing like correspondence. "When a genre is in the process of disintegrating, it migrates from the center to the periphery, and a new phenomenon moves in from the minutiae of literature, its backwoods and lowlands [*задворков и низин*], and takes the previous genre's place at the center."[29]

The publication of "The Literary Fact" announced a new program for the Formalists, who began in the mid-1920s to study journalism, epistolary exchanges, memoirs, and other factographic practices that were situated on the border between life and literature.[30] Taking up "newspapers, journals, and literary almanacs as literary works in their own right," they turned "toward the fact, the document, history—toward material that breaks down or at least conceals traditional form."[31] For Tynianov, documents alone were capable of advancing cultural evolution in the current historical crisis, when "the sense of genre has disappeared."[32] It was telling, he observed, that today's reader ignores poetry and novels and instead goes "straight to the current events, the reviews, the editorials—to the journalistic back alleys [*задворкам*] that are beginning to point toward a new type of journal."[33] Eikhenbaum and Tynianov began following the debates about genre on the pages of *The Journalist* and teaching courses on the newspaper at Leningrad's Institute of the Living Word.[34] They were particularly fascinated by the feuilleton, a discursive hybrid that encapsulated for them "the essential problem of contemporary literature as a whole":[35] smashing against the stylistic codes of literature, the feuilleton "powerfully deformed their literary structure, dynamized them in its own way, rebuilt their elements," wrote their colleague Tomashevsky. This fact-based practice introduced "an element of nervousness, tension, sensationalism" into Russian culture.[36]

At the same time that the Formalists began to study the "super-genre" (*сверх-жанр*) of the newspaper, their own manner of writing criticism itself became more factographic. Shklovsky published books like *Zoo, or Letters Not About Love* (1923) and *Third Factory* (1926), which were part human document and part scholarly treatise; Eikhenbaum combined literary criticism with personal diarism in his essay collection *My Periodical* (1929); and Tynianov published his first historical biography, *Kiukhlia* (1925), a book that Chuzhak heralded as a model of factographic writing on par with Furmanov's *Chapaev*. Indeed, the factographers could not help but see their own work reflected and theorized in the new program of the Formalists. There was a remarkable resonance between the literary fact and the literature of fact. Chuzhak cited Tynianov's "The Literary Fact" in *Novyi Lef* and echoed its arguments in his polemical treatise *"Literature": On the Artistic Politics of the Russian Communist Party*. Teodor Grits likewise urged that "the 'low' [*низкие*], minor forms that never entered into the bright field of scholarly consciousness—the joke, the ocherk, the essay, the feuilleton—need to be studied, since they play a major role in the development of literature. These forms are the points where the literary series intersects with the social and environmental pressures outside of literature."[37] Tynianov's literary "lowlands" became the favorite haunt of the factographers, and his cultural "minutiae" their avowed specialty.

Tynianov's account of the continuous exchange between high and low, center and periphery, clarifies why factography and the ocherk would never find an enduring place in the great pantheon of cultural forms. Factography was neither within the system of literature nor outside of it, per se, but was instead the very mechanism by which this system encounters life and is renewed. When older strategies of writing and artmaking fall out of step with the present, as was the case in the 1920s, factographic practices proliferate to reconnect culture with everyday experience. Factography is not a genre, then, but an operation, a transaction that is endemic to the historical hiatus that Tynianov dubbed the "interval," or "interregnum" (*промежуток*). During this interval, minor, fact-based practices stimulate the metabolism between art and life in order to overcome the stifling "inertia" of an outdated canon, Tynianov wrote. These moments witness an explosion of strange hybrid cultural species. According to Tynianov, even the most basic formal distinctions, such as the one separating verse and prose, lose their purchase in the interval. Kushner might have lamented in his

June 1934 talk that "the genre of the artistic ocherk is undergoing a crisis," but what Kushner failed to grasp was that the ocherk was *itself* the crisis.[38] So many of the labels that were given to the ocherk indeed suggest a practice that is constitutionally, structurally in between. Some called the ocherk a "transfer genre" (*транзитный жанр*), and others described it as a "transitional genre" (*переходный жанр*), although most often, following Tynianov, it was designated an "intervallic genre" (*промежуточный жанр*).[39] As Kurs put it, the literature of fact is "neither fish nor fowl."[40]

Shklovsky counseled writers of the transitional period "to work in newspapers and journals every day, to be unsparing of yourself and caring about the work, to change, to crossbreed with the material, change some more, crossbreed with the material, process it some more—and then there will be literature" (*Third Factory*, 51). This injunction to crossbreed invoked an idiom that was commonly used to discuss factical literature: the language of heredity and genetic science. Writers from across the cultural spectrum saw the newspaper as a laboratory for recombining the species traits of literature. At one extreme were revolutionaries like Tret'iakov, who enthused about the "evolution of genre" as a process of cultural renewal. At the other extreme were conservatives like Karl Kraus, who rejected hybrids like the feuilleton as a "changeling" (*Wechselbalg*) and a "genetic mutation" (*Mißgeburt*) that signaled cultural decline.[41] Somewhere between these poles were figures like Ilya Ehrenburg, who conceded that these artless and amateurish generic crossovers might look awkward at first, and that they may not even turn out to be viable organisms in the end, but who still accepted the fact that Soviet culture could not move forward without intervallic forms like these. For him, the "fatuous hydrocephalus" of mass journalism could hardly be considered good literature, but it was the most significant and forward-looking cultural development of his time, "the embryonic form of a new literary genre."

The role of genetic mutations in the evolution of literature and the conflict between major and minor forms at the moment of the interval were the subjects of Tynianov's brilliant story from 1931, *The Wax Figure*. This piece of "theoretical fiction," as he called it, offers a perfect allegory about the plight, and eventual fate, of the literature of fact. The story narrates two processes that unfold in parallel after the death of Peter the Great: while a group of misfit "genetic deviations" (*уроды*) break out of the sovereign's Enlightenment *Kunstkammer*, the tsar's followers create a likeness (*подобие*) from Peter's death mask to place atop a mechanical statue. On the one hand there are the monsters, genetic-generic miracles that are full of life and that elude classification but that, as singularities, are also unable to reproduce themselves; and on the other hand there is the death mask, the canonical form that has ossified over time and that now replicates itself automatically, without difference. For Tynianov, the aberrations and swerves that proliferate in the interregnum cannot be recuperated into the grand lineage of culture, nor can they even be situated confidently within the linear logic of historical descent. Some of the genetic monsters in *The Wax Figure* represent an evolutionary step backward (Foma is eight-fingered and slow-witted) while others constitute an evolutionary leap forward (Iakov is twelve-fingered and ingenious). Recombinations of the old and the new flourish in the period of the interregnum. But they cannot survive beyond this interval. The "monstrosity" of a "world that has been rendered journalistic will be spared the shame of a progeny that is incapable of living," wrote Kraus: "It cannot reproduce itself."[42] The real-life Iakov about whom Tynianov wrote was, in fact, sterile.[43] Thus, at the story's conclusion, when the frozen likeness of the sovereign is finally installed atop an incorruptible machine, Iakov disappears "to the lowlands . . . to the no-man's-land" (*на Низ . . . на ничьи земли*), never to be seen again.[44] Lacking any conspecific, the escapee from the *Kunstkammer* shares the same fate as the ocherk, the generic one-off that, according to Pertsov, strives to be "closer to life, to a reality that is specific and that resembles only itself [*похожа только на самое себя*], not any previous artistic depictions of another reality."[45]

Throughout the modern era, facts have been regarded as monstrous. Early on, the noun "fact" designated marvelous phenomena such as prodigies, miracles, anomalies, and other theoretical exceptions that exhibited "strangeness and/or irreplicability."[46] They were entities without images, texts with no comparanda, abrupt turns in history. Bacon described facts as "deviating instances, such as the errors of nature, or strange and monstrous objects, in which nature deviates and turns from her ordinary course."[47] For the factographers who strove to make work that would resemble only itself and that would not rely on earlier models, the fact has neither likeness nor precedent. Every artistic image recalls another image, but factography recalls nothing. According to Lukács, Tret'iakov's pseudomorphs were *ungestaltet*, a word rendered aptly in the Russian translation of "Reportage or Portrayal?" as *bezobraznyi*—imageless and shapeless, but also disordered, abnormal, literally monstrous.

When Georges Bataille heard Eisenstein speak in February 1930 about his new factographic film *The Old and the New*, the disciple of *informe* could not help but make this connection.[48] The Soviet director's presentation at the Sorbonne inspired the editor of *Documents* to write "The Deviations of Nature," an essay that celebrated the monster as the embodiment of the unprecedented and the unthinkable, an "irreducible form" that challenged the "Platonic idea." Bataille contrasted Eisenstein's film of fact to the famous composite images of the photographer Francis Galton, which smoothed out the differences between individual faces in conformance with the law of "geometric regularity." As a precedent for factography, Bataille cited *Les Écarts de la nature*, the 1775 collection of engravings depicting genetic prodigies that broke down the taxonomic divisions between species (fig. 5.1). Several months later *Documents* printed a series of stills from *The Old and the New* which confirmed Bataille's claim that this was a film with no images, only singularities. The eccentric angles of cameraman Eduard Tissé dis-figured the peasants, the use of close-ups twisted their faces into bizarre physiognomies, and the extreme anatomical pre-

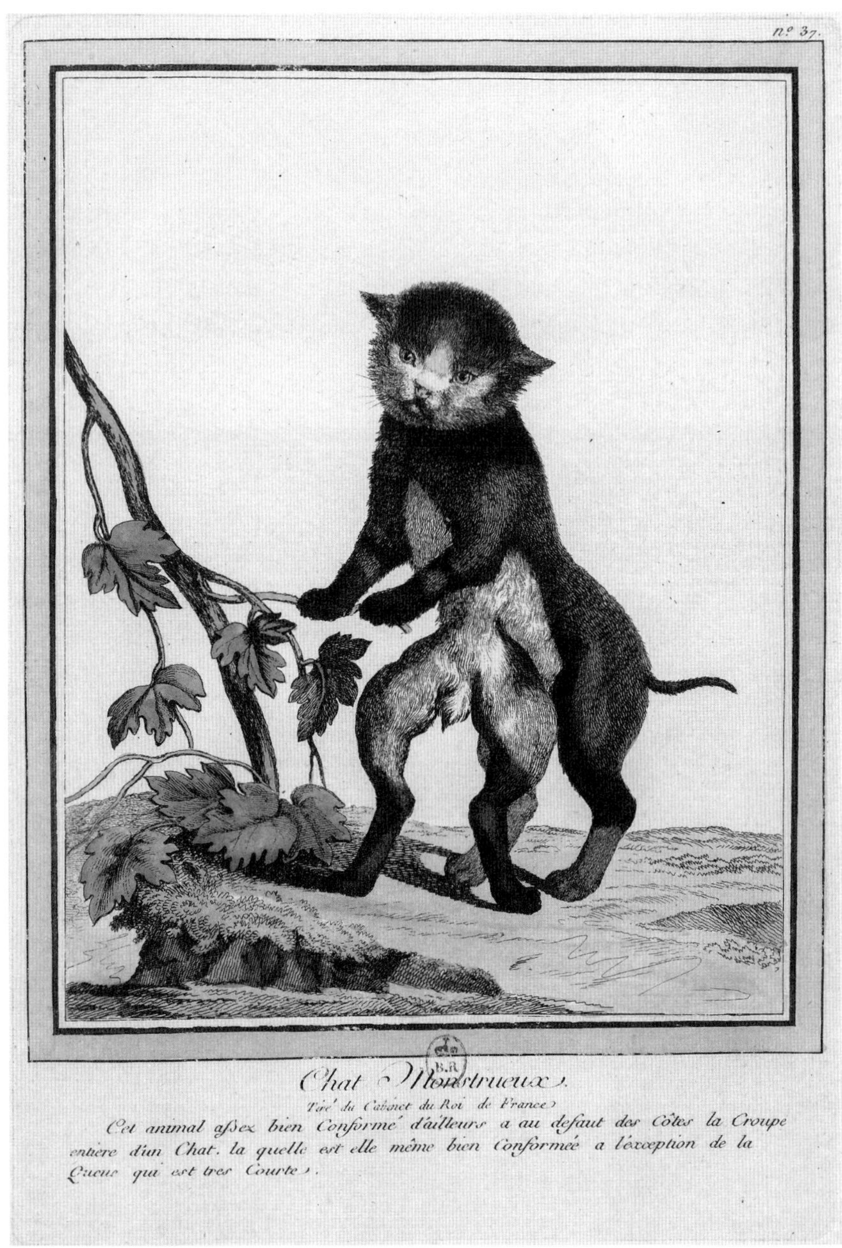

5.1 "A monstrous cat." Nicolas-François Regnault and Geneviève Regnault, *Les Écarts de la nature, ou Recueil des principales monstruosités que la nature produit dans le genre animal*, 1775. Bibliothèque nationale de France, département Estampes et photographie (PETFOL-JF-21).

cision reduced the body to a bundle of organic limbs and functions that erased the distinction between human and animal (fig. 5.2). The Soviet film of fact explodes Enlightenment classifications and "ravishes the senses," Bataille wrote. "The determination of a dialectical development of facts as *concrete* as visible forms would be literally overwhelming." The Platonic conceit of regularity was flouted by Eisenstein's monsters, which did not fit neatly under any abstract concept but instead inhabited the dark interstices between the categories of thought. Biologists may try to theorize these exceptions, but for Bataille, "they remain, no less positively, anomalies and contradictions."[49] As the philosopher

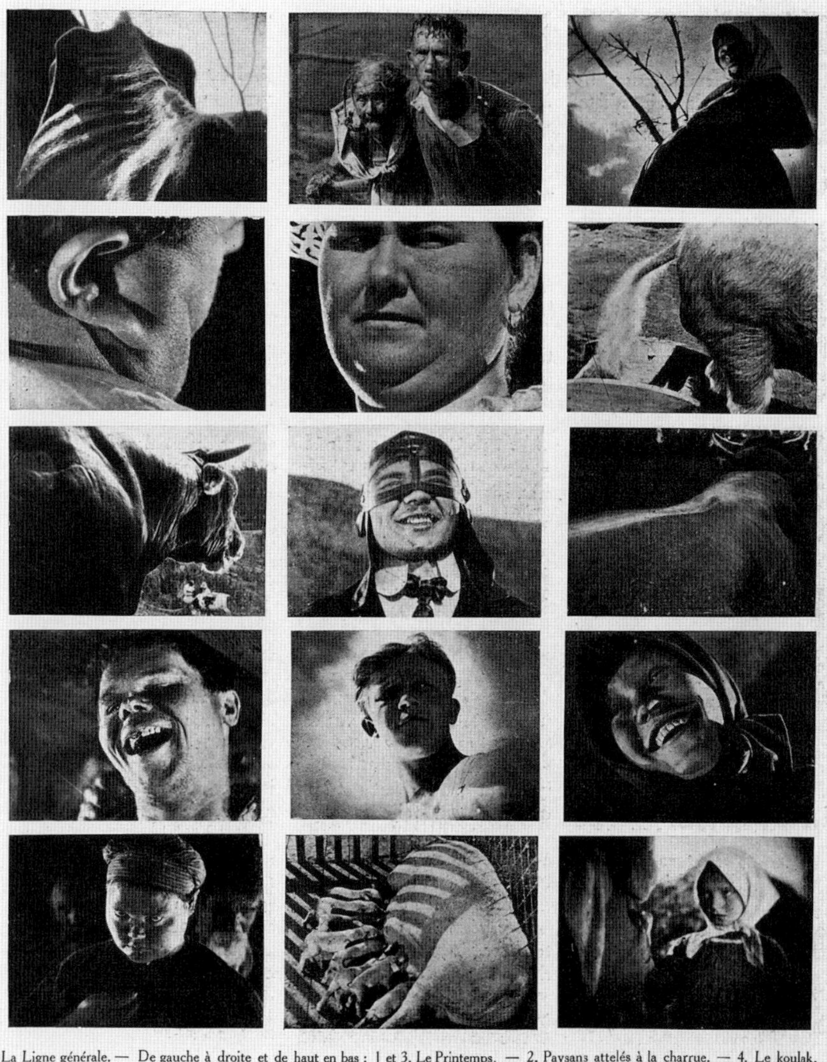
La Ligne générale. — De gauche à droite et de haut en bas : 1 et 3. Le Printemps. — 2. Paysans attelés à la charrue. — 4. Le koulak. 5. La femme du koulak. — 6. Porc. — 7 et 9. Le taureau Fomka. — 10, 12, 13 et 15. Paysans. — 11. Le komsomol: — 14. Truie allaitant.

5.2 Film stills from *The Old and the New* (dir. Sergei Eisenstein, 1929), as published in *Documents*, no. 4 (1930): 219. Getty Research Institute, Los Angeles (84-S596).

of science Georges Canguilhem would later confirm, monsters are "morphological failures" and "transitional forms" that upend established hierarchies of knowledge by exposing the arbitrariness of its divisions.[50] The monster, like the fact, is a sheer positivity that precludes conceptualization.[51]

The ocherk conferences of 1934 came to the same conclusion: theorizing the literature of fact would require a teratology, a science of monsters. Because each work produced by the ocherkist effectively constituted its own class of writing, its own species among the genera of literature, these texts could find no place in the canon of culture. For this reason, factography also had no future. Excluded from the sovereign lineage of artistic forms, these documents could not be replicated and consequently disappeared with the passage of the transitional society that had commissioned them. Despite the impressive efforts of RAPP to elevate the mass ocherk into "the ocherk of the great style," this literary pseudomorph would, like the twelve-fingered prodigy Iakov, eventually return to the cultural lowlands from which it originally emerged.

After months spent prospecting the ocherk at various conferences, when the All-Union Congress of Soviet Writers finally came around in August and everyone was abuzz with talk of great genres, Tret'iakov had the good sense to avoid discussing the ocherk. Instead he spoke on the importance of translation. This, he explained, would assist the export of Soviet ideals to the rest of the world, an achievement that was evidenced by the growing popularity of Fadeev in China, Ivanov in Australia, Mayakovsky in Poland, and Sholokhov in England. His talk pointed out the importance of translating in the other direction as well: everyone at the All-Union Congress was debating James Joyce and whether modernism was inherently fascistic, but how many of these positions were actually informed by a reading of *Ulysses*, which, as Tret'iakov pointed out, still hadn't been translated into Russian? The export-import business of literature aside, Tret'iakov's decision to talk about translation rather than the ocherk signaled a profound recognition that the period of cultural transition was over. For, unlike the ocherk that has no likeness, every act of translation demands likeness, indeed, is premised upon the equivalence of two texts. Just as the ocherk is always singular, every translation is always multiple.[52] Further, every translation assumes a logic of posteriority, a temporality that positions one work as the original and another as its successor. As the factographers already pointed out in their debates with the RAPP at the end of the 1920s, the great novels of proletarian realism were all effectively just translations of earlier works, whether Fadeev's *Rout* (i.e., *War and Peace*) or Gladkov's *Cement* (i.e., tales of Muromets). If the ocherk opens literature to difference and historical rupture, Socialist Realism sets in motion a machine of eternal repetition, an endless play of likeness, translations of translations, in sum, "history as ritual."[53] With his change of topic at the All-Union Congress, Tret'iakov finally acquiesced that the era of the fact had come to an end.

Acknowledgments

For a book about punctuality, this one took entirely too long to write. The intellectual, personal, and institutional debts that I have accrued since its conception in Moscow two decades ago are now almost too numerous to recall. To complicate matters, work on this book has overlapped with another that now reaches completion, making it hard to disentangle the debts of the two projects.

Three dear friends read portions of the manuscript at different stages and offered invaluable feedback that shaped the final book in crucial ways: Jonathan Flatley, who managed to be both generous and exacting; Rachel Haidu, who discerned what I was trying to say far better than I did; and Michael Kunichika, whose wit and integrity I will always seek to emulate. Back at Columbia University years ago Benjamin Buchloh first inspired my thinking about factography; in so many ways this book feels like an extended historical footnote to insights that he arrived at forty years ago through brilliant formal analysis alone. Boris Gasparov encouraged me to take up this marginal subject and set the highest scholarly bar for the work ahead. Conversations and seminars taught with Hal Foster transformed my understanding of the avant-garde and much more. My neighbor Yve-Alain Bois modeled the early Soviet ideal of a fully integrated monistic existence: genius as embodied habitus. Just farther down the road, Serguei Oushakine was a constant interlocutor for me, at once both humorous and opinionated. Two other colleagues at Princeton played a key role at crucial junctures in this project: Caryl Emerson, who helped me through more than one theoretical impasse, and Brooke Holmes, whose profound reflections on temporality informed my own thinking about transition and conjuncture. Chapter 3 would not have been conceivable without the stimulating dialogue and collaboration with Matthew Witkovsky for the *Revoliutsiia! Demonstratsiia!* show. Warm thanks are due to Juliet Koss for the demonstrational models, to Michelle Kuo for the technological determinism, to Stephanie Schwartz for acts of shock labor, to Amy Sillman for the aesthetic condensations, and to Kerstin Stakemeyer for the Proletkul't life-forms. And Yuval Boim made it all possible.

Work on this book unfolded across many different contexts beyond the United States, above all, Russia, Germany, England, France, Canada, and Spain. Colleagues, friends, and collaborators here and abroad gave shape to its claims: Leslie Adelson, Thomas Beard, Katerina Clark, Thomas Eggerer, Darby English, Douglas Greenfield, Anke Hennig, Andreas Huyssen, Gertrud Koch, Ben Lerner, Sam Lewitt, Christine Mehring, Nick Muellner, Molly Nesbit, Kristin Romberg, Marc Siegel, Elena Ulantseva, Juliane Vogel, and Geoffrey Winthrop-Young. This book also benefited from the input of Stefan Andriopoulos, Emily Apter, Leo Bersani, Svetlana Boym, Douglas Crimp, Maria Gough, Jodi Hauptman, Tatjana Hofmann, Denis Hollier, Christina Kiaer, Ethel Mathala de Mazza, Annette Michelson, Jorge Ribalta, Sylvia Sasse, Sven Spieker, Maria Stavrinaki, Susanne Strätling, Dima Vilensky, Dorothea Walzer, Christopher Williams, Georg Witte, and Barbara Wurm. I would also like to thank the archivists at the Russian State Archive of Literature and Art and the librarians at the Institute of Scientific Information on Social Sciences of the Russian Academy of Sciences, both in Moscow. Further gratitude to Chema González, of the Filmoteca Española and the Museo Reina Sofía, for the impetus to look hard at Vertov. My editor at the University of Chicago Press, Susan Bielstein, believed in this project from the outset and made sure it never fell short of her exceedingly high standards. At the very end, Joanna Szupinska, Karen Levine, and Victoria Barry leapt in and pulled it all together. Special thanks—and an apology—go to Eric Banks, who offered thoughts on the manuscript before the ideas had fully coalesced.

Over the years feedback from audiences at the following institutions helped me to distill a set of coherent claims from a sprawl of historical material: the Art Institute of Chicago, Bard College, the Centre Pompidou Paris, Columbia University, the Cooper Union, Cornell University, CUNY Graduate Center, the Free University Berlin, Harvard University, IFK Vienna, the Institute for Cultural Inquiry in Berlin, Ithaca College, Light Industry, Moscow State University, the Museo Reina Sofía, the Museu d'Art Contemporani de Barcelona, the Museum of Modern Art New York, New York University, Northwestern University, Stanford University, University College London, the University of Chicago, the University of Freiburg, the University of Pennsylvania, the University of Rochester, the University of Wisconsin–Madison, the University of Zurich, V-A-C Foundation Moscow, and Vassar College. Colleagues at two of these universities, Cornell and the University of Chicago, provided a home for me beyond Princeton.

Finally, immense gratitude to the Fulbright Foundation, the Social Science Research Council, the American Academy in Berlin, the Alexander von Humboldt Foundation, the American Council of Learned Societies, and the Guggenheim Foundation not just for supporting this work financially, but, in many cases, also for providing scholarly contexts in which to test and refine its theses.

Notes

INTRODUCTION

1. Ernst Bloch, "On the Present in Literature," in *Literary Essays*, translated by Andrew Joron et al. (Stanford, CA: Stanford University Press, 1998), 127; hereafter cited in text as "On the Present."

2. The word *factography* first appears in Nikolai Chuzhak, "The Literature of Life-Construction." To clarify the new term, Chuzhak provides an extensive catalogue of examples:

> The literature of fact is: the sketch and the scientific-artistic (workshop) monograph; the newspaper and facto-montage; the feuilleton of the newspaper and the periodical (also diverse); biography (work on a concrete person); memoires; autobiography and human documents; the essay; the diary; the record of the proceedings of a trial, along with the public debate around the trial; the description of journeys and historical excursions; the recording of an assembly or a meeting in which the interests of social groups, classes, of individuals intersect; the comprehensive correspondence from location (recall the remarkable letter of Serebrianskii to *Pravda* about how they extinguished the oil fire in Baku); a speech that has been structured rhythmically; the pamphlet, parody, satire, etc. etc.

"The Literature of Life-Construction" was first published in two parts in 1928 in *Novyi Lef* no. 10 and no. 11, but because this publication is missing four sections, I cite the complete version that was published one year later: Nikolai Chuzhak, "Literatura zhiznestroeniia. Istoricheskii probeg," in *Literatura fakta. Pervyi sbornik materialov rabotnikov Lefa*, edited by Nikolai Chuzhak (Moscow: Federatsiia, 1929), 60; hereafter cited in text as "Literatura zhiznestroeniia."

3. Nikolai Chuzhak, "More Left Than Lef," in *Russian Futurism through Its Manifestoes, 1912–1928*, edited by Anna Lawton, translated by Anna Lawton and Herbert Eagle (Ithaca, NY: Cornell University Press, 1988), 280; translation modified.

4. Georg Lukács, "Reportage or Portrayal?," in *Essays on Realism*, edited by Rodney Livingstone, translated by David Fernbach (Cambridge, MA: MIT Press, 1980), 59; hereafter cited in text as "Reportage or Portrayal?" Although this essay was written in response to a recent novel by Ernst Ottwalt, specifically, Tret'iakov is invoked in the first paragraph and throughout the remaining text. According to Lukács, the theses in "Reportage or Portrayal?" indeed pertain even more to the Soviet factographer than to Ottwalt: "Tret'iakov's case . . . is even crasser than Ottwalt" (61; translation modified).

5. Rosalind Krauss, "Reinventing the Medium," *Critical Inquiry* 25, no. 2 (1999): 289–305.

6. Michel de Certeau, "The Historiographical Operation," in *The Writing of History*, translated by Tom Conley (New York: Columbia University Press, 1988), 98.

7. Ilja Ehrenburg, "Die heutige russische Literatur," in *Russen in Berlin: Literatur, Malerei, Theater, Film, 1918–1933*, edited by Fritz Mierau (Leipzig: P. Reclam, 1987), 409–10, 404.

8. Sergei Tret'iakov, "Art in the Revolution and the Revolution in Art: Aesthetic Consumption and Production," translated by Devin Fore, *October* 118 (2006): 16; hereafter cited in text as "Art in the Revolution."

9. Sergei Tret'iakov, "Pisatel' na kolkhoze," *Zhurnalist*, no. 1 (1929): 8.

10. Mariia Gal', "Pisatel' vsekh zhanrov (S. Tret'iakov)," *Nashi dostizheniia*, no. 10 (1935): 142–47.

11. Sergej Tretjakov, "Der Schriftsteller im Aufbauwerke," *Slavische Rundschau*, no. 8 (1936): 8–9; hereafter cited in text as "Schriftsteller im Aufbauwerke."

12. See, for example, the testimonies of I. K. Martovitskii, a tractorist at Communist Lighthouse who eventually became one of Tret'iakov's closest friends. I. Martovitskii, "Ia o kommune pisat' budu . . . ," *Literaturnaia gazeta*, no. 47 (1967): 6; A. V. Chukhno and I. K. Martovitskii, *Kolkhoz—shkola kommunizma* (Moscow: Kolos, 1965), 50–59.

13. Sergei Tret'iakov, stenogram of talk on the afternoon of June 8, 1934, *Vsesoiuznoe soveshchanie po khudozhestvennomu ocherku*, Rossisskii gosudarstvennyi arkhiv literatury i iskusstva [RGALI], f. 631, o. 1, d. 70–73.

14. Walt Carmon, "A Soviet Jack-of-All-Trades," *Soviet Russia Today* 6, no. 6 (1937): 19.

15. Sergei Tret'iakov, "New Leo Tolstoy," translated by Kristin Romberg, *October*, no. 118 (2006): 48; hereafter cited in text as "New Leo Tolstoy."

16. I. S. Grossman-Roshchin, "Prestuplenie i nakazanie (likvidatsiia likvidatorov)," *Na lit. postu*, no. 22 (1928): 14. More recently, Maria Zalambani similarly argued that the factographers sought to reconcile two fundamentally incompatible impulses, Formalism and productivism: *Literatura fakta: Ot avangarda k sotsrealizmu* (St. Petersburg: Akademicheskii proekt, 2006).

17. Mikhail Levidov, "Lefu predosterezhenie (druzheskii golos)," *Lef*, no. 1 (1923): 231. "Chuzhak is a party communist, an old Bolshevik, a man from the under-

ground . . . the one true revolutionary among the Lefists": Viacheslav Polonskii, quoted in Nikolai Chuzhak, "Vmesto zakliuchitel'nogo slova. O novom, zhivom, i garmonicheskom," *Novyi Lef*, no. 4 (1928): 24.

18. Viktor Pertsov discusses his early work with Gastev at the Central Institute of Labor in "O moei rabote," in *Sovremenniki. Izbrannye literaturno-kriticheskie stat'i* (Moscow: Khudozhestvennaia literatura, 1980), 2:412.

19. See their coauthored statement about the liquidation of Lef and their decision not to join Mayakovsky's new organization Ref, which, as they put it, "continues to be a salon, a famous association of a few ponderous literary personalities." But "ours is an age of mass organizations": S. Tret'iakov, V. Pertsov, N. Chuzhak, "Ni Lef, ni Ref," *Literaturnaia gazeta*, no. 33 (December 2, 1929): 2. Pertsov discusses the crisis of Lef in mid-1928 in "Maiakovskii," in *Sovremenniki*, 1:125–32.

20. "Like Plato, Tret'iakov believed that there was no place for art in the young socialist state." Boris Pasternak, quoted in Viktor Pertsov, *Maiakovskii. Zhizn' i tvorchestvo (1925–1930)* (Moscow: Nauka, 1972), 220. Gottfried Benn also compared Tret'iakov to Plato in his radio talk from August 28, 1931, "The New Literary Season," *Primal Vision: Selected Writings*, edited by E. B. Ashton (New York: New Directions, 1971), 39–45.

21. Mayakovsky, quoted in I. Terent'ev, "Maiakovskii 'levee lefa," *Novyi Lef*, no. 9 (1928): 48. When Mayakovsky left Lef, he took Nikolai Aseev, Osip Brik, Aleksandr Rodchenko, Vitalii Zhemchuzhnyi, and others with him. Mayakovsky discusses his break with the factographers in "Tovarishchi!" and "Levei Lefa," in *Polnoe sobranie sochinenii v trinadtsati tomax* (Moscow: Khudozhestvennaia literatura, 1959), 12:203–4, 503–6. Chuzhak's response is in "More Left Than Lef." On the break, see L. K. Shvetsova, "*Lef* i *Novyi Lef*," in *Ocherki istorii russkoi sovetskoi zhurnalistiki, 1917–1932*, edited by A. G. Dement'ev (Moscow: Nauka, 1966), 311–44.

22. Sergei Tret'iakov, "To Be Continued," translated by Devin Fore, *October*, no. 118 (2006): 56; hereafter cited in text as "To Be Continued."

23. Pertsov, *Maiakovskii*, 214.

24. Nikolai Chuzhak, "Osoznanie cherez iskusstvo," in *K dialektike iskusstva: Ot realizma do iskusstva, kak odnoi iz proizvodstvennykh form. Teoreticheski-polemicheskie stat'i* (Chita: 1921), 89.

25. Andrei Platonov, "Stenogramma tvorcheskogo vechera Andreia Platonova. Vo Vserossiiskom Soiuze sovetskihkh pisatelei 1 fevralia 1932 g.," *Pamir*, no. 6 (1989): 102.

26. Georg Büchner, *Dantons Tod*, in *Werke und Briefe*, edited by K. Pörnbacher et al. (Munich: DTV, 1988), 110.

27. On the distinction between language and action in the Ur-text of realist mimesis, Thucydides's *History of the Peloponnesian War*, see Adam Parry, *Logos and Ergon in Thucydides* (New York: Arno Press, 1981).

28. Sergej Tretjakov, "Das Wort ist zur Tat geworden," *Unsere Zeit* 6, no. 9 (1933): 99–104.

29. "Only *political superstition* still imagines today that civil life must be held together by the state, whereas in reality, on the contrary, the state is held together by civil life." Karl Marx and Friedrich Engels, *The Holy Family, or Critique of Critical Criticism*, translated by Richard Dixon and Clemens Dutt, in *Collected Works* (London: Lawrence and Wishart, 1975), 4:121.

30. Sergei Tret'iakov, "Evoliutsiia zhanra," *Nashi dostizheniia*, no. 7–8 (1934): 160; hereafter cited in text as "Evoliutsiia zhanra."

31. Guy Debord, *Comments on the Society of the Spectacle*, translated by Malcolm Imrie (London: Verso, 1990), 3.

32. Fredric Jameson, *The Prison-House of Language: A Critical Account of Structuralism and Russian Formalism* (Princeton, NJ: Princeton University Press, 1972), ix.

33. Grossman-Roshchin, "Prestuplenie i nakazanie," 22.

34. Viktor Pertsov, "Grafik sovremennogo Lefa," *Novyi Lef*, no. 1 (1927): 17.

35. Adolf Damaschke, *Aus meinem Leben* (Leipzig: Grethlein Verlag, 1924), 4.

36. Like all of his successors, the first reporter of the Western tradition was able to make sense of his own turbulent times only through recourse to a moment in the future when all of these worldly events had come to their conclusion. In a brilliant text on Dante, Osip Mandelstam consequently observed that these verses "are projectiles [*снаряды*] for capturing the future. They demand commentaries in the *futurum*." Osip Mandelstam, "Conversation About Dante," in *Critical Prose and Letters*, edited by Jane Gary Harris, translated by Jane Gary Harris and Constance Link (Ann Arbor: Ardis, 1979), 420. Kisch writes of Dante and journalism in *Marktplatz der Sensationen* (Mexico: Das Freie Buch, 1942).

Erich Auerbach explained that Dante was the inventor of "the modern European form of artistic mimesis which stresses the actuality of events," a "poet of the secular world" who "had lived in the very midst of important events, participating in them and suffering through them." But the secular poet and proto-journalist could not simply depict events in their immediacy. As a result, "the encounters do not take place in this life, where men are always met with in a state of contingency that manifests only a part of their essence, and where the very intensity of life in the most vital moments makes self-awareness difficult and renders a true encounter impossible." *Dante, Poet of the Secular World*, translated by Ralph Manheim (Chicago: University of Chicago Press, 1961), 83, 134.

37. Boris Agapov, "Predislovie," in *Vchera i segodnia. Ocherki russkikh sovetskikh pisatelei v dvukh tomakh*, edited by Boris Agapov (Moscow: Khudozhestvennaia literatura, 1960), 1:5.

38. Iuda Grossman-Roshchin, "O prirode deistvennogo slova," *Lef*, no. 6 (1924): 94–95.

39. Khrisanf Khersonzky, "Landmarks of Revolutionary Film Culture," in *Lines of Resistance: Dziga Vertov and the Twenties*, edited by Yuri Tsivian, translated by Julian Graffy (Pordenonne: Le Giornate del Cinemo Muto, 2005), 138.

40. This anecdote is recounted in Georges Sorel, *Reflections on Violence*, edited by Jeremy Jennings, translated by Thomas Ernest Hulme and Jeremy Jennings (Cambridge: Cambridge University Press, 1999), 128.

41. Sorel, *Reflections on Violence*, 114–15.

42. Michel Foucault, *The Archaeology of Knowledge*, translated by A. M. Sheridan Smith (New York: Pantheon Books, 1972), 3–17.

43. de Certeau, "The Historiographical Operation," 74.

44. Luis Costa Lima, *Control of the Imaginary: Reason and Imagination in Modern Times*, translated by W. Ronald Sousa (Minneapolis: University of Minnesota Press, 1988), 58.

45. Jacques Le Goff, "Documento/monumento," quoted in Paul Ricoeur, *Time and Narrative*, translated by Kathleen Blarney and David Pellauer (Chicago: University of Chicago Press, 1988), 3:303–4.

46. Erik Reger, *Das wachsame Hähnchen. Polemischer Roman* (Leipzig: Rowohlt, 1932), 7.

47. Etienne Balibar, *On the Dictatorship of the Proletariat* (London: New Left Books, 1977), 132.

48. A. Lezhnev, "Delo o trupe," *Krasnaia Nov'*, no. 5 (1927): 234.

49. Viktor Shklovsky, *Literature and Cinematography*, translated by Irina Masinovsky (Champaign, IL: Dalkey Archive Press, 2008), 11.

50. Roland Barthes, "The Reality Effect," in *The Rustle of Language*, translated by Richard Howard (New York: Hill and Wang, 1989), 146; translation modified.

51. Sergei Tret'iakov, "From Where to Where," in *Russian Futurism Through Its Manifestoes*, 209; hereafter cited in text as "From Where."

52. Peter Sloterdijk, *Literatur und Organisation von Lebenserfahrung. Autobiografien der Zwanziger Jahre* (Munich: Carl Hanser, 1978), 70.

53. Bill Nichols, *Representing Reality: Issues and Concepts in Documentary* (Bloomington: Indiana University Press, 1991), 178.

54. These two phrases are from Sergei Tret'iakov, "Skvoz' neprotertye ochki," *Novyi Lef*, no. 9 (1928): 22; hereafter cited in text as "Skvoz'"; and Tret'iakov, "Evoliutsiia zhanra," 160. According to Gal', this would be Tret'iakov's legacy to the next generation of documentary sketch writers: "Our best ocherkists are 'downright ill' with this longing for knowledge," she writes in "Pisatel' vsekh zhanrov," 145.

55. Agapov, "Predislovie," 1:3. Osip Brik, "Ocherk stikhom," *Nashi dostizheniia* 4 (1936): 138.

56. Maksim Gorky, quoted in Petr Palievskii, "Literatura, Dokument, Fakt," *Inostrannaia literatura*, no. 8 (1966): 205.

57. Sergei Tret'iakov, "Lef and Film. Notes of a Discussion (Extracts)," edited by Ben Brewster, translated by Diana Matias, *Screen* 12, no. 4 (1971–72): 75.

58. Quoted in anonymous, "Uspekhi i pritiazaniia S. Tret'iakova," *Na literaturnom postu*, no. 12 (1931): 32.

59. Tom Vandeputte, *Critique of Journalistic Reason: Philosophy and the Time of the Newspaper* (New York: Fordham University Press, 2020), 14, 28.

60. Peter Kenez, *The Birth of the Propaganda State: Soviet Methods of Mass Mobilization, 1917–1929* (Cambridge: Cambridge University Press, 1985), 224–50.

61. Vladimir Lenin, "The Character of Our Newspapers," in *Collected Works*, 28:96; hereafter cited in text as "Character of Our Newspapers."

62. Viktor Shklovsky, "Zorich," in *Gamburgskii shchet. Stat'i, vospominaniia, esse (1914–1933)* (Moscow: Sovetskii Pisatel', 1990), 359.

63. Grossman-Roshchin, "Prestuplenie i nakazanie," 22.

64. On Machist currents within factography, see Anatolii Tarasenkov, "*Literatura fakta. Pervyi sb. materialov rabotnikov Lefa* pod red. N. Chuzhaka," *Pechat' i revoliutsiia*, no. 8 (1929): 106–10. Along similar lines, Georg Lukács wrote that while reading the works of Tret'iakov or Ottwalt, it is "hard not to recall Mach's 'complexes of sensation,' which, according to him, are what make up 'our reality.'" The "neomachist" factographer writes texts filled with "machist-sounding terminology." Georg Lukács, "Reportage or Portrayal?," 64, 62, 56. Accusations of Machism actually began already in the early years before the establishment of Lef when the Futurists first began to get involved with Proletkul't. One letter printed in *Pravda* in 1920 protested: "Under the guise of 'proletarian culture' they represented to the workers bourgeois views in

philosophy (Machism). And in the artistic sphere they implanted in the workers absurd, distorted tastes (futurism)." Quoted in Zenovia Sochor, *Revolution and Culture: The Bogdanov-Lenin Controversy* (Ithaca, NY: Cornell University Press, 1988), 153.

65. In general, members of the productivist avant-garde were enthusiastic about Bogdanov's philosophical writings but derided his conservative aesthetic tastes, which favored neoclassicism over machine-art. Writing about Bogdanov's "dogged and out-of-date ignorance in the realm of art," Chuzhak described the tektologist as "a formidable philosopher and economist, but a talentless and ignorant critic." Nikolai Chuzhak, "Nerazberikha," in *K dialektike iskusstva*: 110. Three particularly Boganovite texts by Tret'iakov stand out, all from 1923: "From Where"; "Lef i NEP," *Lef*, no. 2 (1923): 70–78; and "Art in the Revolution." For another Bogdanovite statement by a core Lef member, see Boris Arvatov, "Iskusstvo v sisteme proletarskoi kul'ture," in *Iskusstvo i proizvodstvo. Sbornik statei* (Moscow: Proletkul't, 1926), 94–130. On Bogdanov and Chuzhak, see Hans Günther, "Proletarische und avantgardistische Kunst. Die Organisationsästhetik Bogdanovs und die LEF-Konzeption der 'lebenbauenden' Kunst," *Ästhetik und Kommunikation* 12, no. 4 (1973): 62–75.

66. Anatolii I. Mazaev, *Kontseptsiia "proizvodstvennogo iskusstva" 20-x godov* (Moscow: Nauka, 1975), 233.

67. Grossman-Roshchin, "Prestuplenie i nakazanie," 17.

68. Aleksandr Fadeev, "Stolbovaia doroga proletarskoi literatury," *Oktiabr'*, no. 12 (1928): 182.

69. Aleksei Gastev, "Vosstanie kul'tury," in *Kak nado rabotat'. Prakticheskie vvedenie v nauku organizatsii truda*, edited by N. M. Bakhrakh et al. (Moscow: Ekonomika, 1966), 46.

70. Iakov Shafir, "Gazeta i sovremennaia epokha," in *Voprosy gazetnoi kul'tury* (Moscow: Gosudarstvennoe izdatel'stvo, 1927), 34.

71. With the exception of presentations about factography made in the German and British press in the early 1930s, Tret'iakov's contributions to the 1929 anthology *The Literature of Fact* will be his last major theoretical statements about factography in Russian until his 1934 retrospective text "Evoliutsiia zhanra."

72. Georg Lukács, *Lenin: A Study on the Unity of His Thought* (London: Verso, 2009), 41.

73. Viktor Shklovsky, "V zashchitu sotsiologicheskogo metoda," *Novyi lef*, no. 3 (1927): 21. Hegel had argued in his 1801 dissertation that there were only seven planets in our solar system, and when he was confronted with the "fact" of Neptune, which was discovered in 1846, the Idealist apparently responded "all the worse for the facts." When concrete evidence contradicted his theory, Hegel took the side of theory. Chuzhak too mocks Hegel's phrase in "Opyt uchoby na klassike," *Novyi Lef*, no. 7 (1928): 10.

74. Lorraine Daston, "Fear & Loathing of the Imagination in Science," *Daedalus* 134, no. 4 (2005): 28. See also idem, "Baconian Facts, Academic Civility, and the Prehistory of Objectivity," in *Rethinking Objectivity*, edited by Allan Megill (Durham, NC: Duke University Press, 1994), 37–63.

75. See, for example, E. Arnol'di, "Fakty—veshch' upriamaia," *Zhizn' iskusstva*, no. 34 (1929): 6–7; S. Rozval, "Ob upriamykh faktakh," *Zhurnalist*, no. 12 (1929): 658–60, and *Zhurnalist*, no. 22 (1929): 686–87.

76. For an overview of responses, see Hugh Ridley, "Tretjakov in Berlin," in *Culture and Society in the Weimar Republic*, edited by Keith Bullivant (Manchester: Man-

chester University Press, 1977), 150–65. In addition to Benn's "Die neue literarische Saison," there was the trenchant criticism from Johannes Becher, "Unsere Wendung. Vom Kampf um die Existenz der proletarisch-revolutionären Literatur zum Kampf um ihre Erweiterung," *Die Linkskurve* 3, no. 10 (1931): 1–8. An equally negative response comes from Ezra Pound, in "Open letter to Tretjakow, kolkhoznik," *Front*, no. 2 (1931): 124–26.

77. Walter Benjamin, "The Author as Producer," in *Selected Writings*, edited by Marcus Bullock and Michael W. Jennings (Cambridge, MA: Belknap Press, 1996), 2:768–82; hereafter cited in text as "Author as Producer." The phrase "wide-eyed presentation of mere facts" comes from a letter that Adorno wrote to Benjamin, in Theodor W. Adorno and Walter Benjamin, *The Complete Correspondence, 1928–1940*, edited by Henri Lonitz, translated by Nicholas Walker (Cambridge, MA: Harvard University Press, 1999), 283. It is not surprising that Benjamin would be so powerfully drawn to Tret'iakov's project, given his own experiments writing nonlinear documentary history in works like the *Arcades Project*.

78. Siegfried Kracauer, "Der operierende Schriftsteller. Zu Tretjakows Buch *Feld-Herren*," in *Schriften: Aufsätze*, edited by Inka Mülder-Bach (Frankfurt am Main: Suhrkamp, 1990), 5.3:28.

79. Siegfried Kracauer, "Instruktionsstunde in der Literatur. Zu einem Vortrag des Russen Tretjakow," in *Schriften*, 5.2:311. Further texts by Kracauer on Tret'iakov are "Über den Schriftsteller," in *Schriften*, 5.2:343–46, in which Kracauer reiterates that the factographer's chief mistake was that he "wasn't familiar with the German situation" (345); and "Ein Bio-Interview," in *Schriften*, 5.3:52–55.

80. Werner Hamacher, "Journals, Politics," in *Responses: On Paul de Man's Wartime Journalism*, edited by Werner Hamacher, Neil Hertz, and Thomas Keenan (Lincoln: University of Nebraska Press, 1989), 453.

81. Dmitrii Levonevskii, "Literatura fakta," *Zhizn' iskusstva*, no. 3 (1929): 6.

82. Kracauer, "Der operierende Schriftsteller," 28.

83. "The 'Western' Marxism of 1923 lacked a means of expressing the inertia of the infrastructures, the resistance of economic and even natural conditions, and the swallowing-up of 'personal relationships' in 'things.' History as they described it lacked density and allowed its meaning to appear too soon. They had to learn the slowness of mediations." Maurice Merleau-Ponty, *Adventures of the Dialectic*, translated by Joseph Bien (Evanston, IL: Northwestern University Press, 1973), 64.

84. Hans Ulrich Gumbrecht, *Our Broad Present: Time and Contemporary Culture* (New York: Columbia University Press). Similarly, the anti-historicist method of media archaeology today can be linked to the expansion of digital culture over the last two decades.

85. Kracauer writes that

> although Tret'iakov's notions . . . find no immediate application in our conditions because of course we don't find ourselves in the stage of socialist construction, they can be used to engage critically with various forms of literary expression that are native here. Above all with the form of *reportage*. Tret'iakov's methods are superior to those of the latter because they don't show matter from a perspective that is more or less subjectively conditioned, but instead transform matter in the process of presenting it. Of course, operating in accordance with the Russian example is not

possible for our writers at the present moment; but Tret'iakov's efforts can nonetheless prompt some of our authors finally to interrogate their *relationship to practice*. . . . At the very least, Tret'iakov's book [*Die Feld-Herren*] can direct the attention of many writers to the question of how to understand the urgent necessity of fusing theory with practice.

"Der operierende Schriftsteller," 28.

86. "Liberal conceptions of objectivity, independence or freedom of the press were overtly dismissed as an ideological fiction in Bolshevik journalism." Jeremy Hicks, "From Conduits to Commanders: Shifting Views of Worker Correspondents, 1924–1926," *Revolutionary Russia* 19, no. 2 (2006): 133.

87. Sergei Tret'iakov, "S. Tretjakov," *Die Literatur in der Sowjetunion* 7/8 (1934): 135. For more about audience responses during his 1931 tour, see Sergei Tret'iakov, "Eine Sache der Ehre—eine Sache des Ruhms," in *Rote Arbeit: Der neue Arbeiter in der Sowjetunion*, edited by Jürgen Kuczynski (Berlin: Historia-Foto, 1931), 60–88.

88. For his critique of tourism, see Sergei Tret'iakov, *Vyzov. Kolkhoznye ocherki* (Moscow: Federatsiia, 1930; hereafter cited in text as *Vyzov*); and S. Tretyakow, "Report." See also Maria Gough, "Radical Tourism: Sergei Tret'iakov at the Communist Lighthouse," *October* 118 (2006): 159–78.

89. Alfred H. Barr, "Russian Diary 1927–28," *October* 7 (1978): 31.

90. On the "subjectivism" of Chuzhak and Tret'iakov, see Aleksandr Voronsky, "Art as the Cognition of Life, and the Contemporary World (Concerning Our Literary Disagreements)," in *Art as the Cognition of Life: Selected Writings, 1911–1936*, edited and translated by Frederick S. Choate (Oak Park, MI: Mehring Books, 1998), 102–16.

91. Alexander Bogdanov, *Empiriomonism*, edited and translated by David G. Rowley (Leiden: Brill, 2020), 269. For Bogdanov, truth was the result not of the mind's accurate "reflection" of the world but of the correspondence (*соответсвие*, *совпадение*) between the grammar of consciousness and that of reality. The experience of truth was an effect of the structural resonance between individual and world that Mach called *Mitstimmung*. See V. I. Lenin on *sovpadenie* and *Mitstimmung* in *Materialism and Empirio-criticism*, translated by Abraham Fineberg, in *Collected Works* (Moscow: Progress, 1962), 14:114.

92. The argument that factography represents a transition from the avant-garde to Socialist Realism is central to Zalambani, *Literatura fakta*; Elizabeth Papazian, *Manufacturing Truth: The Documentary Moment in Early Soviet Culture* (DeKalb: Northern Illinois University Press, 2009); and, most recently, a special issue of *Russian Literature* dedicated to Tret'iakov, whose editors write that "the logical conclusion of this approach is the Socialist Realism of the 1930s." Tat'iana Hofmann, Denis Ioffe, and Hans Günther, "Sergei Tret'iakov: Estetika politicheskogo dokumentalizma i produktivizma. Vvedenie," *Russian Literature*, no. 103–5 (2019): 12.

93. Nikolai Chuzhak, "Ruzh'e, kotoroe ne streliaet," RGALI, f. 340, o. 1, d. 18. Also see Nikolai Chuzhak, *"Literatura": K khudozhestvennoi politike RKP* (Moscow: Vserossiiskii Proletkul't, 1924); and Chuzhak, "Chto kul'tlivirovat'? (k diskussii o politike RKP v khudozhestvennoi literature)," *Pravda* (6 February 1924): 5.

94. "Dada could be understood essentially as a school of 'subjective' positivism, in contrast to the 'objective' positivism of logical empiricism. Both positivisms intersect in their radical semantic cynicism. Dada speaks of *nonsense* in an existential regard; the

logical positivists speak of *senselessness* with regard to (e.g. metaphysical) statements." Peter Sloterdijk, *Critique of Cynical Reason*, translation by Michael Eldred (Minneapolis: University of Minnesota Press, 1987), 408. On the "tyranny of the particular" in the Documents circle, see Denis Hollier, "The Use-Value of the Impossible," in *Absent Without Leave: French Literature Under the Threat of War*, translated by Catherine Porter (Cambridge, MA: Harvard University Press, 1997), 125–44.

95. Giorgio Agamben, "The Passion of Facticity," in *Potentialities: Collected Essays in Philosophy*, translated by Daniel Heller-Roazen (Stanford, CA: Stanford University Press, 1999), 189. Daston likewise observes that "one of the most striking features of the new-style scientific facts of the seventeenth century is how swiftly and radically they broke with the etymology that connected them to words like 'factory' and other sites of making and doing." Daston, "Fear & Loathing of the Imagination in Science," 18.

96. Sergei Tretyakov, "From the Editor," translated by John E. Bowlte, in *Photography in the Modern Era*, 270; translation modified. See also Sergei Tret'iakov, "K probleme soderzhanii," *Oktiabr' mysli*, no. 5 (1923): 3.

97. Iuda Grossman-Roshchin, "Sotsial'nyi zamysel futurizma," *Lef*, no. 4 (1924): 112.

98. Louis Althusser, "The Only Materialist Tradition, Part I: Spinoza," translated by Ted Stolze, in *The New Spinoza*, edited by Warren Montag and Ted Stolze (Minneapolis: University of Minnesota Press, 1998), 13.

99. Platon Kerzhentsev, *Gazeta. Organizatsiia i tekhnika gazetnogo dela*, 2nd ed. (Moscow: Gosizdat, 1925), 6; hereafter cited in text as *Gazeta*.

100. Viktor Pertsov, "Anekdot," *Novyi Lef*, no. 2 (1927): 41. Soviet critics working in the field of newspaper studies in the 1920s also proposed the joke as a discursive model for journalists to emulate. Iakov Shafir, who explored the connection between the news and Freud's *Wit and Its Relation to the Unconscious*, argued that both the news and the joke rely on the principle of condensation (*сгущение*, or *Verdichtung*). Shafir, *Ot ostroty do pamfleta* (Moscow: Rabotnik prosveshcheniia, 1925).

101. Daston, "Fear & Loathing of the Imagination in Science," 18. Catherine Gallagher likewise writes: "Before the scientific revolution, contingency was thought to be a characteristic of facts in general: the word *fact* was used mainly to describe the time-bound and particular deeds of humankind as opposed to the eternal and general truths of nature. . . . The stark opposition between everlasting truths and contingent facts . . . became blurrier, yet the difference between widely applicable principles and contingent occurrences survives in distinctions between facts and explanations, generalizations, meanings, hypotheses, and laws." In "Facts, Fictions, Counterfactuals," *PMLA* 134, no. 5 (2019): 1129.

102. William R. Dennes, "Fact and Interpretation," in *Studies in the Nature of Facts* (Berkeley: University of California Press, 1932), 99. Dennes, a Spinoza scholar, observes that "to deny that facts are events, and events facts" leads to an "indefensible identification of fact and truth" (97).

103. Lorraine Daston, "Marvelous Facts and Miraculous Evidence in Early Modern Europe," *Critical Inquiry* 18, no. 1 (1991): 93–124.

104. V. I. Lenin, "Letters from Afar," in *Collected Works*, 23:297.

105. Louis Althusser, *Philosophy of the Encounter: Later Writings, 1978–87*, edited by François Metheron and Oliver Corpet, translated by G. M. Goshgarian (London: Verso, 2006); hereafter cited in text as *Philosophy of the Encounter*.

106. Karl Marx, *Difference Between the Democritean and Epicurean Philosophy of Nature*, in Marx and Engels, *Collected Works*, 1:90.

107. Sergei Tret'iakov, "Ferz' ili peshka," *Revoliutsiia i kul'tura*, no. 1 (1928): 50; hereafter cited in text as "Ferz' ili peshka."

108. Viktor Shklovsky, "Mistakes and Inventions," in *The Film Factory: Russian and Soviet Cinema in Documents*, edited and translated by Richard Taylor (Cambridge, MA: Harvard University Press, 1988), 180–83.

109. Quoted in Jane Burbank, *Intelligentsia and Revolution: Russian Views of Bolshevism, 1917–1922* (Oxford: Oxford University Press, 1986), 4.

110. Aleksandr Kurs, "Informatsiia (reportazh)" [Parts I and II], *Zhurnalist*, no. 1 (1929): 43; Part III in *Zhurnalist*, no. 2 (1929): 53–56; hereafter cited in text as "Informatsiia (reportazh)."

111. Hans-Jörg Rheinberger, "Difference Machines: Time in Experimental Systems," *Configurations*, no. 23 (2015), 166–67. Importantly, the scientific experiment is less oriented toward the future so much as it is oriented away from the present. The "time trajectory" of the experiment "does not point toward something, but rather away from the current state of the art. Historian of science Thomas Kuhn addressed this precise point when he said that research is 'a process driven from behind.' It is not a teleological enterprise, as is often suggested; certainly, you can have a goal in mind, and as a rule one must if one carries out research, but the end result defies again and again our capacity to anticipate" (167).

112. Il'ia Dukor, "S. Tret'iakov," *Na literaturnom postu*, no. 18 (1928): 50; hereafter cited in text as "S. Tret'iakov."

113. This phrase is from Lorraine Daston, *Classical Probability in the Enlightenment* (Princeton, NJ: Princeton University Press, 1988), 60.

114. This was a favorite idiom of Tret'iakov that comes up in other texts, including "The Industry Production Screenplay," edited by Masha Salazkina, translated by Mihaela Mihailova, *Cinema Journal* 51, no. 4 (2012): 135; hereafter cited in text as "Industry Production Screenplay."

115. Like that of the factographer, the mind of the gambler is focused entirely upon the current moment:

> the peculiar capacity of the game to provoke presence of mind through the fact that, in rapid succession, it brings to the fore constellations which work—each one wholly independent of the others—to summon up in every instance a thoroughly new, original reaction from the gambler. This fact is mirrored in the tendency of gamblers to place their bets, whenever possible, at the very last moment—the moment, moreover, when only enough room remains for a purely reflexive move. Such reflexive behavior on the part of the gambler rules out an "interpretation" of chance. The gambler's reaction to chance is more like that of the knee to the hammer in the patellar reflex.

Walter Benjamin, *The Arcades Project*, edited by Rolf Tiedemann, translated by Howard Eiland and Kevin McLaughlin (Cambridge, MA: Harvard University Press, 1999), 512–13. The reflexes of factography and the foreclosure of interpretation will be explored in the second chapter of this book.

CHAPTER 1

1. Leon Trotsky, "On Stenography," in *Problems of Everyday Life, and Other Writings on Culture & Science* (New York: Monad Press, 1973), 230.

2. Sergei Tret'iakov, "Moskva–Pekin (put'fil'ma)," *Lef*, no. 3 (1925): 33; hereafter cited in text as "Moskva–Pekin."

3. Georg Simmel, "Das Abenteuer," in *Philosophische Kultur. Gesammelte Essays* (Leipzig: Alfred Kröner, 1919), 20.

4. Aleksei Gastev, "Vremia," in *Kak nado rabotat'*, 63; hereafter cited in text as "Vremia."

5. "Absolute representation, the total transparency between the representative and the represented, means the extinction of the relationship of representation." Ernesto Laclau, *New Reflections on the Revolution of Our Time*, translated by Jon Barnes (London: Verso, 1990), 38. On Tret'iakov's attempt to align event and writing, see Armen Avanessian and Anke Henning, *Präsens: Poetik eines Tempus* (Zurich: Diaphanes, 2012), 35–42.

6. On photography as a model for the factographers, see Leah Dickerman, "The Fact and the Photograph," *October*, no. 118 (2006): 132–52; Erika Wolf, "The Author as Photographer: Tret'iakov's, Erenburg's, and Il'f's Images of the West," *Configurations* 18, no. 3 (2010): 383–403; and Katherine M. H. Reischl, "'Where I Have Been with My Camera': Sergei Tret'iakov and Developing Operativity," *Russian Literature*, no. 103–5 (2019): 119–43.

7. Henri Bergson, *Creative Evolution*, translated by Arthur Mitchell (New York: The Modern Library, 1944), 332, 331. For modern science, time "has no natural articulations. We can divide it as we please. All moments count. None of them has the right to set itself up as a moment that represents or dominates the others" (332).

8. Brik's story begins when the appropriately named Leaguist Dmitrii Minutkin enjoins the hero: "You should become a Leaguist. You'll never have enough time to do anything in Moscow if you don't draw up a complete schedule of all of your activities that breaks down all of the times precisely." Such lines likely inspired Tret'iakov's "Moscow–Beijing." After the protagonist joins the League, the film features numerous shots of clocks, close-ups of the chronocard with his daily schedule broken down by hour, and, of course, many fast-motion sequences depicting hectic life in Moscow. Osip Brik and Sergei Iutkevich, "Prikliucheniia el'vista. Rezhisserskii stsenarii," *Kinovedicheskie zapiski*, no. 62 (2003): 83–95.

9. Tret'iakov would praise Kerzhentsev the "NOTist" and "the creator of the League of Time," although, as with Bogdanov, the factographers were disappointed with Kerzhentsev's traditional taste in art. Sergei Tret'iakov, "Vot spasibo," *Novyi Lef*, no. 5 (1927): 45–47.

10. Aleksei Gastev, "B'et chas," in *Poeziia rabochego udara* (Moscow: Khudozhestvennaia literatura, 1971), 248.

11. Kerzhentsev discusses meetings in "Vremia stroit aeroplany," in *Printsipii organizatsii. Izbrannye proizvedeniia* (Moscow: Ekonomika, 1968), 335–84. Gastev discusses delays in meetings in "Vremia."

12. I. Kan, "Vremia i kul'tura," *Vremia*, no. 4 (1924): 24, 26.

13. E. P. Thompson, "Time, Work-Discipline, and Industrial Capitalism," *Past*

and Present, no. 38 (1967): 56–97. Echoing Kan, Thompson writes: "It is well known that among primitive peoples the measurement of time is commonly related to familiar processes in the cycle of work or of domestic chores. Evans-Pritchard has analysed the time-sense of the Nuer: 'The daily timepiece is the cattle clock, the round of pastoral tasks, and the time of day and the passage of time through a day are to a Nuer primarily the succession of these tasks and their relation to one another'" (58).

14. Reinhart Koselleck, *Sediments of Time: On Possible Histories*, translated and edited by Sean Franzel and Stefan-Ludwig Hoffmann (Stanford, CA: Stanford University Press, 2018).

15. Hartmut Rosa, "Social Acceleration: Ethical and Political Consequences of a Desynchronized High-Speed Society," in *High-Speed Society: Social Acceleration, Power, and Modernity*, edited by Hartmut Rosa and William E. Scheuerman (University Park: Pennsylvania State University Press, 2009), 13–14.

16. Hartmut Rosa explains: "Contrary to a widespread opinion, modernity has not just established a single, unitary form of abstract, linear time that synchronizes its various subsystems. Rather, the process of functional differentiation has resulted in a series of almost autopoietic subsystems like the economy, science, law, politics, the arts, and so on, all of which follow their own temporal rhythms, patterns, and horizons. Just as there is no unifying social or substantial center governing the subsystemic operations, there is also no integrating temporal authority, and this, in turn, results in increasing temporal desynchronization." "Social Acceleration," 104.

17. Hartmut Rosa, *Social Acceleration: A New Theory of Modernity*, translated by Jonathan Trejo-Mathys (New York: Columbia University Press, 2013), 84.

18. Benjamin writes:

> A feeling for the value of time, notwithstanding all "rationalization," is not met with even in the capital of Russia. Trud, the trade-union institute for the study of work, under its director, Gastiev, launched a poster campaign for punctuality. From earliest times a large number of clockmakers have been settled in Moscow. Like medieval guilds, they are crowded in particular streets, on the Kuznetsky Bridge, on Ulitsa Gertsena. One wonders who actually needs them. "Time is money"—for this astonishing statement posters claim the authority of Lenin, so alien is the idea to the Russians. They fritter everything away. (One is tempted to say that minutes are a cheap liquor of which they can never get enough, that they are tipsy with time.) If on the street a scene is being shot for a film, they forget where they are going and why, and follow the camera for hours, arriving at the office distraught. In his use of time, therefore, the Russian will remain "Asiatic" longest of all.

Further: "The real unit of time is the *seichas*. This means 'at once.' You can hear it ten, twenty, thirty times, and wait hours, days, or weeks until the promise is carried out. By the same token, you seldom hear the answer no. Negative replies are left to time. Time catastrophes, time collisions are therefore as much the order of the day as *remonte*. They make each hour superabundant, each day exhausting, each life a moment." Walter Benjamin, "Moscow," in *Selected Writings*, 2:31–32.

19. Kan, "Vremia i kul'tura," 29.

20. Martin Heidegger, *The Concept of Time*, translated by William McNeill (Oxford: Blackwell, 1992), 17E.

21. John Durham Peters, *The Marvelous Clouds: Toward a Philosophy of Elemental Media* (Chicago: University of Chicago Press, 2015), 221.

22. Bernhard Siegert, "Longitude and Simultaneity in Philosophy, Physics, and Empires," *Configurations*, no. 23 (2015): 162.

23. A similar distinction comes up in Bloch, who differentiated in 1932 between "objective contemporaneity" (the "technological blessing") and "subjective contemporaneity" (the condition of "free revolutionary action"). Ernst Bloch, "Non-Contemporaneity and Obligation to Its Dialectic," in *Heritage of Our Times*, translated by Neville and Stephen Plaice (Oxford: Polity, 1991), 97–148.

24. I. Matsa, "'Seichas'.—'Nu, ladno . . . nichego,'" *Vremia*, no. 6 (1924): 31.

25. Carl Schmitt, *Political Romanticism*, translated by Guy Oakes (Cambridge, MA: MIT Press, 1986). In categorically rejecting the arbitrariness of the Now, the factographers distinguished themselves from other Presentist avant-gardes such as the Dadaists. Like the factographers, the Dadaists walked upon the "slippery plank of the present," as Maria Stavrinaki puts it, but the Dadaists' decisionistic conception of time ultimately precluded collective politics. *Dada Presentism: An Essay on Art & History*, translated by Daniela Ginsburg (Stanford, CA: Stanford University Press, 2016), 30. If Dada and Surrealism pursue what Schmitt called a "subjectified occasionalism," the factographers instead pursued a "objectified occasionalism" that was oriented toward intersubjective experience and facilitated the synchronization of collective endeavor.

26. Benjamin, "Moscow," 32.

27. F. Dunaevskii, "Psikhologiia opozdaniia," *Vremia*, no. 1 (1923): 19–23.

28. Gastev, "Snariazhaites', montery!," in *Poeziia rabochego udara*, 230.

29. Gleb Krzhizhanovskii, "Planovaia rabota SSSR," *Vremia*, no. 3 (1923): 5. For Krzhizhanovskii, the precise analytics of time was just as important for Russian economic and cultural modernization as the mapping of space: "Alongside these spatial coordinates, we continuously track the effect of our work in determinate calendrical segments as well, never for a minute allowing the lines of the fourth dimension—the coordinate of time—to slip out of our sights."

30. Kerzhentsev, "Vremia stroit aeroplany," 336.

31. A. Kaktyn', "Vremia, kak ekonomicheskii faktor," *Vremia*, no. 1 (1923): 7.

32. The first figure comes from Kerzhentsev, "Vremia stroit aeroplany," 335. The second figure comes from a leader of the League cell at Moscow State University. L. Tamarchenko, "Iazyk tsifr," *Vremia*, no. 6 (1924): 46–47.

33. Evgenii Al'perovich, "Khronometrazh," *Vremia*, no. 7 (1924): 26.

34. V. I. Lenin, "'Left-Wing' Communism: An Infantile Disorder," in *Collected Works*, 31:96.

35. Aron Zalkind, "Psikhlogiia cheloveka budushchego," in *Zhizn' i tekhnika budushchego*, edited by Ark. A-n and E. Kol'man (Moscow: Moskovskii rabochii, 1928), 456.

36. Karl Marx and Friedrich Engels, *The German Ideology*, in Marx and Engels, *Collected Works*, 5:47.

37. Gastev, "Snariazhaites', montery!," 230.

38. Gal', "Pisatel' vsekh zhanrov. S. Tret'iakov," 144.

39. Sergei Tret'iakov, "Chto pishut dramaturgi," *Rabis*, no. 11 (1929): 11.

40. Montaigne writes:

> I do not portray his being, I portray his passage; not a passage from one ago to

another or, as the common people say, from seven years to seven years, but from day to day, from minute to minute. I must suit my story to the hour, for soon I may change, not only by chance but also by intention. It is a record of various and variable occurrences, an account of thoughts that are unsettled and, as chance will have it, at times contradictory, either because I am then another self, or because I approach my subject under different circumstances and with other considerations. Hence it is that I may well contradict myself, but the truth, as Demades said, I do not contradict.

Michel de Montaigne, "On Repentance," in *Essays*, translated by J. M. Cohen (London: Penguin, 1993), 235.

41. Roland Barthes, *Writing Degree Zero*, translated by Annette Lavers and Colin Smith (New York: Hill and Wang, 2012), 76.

42. Karel Čapek, "In Praise of Newspapers," in *In Praise of Newspapers and Other Essays on the Margin of Literature*, translated by M. and R. Weatherall (London: Allen, 1951), 9–10; translation modified.

43. Egon Erwin Kisch, "Die Mutter des Mörders und ein Reporter," in *Der rasende Reporter* (Berlin: Aufbau, 1995), 342.

44. Gitelman explains: "The fleeting currency of news, the ephemerality of the papers, rendered them more like speech acts and less like print artifacts, while their tangibility conversely rendered them 'hard' evidence in black and white. Materially, newspapers were print. Legally, however, they tended to resemble vocal performances more than they did authored forms. According to a precedent established by the U.S. Supreme Court in 1829, nothing with 'so fluctuating and fugitive a form' could possess copyright, which the Constitution reserved for 'more fixed, permanent, and durable' expressions." Lisa Gitelman, *Always Already New: Media, History, and the Data of Culture* (Cambridge, MA: MIT Press, 2006), 28.

45. S. Ingulov, "Kak chitat' gazetu?," *Vremia*, no. 3 (1924): 48. This essay ("How to Read a Newspaper?") was printed opposite Nadezhda Krupskaia's "How to Read a Book?," which described a very different experience of time.

46. Kracauer, "Über den Schriftsteller," 344–54.

47. Nikolai Chuzhak, "Tvorchestvo slova," in *K dialektike iskusstva*, 15. "Presentification" is the term that Hans Ulrich Gumbrecht uses to describe the effect of "À une passante" by Baudelaire, the famous poet of modern life. *Production of Presence: What Meaning Cannot Convey* (Stanford, CA: Stanford University Press, 2004), 103.

48. Henri Lefebvre, *Critique of Everyday Life*, translated by John Moore (London: Verso, 1991), 2:224. What results is "the reign of an enormous tautology": Maurice Blanchot, "Everyday Speech," in *The Infinite Conversation*, translated by Susan Hanson (Minneapolis: University of Minnesota Press, 1993), 240.

49. Roman Jakobson, "Closing Statement: Linguistics and Poetics," in *Style in Language*, edited by T. A. Sebeok (New York: Wiley, 1960), 355.

50. Niklas Luhmann, *The Reality of the Mass Media*, translated by Kathleen Cross (Cambridge: Polity Press, 2000), 21.

51. Charles Madge, "Press, Radio, and Social Consciousness," in *The Mind in Chains: Socialism and the Cultural Revolution*, edited by C. Day Lewis (London: Frederick Muller, 1937), 148.

52. Tom Harrison, Humphrey Jennings, and Charles Madge, "Anthropology at Home," letter to *The New Statesman and Nation* (January 30, 1937).

53. Looking back on the factographic project, Tret'iakov would again reiterate this phrase: "It often seemed to me as if the newspaper was the all-encompassing epic of our age, just like the Iliad and the Odyssey were the epics of the ancient Greeks or the Bible was the epic of the ancient Jewish tribes. For the newspaper doesn't just reflect the present moment in words: it exerts an active influence upon this present and transforms it." Sergej Tretjakow, "Autobiographie" [1932], in *Lyrik, Dramatik, Prosa*, edited by Fritz Mierau (Frankfurt am Main: Röderberg, 1972), 16.

54. Sergej Tretjakow, "Mein erstes Gedicht" [1932], in *Lyrik, Dramatik, Prosa*, 11.

55. Dukor discusses Tret'iakov's shorthand formulations, which combine telegrammatic neologisms with stump-compounds, in "S. Tret'iakov," 48. These "compacts," as Tret'iakov called them, are further explored in D. A. Rachkov, "Is istorii stanovleniia sovetskoi poezii na dal'nem vostoke (Dal'nevostochnyi period S. Tret'iakova i P. Neznamova)," *Voprosy sovetskoi literatury* 13 (1965): 93–112.

56. This is Chuzhak's characterization of "Through Clouded Glasses" in an editor's footnote to the reprint of Tret'iakov's sketch in *Literatura fakta*, 227.

57. Aleksei Gastev, "Novaia kul'turnaia ustanovka," in *Kak nado rabotat'*, 93; hereafter cited in text as "Novaia kul'turnaia ustanovka." On Kerzhentsev and stenography, see Solomon Levin, "Stenografiia v obikhode zhurnalista," *Zhurnalist*, no. 10 (1928): 34–35.

58. "Ot redaktsii," *Vremia*, no. 1 (1923): 48.

59. Trotsky, "On Stenography," 231.

60. Trotsky, "On Stenography," 230.

61. Roland Barthes, *The Preparation of the Novel*, translated by Kate Briggs (New York: Columbia University Press, 2011), 263–65; hereafter cited in text as *Preparation of the Novel*.

62. Mikhail Kol'tsov, "'Svoeiu sobstvennoi rukoi' ili . . . mashinkoi?," *Zhurnalist*, no. 13 (1924): 24.

63. Ia. T-d, "Lakonizm v iskusstve," *Vremia*, no. 3 (1924): 24–27.

64. Nikolai Tarabukin, "Foto-reklama i foto-plakat," *Vremia*, no. 10–11 (1924): 45. When Tarabukin revised this text and republished it the following year, first in Chuzhak's *Proletkul't Al'manakh* and then as the concluding chapter to his *Iskusstvo dnia* (*Art of the Day*), the expanded version explored the distinction between painterly realism and photography as an instrument of scientific inquiry.

65. Aleksandr Rodchenko, "Against the Synthetic Portrait, For the Snapshot," translated by John E. Bowlte, in *Photography in the Modern Era*, 239–40. Susan Sontag likewise explained that "the photograph is a thin slice of space as well as time. In a world ruled by photographic images, all borders ('framing') seem arbitrary. Anything can be separated, can be made discontinuous, from anything else." *On Photography* (New York: Farrar, Straus & Giroux, 1973), 22.

66. Ron Burnett, *Cultures of Vision: Images, Media, and the Imaginary* (Bloomington: Indiana University Press, 1995), 59.

67. Nikolai Chuzhak, "Bez rulia i bez vetril," *Oktiabr' mysli*, no. 1 (1924): 38–47. The critique of the "spiritism" of mimetic realism is in "Literatura proletariev," *Oktiabr' mysli*, no. 5–6 (1924): 40–52, esp. 43. See also Chuzhak's tirade against depictivism and representationalism as "sores" on the organism of proletarian literature in *"Literatura". K khudozhestvennoi politike RKP*, 100. On the Futurist crusade against the novel's "provincial reflectionism with respect to everyday life," see also I. Ioffe, *Krizis sovremen-*

nogo iskusstva (Leningrad: Priboi, 1925), 27. Ioffe's study already predicts that the great novel will be replaced by lesser factographic genres like the telegram, the radio transmission, and the feuilleton.

68. Nikolai Chuzhak, "A Writer's Handbook," translated by Devin Fore and Douglas Greenfield, *October*, no. 118 (2006): 83; hereafter cited in text as "Writer's Handbook."

69. To this day, Chuzhak has a reputation as a vulgar sociologist of art, but his functionalist approach to cultural production actually aligned him more closely with the work of the Formalists. Indeed, the influences of Tynianov, Shklovsky, and Jakobson on Chuzhak are profound. The original table of contents for his edited 1929 volume *The Literature of Fact* promised a breviary of Formalist criticism: see "Po knigam i zhurnalam: Literatura fakta," *Novyi Lef*, no. 10 (1928): 45–47.

70. Chuzhak, "Chto kul'tlivirovat'?," 5.

71. On the purported "cult of description" among the factographers, see N. Berkovskii, "Bor'ba za prozu" [Part I], *Na lit. postu*, no. 23 (1928): 26–36. Much subtler is Georg Lukács, "Narrate or Describe?," in *Writer and Critic and Other Essays*, edited and translated by Arthur Kahn (London: Merlin Press, 1970), 110–48; hereafter cited in text as "Narrate or Describe?" Unfortunately for our purposes, the 1970 English translation of Lukács's "Narrate or Describe?" omits the final section (VII) of the German original, which turns to recent developments in Soviet literature and culminates in a critique of Tret'iakov's factographic work, and of his notorious "biography of the thing" in particular. Georg Lukács, "Erzählen oder Beschreiben?," in *Werke: Probleme des Realismus I* (Neuwied am Rhein: Luchterhand, 1962), 4:197–242; hereafter cited in text as "Erzählen oder Beschreiben?"

72. Chuzhak responds to the critics who complained about the Lefists' lack of imagery and their abstractness (*беспредметничество*, or "non-objectivism") in "'V rode otkrytogo pis'ma . . .' Vol'noe podrazhanie Lunacharskomu," *Pravda* (January 5, 1924): 7.

73. Iurii Tynianov, "Illiustratsii," *Kniga i revoliutsiia*, no. 4 (1923): 15–19.

74. Maksim Gor'kii, "O sotsialisticheskom realizme" (1933), quoted in Evegeny Dobrenko, *The Making of the Soviet Writer: Social and Aesthetic Origins of Soviet Literary Culture*, translated by Jesse M. Savage (Stanford, CA: Stanford University Press, 2001). On Gorky's elevated point of view, see also Papazian, *Manufacturing Truth*, 133–37.

75. Andreas Guski, "Der Präzeptor unterwegs: Gor'kijs Reiseskizzen 'Durch die Union der Sowjets,'" in *Flüchtige Blicke. Relektüren russischer Reisetexte des 20. Jahrhunderts*, edited by Wolfgang Kissel (Bielefeld: Aisthesis, 2009), 213. As Guski observes, "eating, drinking, sleeping, corporeal or mental dispositions: all of this is removed indefinitely" (216).

76. Maksim Gor'kii, "Po soiuzu sovetov," in *Polnoe sobranie sochinenii v dvadtsati piati tomakh* (Moscow: Nauka, 1974), 20:116.

77. Gal', "Pisatel' vsekh zhanrov," 145.

78. André Breton, "Manifesto of Surrealism," in *Manifestoes of Surrealism*, translated by Richard Seaver and Helen R. Lane (Ann Arbor: University of Michigan Press, 1972), 29–30.

79. Dunaevskii, "Psikhologiia opozdaniia," 20.

80. Viktor Pertsov, "Udarnyi tsekh sovetskoi literatury," in *Pisatel' na proizvodstve. Opyt postanovki voprosa* (Moscow: Federatsiia, 1931), 165.

81. Oskar Maria Graf, "Gegen den Dichter von Heute," in *Neue Sachlichkeit. Quel-*

len und Dokumente, edited by Sabine Becker (Cologne: Böhlau, 2000), 2:48.

82. Nikolai Chuzhak, "Opyt ucheby na klassike," *Novyi Lef*, no. 7 (1928): 9, 11, 16.

83. Nikolai Chuzhak, "Iskusstvo byta," *Sovetskoe iskusstvo*, no. 4–5 (1925): 10.

84. Chuzhak, "Opyt ucheby na klassike," 10, 14. Chuzhak was not the only one to notice Gorky's evasiveness: "A specific characteristic of Gorky's style is the polysemy of the word." V. Keldysh, "Gorkii o sotsialisticheskom realizme," in *Iz istorii sovetskoi esteticheskoi mysli. Sbornik statei*, edited by Ivan Matsa (Moscow: Iskusstvo, 1967), 460. Chuzhak's distinction between construction and cognition originates in a polemic with Voronsky, who had famously defined art as "the cognition of life." For Voronsky, cognition is, and must always be, out of sync with the present. "Man first cognizes, then he acts, 'he builds,'" writes Voronsky in "Art as the Cognition of Life, and the Contemporary World" (105). To propose that construction and cognition might coincide, as Chuzhak did, leads to pure relativism (110).

85. A. Kurs, "Daem otvety na vsiakie muchitel'nye lit-voprosy," *Nastoiashchee*, no. 1 (1929): 8–13. Sergei Eisenstein, "Dynamic Mummification: Notes for a General History of Cinema," in *Notes for a General History of Cinema*, edited by Naum Kleiman and Antonio Somaini, translated by Margo Shohl Rosen et al. (Amsterdam: Amsterdam University Press, 2016), 183–84. Elsewhere, Eisenstein observed that "the mistake of [the documentarists of the 1920s] was that, in propagandizing for the fact, they failed to see that, in that period, the fact was at the same time an *image* [*факт является одновременно* образом]." Eisenstein, "Vystuplenie na vsesoiuznom tvorcheskom soveshchanii rabotnikov sovetskoi kinematografii," in *Izbrannye proizvedeniia* (Moscow: Iskusstvo, 1964), 2:97–98.

86. L. Kozlov, "Avtora, avtora! . . . ," *Inostrannaia literatura*, special issue *Literatura, dokument, fakt*, no. 8 (1966): 197.

87. Sergei Tret'iakov, "Obrazoborchestvo," *Novyi Lef*, no. 12 (1928): 43. Decades after the factographer's death, Pertsov would still recall that Tret'iakov rejected "the image in art the way that iconoclasts rejected worship through images. In his futurism, and as an adherent of the 'literature of fact,' S. Tret'iakov looked at times like an iconoclast." Viktor Pertsov, "Sergei Tret'iakov," in Sergei Tret'iakov, *Den Shi-Khua, Liudi odnogo kostra, Strana perekrestok* (Moscow: Sovetskii pisatel', 1962), 21.

88. Jacques Rancière, *The Future of the Image*, translated by Gregory Elliott (London: Verso, 2007), 19.

89. Allan Paivio, *Imagery and Verbal Processes* (New York: Holt, Rinehart and Winston, 1971), 1–10. The best overview of twentieth-century research on reading and the imagination is Ellen Esrock, *The Reader's Eye: Visual Imaging as Reader Response* (Baltimore: Johns Hopkins University Press, 1994).

90. I. Beksler, "Fedor Mikhailovich Reshetnikov," in *Literaturnaia entsiklopediia*, edited by V. M. Friche (Moscow: Izd-vo Kommunisticheskoi akademii, 1930).

91. Georg Lukács, *The Theory of the Novel*, translated by Anna Bostock (Cambridge, MA: MIT Press, 1971), 60.

92. Roman Jakobson, "On Realism in Art," in *Language in Literature*, edited by Krystyna Pomorska and Stephen Rudy (Cambridge, MA: Belknap Press, 1987), 21, 26.

93. Nikolai Chuzhak, "Ot illiuzii k materii. Po povodu Reviziia LEF'a," in *Reviziia levogo fronta*, edited by Viktor Pertsov (Moscow: Vserossiiskii Proletkul't, 1925), 119.

94. Nikolai Chuzhak, "Diskussiia o literaturno-khudozh. taktike gruppy *Na literaturnom postu*: 'I shefstvuia vazhno,'" *Zhizn' iskusstva*, no. 27 (1927): 4.

95. Alain Robbe-Grillet, "A Future for the Novel," in *For a New Novel: Essays on Fiction*, translated by Richard Howard (Evanston, IL: Northwestern University Press, 1989), 21.

96. Quoted in Jacques Catteau, *Dostoevsky and the Process of Literary Creation*, translated by Audrey Littlewood (Cambridge: Cambridge University Press, 1989), 193.

97. Georg Lukach, "Reportazh ili obrazotvorchestvo? Kriticheskie zamechaniia po povodu romana Otval'ta," translated by I. Barkhash, *Internatsional'naia literatura*, no. 1 (1933): 91–104. Ottwalt's response appeared in the following issue: Ernst Otwal't, "Roman fakta (otvet Lukachu)," *Internatsional'naia literatura* no. 2 (1933): 105–9.

98. Anselm Haverkamp points out that the Russian Formalists did not distinguish rigorously between metaphor and the image as such. "Einleitung," in *Theorie der Metapher*, edited by Anselm Haverkamp (Darmstadt: Wissenschaftliche Buchgesellschaft, 1983), 1. It warrants mention here that, unlike the English word "image," which is associated specifically with a visual mode of representation, the Russian word *obraz* suggests trope more generally (a common translation for *obraz* is "figure"). For a useful overview of scholarship on metaphor at the time of factography, see N. N. Volkov, "Chto takoe metafora?," in *Khudozhestvennaia forma*, edited by A. G. Tsires (Moscow: GAKhN, 1927), 81–124.

99. Iurii Tynianov, "Slovar' Lenina-polemista," *Lef*, no. 5 (1924): 98–99; hereafter cited in text as "Slovar.'"

100. Michel Leiris, *Brisées: Broken Branches*, translated by Lydia Davis (San Francisco: North Point Press, 1989), 18.

101. Haverkamp, "Einleitung," 2. Likewise: "Metaphor is not one figure of discourse among others, but the transference principle common to all of them." Paul Ricoeur, *The Rule of Metaphor*, translated by Robert Czerny (Toronto: University of Toronto Press, 1977), 237.

102. Martin Heidegger, *The Principle of Reason*, translated by Reginald Lilly (Bloomington: Indiana University Press, 1991), 48.

103. Shpet discusses the image-word (*слово-образ*) and the term-word (*слово-термин*) in *Esteticheskie fragmenty* (Peterburg: Kolos, 1923), 3:32–35. Grigorii Vinokur, "Poeziia i nauka," in *Chet i nechet: Al'manakh poezii i kritiki* (Moscow: Avtorskoe Izdanie, 1925), 21–31. Ricoeur confirms this opposition: "Technical language and poetic language constituted two ends of a single scale. One end is occupied by univocal meanings anchored in definitions. At the other end, no meaning stabilizes outside of the 'movement among meanings.'" *The Rule of Metaphor*, 78.

104. S. I. Kartsevskii, *Iazyk, voina, i revoliutsiia* (Berlin: Russkoe universal'noe izdatel'stvo, 1923), 67.

105. Aleksei Kruchenykh, "Declaration of the Word as Such," in *Russian Futurism Through Its Manifestoes*, 67.

106. The Lefist Grigorii Vinokur defends the newspaper's complex linguistic technology (*лингвистическая технология*) against the "simplificationists" of language in "Iazyk nashei gazety," *Lef*, no. 6 (1924): 117–40. His brilliant critique of purism had appeared in the journal two issues prior: "O purizme," *Lef*, no. 4 (1924): 156–71.

107. Aleksandr Luria, *The Mind of a Mnemonist: A Little Book About a Vast Memory*, translated by Lynn Solotaroff (Cambridge, MA: Harvard University Press, 1987), 113, 121.

108. Richard Stites, *Revolutionary Dreams: Utopian Vision and Experimental Life*

in the Russian Revolution (Oxford: Oxford University Press, 1988), 235.

109. Theodor W. Adorno, "On the Use of Foreign Words," in *Notes to Literature*, edited by Rolf Tiedemann, translated by Shierry Weber Nicholsen (New York: Columbia University Press, 1992), 2:290, 287, 288, 290, 291, 287. Although Adorno does not directly mention the language of the daily press in the final version of the essay, he explained in a letter to Walter Benjamin that his reflections were meant as a defense of "the language-chaos of the newspapers." See the editorial note in Walter Benjamin, *Gesammelte Schriften*, edited by Rolf Tiedemann and Hermann Schweppenhäuser (Frankfurt am Main: Suhrkamp, 1972–), II.3:1437.

110. Mikhail Bekker, "Problema khudozhestvennogo ocherka," *Na literaturnom postu*, no. 13 (1929): 56.

111. Viktor Shklovsky, *A Hunt for Optimism*, translated by Shushan Avagyan (Champaign, IL: Dalkey Archive Press, 2012), 5; translation modified; hereafter cited in text as *Hunt for Optimism*.

112. Tret'iakov, quoted in "Na vsesoiuznom soveshchanii po khudozhestvennomu ocherku," *Literaturnaia gazeta*, no. 74 (June 12, 1934): 3. Reading over Tret'iakov's dispatches from the kolkhoz, Shklovsky had written earlier that year that "the image is usually presented weakly and tersely, only mentioned in passing as a transition between pieces." As a result of their diminished image-content, "Tret'iakov's sketches became unconcrete [*неконкретными*]." Shklovsky, "Ocherki ob ocherkakh," *Literaturnaia gazeta*, no. 43 (April 8, 1934): 2.

113. Chuzhak's insight about Gorky was confirmed many decades later, and in a very different geopolitical context, when Dutch research psychologists conducted experiments in the 1980s—a decade far more sympathetic to figuration than the 1920s—which demonstrated that readers of Gorky who were instructed to focus on the imagery of the text were then able to recall the general contours of the story better than the test group that was instructed to focus on informational accuracy. C. Giesen and J. Peeck, "Effects of Imagery Instruction on Reading and Retaining a Literary Text," *Journal of Mental Imagery* 8, no. 2 (1984): 87.

114. Adorno, "On the Use of Foreign Words," 287.

115. Leon Trotsky, "Alas, We Are Not Accurate Enough!," in *Problems of Everyday Life*, 116.

116. Aleksei Gastev, "Kak nado rabotat'," in *Kak nado rabotat'*, 122.

117. Quoted in Kornelii Zelinskii, "Konstruktvizm i sotsializm," in *Biznes. Sbornik Literaturnogo Tsentra Konstruktivistov*, edited by K. Zelinskii and I. Sel'vinskii (Moscow: Gosudarstvennoe izd-vo, 1929), 62.

118. Viktor Pertsov, "Nekrolog, kak forma professional'noi kharakteristiki," in *Literatura zavtrashnego dnia* (Moscow: Federatsiia, 1929), 7.

119. Carl Einstein, *Die Kunst des 20. Jahrhunderts* (Leipzig: Philipp Reclam, 1988), 273, 271. Along similar lines, Shklovsky wrote that "the constructivists wanted to be Futurists without errors [*футуристами без ошибок*]" (*A Hunt for Optimism*, 130).

120. Vsevolod Meyerhold, *Meyerhold on Theater*, edited and translated by Edward Braun (London: Bloomsbury Methuen, 2017), 49, 41.

121. Meyerhold shared Arthur Schopenhauer's dislike of facsimiles: "Wax figures have no aesthetic impact even though they represent the closest imitation of nature. It is impossible to regard them as artistic creations, because they leave nothing to the imagination of the spectator." *Meyerhold on Theater*, 25.

122. M. Zagorskii, "Rychi, Kitai," *Zhizn' iskusstva*, no. 6 (1926): 11–12.

123. Benjamin, "Surrealism," 208.

124. Petr Palievskii, "Rol' dokumenta v organizatsii khudozhestvennogo tselogo," in *Problemy khudozhestvennoi formy sotsialisticheskogo realizma*, edited by N. K. Gei et al. (Moscow: Nauka, 1971), 400.

125. Shklovsky, *Literature and Cinematography*, 53–54.

126. Siegfried Kracauer, "Photography," in *The Mass Ornament: Weimar Essays*, edited and translated by Thomas Y. Levin (Cambridge, MA: Harvard University Press, 1995), 51, 52, 58, 59, 62.

127. Wolfgang Iser, "Context-Sensitivity and Its Feedback: The Two-Sidedness of Humanistic Discourse," in *Emergenz: Nachgelassene und verstreut publizierte Essays*, edited by Alexander Schmitz (Konstanz: Konstanz University Press, 2013), 220. K. Ludwig Pfeiffer likewise observes that if "reflective-imaginative thought is no longer activated, then the contribution of the 'imagined' that is necessary for the representation of even the most elementary experiences is eventually lost." In an age of ultra-precise technical media, "image and image content melt into a pseudorealism that economizes the 'effort of imagining.'" "Dimensions of Literature," in *Materialities of Communication*, edited by Hans Ulrich Gumbrecht and K. Ludwig Pfeiffer, translated by William Whobrey (Stanford, CA: Stanford University Press, 1994), 47.

128. Erik Reger, "Die Erneuerung des Menschen durch den technischen Geist. Oder: Das genau gebohrte Loch," in *Kleine Schriften*, edited by Erhard Schütz (Berlin: Argon, 1993), 1:61.

129. Roman Jakobson, "On a Generation That Squandered Its Poets," in *Language in Literature*, 277.

130. There is hardly a single statement by the factographers that does not attack imagining or the imagination, that realm of inner experience that constituted the greatest obstacle to their efforts to connect with the present. Just two years after *Novyi Lef* closed, the editors of the journal *The Present* summarized the factographic episode: "The Lefists tried to reevaluate [*переоценить*] all of the very 'eternal' provisions of art. Imagination, contrivance, invention, fantasy . . . were put into question by the Lefists. . . . Questions about the relationship of art to actual reality arose for many, and the Lefists were correct to undertake this reevaluation, but the problem was that they did it in the wrong way. They slid into base empiricism. They opposed the artistic image to the fact as such; they opposed imagination and invention to the precise recording of the fact, to factography; they threw out generalization and abstraction entirely." "Novyi god 'Nastoiashchego,'" *Nastoiashchee*, no. 1 (1930): 8.

131. Chuzhak outlines the program of "future-exactism" in "K zadacham dnia," *Lef*, no. 2 (1923): 152.

132. Nikolai Aseev, quoted in Pertsov, *Sovremenniki*, 127.

133. Il'ia Erenburg, "Romantizm nashikh dnei," in *Belyi ugol', ili slezy Vertera* (Leningrad: Priboi, 1928), 16–17.

134. According to Tzvetan Todorov, the nineteenth-century fantastic flourished in the gap between experience and knowledge. This mode was characterized by an element of uncertainty, a moment of vacillation when the reader cannot decide whether events are hallucinated or real, supernatural or scientific. *Tzvetan Todorov, The Fantastic: A Structural Approach to a Literary Genre*, translated by Richard Howard (Ithaca, NY: Cornell University Press, 1975).

135. Il'ia Erenburg, "Materializm fantastiki," in *Belyi ugol'*, 42.

136. Theodor W. Adorno, "'Beautiful Passages' in Beethoven," quoted in Shierry Weber Nicholsen, *Exact Imagination, Late Work: On Adorno's Aesthetics* (Cambridge, MA: MIT Press, 1997), 20. Commenting on Adorno, Susan Buck-Morss would thus describe fantasy as a "dialectical concept which acknowledged the mutual mediation of subject and object without allowing either to get the upper hand." *The Origin of Negative Dialectics: Theodor W. Adorno, Walter Benjamin and the Frankfurt Institute* (New York: Free Press, 1977), 86.

137. Theodor W. Adorno, "The Actuality of Philosophy," translated by Benjamin Snow, *Telos*, no. 31 (1977): 131, 132–33.

138. Erenburg, "Materializm fantastiki," 41. In a discussion of early film, Friedrich Kittler likewise observed: "A new imaginary sphere emerged. It was no longer literary, as in the Romantic period, but rather technogenic. Tzvetan Todorov's theory that the fantastic in literature died after it was elucidated by Freud and psychoanalysis is partly false: the fantastic experienced a triumphant resurrection through film." *Optical Media: Berlin Lectures 1999*, translated by Anthony Enns (Cambridge: Polity Press, 2010), 166.

139. "Nothing is more fickle than a colourless writing. Mechanical habits are developed in the very place where freedom existed, a network of set forms hem in more and more the pristine freshness of discourse." Barthes, *Writing Degree Zero*, 78.

140. In geometry, every spatial aspect of a form—shape, area, angle, scale, and so on—corresponds to a precise numerical value. It constitutes an empirical mathematics whose objects are at once both fully rationalized and spontaneously *anschaulich* (sensuously intelligible). Geometry thereby provides one possible answer to the question "How can the subjective egological evidence of sense become objective and intersubjective?" Jacques Derrida, *Edmund Husserl's* Origin of Geometry*: An Introduction*, translated by John P. Leavey Jr. (Lincoln: University of Nebraska Press, 1989), 63.

141. In his commentary to "Through Clouded Glasses," Chuzhak would characterize this as "the first step in connecting our theory with a scientific-biological system." *Literatura fakta*, 227.

142. On Tret'iakov's critique of orientalist exotica, see Edward Tyerman, *Internationalist Aesthetics: China and Early Soviet Culture* (New York: Columbia University Press, 2022).

143. Joel Snyder, "Visualization and Visibility," in *Picturing Science, Producing Art*, edited by Caroline Jones and Peter Galison (New York: Routledge, 1998), 388.

144. Karmen would later explain that "Moscow at Night during October Days" reflected his increasing preoccupation with capturing time on the photographic plate. He would soon abandon still photography entirely and start a career as a documentary filmmaker. *Roman Karmen v vospominaniiakh sovremennikov*, edited by A. L. Vinogradov (Moscow: Iskusstvo, 1983), 119–20.

145. Sergei Tret'iakov, "Gazeta na shestakh," *Novyi Lef*, no. 10 (1927): 18–19; hereafter cited in text as "Gazeta na shestakh."

146. I. Ch., "Kak ispol'zovali deistvennikov," *Novyi L*ef, no. 10 (1927): 10–14.

147. "Who has not crammed, running from corner to corner in a four-walled enclosure book in hand? / Who has not drummed rhythmically with his fist, memorising 'Surplus value is . . .' / In other words who has not given visual stimulation a helping hand by including some sort of motor rhythm in order to memorise abstract truths?"

Sergei Eisenstein, "Perspectives," in *Selected Works*, edited and translated by Richard Taylor (London: BFI, 1988), 1:157.

CHAPTER 2

1. Andrey Platonov, *The Foundation Pit*, translated by Robert Chandler, Elizabeth Chandler, and Olga Meerson (New York: New York Review of Books, 2009), 53.

2. Tarasenkov, "*Literatura fakta*," 106, 107.

3. Fedor Ivanov, "Fetishisty fakta," *Krasnaia nov'*, no. 7 (1929): 234.

4. Sergei Tret'iakov, "Knige," in *Iasnysh. Stikhi* (Chita: Ptach, 1922), 3.

5. S. Vysheslavtseva, "O motornykh impul'sakh stikha," in *Poetika. Sbornik statei* 3 (1927): 58. She describes the phenomenon of poetic contagion thus: "Our vocal apparatus is connected to the nervous and the muscular system as a whole through countless of the finest threads. Thanks to this fact, there exists an extremely intimate interconnection between the motor-vocal and general motor sensation: one series of sensation at times penetrates another in a parallel fashion, the intensity of certain sensations is accompanied by an increase in the intensity of others, a change in the overall character of the first ones is reflected in the overall character of the second" (48).

6. Sergei Tret'iakov, "The Theater of Attractions," translated by Kristen Romberg, *October* 118 (2006): 26, 21; hereafter cited in text as "Theater of Attractions." Eisenstein is typically credited for introducing the theory of the "attraction" into Russian theater and cinema, but the concept was one that he and Tret'iakov developed together.

7. Sergei Tret'iakov, "'Zemlia dybom': tekst i rechemontazh," *Zrelishcha*, no. 27 (1923): 7.

8. Tret'iakov explained at the 1934 ocherk conference that his interest in the physical and psychoacoustic aspects of the word had originated in his work as a Futurist poet: *Vsesoiuznom soveshchanii po khudozhestvennomu ocherku* (June 8, 1934), in RGALI, f. 631 (SSP), o. 1, d. 70–73, l. 120.

9. Raketa, "Opyt teatral'noi raboty. *Na vsiakogo mudretsa dovol'no prostoty*," *Gorn*, no. 8 (1923): 57–58.

10. Mel Gordon and Alma Law, "Eisenstein's Early Work in Expressive Behavior: The Montage of Movement," *Millenium Film Journal*, no. 3 (1979): 27. See also Mel Gordon, "Eisenstein's Later Work at the Proletkult," *The Drama Review* 22, no. 3 (1978): 108.

11. Chuzhak, *"Literatura". K khudozhestvennoi politike RKP*, 99.

12. Voronsky, "Art as the Cognition of Life," 107.

13. Sergei Tret'iakov, "S novym godom! S *Novym Lefom*!," *Novyi Lef*, no. 1 (1928): 2.

14. Tikhon Churilin, "Pokhvala literaturnoi negramotnosti. Khod k obsledovaniiu obrashcheniia s khudozhestvennoi literaturoi," *Na putiiakh iskusstva. Sbornik statei*, edited by V. M. Bliumenfel'd, V. F. Pletnev, and N. F. Chuzhak (Moscow: Proletkul't, 1926), 125, 129. This essay singles out Tret'iakov as the most advanced among the circle of Futurists who are developing a new method of "verbal-artistic materialism."

15. Lenin, *Materialism and Empirio-criticism*, 51. The first chapter of the book, titled "Sensations and Complexes of Sensations," offers a detailed critique of the Machist concept of sensation and a defense of the epistemology of the image. For Lenin, "our sensations, our consciousness are only an *image* of the external world [образ *внешнего мира*]" (69).

Emma Widdis's important study *Socialist Senses* reconstructs the avant-garde projects that explored the affective stratum of *oshchushchenie* and that Widdis, in turn, contrasts with the succeeding school of Socialist Realism that sought to reassert the sovereignty of the eye over other sense organs. *Socialist Senses: Film, Feeling, and the Soviet Subject, 1917–1940* (Bloomington: Indiana University Press, 2017), 5. According to Edward Tyerman, Tret'iakov's internationalist aesthetic was based on the practice of connecting people through sensory experience. *Internationalist Aesthetics*, 14–28.

16. "Ot redaktsii," *Proletarskaia kul'tura*, no. 3 (1919): 36.

17. On Lef's "world-sensation," see also Sergei Tret'iakov, "LEF i NEP," *Lef*, no. 2: 70–78.

18. Churilin, "Pokhvala literaturnoi negramotnosti," 130.

19. V. M. Bekhterev, *Collective Reflexology: The Complete Edition*, edited by Lloyd Strickland, translated by Eugenia Lockwood and Alisa Lockwood (New York: Routledge, 2001), 118.

20. Mikhail Gus, *Informatsiia v gazete. Opyt prakticheskikh posobii* (Moscow: Gosudarstvennoe izd-vo, 1930), 88; hereafter cited in text as *Informatsiia v gazete*.

21. Ilia Ehrenburg, *A vse-taki ona vertitsia* (Moscow: Gelikon, 1922), 99–100.

22. Shafir, "Poznai svoego chitatelia," in *Voprosy gazetnoi kul'tury*, 184–85.

23. I. Starobogatov, "Problemy gazetnoi verstki," in *Problemy gazetovedeniia. Sbornik pervyi*, edited by D. Bentsman, Iu. Bocharov, and M. Gus (Moscow: GIZh, 1930), 129.

24. Mikhail Gus, "Problemy izucheniia gazetnogo iazyka," in *Problemy gazetovedeniia*, 64.

25. Many of Lissitzky's strategies for the Cologne exhibition responded to the suggestions made in the monthly *Journalist* column that ran on Pressa starting already in December 1927. See, in particular, Krasnov, "Keln'skaia vystavka pechati 'Pressa': 'Samoe sil'noe i samoe grandioznoe,'" *Zhurnalist*, no. 11 (1928): 21–23; and anon., "Keln'skaia vystavka pechati 'Pressa': Podgotovka sovetskogo pavil'ona," *Zhurnalist*, no. 1 (1928): 32–33.

Gus in turn recognized their brief to be "showing the particularity of our press" to an audience who could not understand its actual contents. See "Uchastie SSSR na Mezhdunaronnoi vystavke pechati v Kël'ne" from "Iz otcheta otdela vystavok VOKS o vystavochnoi rabote v 1927–1928 gg.," in *Vystavochnye ansambli SSSR 1920–1930-e gody. Materialy i dokumenty* (Moscow: Galart, 2006), 126–27. For Gus's reflections on his collaboration with Lissitzky, including a detailed account of Gorky's visit to Pressa, see Mikhail Gus, *Bezumie svastiki* (Moscow: Sovetskii pisatel', 1971), 41–51.

26. *Frankfurter Zeitung* (May 29, 1928), quoted in *Katalog des Sowjet-Pavillons auf der internationalen Presse-Ausstellung Köln*, edited by Mikhail Gus (Cologne: Dumont, 1928), 108.

27. *Manchester Guardian* (June 16, 1928), quoted in *Katalog des Sowjet-Pavillons*, 109.

28. A. Khalatov, "Vorwort," in *Katalog des Sowjet-Pavillons*, 5. Already in 1920 Lissitzky had rejected the metaphysics of acoustic speech in favor of motor optics: "The book finds its channel to the brain through the eye, not through the ear; in this channel the waves rush through with much greater speed and pressure than in the acoustic channel." El Lissitzky, "Our Book," translated by Helene Aldwinckle and Mary Whittall, in *Graphic Design Theory: Readings from the Field*, edited by Helen Armstrong (Princeton, NJ: Princeton University Press, 2009), 29.

29. On Lissitzky's campaign against phonetic writing as an anticipation of Derrida's critique of metaphysics, see Yve-Alain Bois, "El Lissitzky: Reading Lessons," translated by Christian Hubert, *October* 11 (1979): 113–28.

30. *Manchester Guardian* (June 16, 1928), quoted in *Katalog des Sowjet-Pavillons*, 109.

31. *Berliner Tageblatt* (May 26, 1928), quoted in *Katalog des Sowjet-Pavillons*, 107.

32. See, for example, Gus's Rubakinite anthology *Problemy gazetovedeniia*. For a critique of Rubakin's influence on Gus's group, see M. Bochacher, "O metodologii gazetovedeniia," *Zhurnalist*, no. 5 (1930): 156.

33. The first quote is from N. Rubakin and M. Bethman, "On Bibliopsychology: The Psychology of the Public Library," in *Nicholas Rubakin and Bibliopsychology*, edited by S. Simsova (London: Clive Bingley, 1968), 11. The second quote is from D. Balika, "Chitatel' i kniga," *Krasnyi bibliotekar'*, no. 10 (1926): 105.

34. Nikolai Rubakin, "The 'Special Method' of Bibliopsychology," in *Nicholas Rubakin and Bibliopsychology*, 32.

35. Balika, "Chitatel' i kniga," 104–5.

36. Shafir, "Zagolovok," in *Voprosy gazetnoi kul'tury*, 177–79.

37. Nikolai Rubakin, "Rabota biblioekaria s tochki zreniia biblio-psikhologii," in *Chitatel' i kniga. Metody ikh izucheniia*, edited by Ia. V. Rivlin, N. A. Rubakin, and B. O. Borovich (Khar'kov: Trud, 1925), 50–51. Here, as elsewhere, Rubakin uses the word "book" to designate all print media.

38. Quoted in Daniel Schacter, James Eric Eich, and Endel Tulving, "Richard Semon's Theory of Memory," in Schacter, *Forgotten Ideas, Neglected Pioneers: Richard Semon and the Story of Memory* (London: Taylor & Francis, 2001), 256.

39. Ol'gin, "O Kel'ne i o 'Presse' konkretno," *Zhurnalist*, no. 3 (1928): 45.

40. *Frankfurter Zeitung*, quoted in *Katalog des Sowjet-Pavillons*, 108.

41. See, for example, A. Basler, "Über das Sehen von Bewegungen: I. Mitteilung. Die Wahrnehmung kleinster Bewegungen," *Pflügers Archiv für Physiologie*, no. 115 (1906): 582–601; and A. Basler, "Über das Sehen von Bewegungen: II. Mitteilung. Die Wahrnehmung kleinster Bewegungen bei Ausschluss aller Vergleichsgegenstände," *Pflügers Archiv für Physiologie*, no. 124 (1908): 313–35. More recently, see Jerome Y. Lettvin, "On Seeing Sidelong," *The Sciences* 16 (1976): 10–20; and Marc Boucher, "A Study on Proprioception and Peripheral Vision in Synesthesia and Immersion," *Leonardo* 50, no. 2 (2017): 144–51.

42. Khalatov, "Vorwort," 5.

43. Lissitzky, "Do Not Separate Form from Content!," in *El Lissitzky. 1890–1941* (Cambridge, MA: Harvard University Press, 1987), 62.

44. Sergei Tret'iakov, "Biografiia moego stikha," in *15 let russkogo futurizma*, edited by Aleksei Kruchenykh (Moscow: Vserossiiskii soiuz poetov, 1928), 56.

45. Theodor W. Adorno, *Kierkegaard: Construction of the Aesthetic*, translated by Robert Hullot-Kentor (Minneapolis: University of Minnesota Press, 1989), 46.

46. Ernst Jünger, *The Worker: Dominion and Form*, edited by Laurence Paul Hemming, translated by Bogdan Costea and Laurence Paul Hemming (Evanston, IL: Northwestern University Press, 2017), 167–68, 170, 85; translation modified.

47. Gastev reiterated the primacy of observation above all other cultural qualifications in his introduction to Nikolai Dmitrievich Levitov, *Nabliudatel'nost'* (Moscow: TsIT, 1924), 3; hereafter cited in text as *Nabliudatel'nost'*. Members of the League of

Time similarly proclaimed the "power of observation" to be the most valuable of all contemporary skills: see A. Denisov, "Vremia—NOT," in *Vremia*, no. 4 (1923): 55.

48. Lorraine Daston and Elizabeth Lunbeck, "Introduction: Observation Observed," in *Histories of Scientific Observation* (Chicago: University of Chicago Press, 2011), 3.

49. The primary source for Levitov's definition of *nabliudatel'nost'* was the work of the German experimental psychologist Ernst Meumann, above all the chapter on "Das beobachtende Merken" in the classic study *Ökonomie und Technik des Gedächtnisses: Experimentelle Untersuchungen über das Merken und Behalten* (Leipzig: J. Klinkhardt, 1908).

50. See the descriptions of these tests in L. Braginskii, "Vospitanie nabliudatel'-nosti," *Oktiabr' mysli*, no. 2 (1924): 62–65.

51. Walter Benjamin, "The Work of Art in the Age of Its Mechanical Reproducibility," in *Selected Writings*, 4:267. For Benjamin, this state of alert distraction finds its opposite not in attention but in contemplation. As Carolin Duttlinger explains, "Benjamin's own model of distraction goes far beyond the goal of passive exposure," but combines features of active and passive perception. "Between Contemplation and Distraction: Configurations of Attention in Walter Benjamin," *German Studies Review* 3, no. 1 (2007): 42. See also Howard Eiland, "Reception in Distraction," *boundary 2*, no. 30 (2003): 51–66.

52. Evgenii Al'perovich, "Khronometrazh," *Vremia*, no. 7 (1924): 26.

53. Shafir, "Gazeta i sovremennaia epokha," 34.

54. Immanuel Kant, *Anthropology from a Pragmatic Point of View*, edited and translated by Robert B. Louden (Cambridge: Cambridge University Press, 2006), 100–102.

55. Stanley Cavell, "The Fact of Television," *Daedalus* 111, no. 4 (1982): 93, 92.

56. On the clock and Heidegger's *Wachsein*, see Peters, *The Marvelous Clouds*, 241–43.

57. Ingulov, "Kak chitat' gazetu?," 48.

58. Luhmann, *The Reality of the Mass Media*, 22.

59. Benjamin, "Surrealism," 218.

60. René Fülöp-Miller, *The Mind and Face of Bolshevism: An Examination of Cultural Life in Soviet Russia*, translated by F. S. Flint and D. F. Tait (New York: A. A. Knopf, 1928), 155.

61. H. S. Curtis, "Automatic Movements of the Larynx," *American Journal of Psychology*, no. 11 (1900): 237.

62. Ana Hedberg Olenina, *Psychomotor Aesthetics: Movement and Affect in Modern Literature and Film* (Oxford: Oxford University Press, 2020), 92. For a contemporaneous discussion of these issues in Formalism, see M. Grigor'ev, "Biologicheskii uklon v literaturovedenii (Kritika biologicheskikh poniatii v literaturovedenii)," *Na literaturnom postu*, no. 3 (1928): 24–30. According to Grigor'ev, the Formalists consider the literary work as a "record of a motor scheme" and see the process of reading as "a reenactment of the movements that are recorded" (24).

63. Nikolai Chuzhak et al., "Proletarskaia kul'tura. Tezisy," *Al'manakh Proletkul'ta* (1925): 14. Although this essay appeared in the *Al'manakh* without attribution of authorship, Chuzhak claimed at the 1925 Lef conference to have written it.

64. S. T-ov, "Pererozhdenie ili velikoe istoricheskoe utverzhdenie?," *Oktiabr' mysli*, no. 5: 2. On the unification of physical and mental labor in factography, see also Viktor

Pertsov, *O chem i kak pisat' rabochemu pisateliu* (Moscow: Khudozhestvennaia literatura, 1931), 9–10.

65. Bekhterev's essay is discussed in Shafir, "Protsess chteniia i izuchenie chitatelia," in *Voprosy gazetnoi kul'tury*, 179.

66. Vladimir Bekhterev, "Umstvennyi trud s refleksologicheskoi tochki zreniia i izmerenie sposobnosti k sosredotocheniiu," in *Refleksologiia truda*, edited by A. A. Press (Moscow: Gosudarstvennoe izd-vo, 1926), 53–97.

67. Quoted in Michael Dewey, "Revolution, Philologie und 'literarischer Alltag," in Boris Eichenbaum, *Mein Zeitbote. Belletristik, Wissenschaft, Kritik, Vermischtes* (Leipzig: Gustav Kiepenheuer, 1987), 219.

68. Zakharii I. Chuchmarev, "Opyt eksperimental'noi khudozhestvennoi kritiki," *Sovetskoe iskusstvo*, no. 9 (1925): 22. See Chuchmarev's major essay on Formalism, "Sotsiologichnyi metod v istorii i teorii literatury," *Chervonyi shliakh*, no. 7–8 (1926): 208–32.

69. Z. I. Chuchmarev and V. A. Lavrova, *Psikhofiziologicheskoe issledovanie truda telegrafistov-klopferistov* (Khar'kov: Ukrainskii gosudarstvennyi psikho-nevrologicheskii institut, 1927), 13, 31.

70. Chuchmarev, "Opyt eksperimental'noi khudozhestvennoi kritiki," 27, 24–25.

71. In subsequent versions of this experiment, Chuchmarev added a device for measuring galvanic skin activity, a physiological response that has been foregrounded in more recent research on affect. Brian Massumi, "The Autonomy of Affect," in *Parables for the Virtual: Movement, Affect, Sensation* (Durham, NC: Duke University Press, 2002), 23–45.

72. Robert Brain, *The Pulse of Modernism: Physiological Aesthetics in Fin-de-Siecle Europe* (Seattle: University of Washington Press, 2015), 20–21.

73. Chuchmarev, "Opyt eksperimental'noi khudozhestvennoi kritiki," 28.

74. Wilhelm Wundt, *Outlines of Psychology*, translated by Charles Hubbard Judd (London: Williams & Norgate, 1897), 197. On the reception of these experiments in Russia and elsewhere, see David K. Robinson, "Reaction-Time Experiments in Wundt's Institute and Beyond," in *Wilhelm Wundt in History. The Making of a Scientific Psychology*, edited by Robert W. Rieber and David K. Robinson (London: Kluwer, 2001), 161–204.

75. Sergei Eisenstein, "More Notes for a Film of *Capital*," translated by Michael Kunichika, forthcoming in *October*. See also Irina Sirotkina, "The Ubiquitous Reflex and Its Critics in Post-Revolutionary Russia," *Berichte zur Wissenschaftsgeschichte* 32 (2009).

76. R. V. L. Hartley, "Transmission of Information," *Bell Systems Technical Journal* (July 1928): 538.

77. Chuchmarev and Lavrova, *Psikhofiziologicheskoe issledovanie truda telegrafistov-klopferistov*, 4, 7, 143, 47.

78. On the "factical materials" that were the basis for Mayakovsky's poem, collected during his time working at ROSTA during the Civil War, see V. F. Zemskov, "Reka po imeni 'Fakt' (nekotorye istoricheskie istochniki poemy 'Khorosho!')," in *Poema Maiakovskogo "Khorosho!" Sbornik statei* (Moscow: Izd-vo Akademii nauk, 1958), 177–212.

79. Valer'ian Pletnev, "Na ideologicheskom fronte," *Pravda*, no. 217 (September 27, 1922): 3. His article followed an item in *Pravda* on the Russian Telegraph Agency ROSTA. For Pletnev, the transformation of language into electrical-telegraphic

impulses breaks down bourgeois dualisms. He predicts that "an artist's ability to think generally and monistically will become just as necessary as breathing, eating and drinking" (3).

80. P. Ia. Chernykh, "Russkii iazyk i revoliutsiia," in *Sovremennyi techeniia v lingvistike* (Irkutsk: Vlast' truda, 1929), 60, 61.

81. Iosif Burdianskii, "K lakonizmu," *Vremia*, no. 3 (1923): 28.

82. Jonathan Sterne, "Compression: A Loose History," in *Signal Traffic: Critical Studies of Media Infrastructures*, edited by Lisa Parks and Nicole Starosielski (Urbana: University of Illinois Press, 2015), 33–34.

83. Kenez, *The Birth of the Propaganda State*, 231.

84. L. D. Trotskii, "Kak pisat' stat'i," *Zhurnalist*, no. 8–9 (1925): 18.

85. Vinokur, "Iazyk nashei gazety"; and L. D. Trotskii, "Za kachestvo zhurnalistiki," *Zhurnalist*, no. 8–9 (1926): 18. On electrical tension in newspaper language, see Mikhail Gus's lecture "Predmet, zadachi i metody izucheniia gazetnogo iazyka," *Zhurnalist*, no. 5 (1927): 59–61.

86. Vitalii Kostomarov, *Russkii iazyk na gazetnoi* polose (Moscow: Izd-vo Moskovskogo universiteta, 1971), 60–89; Irina Lysakova, *Iazyk gazety i tipologiia pressy* (St. Petersburg: Filologicheskii fakultet SPBGU, 2005), 225ff.

87. Vinokur, "Iazyk nashei gazety," 123. Compression would become a key feature of factography in turn: the ocherk is "a distinct kind of creation in which the *many, the great and the important is stated in few words*, in a terribly compact [*страшно сжатом*], condensed form." G. Vovsy, "Ob ocherke voobshche i ob ocherkakh Zhigi v chastnosti," *Literatura i iskusstvo*, no. 3–4 (1930): 105.

88. Chuzhak, "Tvorchestvo slova," 15–17. According to Chuzhak, the telegraph overturned the tenets of Lessing's *Laocoon*, which had famously argued that literature's defining quality was its temporal duration.

89. Vinokur, "Iazyk nashei gazety," 123.

90. Daniel Weiss, "Was ist neu am 'Newspeak,'" *Slavistische Linguistik*, edited by Renate Rathmayr (Munich: Otto Sagner, 1986), 274.

91. Kornelii Zelinskii, *Poeziia kak smysl. Kniga o konstruktivizme* (Moscow: Federatsiia, 1929). Not for nothing did every one of the factographers, from Tret'iakov to Kushner to Agapov, begin their literary career as a poet: writing poetry provided an ideal training in verbal economy and syntactic supersaturation. Decades later Agapov, who was a member of Zelinskii's Literary Center of Constructivists in the 1920s, would likewise write that "tectonically, the ocherk is closest to lyrical verse." Boris Agapov, "Khozaistvo dokumentalista," *Voprosy literatury*, no. 11 (1960): 169.

92. Quoted in Fritz Mierau, "Tatsache und Tendenz. Der 'operierende' Schriftsteller Sergej Tretjakow," in *Lyrik, Dramatik, Prosa*, 449.

93. Arvatov likened the trans-sense language of Kruchenykh and Khlebnikov to "the telegraph code adopted for communication between industrial firms." Boris Arvatov, "Rechetvorchestvo," in *Sotsiologicheskaia poetika* (Moscow: Federatsiia, 1928), 130.

94. Iakov Shafir, "Iazyk gazety," in *Voprosy gazetnoi kultury*, 130.

95. Gus, *Informatsiia v gazete*, 209. Italics added.

96. Grigorii Vinokur, "Odin iz voprosov iazykovoi politiki," in *Kul'tura iazyka* (Moscow: Federatsiia, 1929), 161.

97. Vinokur, "Iazyk nashei gazety," 131.

98. Vinokur, "Iazyk nashei gazety," 125.

99. Vitalii Kostomarov, "Lingvisticheskii status massovoi kommunikatsii," in *Psikholingvisticheskie problemy massovoi kommunikatsii*, edited by A. A. Leont'ev (Moscow: Nauka, 1974), 60; Françoise Thom, *Newspeak: The Language of Soviet Communism*, translated by Ken Connelly (London: Claridge Press, 1989), 101.

100. Recent research confirms that the affective responses of the body are faster than thought. Consciousness, again, is just matter on a delay: "Thought lags behind itself. It can never catch up with its own beginnings. The half-second of thought-forming is forever lost in darkness. All awareness emerges from a nonconscious thought-o-genic lapse indistinguishable from movements of matter" (Massumi, "The Autonomy of Affect," 195). A useful overview of scientific research into the temporality of consciousness can be found in Michael I. Posner, *Chronometric Explorations of Mind* (Hillsdale, NJ: L. Erlbaum Associates, 1978).

101. L. S. Vygotsky, "Consciousness as a Problem in the Psychology of Behavior," in *Undiscovered Vygotsky: Etudes on the Pre-History of Cultural-historical Psychology*, edited and translated by Nikolai Veresov (Frankfurt am Main: Peter Lang, 1999), 279.

102. Chuchmarev and Lavrova, *Psikhofiziologicheskoe issledovanie truda telegrafistov-klopferistov*, 188.

103. Aleksei Gastev, "Ustanovka proizvodstva metodom TsIT," in *Trudovye ustanovki*, edited by Iu. A. Gastev and E. A. Petrov (Leningrad: Ekonomika, 1973), 168. This definition of consciousness as feedback appears in other essays by Gastev as well, where he describes the human as "a machine with the most precise autoregulator: the brain" and the brain as a "beautiful autoregulator." *Trudovye ustanovki*, 123, 194. Gastev explored a basic principle of second-wave cybernetics long before scientists like Heinz von Foerster proposed that consciousness resulted from autopoietic closure and feedback.

104. Bernhard Siegert, *Relays: Literature as an Epoch of the Postal System*, translated by Kevin Repp (Stanford, CA: Stanford University Press, 1999), 12.

105. Katerina Clark describes spontaneity and consciousness as "one of the key binary oppositions in Russian culture" in *The Soviet Novel: History as Ritual* (Bloomington: Indiana University Press, 2000), 20.

106. Vladimir Bazarov, "Material kollektivnago opyta i organizuiushchiia ego formy," in *Ocherki filosofii kollektivizma. Sbornik pervyi* (St. Petersburg: Znanie, 1909): 151–52, 153, 149, 151.

107. Paul Virilio, *The Vision Machine*, translated by Julie Rose (London: BFI, 1994), 3.

108. The discussion of Jung appears only in the Ukrainian version of Chuchmarev's text: "Sproba eksperimental'noi khudozhestvennoi kritiki," *Chervonyi shliakh*, no. 11–12 (1925), 193.

109. Roman Jakobson, "Language in Relation to Other Communication Systems" (The Hague: Mouton, 1971), 2:705.

110. Charles S. Peirce, *The Essential Peirce: Selected Philosophical Writings*, edited by Nathan Houser and Christian J. W. Kloesel (Bloomington: Indiana University Press, 1992), 163, 226, 14, 380.

111. Boris Eikhenbaum, "How Gogol's 'Overcoat' Is Made," in *Gogol from the Twentieth Century: Eleven Essays*, edited and translated by Robert A. Maguire (Princeton, NJ: Princeton University Press, 1974), 279–80; translation modified. Formalists of other traditions made similar claims. For example, in 1925 the New Critic I. A.

Richards distinguished between the "auditory image" of language and the "image of articulation," a term which he glossed as "the feel in the lips, mouth, and throat, of what the words would be like to speak":

> Too much importance has always been attached to the sensory qualities of images. What gives an image efficacy is less its vividness as an image than its character as a mental event peculiarly connected with sensation. It is, in a way which no one yet knows how to explain, a relic of sensation and our intellectual and emotional response to it depends far more upon its being, through this fact, a representative of a sensation, than upon its sensory resemblance to one. An image may lose almost all its sensory nature to the point of becoming scarcely an image at all, a mere skeleton, and yet represent a sensation quite as adequately as if it were flaring with hallucinatory vividity. In other words, what matters is not the sensory resemblance of an image to the sensation which is its prototype, but some other relation, at present hidden from us in the jungles of neurology.

Principles of Literary Criticism (New York: Harcourt, Brace & World, 1925), 119–20.

112. Tynianov, "Illiustratsii," 18.

113. Igor' Terent'ev, "'Khochu rebenka.' Plan postanovki," *Novyi Lef*, no. 12 (1928), 33.

114. Sergei Tret'iakov, "Khochu rebenka! Kino-libretto," in *Khochu rebenka! P'esy, stsenarii, diskussii*, edited by Tat'iana Khofman and Eduard Jan Ditschek (St. Petersburg: Aleteia, 2018), 205, 198.

115. Tret'iakov, "Pererozhdenie ili velikoe istoricheskoe utverzhdenie," 3.

116. Wilhelm Ostwald, *Große Männer: Studien zur Biologie des Genies* (Leipzig: Akademische Verlagsgesellschaft, 1910), 371–73.

117. Sergei Tret'iakov, "Ich will ein Kind! Zweite Fassung," translated by Ernst Hube, adapted by Bertolt Brecht, in *Ich will ein Kind! Zwei Stückfassungen und ein Film-Libretto*, edited by Tatjana Hofmann and Eduard Jan Ditschek (Berlin: Kadmos, 2019), 174, 186–87. The original Russian for the second version of *I Want a Baby* is lost; all that remains is the German translation by Hube and Brecht.

118. Jimena Canales, *A Tenth of a Second: A History* (Chicago: University of Chicago Press, 2009).

119. Viktor Pertsov, "Slovo—zritel'nyi obraz—budushchee," *Al'manakh proletkul'ta* (Moscow: Vserossiiskii Proletkul't, 1925), 89, 86, 90, 88. Viktor Pertsov discusses Ostwald in "Proizvodstvennaia psikhologiia i khudozhestvennaia literatura," in *Literatura zavtrashnego dnia*, 28–47.

120. Pertsov, "Slovo—zritel'nyi obraz—budushchee," 93.

121. Dziga Vertov, "We: Variant of a Manifesto," in *Kino-Eye: The Writings of Dziga Vertov*, edited by Annette Michelson, translated by Kevin O'Brien (Berkeley: University of California Press, 1984), 7.

122. Starting in the 1920s, Miles Tinker began publishing legibility experiments under the rubric of "the hygiene of reading." This work eventually led to the books *The Legibility of Print* (Ames: Iowa State University Press, 1963) and *Bases for Effective Reading* (Minneapolis: University of Minnesota Press, 1965).

123. Laszlo Moholy-Nagy, *Vision in Motion* (Chicago: Paul Theobold, 1946), 307.

124. Pertsov, "Slovo—zritel'nyi obraz—budushchee," 88. The next year Pertsov would continue his studies of language velocity and the newspaper in "Slovo-dvigateli," *Zhurnalist*, no. 8–9 (1926): 24.

125. V. A. Kuz'michev, *Pechatnaia agitatsiia i propaganda* (Moscow: Gosudarstvennoe izd-vo, 1930), 167. Like many of his contemporaries, Kuz'michev equates consciousness with braking: "Gesture, facial expression, and thought: all of these are motor reflexes that have been braked and delayed (at the highest level of life's development, they are delayed by consciousness)." He continues: "Along its pathway, every psychic process encounters moments of braking that either slow down the flow of the process or even transform completely. This 'braking' is variable, depending on the social conditions."

126. Viktor Pertsov, "Ob"em khudozhestvennogo proizvedeniia i biudzhet vremeni russkogo rabochego," in *Literatura zavtrashnego dnia*, 117. Like many of his contemporaries, Pertsov based his calculations on the studies of the economist Stanislav Strumilin, *The Time Budget of the Russian Worker* (1923) and *The Life of the Worker in Numbers* (1924).

127. Pertsov, "Slovo—zritel'nyi obraz—budushchee," 91.

128. Walter Benjamin, "One Way Street," in *Selected Writings*, 1:444; translation modified; hereafter cited in text as "One Way Street."

129. A. Popova, "Nashim protivnikam," *Nastoiashchee*, no. 2 (1929): 7.

130. Sergei Tret'iakov, "The Writer and the Socialist Village," translated by Devin Fore, *October* 118 (2006): 63–70; hereafter cited in text as "Writer and Socialist Village."

131. Becher, "Unsere Wendung," 5.

132. Boris Kushner, "Prichiny otstavaniia," *Krasnaia nov'*, no. 11 (1930): 136, 137. His thesis about the delay resonated with all of the factographers, not just Tret'iakov. Agapov, for example, observed that "the life that surrounds us is moving unbelievably quickly, is utterly changing the face of our nation, and the scientific conception of the world is changing just as utterly. How is it possible to catch up with this rapid change in the material world and in our very conception of it? I think that, for a time, literature must, as a rule, lag behind life." Boris Agapov, "Rech' B. N. Agapova," in *Pervyi vsesoiuznyi s"ezd sovetskikh pisatelei 1934. Stenograficheskii otchet*, edited by I. K. Luppol, M. M. Rozental', and S. M. Tret'iakov (Moscow: Khudozhestvennaia literatura, 1934), 604.

For a RAPPist defense of aesthetic mediation and the delay of art, see G. Vovsy, "Ob ocherke voobshche i ob ocherkakh Zhigi v chastnosti."

133. Lidiia Ginzburg, *Vsesoiuznoe soveshchanie po khudozhestvennomu ocherku* (June 8, 1934), l. 48–50.

134. Ivanov, "Fetishisty fakta," 230.

135. John Grierson, "Postwar Patterns," in *Hollywood Quarterly: Film Culture in Postwar America, 1945–1957*, edited by Eric Smoodin and Ann Martin (Berkeley: University of California Press, 2002), 96. Grierson's reconciliation with the "creative method" of art in the 1930s would clear up this confusion.

136. Vladimir Mayakovsky, *How to Make Verse* (Willimantic, CT: Ardis, 1976), 53, 56, 57.

137. Tret'iakov's talk at the conference is published as an appendix to Zalambani, *Literatura fakta*, under the title "Ob evoliutsii sovetskogo ocherka," 175; hereafter cited in text as "Ob evoliutsii sovetskogo ocherka." Decades after Tret'iakov's death, Pertsov would still recall that he "was sometimes too direct, attempting to replace the image

with the fact." Viktor Pertsov, "Sergei Tret'iakov," in Tret'iakov, *Den Shi-Khua, Liudi odnogo kostra, Strana perekrestok*, 21.

138. Sergei Tret'iakov, "Sowjetschriftsteller über sich selbst," *Literatur der Sowjetunion*, no. 7–8 (1934): 135. On *operativnost'*, see the series on the subject that ran in the second half of 1931 in *Zhurnalist*. Vladimir Bogushevskii, in particular, was credited for popularizing the term in the Soviet Union through his public lectures and essays such as "Sushchestvo i forma gazetnoi operativnosti," *Zhurnalist*, no. 9 (1931): 8–13. Just as Tret'iakov was criticized by Lukács for reducing the brief of art to ephemeral "practicism," Bogushevskii was attacked for his "formalist" presentism: see V. Nodel', "Operativnost' voobshche i operativnost' segodnia," *Zhurnalist*, no. 12 (1931): 14–16.

139. Tret'iakov, "Autobiographie," 16.

140. Viktor Shklovsky, "Togda i seichas," in *Literatura fakta*, 124. For Shklovsky, the situation recalls Nikolai Akhsharumov's nineteenth-century juridical fiction *Naturshchitsa*, in which "an imaginary woman on trial protests against the fate that the author has assigned to her" (123).

141. Sergei Tret'iakov, "O tom zhe," in *Literatura fakta*, 195–99.

142. Kushner writes about his own time at the Communist Lighthouse in "Kommunisticheskii maiak," *Novyi mir*, no. 2 (1929): 241–46. In his essay on Tret'iakov, Benjamin noted that *The Summons* "is said to have had considerable influence on the further development of collective agriculture." "Author as Producer," 770.

143. Sergei Tret'iakov, "S. Tretjakow," in *Die Arbeit des Schriftstellers: Aufsätze, Reportagen, Porträts*, edited by Heiner Boehncke (Reinbek bei Hamburg: Rowohlt, 1972), 141.

144. Tret'iakov, *Vsesoiuznoe soveshchanie po khudozhestvennomu ocherku* (June 5, 1934), l. 106.

145. Boris Agapov, "Zakliuchenie," in *Tekhnicheskie rasskazy* (Moscow: Khudozhestvennaia literatura, 1936), 298.

146. Viktor Pertsov, "Novyi tip pisatelia," 43.

147. Bazarov, "Material kollektivnago opyta i organizuiushchiia ego formy," 151.

148. Ernst Mach, *The Analysis of Sensations*, translated by C. M. Williams (Chicago: Open Court Publishing, 1914), 19.

149. Ernst Bloch, "Self-Portrait Without Mirror," in *Literary Essays*, 195, 194.

150. Ernst Bloch, "Great Moments That Pass Unnoticed," in *Literary Essays*, 196.

151. L. Varpakhovskii, "Sergei Tret'iakov, *Vyzov. Kolkhoznye ocherki*," *Literatura i iskusstvo*, no. 4 (1930): 18.

152. Dziga Vertov, "O s"emke siuzhetov kinokhroniki," in *Iz naslediia*, edited by A. S. Deriabin (Moscow: Eizenshtein tsentr, 2004), 2:22.

153. Deleuze, *Cinema 1, The Movement-Image*, translated by Hugh Tomlinson and Barbara Habberjam (Minneapolis: University of Minnesota Press, 1986), 40.

154. Sergei Tret'iakov, "Our Cinema," translated by Devin Fore, *October* 116 (2006): 41.

155. Sergei Tret'iakov, "Foto-apparat—zhurnalistu!," *Sovetskoe foto*, no. 9 (1927): 260.

156. Sergei Tret'iakov, "Moi zritel'nyi dnevnik," *Sovetskoe foto*, no. 2 (1934): 24.

157. Osip Brik, "The Picture, the Photograph, and the Movie Still," *Russian Literature Triquarterly*, no. 7 (1973): 193.

158. Susan Schuppli, *Material Witness: Media, Forensics, Evidence* (Cambridge, MA: MIT Press, 2020), 22.

159. Eyal Weizman, *Forensic Architecture: Violence at the Threshold of Detectability* (Brooklyn, NY: Zone Books 2017), 39–40.

CHAPTER 3

1. Ilja Ehrenburg, "Randbemerkungen zur heutigen russischen Literatur," *Slavische Rundschau*, no. 2 (1930): 86.

2. Roland Barthes, *Mythologies*, translated by Richard Howard (New York: Hill and Wang, 2012), 118.

3. The most concise critiques of psychologistic art and literature are: Sergei Tret'iakov, "The Biography of the Object," translated by Devin Fore, *October*, no. 118 (2006): 57–62; Viktor Pertsov, "Nekrolog, kak forma professional'noi kharakteristiki" and "Proizvodstvennaia psikhologiia i khudozhestvennaia literatura," in *Literatura zavtrashnego dnia*, 7–47; Nikolai Chuzhak, "Garmonicheskaia psikhopatiia," *Chitatel' i pisatel'* (December 24, 1927): 2; and Chuzhak, "Vmesto zakliuchitel'nogo slova (o novom, o zhivom, o garmonicheskom)," *Novyi Lef*, no. 4 (1928): 16–23. Osip Beskin, the chair of the editorial board for the General Directorate for Political Education (*Glavlitprosvet*), replied to Chuzhak in "Dogmaticheskaia kastratsiia," *Chitatel' i pisatel'* (January 7, 1928): 7.

4. Gilles Deleuze, "Whitman," in *Essays Critical and Clinical*, translated by Daniel Smith and Michael Greco (Minneapolis: University of Minnesota Press, 1997), 57, 60.

Ippolit Sokolov discusses the "Whitman-Derzhavian style" of *A Sixth Part* in "On the Film *A Sixth Part of the World*," in *Lines of Resistance*, 236. On the ode as a structural model for *A Sixth Part*, see Michael Kunichika, "'The Ecstasy of Breadth': The Odic and the Whitmanesque Style in Dziga Vertov's *One Sixth of the World* (1926)," *Studies in Russian and Soviet Cinema* 6, no. 1 (2012): 53–74. Vertov was not the only filmmaker to propose the ode as a formal solution to the problem of documentary particularism. The incantatory voice-over of Pare Lorentz's 1937 film *The River*, for example, likewise reminded historian of technology Lewis Mumford of the poetry of Walt Whitman. Lorentz's film is "the first evocation since Whitman that gives one a sense of the length and the breadth of the continent, of the realities of everyday life, of the good fortunes and mischances of our people." Quoted in Finis Dunaway, *Natural Visions: The Power of Images in American Environmental Reform* (Chicago: University of Chicago Press, 2005), 74.

5. Ia. M. Tolchan, "S Vertovym bylo udivitel'no legko," in *Dziga Vertov v vospominaniiakh sovremennikov*, edited by E. I. Vertov-Svilova and A. L. Vinogradov (Moscow: Iskusstvo, 1976), 124.

6. Michael Kunichika, *Our Native Antiquity: Archaeology and Aesthetics in the Culture of Russian Modernism* (Boston: Academic Studies Press, 2015), 267–68. As Aristotle observed long ago, the eye-opening experience of wonder (θαυμάζειν, *thaumazein*) was the sensory origin of all higher philosophy.

7. Clifford Geertz, "Thick Description: Toward an Interpretive Theory of Culture," in *The Interpretation of Cultures: Selected Essays* (New York: Basic Books, 1973), 26.

8. Sokolov, "On the Film *A Sixth Part of the World*," 234.

9. Noël Burch, "A Primitive Mode of Representation?," in *Life to Those Shadows*,

translated and edited by Ben Brewster (Berkeley: University of California Press, 1990), 186–201.

10. Dziga Vertov, "Front kino-glaza," in *Iz naslediia*, 2:103.

11. On structural linguistics and modernism, see Yve-Alain Bois, "The Semiology of Cubism," in *Picasso and Braque: A Symposium*, edited by Lynn Zelevansky (New York: Museum of Modern Art, 1992), 169–208; and Rosalind Krauss, "The Motivation of the Sign," in *Picasso and Braque*, 261–86.

12. Dziga Vertov, "Chetyre zadachi 'Cheloveka s kinoapparatom,'" in *Iz nasledija*, 2:155.

13. Ivo Osolsobě, "Die Ostension als Grenzfall menschlicher Kommunikation und ihre Bedeutung für die Kunst (Part I)," *Balagan: Slavisches Drama, Theater und Kino* 7, no. 2 (2001): 48.

14. Thomas Sebeok, quoted in Ivo Osolsobě, "Ostension nach 35, genauer gesagt nach 1613 Jahren," in *Balagan: Slavisches Drama, Theater und Kino* 8, no. 1 (2002): 60.

15. Sergei Tret'iakov, "Pro karman," *Pioner*, no. 8 (1932): 14.

16. Sergei Tret'iakov, "A dal'she?," RGALI, f. 2886, o. 1, d. 1, n.p.

17. Viktor Shklovsky, "Where Is Dziga Vertov Striding?," in *The Film Factory*, 152.

18. Roman Jakobson, "Entretien sur le cinéma," in *Cinéma: Théorie, Lectures* (Paris: Klincksieck, 1973), 63. Here Jakobson was adapting the distinction that he made between metaphor and metonymy in his influential 1956 essay "Two Aspects of Language and Two Types of Aphasic Disturbances."

19. Sergei Tret'iakov, *Den Shi-Khua. Bio-interv'iu* (Moscow: Molodaia gvardiia, 1930), 3; hereafter cited in text as *Den Shi-Khua*.

20. Karl Marx and Friedrich Engels, *The Holy Family*, in Marx and Engels, *Collected Works*, 4:127.

21. Joseph Roth, "Schluß mit der 'neuen Sachlichkeit'!," in *Werke*, edited by Klaus Westermann (Cologne: Kiepenheuer & Witsch, 1989), 3:159.

22. Osolsobě associates ostension with all variety of institutions that put artifacts on display, from World Fairs, shop windows, and museums to zoos and military parades. The humorous list that he proposes devolves into Borgesian nominalism:

> Exhibitions, vitrines, the display of commodities, installations of collections, inspections, parades, screenings, performances . . . demonstrations in every sense of the word (the wrecks that are left behind in some streets in the USA in order to explicitly designate places with frequent accidents), zoos, botanical gardens, striptease, clothing, fashion, artistry, spectator sports, sport competitions, public appearances, victories, high heels, skirt length, clothing in general, exposés in general, presentation upon review, removing masks as a masquerade, façades, rococo wigs, new hairstyles, haircuts, full beards, decoration, tattoos, fashionable mirrored sunglasses—in sum, every display of things, both mobile and immobile; every display of people, both living and dead, both newborn and executed, both denounced and celebrated, those declared welcome (consider the obligatory photograph of a child in the arms), those ceremoniously mourned: all of this belongs to the common (or relatively common) phenomena of our everyday Balnibarbi. And all of this is ostension.

"Die Ostension als Grenzfall" (Part I): 54. For Osolsobě, ostension puts its user in the land of the Balnibarbi from *Gulliver's Travels*, a tribe of radical empiricists who had abolished language and who communicated with each other instead by pointing to reference objects that they carried around with them in great bags.

23. Sokolov, "On the Film *A Sixth Part of the World*," 237. "There is no coherence, connection, or intensification in the succession of sequences" (236).

24. Tarasenkov, "*Literatura fakta*," 108.

25. These canonical lines were referenced by factographers like Pertsov, who emphasized the "power of example" (*сила примера*): "The education of the masses through the use of concrete examples and models from all realms of life: herein lies one of the primary tasks of the press according to Lenin." "Novyi tip pisatelia," *Pisatel' na proizvodstve*, 15–16. Lenin's injunction was also gospel for the theorists working in newspaper studies. Mikhail Gus, for example, stipulated that journalists had to learn "to agitate not through fabulation but through showing [*не рассказом, а показом*], not through words but through facts and examples." *Informatsiia v gazete*, 204.

26. Lenin had started to abandon the anti-positivist stance of *Materialism and Empirio-criticism* already during World War I, although it was the October Revolution that caused him finally to reverse the priority he once gave to philosophy over experience. He eventually lost faith in the arguments of *Materialism and Empirio-criticism*, a work to which he made few references after the revolution and which he reprinted only once in his lifetime despite high demand for the book. He eventually arrived at an interventionist theory of knowledge—a quasi-Bogdanovite "practicism" that anticipated Tret'iakov's own method of operativism: "The activity of man, who has constructed an objective picture of the world for himself, *changes* external actuality, abolishes its determinateness (= alters some sides or other, qualities, of it), and thus removes from it the features of Semblance, externality and nullity, and makes it as being in and for itself (= objectively true)." Vladimir Lenin, *Collected Works*, 38:217–18. On the return of concretion in Lenin's later thought, see Robert Mayer, "Lenin and the Practice of Dialectical Thinking," *Science & Society* 63, no. 1 (1999): 40–62.

27. Vladimir Lenin, "Letters on Tactics: First Letter. Assessment of the Present Situation," in *Collected Works*, 24:45; hereafter cited in text as "Assessment of the Present Situation." Chuzhak quotes this letter in, for example, *Fetishizm kul'tury* (Moscow: Moskovskii rabochii, 1925), 52.

28. Henri Bergson, *Creative Evolution*, translated by Arthur Mitchell (New York: Holt and Company, 1911), 51.

29. Jacques Derrida, "My Chances/*Mes Chances*: A Rendezvous with Some Epicurean Stereophonies," in *Psyche: Inventions of the Other*, edited by Peggy Kamuf and Elizabeth Rottenberg (Stanford, CA: Stanford University Press, 2007), 349.

30. Vladimir Lenin, "Better Fewer, but Better," in *Collected Writings*, 33:497.

31. Edward Tyerman highlights a variation of the Goethean phrase: "Fantasy is more grey than reality," wrote Tret'iakov. *Internationalist Aesthetics*, 27.

32. Peters, *Marvelous Clouds*, 190–91.

33. Stephen E. Hanson, *Time and Revolution: Marxism and the Design of Soviet Institutions* (Chapel Hill: University of North Carolina Press, 1997), 124–25.

34. Heidegger's reflections on care (*Sorge*) illuminate Lenin's concept of *забота*. For Heidegger, care is unique among emotional attachments for expanding the ambit concern beyond the immediate environment, even extending this bond to those situated at other historical moments. It is, importantly, a bond that is established by

the clock: "Utilizing the clock is a particular way of being temporal [*Zeitlichsein*], that is, a way of taking care of Dasein [*Besorgen des Daseins*]." Further: "Whether the clock allows us to tell the time with precision or provides only an approximation makes no essential difference to the ontological characteristics of that being-in to which it owes its 'invention' and further development. The clock exists because the being-in that identifies the now encounters 'time' in a worldly manner. 'Time' exists because Dasein is constituted through Dasein's facticity as presencing immersion in the world, in other words as care [*als Sorgen*]." Martin Heidegger, *The Concept of Time: The First Draft of Being and Time*, translated by Ingo Farin (London: Continuum, 2011), 61–62.

35. The Russian translation of Nietzsche's *Thus Spoke Zarathustra* could be found in Lenin's personal library in the Kremlin. In that book, Nietzsche cajoled the reader:

> You crowd around your neighbor and you have pretty words for it. But I say to you: your love of the neighbor [*liubov' k blizhnemu*] is your bad love of yourselves.
>
> . . .
>
> Do I recommend love of the neighbor to you? I prefer instead to recommend flight from the neighbor and love of the farthest! Higher than love of the neighbor is love of the farthest and the future [*liubov' k dal'nemu i budushchemu*]; higher still than love of human beings is love of things and ghosts.

Friedrich Nietzsche, *Thus Spoke Zarathustra*, edited by Robert Pippin, translated by Adrian del Caro (Cambridge: Cambridge University Press, 2006), 44. Russian translation as *Tak govoril Zaratustra*, translated by V. Izraztsov (St. Petersburg: Probuzhdenie, 1913).

Kerzhentsev discusses how to expand the ambit of concern beyond the nuclear family in *K novoi kul'ture* (Leningrad: Gosudarstvennoe izd-vo, 1921), 84.

36. Étienne Balibar, "The Vacillation of Ideology in Marxism," in *Masses, Classes, Ideas: Studies on Politics and Philosophy Before and After Marx*, translated by James Swenson (London: Routledge, 1994), 236.

37. Milda Grignau exemplifies this expanded ambit of care. When the agronomist is asked how it is possible for her to love the grain that she has engineered as much as her own son, she responds, "I love all of my products."

38. Sergei Tret'iakov, "'Eine Sache der Ehre—eine Sache Ruhmes,'" in *Rote Arbeit. Der neue Arbeiter in der Sowjetunion*, edited by Jürgen Kuczynski (Berlin: Historia-Foto, 1931), 70, 67, 69, 67. This article focuses specifically on shock-work, a direct outgrowth of the subbotnik movement.

39. Nelson Goodman, *Languages of Art* (Indianapolis: Hackett, 1976), 57.

40. The Latin verb *ostendere* first appears in Augustine's treatise "Concerning the Teacher" (*De magistro*). Augustine invented the term to designate acts of instruction in which a teacher defines a word for a child by pointing to the corresponding object. To this day, the didactic ostension of exempla continues to be a cornerstone of pedagogical practice. Ivo Osolsobě, "Ostension," in *Encyclopedic Dictionary of Semiotics*, edited by Thomas Sebeok (Berlin: De Gruyter, 1986), 3:656.

41. E. Mikulin, "Gody i dni," quoted in L. A. Az'muko, "Eshche raz o 'literature fakta' (K voprosy ob evoliutsii teoreticheskikh vzgliadov S. M. Tret'iakova vo vtoroi polovine 20-khx godov)," in *Problemy stanovleniia sotsialisticheskogo realizma v russkoi i zarubezhnoi literature*, edited by N. V. Kovrigina (Irkutsk: 1972), 59.

42. Kerzhentsev, *K novoi kul'ture*, 34.

43. Lisa Gitelman, *Paper Knowledge: Toward a Media History of Documents* (Durham, NC: Duke University Press, 2014), 1. Gitelman dubs this the "know-show function" of documentation.

44. Within the conjunctural alignment, "the focus is no longer on the dichotomy between 'surface' and 'essence,' but on the complex formation of the historical moment." Juha Koivisto, Mikko Lahtinen, and Alexis Petrioli, "Konjunktur, politisch-historische," in *Historisch-kritisches Wörterbuch des Marxismus*, edited by Wolfgang Fritz Haug, Frigga Haug, and Peter Jehle (Berlin: Argument, 1994–), 7:1518.

45. Ludwig Wittgenstein, *Tractatus logico-philosophicus* (Berlin: Akademie, 2001), 4.121 and 4.1212. On silence and showing in Wittgenstein, see Lambert Wiesing, "Zeigen, Verweisen und Präsentieren," in *Politik des Zeigens*, edited by Karen van den Berg and Hans Ulrich Gumbrecht (Munich: Fink, 2010), 15–27.

46. This strategy was outlined already in Marx's *Grundrisse*, where "thinking in the conjuncture and through the singularity of specific cases" presumed "a standpoint where politics can never be fully derived from a pre-established theory and is always eccentric to it." Luca Basso, *Marx and Singularity: From the Early Writings to the Grundrisse*, translated by Arianna Bove (Leiden: Brill, 2012), 5.

47. Maksim Gor'kii, "Beseda s pisateliami-udarnikami," in *Sobranie sochinenii* (Moscow: Khudozhestvennaia literatura, 1953), 26:79.

48. Iurii Libedinskii, quoted in Osip Brik, "Blizhe k faktu," *Novyi Lef*, no. 2 (1927): 32; hereafter quoted in text as "Blizhe k faktu."

49. B. Mikhailov, "Za kachestvo pokaza geroev truda," *Na lit. postu*, no. 31–32 (1931): 51.

50. Kurs, "Daem otvety na vsiakie muchitel'nye lit-voprosy," 11. This programmatic essay railed against RAPP's "spurious, idealist views about generalization . . . [which] consists of taking qualities that are present in various people and pasting them together into a 'type'" (10).

51. See, for example, the entries for *zhenshchina* and *muzhchina* in V. V. Vinogradov, *Istoriia slov*, edited by N. Iu. Shvedova (Moscow: Tolk, 1994).

52. Giorgio Agamben, *The Signature of All Things: On Method*, translated by Luca D'Isanto with Kevin Attell (Brooklyn, NY: Zone Books, 2009), 22. Through its material specificity, the paradigm interrupts "the logic of the metaphorical transfer of meaning" (18). The paradigm cannot be defined using language that is external to it, but instead can only be designated through direct ostension: "The rule (if it is still possible to speak of rules here) is not a generality preexisting the singular cases and applicable to them, nor is it something resulting from the exhaustive enumeration of specific cases. Instead, it is the exhibition alone of the paradigmatic case that constitutes a rule, which as such cannot be applied or stated" (21).

53. Viktor Pertsov, "Otvety na zapiski," in *Pisatel' na proizvodstve*, 205.

54. Sergei Tret'iakov, "Blizhe k gazete," in *Literatura fakta*, 212. As Tret'iakov explained in this talk, the writers of VAPP are mistaken to think that "the writer has to be something greater than just a recorder of facts: they believe that the writer should be a synthesizer, should have the ability to produce generalizations, and that this puts him above the newspaper journalist." See Teodor Grits's analysis of Tret'iakov's discussion of *shchiny* in this 1928 talk: "Tribuna i kuluary," *Novyi Lef*, no. 6 (1928): 40–44. Chuzhak too promoted the *shchina* as a counterstrategy to the typologies of the novel in "A Writer's Handbook," 87.

55. Ostension generates "ad hoc concepts"—makeshift placeholders for ideas that, according to cognitive scientists, will subsequently be filled in by a process of backward inference that specifies what was initially indeterminate. Deirdre Wilson and Dan Sperber, "Relevance Theory," in *The Handbook of Pragmatics*, edited by Laurence Horn and Gregory Ward (Malden, MA: Blackwell, 2004), 618.

56. A. M. Selishchev, *Iazyk revoliutsionnoi epokhi: Iz nabliudenii nad russkim iazykom (1917–1926)* (Moscow: Editorial URSS, 2003), 177. Selishchev describes the operation of *shchiny*: "These designations are formed from the names of people whose relationship to the designated phenomena serve as a distinctive sign for these phenomena."

57. Sergeiy Sandler, "A Strange Kind of Kantian: Bakhtin's Reinterpretation of Kant and the Marburg School," *Studies in Eastern European Thought*, no. 67 (2015): 166.

58. On Bakhtin's struggle with "fatal theoreticism," see Greg Marc Nielsen, *The Norms of Answerability: Social Theory Between Bakhtin and Habermas* (Albany: State University of New York Press, 2002), 89–108.

59. Mikhail Bakhtin, *Toward a Philosophy of the Act*, translated by Vadim Liapunov (Austin: University of Texas Press, 1993), 39, 8, 20.

60. Bakhtin, *Toward a Philosophy of the Act*, 30. Bakhtin also observes that "the compellently 'actual' face of the event is determined for me myself from my own unique place." From there he arrives at philosophical nominalism: "If the 'face' of the event is determined from the unique place of a participative self, then there are as many different 'faces' as there are different unique places" (45).

61. Althusser, "The Only Materialist Tradition, Part I: Spinoza," 8.

62. Pierre Vilar, "Marxist History, A History in the Making: Towards a Dialogue with Althusser," in *Althusser: A Critical Reader*, edited by Gregory Elliott (Oxford: Blackwell, 1994), 20. "Knowledge . . . is only ever produced by an 'exceptional' encounter . . . in other words, it is produced by a historical conjuncture in which several distinct practices intervene" (*Philosophy of the Encounter*, xl).

63. The most important philosophers to explore the post-Kantian "modal collapse" are Alexius Meinong and Ernst Mally. In her study of the proletarian novel, Katerina Clark proposes a similar phrase, "modal schizophrenia." See *The Soviet Novel: History as Ritual* (Chicago: University of Chicago Press, 1981), 36–45. If, as Clark explains, the cultural production of the transitional period oscillates restlessly between *what is* (fact) and *what ought to be* (utopia), the two practices of factography and the proletarian novel each privilege one of these two moments, either the present and or the future. See n106 below.

64. Bakhtin, *Toward a Philosophy of the Act*, 20.

65. Agapov, "Khozaistvo dokumentalista," 169.

66. Sergei Tret'iakov, *Strana A-E* (Moscow: Molodaia gvardiia, 1932), 137. He repeats this anecdote in "Der Schriftsteller im Aufbauwerke," 1.

67. Bloch, "Marxism and Poetry," in *Literary Essays*, 119.

68. On the demonstration genre, see Viktor Pertsov, "'Igra' i demonstratsiia," *Novyi Lef*, no. 11–12 (1927): 33–44.

69. European observers were perplexed and intrigued by this method. Benjamin observed that "some of the actors taking part in Russian films are not actors in our sense but people who portray themselves and primarily in their own work process"

("The Work of Art in the Age of Its Technological Reproducibility," 262). See also Rudolf Arnheim's discussion of this technique in *Film as Art* (Berkeley: University of California Press, 1957), 138. Joris Ivens, with whom Tret'iakov collaborated on the film *Komsomol: A Poem of Heroes* (1932), would develop this device of documentary reenactment. In his 1940 essay, "Collaboration in Documentary," Ivens described a setup almost identical to Tret'iakov's account of filming a woodcutter:

> Our farm film presented material that seemed to demand re-enactments. . . . In choosing the people who were to play the roles (of themselves—the farmer as the farmer, his sons as the farmer's sons, etc.), the first visual impression is very important. . . . The writer must employ his imagination to manipulate the real personal characteristic of the new actors—searching them with seemingly careless observations. He must learn thereby, for example that the farmer takes special pride in the sharpness of his tool blades, and therefore suggest a toolshed scene which will make use of that fact. The key to this approach, I think, is that a real person, acting to play himself, will be more expressive if his actions are based on his real characteristics.

Joris Ivens, "Collaboration in Documentary," in *The Documentary Film Reader: History, Theory, Criticism*, edited by Jonathan Kahana (Oxford: Oxford University Press, 2016), 815. On his collaboration with Ivens, see Sergei Tret'iakov, "Ioris Ivens," *Iunii proletarii*, no. 25–26 (1932): 17–18.

70. Rancière, *The Future of the Image*, 26, 22, 29.

71. Sergei Tret'iakov, "Iskusniki iz Kuznitsy," *Lef*, no. 3 (1923): 146.

72. Sergei Tret'iakov, "Po povodu 'Protivogazov,'" *Lef*, no. 4 (1923): 108.

73. "Lef is less interested in types that spontaneously appear than in exempla, the human 'standards' that are taken from some or other realm of industry." Sergei Tret'iakov, "Lef i marksizm," *Lef*, no. 4 (1924): 214.

74. Victor F. Lenzen, "The Contributions of Charles S. Peirce to Metrology," *Proceedings of the American Philosophical Society* 109, no. 1 (1965): 29–46.

75. Agamben, *The Signature of All Things*, 17.

76. On Tret'iakov's exhibition of standards, see Fritz Mierau, "Standard auf der Bühne, oder Fiasko dreier Meister. Tretjakows 'Ich will ein Kind haben,'" in *Zwölf Arten die Welt zu beschreiben. Essays zur russischen Literatur* (Cologne: Röderberg, 1988), 100–108.

77. Friedrich Engels, *Ludwig Feuerbach and the End of Classical German Philosophy*, in Marx and Engels, *Collected Works*, 26:384. Chuzhak quotes Solov'ev's definition of art as "any tangible representation of any object or phenomenon from the point of view of its ultimate state or in the light of the future world": "K estetike marksizma," in *K dialektike iskusstva*, 25.

78. Nikolai Chuzhak, "Vvedenie," in *K dialektike iskusstva*, 3–8.

79. By using what he called "dialectical models," Chuzhak argued that it is possible to grasp flickering, transitional phenomena that are still in their nascent state. See Chuzhak, "K zadacham dnia," 145–46.

80. Aleksandr Bogdanov, *Voprosy sotsializma* (Moscow: Izd-vo pisatelei, 1918), 86.

81. Michel Foucault writes that heterotopias are "real places . . . which are something like counter-sites, a kind of effectively enacted utopia in which the real sites, all the other real sites that can be found within the culture, are simultaneously represented,

contested, and inverted." "Of Other Spaces," translated by Jan Miskowiec, *Diacritics* 16, no. 1 (1986): 24.

82. Nikolai Chuzhak, "Proletarskaia kul'tura. Tezisy pod redaktsiei Nauchnoi Komissii Proletkul'ta," in *Al'manakh Proletkul'ta*, 19.

83. Boris Arvatov, "Utopiia ili nauka," in *Ob agit- i proziskusstve* (Moscow: Federatsiia, 1930), 62. Arvatov's essay was a rejoinder to revolutionary maximalists who argued that radical art could not be realized during the transitional period, but had to wait until a fully communist society had been established.

84. Nikolai Chuzhak, "Krivoe zerkalo. Lef v prelomlenii 'Lefa,'" *Krasnyi oktiabr'*, no. 2 (1924): 44. On the use of standards in *Gasmasks*, also see the second installment of Nikolai Chuzhak's serial essay "Iskusstvo v nashi dni," *Zhizn' iskusstva*, no. 25 (1925): 6.

85. Chuzhak, "K estetike marksizma," 25.

86. Nikolai Chuzhak, "Pod znakom zhiznestroeniia," *Lef*, no. 1 (1923): 15. The quoted passages in Chuzhak's text are from Marx's *Capital*. The next year, Chuzhak would again write of "the methods of *tomorrow* that have not yet been *revealed* in reality, but that are already visible in its subsoil, where they tirelessly 'experiment' with material." Sometimes the way forward proceeds not through the positive but through the negative, he wrote there: one must use "even those devices that have already theoretically been negated [by the working class]." He concludes: "The defining feature of Lef is its *groping* [*нащупывания*] of the *dialectical* elements of '*tomorrow*' in the present day." Chuzhak, "Dva lefo-estestva," *Oktiabr' mysli*, no. 5 (1924): 3.

Most critics didn't know what to do with Chuzhak's dialectically involuted writing. Voronsky, for example, mocked this perplexing passage in "Under the Sign of Life-Construction." As Voronsky explained, Chuzhak proclaims that "the task of proletarian art is not the recording of what has been deposited by everyday life, but the exposition of the 'antithesis,' the depiction of life 'in its movement.'" But this leads Chuzhak to embrace "an immediate reality which already ceases to be an immediate reality." Voronsky, "Art as the Cognition of Life, and the Contemporary World," 106, 107.

87. Nikolai Chuzhak, "Ob etoi knige i o nas," in *Literatura fakta*, 8.

88. Bekker, "Problema khudozhestvennogo ocherka," 59.

89. V. Kuz'michev, "Za marksistskuiu nauku o gazete," in *Problemy gazetovedeniia*, 23–24.

90. Chuzhak, "Osoznanie cherez iskusstvo," 89.

91. Viktor Pertsov, "Basnia i nravouchenie. O sovetskoi bytovoi fil'me," *Kino*, no 7 (1927): 2.

92. Viktor Pertsov, "O polozhitel'nom tipe," in *Literatura zavtrashnego dnia*, 63.

93. Pertsov, "Basnia i nravouchenie," 2.

94. Novitskii, "*Khochu rebenka*—Obsuzhdenie v Glavrepertkome, 4 dekabria 1928 goda," *Sovremennaia dramaturgiia*, no. 2 (1988): 238.

95. Ivan Matsa, "Tvorcheskii metod v proletarskom iskusstve," *Literatura i iskusstvo*, no. 3–4 (1930): 27.

96. Sergei Tret'iakov, "Rabkor i stroitel'stvo," in *Literatura fakta*, 213.

97. Tret'iakov, "Blizhe k gazete," 212.

98. Clark, *The Soviet Novel*, 36–45.

99. *Nastoiashchee*, no. 1 (January 1928): 3.

100. Popova, "Nashim protivnikam," 7.

101. Wilhelm Dilthey, *Introduction to the Human Sciences: An Attempt to Lay a Foundation for the Study of Society and History*, translated by Ramon J. Betanzos (Detroit: Wayne State University Press, 1988), 161.

102. S. Tretjakow, "Die Tasche," *Unsere Zeit* 6, no. 3 (1933): 170.

103. Pertsov, "Basnia i nravouchenie," 2.

104. Lydiya Ginzburg, *On Psychological Prose*, edited and translated by Judson Rosengrant (Princeton, NJ: Princeton University Press, 1991), 8.

105. Viktor Shklovsky, *Knight's Move*, translated by Richard Sheldon (London: Dalkey Archive Press, 2005), 4; translation modified.

106. Benjamin, "Moscow," 22. Benjamin concludes that "someone who wishes to decide 'on the basis of facts' will find no basis in the facts" because the facts are themselves fundamentally multivalent.

107. Iurii Lotman, *Nepredskazuemye mekhanizmy kul'tury*, edited by T. D. Kuzovkina (Talinn, Estonia: Talinn University Press, 2010), 46, 50; hereafter cited in text as *Nepredskazuemye mekhanizmy kul'tury*. For Lotman Russian culture is one that is inherently prone to the "explosion," to leaps and discontinuity, because of its binary extremism. Russian culture lacks the axiologically neutral space that distinguishes the ternary cultures of Western Europe. This binary cultural logic, Lotman adds, establishes the unique historical temporality that is specific to Russia: there, development does not follow historical continuity but is an oscillation between extremes. Continuity and gradualism are alien to Russian history, which instead tends toward "total eschatological change."

108. Iurii Lotman and Boris Uspenskii, "Binary Models in the Dynamics of Russian Culture," in *The Semiotics of Russian Cultural History: Essays*, edited and translated by Alexander D. Nakhimovsky and Alice Stone Nakhimovsky (Ithaca, NY: Cornell University Press, 1985), 37.

109. Juri Lotman, *Culture and Explosion*, edited by Marina Grishakova, translated by Wilma Clark (Berlin: Mouton de Gruyter, 2004), 145–46.

110. In Althusser's influential account, social contradictions express themselves in one of two ways depending on the political configuration of the given moment. During non-revolutionary times antagonisms are articulated through the mechanism of displacement (*Verschiebung*), whereas revolutionary situations are instead characterized by condensation (*Verdichtung*). For Althusser, "in periods of stability the essential contradictions of the social formation are neutralized by displacement; in a revolutionary situation, however, they may condense or fuse into a revolutionary rupture." Ben Brewster, "Glossary," in Althusser and Balibar, *Reading Capital*, 349.

Freud used the term *Verdichtung* to describe a condition of semantic multivalence found in the dream: condensation entails the overlay, within a single image, of a number of distinct and even at times logically irreconcilable meanings. Combining Freud with Lenin, Althusser associated this mechanism of semantic condensation with the condition of historical overdetermination that generates revolutionary action.

111. T. J. Clark, *Farewell to an Idea: Episodes from a History of Modernism* (New Haven, CT: Yale University Press, 1999), 242.

112. Only after this sudden leap has taken place and the new state has stabilized can the course of history be explained. Whereas before there was only the unpredictability of a continuously unfolding present, retrospective consciousness is now able to discern regularity and continuity. Thus, the revolutionary moment concludes "by passing into a state of gradual movement. What was united in one integrated whole is scattered into

different (opposing) elements. . . . The catastrophically explosive becomes the historically inevitable: a logical consequence of this approach is the eschatological myth of the movement of history towards its inevitable conclusion" (*Culture and Explosion*, 158). What previously presented itself at the moment of coalescence as a unity of contradictions begins now to differentiate itself logically into distinctive parts, into a clear sequence of causes and effects. After the ex-/implosion, "subsequent movement along different trajectories causes the particles to move further and further away from each other to the extent that variations of *one* object are transformed into a collection of *different* objects" (*Culture and Explosion*, 135).

113. Konstantin Feldman, "Die Generallinie," in *Die ungewöhnlichen Abenteuer des Dr. Mabuse im Lande der Bolschewiki*, edited by Oksana Bulgakowa (Berlin: Freunde der deutschen Kinemathek, 1995), 112.

114. Eisenstein, "Vystuplenie i zakliuchitel'noe slovo na Vsesoiuznom tvoricheskom soveshchanii rabotnikov sovetskoi kinematografii," in *Izbrannye proizvedeniia v shesti tomakh* (Moscow: Iskusstvo, 1964), 2:101.

115. Iurii Lotman, *Semiotics of Cinema*, translated by Mark E. Suino (Ann Arbor: University of Michigan Press, 1976), 53, 52; translation modified. Lotman compares the effect to that of Iurii Liubimov's *Listen!*, the 1967 play in which the role of Mayakovsky was performed by five different actors who were often on stage at the same time (54).

116. Heinrich Wölfflin, *Principles of Art History: The Problem of the Development of Style in Later Art*, translated by M. D. Hottinger (New York: Bell and Sons, 1932), 11.

117. Vladimir Lenin, "Karl Marx (A Brief Biographical Sketch with an Exposition of Marxism)," in *Collected Works*, 21:75.

118. Ehrenburg, "Randbemerkungen zur heutigen russischen Literatur," 81–82.

119. Goethe's *Faust* was quoted by everyone in the early revolutionary epoch, from Bukharin and Lenin to Trotsky and Vinokur.

120. Ehrenburg singles out the worker correspondence of the newspaper as "the first outline of a new kind of poem." He writes that "modern literature would be unthinkable without the newspaper." Ehrenburg, "Randbemerkungen zur heutigen russischen Literatur," 85, 87, 84.

CHAPTER 4

1. Lukács, "Narrate or Describe?," 131.

2. Reger, *Das wachsame Hähnchen. Eine Vivisektion der Zeit.*

3. Viktor Shklovsky, "Sergei Eizenshtein i neigrovaia fil'ma," *Novyi Lef*, no. 4 (1927): 34.

4. Alain Robbe-Grillet, "On Several Obsolete Notions," in *For a New Novel: Essays on Fiction*, translated by Richard Howard (Evanston, IL: Northwestern University Press, 1989), 32.

5. Tret'iakov, "The Biography of the Object," 59, 58.

6. Viktor Shklovsky, "K tekhnike vne-siuzhetnoi prozy," in *Literatura fakta*, 222; hereafter cited in text as "K tekhnike vne-siuzhetnoi prozy."

7. Viktor Shklovsky, "Prestuplenie epigona. *Prestuplenie Martyna*—roman Bakhmet'eva," in *Literatura fakta*, 130–31.

8. Shklovsky, "Togda i seichas," 123.

9. Sergei Tret'iakov, "Nuzhno predostrech'," in *Literatura fakta*, 209.

10. Vladimir Trenin, "Intelligentnye partizany (formal'nyi kommentarii k stat'e O. M. Brika 'Razgrom Fadeeva')," in *Literatura fakta*, 94.

11. Trenin, "Intelligentnye partizany," 94–98.

12. Petr Neznamov, "Dradedamovyi byt (*Natal'ia Tarpova*—roman S. Smenova)," in *Literatura fakta*, 98–105; and "Derevnia krasivogo opereniia (*Bruski*—roman F. Panferova)," in *Literatura fakta*, 105–13.

13. Chuzhak, "Diskussiia o literaturno-khudozh. taktike gruppy *Na literaturnom postu*: 'I shefstvuia vazhno,'" 4–5.

14. Shklovsky, "Prestuplenie epigona."

15. Osip Brik, "Pochemu ponravil'sia 'Tsement,'" in *Literatura fakta*, 84–88.

16. Teodor Grits, "Periodicheskie droby," *Novyi Lef*, no. 3 (1928): 44–45.

17. Viktor Shklovsky, "The Relationship between Devices of Plot Construction and General Devices of Style," in *Theory of Prose*, translated by Benjamin Sher (London: Dalkey Archive Press, 1990), 16.

18. Osip Brik, "Fiksatsiia fakta," *Novyi Lef*, no. 11–12 (1927): 48.

19. Sergei Tret'iakov, "Konkretnye nositeli zla ili konkretnye kozly otpushcheniia," in *Kinematograficheskoe nasledie. Stat'i, ocherki, stenogrammy vystuplenii, doklady, stsenarii* (St. Petersburg: Nestor-istoriia, 2010), 77.

20. Variations of these formulas in Tret'iakov, "The Industry Production Screenplay," 134; and "Nuzhno predostrech'," 211.

21. Brik, "Fiksatsiia fakta," 50.

22. Chuzhak, "Iskusstvo v nashi dni," 3.

23. See Chuzhak's discussion of "facto-montage" in "Literatura zhiznestroeniia." Agapov discusses the factographic search for "patterns" and "regularities" (*закономерности*) in "Tekhnika, chelovek, sistema," *Nashi dostizheniia*, no. 7–8 (1934): 174–77; and again in "V poiskakh nastoiashchego vremeni," in *Tekhnicheskie rasskazy* (Moscow: Khudozhestvennaia literatura, 1936), 9–30.

24. Karl Mannheim, "On the Interpretation of *Weltanschauung*," in *Essays on the Sociology of Knowledge*, edited by Paul Kecskemeti (London: Routledge, 1952), 57.

25. Viacheslav Ivanov, "Montazh kak printsip postroeniia v kul'ture pervoi poloviny XX v.," in *Montazh. Literatura, iskusstvo, teatr, kino*, edited by B. V. Raushenbakh (Moscow: Nauka, 1988), 130.

26. "Herein lies the production-based inseparability of the sum total of content and form from *ideology*." Eisenstein, "Perspectives," 154.

27. Accounts of the history of the ocherk found in the standard Soviet reference work *Literaturnaia entsiklopediia*, for example, credit Lef with reviving the genre. On the ocherk's place within the system of literature, see Leonid Heller, "Le mirage du vrai. Remarques sur la littérature factographique en Russie," *Communications*, no. 71 (2001): 143–77.

28. Martin Schneider discusses some of the institutional bodies working on the ocherk in the early Soviet period in "Die operative Skizze Sergej Tret'jakovs. Futurismus und Faktographie in der Zeit des 1. Fünfjahrplans" (PhD diss., Ruhr Universität Bochum, 1983), 82, 158.

29. One such exhibition was *Pisatel' i kolkhoz*, which opened in Moscow's State Museum of Literature.

30. Gorky discusses this etymology in his most famous statement on the ocherk, a 1929 letter to the ocherkist Ivan Zhiga. He writes there: "Speaking about the ocherk as

a lit. form, [one] should begin with the verb *to trace, to outline* [*чертить, очерчивать*]. The ocherk is equivalent and tantamount to the 'sketch,' a drawing made with a pencil or a pen for memory's sake." *Polnoe sobranie sochnienii*, 19:85.

31. Vovsy, "Ob ocherke voobshche i ob ocherkakh Zhigi v chastnosti," 106.

32. Agapov, "Khozaistvo dokumentalista," 168; Vladimir Stavskii, "Ob ocherke i ocherkiste," *Na pod"eme*, no. 5 (1931): 14; and Pertsov, "Udarnyi tsekh sovetskoi literatury," in *Pisatel' na proizvodstve*, 165.

33. Lorraine Daston, "Why Are Facts Short?," in *A History of Facts*, edited by Lorraine Daston, Staffan Müller-Wille, and H. Otto Sibum (Berlin: Max Planck Institute, 2001), 6–7.

34. P. K. F., "Ocherk," in *Literaturnaia entsiklopediia v 11 tomakh*, edited by A. Lunacharskii (Moscow: Kommunisticheskaia akademiia, 1929–1939), 8:210.

35. Osip Brik, "Razlozhenie siuzheta," in *Literatura fakta*, 220.

36. Roland Barthes, "The Sequence of Actions," in *The Semiotic Challenge*, translated by Richard Howard (New York: Hill and Wang, 1988), 139, 141.

37. Wlad Godzich, *Narrative as Communication* (Minneapolis: University of Minnesota Press, 1989), vi. According to Godzich, Barthes uses the term *prohairesis* "to denote the future projection of a course of action, and simplifies its meaning to the rational determination of the result of an action. He recognizes, however, that nothing is more difficult than to arrive at such a determination unless one knows beforehand what the outcome of the entire sequence of actions is going to be. Armed with this knowledge, the analyst reads backward as it were and discards those elements that will prove unproductive, keeping only those that will contribute to the general result" (vi).

38. Barthes, "The Sequence of Actions," 141.

39. Sergei Tret'iakov, "Piatiletku pod ob"ektiv," *Literaturnaia gazeta*, no. 34 (December 9, 1929): 1.

40. Gal', "Pisatel' vsekh zhanrov," 144.

41. Mikhail Ritman, "Protiv faktografii, za proletarskii ocherkizm (O knige ocherkov S. Tret'iakova 'Vyzov')," *Na pod"em*, no. 1 (1930): 170.

42. Sergei Bulgakov, quoted in Nikolai Bukharin, *Historical Materialism: A System of Sociology* (Moscow: International Publishers, 1925), 49.

43. Boris Agapov, "Iskusstvo ostaetsia," *Inostrannaia literatura*, no. 8 (1966): 202. In the Russian cultural tradition, *realia* are associated with mundane, external reality, in contrast to the "higher," symbolic reality of *realiora*. See Michael Wachtel, *Russian Symbolism and Literary Tradition: Goethe, Novalis, and the Poetics of Vyacheslav Ivanov* (Madison: University of Wisconsin Press, 1995), 64–67.

44. Wolfgang Ernst, *Digital Memory and the Archive*, edited by Jussi Parikka (Minneapolis: University of Minnesota Press, 2013), 30. Ernst explains: "Between counting and telling, such sequences are well known from nonliterary accounts of history. Gregory of Tours, in the early medieval period, wrote a history of mankind year by year (*cunctam annorum congeriem connotare*), with the connotation of *connotare* being both 'telling' and mathematical counting in discrete leaps. Today historiography rigorously separates narrated time from calculated time, but early medieval Europe read them together" (148). Along similar lines, the historian Hayden White observes that the austere recordkeeping of the medieval chronicle forecloses "metaphoric or paradigmatic consciousness." "The Value of Narrativity in the Representation of Reality," *Critical Inquiry* 7, no. 1 (1980): 19.

45. Ernst points out that modern mechanical clock-time resembles the time of medieval annals, both of which presume "a nonnarrative, nonsubjective kind of temporal processing." Wolfgang Ernst, "Ticking Clock, Vibrating String: How Time Sense Oscillates Between Religion and Machine," in *Deus ex Machina: Religion, Technology, and the Things in Between*, edited by Jeremy Stolow (New York: Fordham University Press, 2013), 51.

46. Gastev, "Vosstanie kul'tury," 32.

47. Aleksandr Bogdanov, *Tektology: Book 1*, edited by Peter Dudley (Hull: Centre for Systems Studies, 1996), 31.

48. John Durham Peters, "Calendar, Clock, Tower," in *Deus in Machina*, 32.

49. Peters, *The Marvelous Clouds*, 218.

50. Robert Bird, *Revolution Every Day: Calendar, 1917–2017*, edited by Robert Bird, Christina Kiaer, and Zachary Cahill (Chicago: Smart Museum of Art, 2017), entry for May 10.

51. Peters, *The Marvelous Clouds*, 213.

52. Grigorii Boltianskii, "Kino-Eye and the Kinocs," in *Lines of Resistance*, 115.

53. Iurii Tynianov, "Interlude," in *Permanent Evolution*, 175.

54. Osip Mandelstam, "The End of the Novel," in *The Complete Critical Prose and Letters*, edited by Jane Gary Harris, translated by Jane Gary Harris and Constance Link (Ann Arbor: Ardis, 1979), 198.

55. Walter Benjamin, "The Storyteller," in *Selected Writings*, 3:156.

56. For Brooks, narrative is anything life-affirming. Rather, it expresses a repetition compulsion that forecloses perception of the new:

> Repetition in all its literary manifestations may in fact work as a "binding," a binding of textual energies that allows them to be mastered by putting them into serviceable form, usable "bundles," within the energetic economy of the narrative. . . . repetition, repeat, recall, symmetry, all these journeys back in the text, returns to and returns of, that allow us to bind one textual moment to another in terms of similarity or substitution rather than mere contiguity. Textual energy, all that is aroused into expectancy and possibility in a text, can become usable by plot only when it has been bound or formalized. . . . To speak of "binding" in a literary text is thus to speak of any of the formalizations, blatant or subtle, that force us to recognize sameness within difference.

Peter Brooks, *Reading for the Plot: Design and Intention in Narrative* (New York: Knopf, 1984), 101.

57. Roland Barthes, *Roland Barthes by Roland Barthes*, translated by Richard Howard (New York: Hill and Wang, 2010), 148.

58. Edward Tyerman writes: "We are not given a conclusive judgment on Deng's character—one that would valorize the bio-interview as a technique for producing and judging revolutionary selves. Instead, the reader is led to understand that this text has been generated from the intersection of multiple partial perspectives, none of which can lay claim to conclusive epistemological authority." *Internationalist Aesthetics*, 191.

59. Tret'iakov, *Vsesoiuznoe soveshchanie po khudozhestvennomu ocherku* (June 5, 1934), l. 105.

60. Lunacharsky made this point in the introduction to his *Revolutionary Silhou-*

ettes of 1923, a collection of biographical profiles that was held in high regard by the factographers, Pertsov above all. Lunacharsky observed there that writing "memoirs at a time when not a single event of the revolution had cooled down—we were still living in its very crucible—was simply impossible." This was so because "any premature description of those events" would necessarily be "too subjective." Anatoly Lunacharsky, *Revolutionary Silhouettes*, translated by Michael Glenny (London: Penguin Press, 1967), 3.

61. Benjamin, "Moscow," 29.

62. The title page of *Den Shi-Khua* actually credits another author in addition to Den and Tret'iakov: Tin Iuin-Pin, whose divergent testimony offers another perspective.

63. Pertsov, "Sergei Tret'iakov," 6.

64. Walter Benjamin, "The Crisis of the Novel," in *Selected Writings*, 2:300.

65. Boris Agapov, "V poiskakh nastoiashchego vremeni," *Literaturnyi kritik*, no. 7–8 (1934): 189–202.

66. Wolfgang Ernst, "Kittler Time," translated by Yuk Hui and James Burton, in *Media After Kittler*, edited by Eleni Ikoniadou and Scott Wilson (London: Rowman & Littlefield, 2015), 59.

67. The designation *казус* (as distinct from *случай*) comes up in "Moscow–Beijing" and "The Industry Production Screenplay." It also figures prominently in Tret'iakov's review of Ernst Ottwalt's reportage novel about the German justice system *Denn sie wissen was sie tun*, where he endorses Ottwalt's method for delivering "casus after casus": "Kniga bol'shoi oblichitel'noi sily. Ernst Ottval'd, *Znaiut, chto tvoriat*'," *Pravda*, no. 302 (November 1, 1934): 4.

68. André Jolles, *Simple Forms*, translated by Peter J. Schwartz (London: Verso, 2017), 153; hereafter cited in text as *Simple Forms*.

69. Sergei Tret'iakov, "Bert Brecht," in *Den Shi-Khua, Liudi odnogo kostra, Strana perekrestok*, 480.

70. John Forrester discusses the disappearance of casuistic thinking ("the moral science devoted to the singular case") with the turn to Kantian universalism in Forrester, "If *p*, Then What? Thinking in Cases," *History of the Human Sciences* 9, no. 3 (1996): 18–19.

71. Tret'iakov, "Konkretnye nositeli zla ili konkretnye kozly otpushcheniia," 78.

72. Fredric Jameson, *Brecht and Method* (London: Verso, 1998), 128.

73. Mikhail Luzgin, "Ob ocherke," in *Za boevoi khudozhestvennyi ocherk* (Leningrad: Izd-vo Pisatelei, 1931), 80.

74. Mikhail Luzgin, "V bor'be za proletarskii ocherk," *Literaturnaia ucheba*, no. 9 (1931): 31.

75. Mikhail Kol'tsov, "Pamflet i ocherk," *Nashi dostizheniia*, no. 7–8 (1934): 172.

76. Viktor Shklovsky, "Neskol'ko slov o chetyrekhstakh millionakh (O knige S. Tret'iakova 'Chzhungo')," *Novyi Lef*, no. 3 (1928): 44.

77. Hermann Broch, "Das Weltbild des Romans," in *Gesammelte Werke*, edited by Hannah Arendt (Düsseldorf: Rhein-Verlag, 1955), 6:224–25.

78. Thomas Mann, *Joseph and His Brothers*, translated by John E. Woods (New York: Knopf, 1956), 1209–10.

79. John Grierson, "The Course of Realism," in *Grierson on Documentary*, 201.

80. John Grierson, "The Russian Cinema," in *Grierson on the Movies*, edited by Forsyth Hardy (London: Faber & Faber, 1981), 141–42.

81. Osip Brik, "Protiv romantiki," *Novyi Lef*, no. 10 (1927): 2.

82. Berkovskii, "Bor'ba za prozu" (Part I): 31.

83. Tret'iakov discusses this bureaucratic affect in "Samyi nuzhnyi (Kto stroitel' sotsializma)," *Komsomol'skaia Pravda* (July 4, 1928): 2.

84. Sergei Tret'iakov, "Anketa o nauchnoi fil'me," *Kino*, no. 17 (1927): 3.

85. Roland Barthes, "From Work to Text," in *The Rustle of Language*, translated by Richard Howard (Berkeley: University of California Press, 1989), 63.

86. Osip Brik, "Za politiku!," *Novyi Lef*, no. 1 (1927): 22.

87. Arthur Conan Doyle, *The Sign of Four*, in *Sherlock Holmes: The Novels* (New York: Penguin, 2015): 239.

88. Marjorie Nicolson, "The Professor and the Detective," *The Atlantic* 143 (1929): 485. Brecht likewise celebrated detective fiction for opening plot to accident and objective facts. Bertolt Brecht, "Über die Popularität des Kriminalromans," in *Werke*, edited by Werner Hecht et al. (Frankfurt am Main: Suhrkamp, 1993), 22:504–10.

89. Gus, *Informatsiia v gazete*, 166.

90. Alexander Kluge, "Thesen 1-4," in *In Gefahr und größter Not bringt der Mittelweg den Tod. Texte zu Kino, Film, Politik*, edited by Christian Schulte (Berlin: Vorwerk, 1999), 155.

91. Bekker, "Problema khudozhestvennogo ocherka," 55.

92. Shklovsky's account of estrangement presumes a similar economy of seriality and deviation, or, in his particular analysis, of rhythm and its violation. As he writes in "Art as Device," "poetic rhythm consists in the distortion of prosaic rhythm," that is, in "disrupting rhythm . . . unpredictably." Viktor Shklovsky, "Art as Device," in *Viktor Shklovsky: A Reader*, edited and translated by Alexandra Berlina (New York: Bloomsbury, 2017), 96. Recognizing the resonances between the Formalist account of aesthetic experience and contemporary cybernetic theory, Umberto Eco wrote in 1976 that Shklovsky's device of defamiliarization "anticipates by some thirty years the analogous conclusions of so-called 'informational aesthetics.'" Umberto Eco, *A Theory of Semiotics* (Bloomington: Indiana University Press, 1976), 264.

93. Arkadii Ursul, *Problema informatsii v sovremennom nauke* (Moscow: Nauka, 1975), 11–31. Just a few years after Kurs, mathematician Andrei Kolmogorov likewise equated informational value to the degree of non-recurrence. For him, information could thus be calculated stochastically according to the same formulas that were used to calculate entropy in physics.

94. Gregory Bateson, "A Re-Examination of 'Bateson's Rule,'" in *Steps to an Ecology of Mind* (Chicago: University of Chicago Press, 2000), 315.

95. Luhmann, *Reality of the Mass Media*, 19.

96. B. Reznikov, "O knige t. Gusa *Informatsiia v gazete*," *Zhurnalist*, no. 18 (1930): 31.

97. B. Reznikov, "Gazetnaia nauka v svete marksizma," *Zhurnalist*, no. 14 (1930): 23. On Germanism versus Americanism in the news, see E. Brom, "Zhurnalistika kak nauka. Germanizm ili amerikanizm?," *Zhurnalist*, no. 7–8 (1927): 11–12.

98. Reznikov, "O knige t. Gusa *Informatsiia v gazete*," 29.

99. Thom, *Newspeak*, 100; Weiss, "Was ist neu am 'Newspeak,'" 274.

100. V. G. Kostomarov, *Russkii iazyk na gazetnoi polose* (Moscow: Moskovskii universitet, 1971). For an overview of Kurs's work in newspaper studies, see Elena Kapinos, "'Gazetchik' A. L. Kursa," *Siuzhetologiia i siuzhetografiia*, no. 1 (2018): 81–103.

101. From Tret'iakov, Chuzhak, Pertsov, and Shklovsky to Mayakovsky, Brik, Aseev, and Neznamov, nearly all Lefists were regular contributors to *The Journalist* during the interval in the mid-1920s when *Lef* (1923–25) had closed and its successor *Novyi Lef* (1927–28) had not yet launched. Even the artists close to Lef contributed to *The Journalist*: fresh back from Pressa, Lissitzky gave the journal a new cover design in January 1929.

102. *The Present* subscribed to all of the central tenets of the factographic program, from the commitment to actuality to the categorical opposition to fiction. And *Novyi Lef* returned the admiration: Chuzhak, Pertsov, Shklovsky, and Tret'iakov all heaped praise on the editors of *The Present*, and on Kurs in particular. "The literature of fact is growing," Chuzhak wrote in a 1928 *Novyi Lef* editorial dedicated to the Presentists: "In Novosibirsk there is an excellent journal *The Present*, and this journal works entirely on the basis of the fact." Chuzhak, "Goni fakty i dver' . . . ," *Novyi Lef*, no. 8 (1928): 44–45. Pertsov too enthused about *The Present*, which he singled out as "the only mass journal in the republic that doesn't publish 'generalized stories,' [but] concrete stories, 'stories about facts.'" Pertsov, "Pamflet—oruzhie klassa," *Chitatel' i pisatel'*, no. 26 (1928): 3. Finally, Tret'iakov dedicated an entire editorial in *Novyi Lef* to Kurs's journal, praising its "orientation toward the fact" and its commitment to publishing "fearless essays and notes complete with reference to all names and addresses—essays that hit the moving targets of our reality." Sergei Tret'iakov, "Nastoiashchee *Nastoiashchee*," *Novyi Lef*, no. 5 (1928): 43.

103. Aleksandr Kurs, "Activist Cinema," in *Lines of Resistance*, 147–51. Along similar lines, Shklovsky wrote about *A Sixth Part*: "Vertov thought he would replace the repetitions of plot with lyrical repetitions, having cut pieces off from the context that defined them and presenting them as a continuous refrain. But the device didn't work out." Shklovsky, "Neskol'ko slov o chetyrekhstakh millionakh," 44.

104. Viktor Pertsov, "Otvety na zapiski," 205.

105. On mathematical patterns and quantitative modeling in Vertov, see Lev Manovich, "Visualizing Vertov," *Russian Journal of Communication* 5 (2013): 44–55; and Adelheid Heftberger, *Kollision der Kader. Dziga Vertovs Filme, die Visualisierung ihrer Strukturen und die Digital Humanities* (Munich: text + kritik, 2006).

106. Sergei Tret'iakov, *Vsesoiuznoe soveshchanie po khudozhestvennomu ocherku*, l. 37.

107. Sergei Tret'iakov, "Obrabotka lozunga," *Gorn*, no. 9 (1923): 122.

108. Iurii Tynianov, "Kino–slovo–muzyka," in *Literaturnaia evoliutsiia. Izbrannye trudy*, edited by V. Novikov (Moscow: Agraf, 2002), 470.

109. For the modern scientist—and the cinematograph in turn—time "has no natural articulations. We can divide it as we please. All moments count. None of them has the right to set itself up as a moment that represents or dominates the others." Bergson, *Creative Evolution*, 332.

110. "Like science, [cinema] breaks down material phenomena in tiny particles . . . It is quite possible indeed that the construction of the film image from shots of minute phases of movement favors the . . . tendency toward decomposing given wholes." Siegfried Kracauer, *Theory of Film: The Redemption of Physical Reality* (New York: Oxford University Press, 1960), 50.

111. Tret'iakov, "Konkretnye nositeli zla ili konkretnye kozly otpushcheniia," 77.

112. Rodchenko, "Against the Synthetic Portrait, For the Snapshot," 238–39.

113. Dziga Vertov, "O s"emke siuzhetov kinokhroniki," *Iz naslediia*, 2:24.

114. Grierson, "The Russian Cinema," 139.

115. Sergei Tret'iakov, "Kak pishut ocherki," *Pionerskaia pravda*, no. 30 (July 13, 1929): 4.

116. This is Mikhail Luzgin's assessment of Kushner in "Za boevoi khudozhestvennyi ocherk," 26.

117. Iakov Shafir, "Pochemu nekotorye protiv pomeshcheniia roman v gazete," in *Rabochaia gazeta i ee chitatel'. Itogi odnoi ankety* (Moscow: Rabochaia gazeta, 1926), 201–2.

118. A. Men'shoi, "Kerzhentsev, NOT i gazeta," *Zhurnalist*, no. 8 (1923): 30.

119. S. Novgorodskaia, "O kartochnykh sistemakh," *Vremia*, no. 3: 31–32.

120. "V nomere," *Novyi Lef*, no. 10 (1927): 48.

121. Lissitzky, "Our Book," 30.

122. El Lissitzky, "Do Not Separate Form from Content!," in *El Lissitzky, 1890–1941* (Cambridge, MA: Harvard University Press, 1987), 62.

123. Paul Otlet, "Transformations in the Bibliographic Apparatus of the Sciences," in *International Organization and Dissemination of Knowledge*, edited and translated by W. Boyd Rayward (Amsterdam: Elsevier, 1990), 149. Otlet's book appeared in the Orga-biblioteka series of Gastev's Central Institute of Labor: *Organizatsiia nauchnoi raboty* (Moscow: TsIT, 1925).

124. Paul Otlet, "The International Organisation of Bibliography and Documentation," in *International Organization and Dissemination of Knowledge*, 187.

125. Paul Otlet, *Traité de Documentation: Le Livre sur le Livre* (Brussels: Editiones Mundaneum, 1934), 370. Otlet's opus shows his impressive knowledge of the Soviet cultural scene. In it, Otlet quotes Fadeev's *Rout* and Zamiatin (367) in addition to citing Mayakovsky's *How Verses Are Made* (371). His discussion of cinema as an "instrument of attraction" that "economizes mental labor" is an unmistakable reference to Eisenstein (224). Otlet also visited Lissitzky's installation at the Pressa show in Cologne: see his review "Cologne & Pressa," *Le Mouvement Communal*, no. 97 (1928): 643–46.

126. Dziga Vertov, "On the Organization of a Creative Laboratory," in *Kino-Eye*, 140; Lissitzky, "Do Not Separate Form from Content!," 62.

127. For an overview of these institutions, see K. B. Gel'man-Vinogradov, "Nauchno-informatsionnaia deiatel'nost' uchrezhdenii akademii nauk SSSR v pervye gody sovetskoi vlasti," *Nauchno-tekhnicheskaia informatsiia*, no. 11 (1967): 19–25.

128. André Leroi-Gourhan, *Gesture and Speech*, translated by Anna Bostock Berger (Cambridge, MA: MIT Press, 1993), 264. In contrast to the "sequentially arranged works" that preceded it, the card system is capable of "indefinite enrichment and reconstruction," he explained (262, 265).

129. Shklovsky, "Neskol'ko slov o chetyrekhstakh millionakh," 44.

130. Jean-François Lyotard, *The Postmodern Condition: A Report on Knowledge*, translated by G. Bennington and B. Massumi (Manchester: Manchester University Press, 1984), 19. Similarly: "So far in Western culture, narrative has been the primary mode of processing archivally stored data in the name of history, which, on the surface of so-called multimedia, continues in the form of stories." Ernst, *Digital Media and the Archive*, 71.

131. Aleksandr Bogdanov, "Chto takoe proletarskaia poeziia?," in *O proletarskoi kul'ture 1904–1924* (Moscow: Kniga, 1924), 127.

132. Sergei Tret'iakov, "Zhivoi 'zhivoi' chelovek (O knige V. K. Arsen'eva *V debriakh Ussuriiskogo kraia*)," in *Literatura fakta*, 243.

133. Kracauer, "Über den Schriftsteller," 345.

134. Kracauer, *Theory of Film*, 213.

135. Tret'iakov, *Vsesoiuznoe soveshchanie po khudozhestvennomu ocherku*, l. 121.

136. Palievskii, "Rol' dokumenta v organizatsii khudozhestvennogo tselogo," 391.

137. Heartfield recalled how he and his brother, the publisher Wieland Herzfelde, put Den Shi-Khua on the cover of the German translation purely by accident. Tret'iakov sent a number of photographs to Malik Press for the cover image, although he didn't identify any of their subjects by name. "Then he was stunned and delighted that we chose a photo for the dust-jacket showing the Chinese student whose life was the subject of the book as he stood in front of many Chinese scrolls with proclamations," explained Heartfield. "We truly had no idea that the Chinese man in the photo was Den Shi-Khua." Quoted in Fritz Mierau, *Erfindung und Korrektur* (Berlin: Akademie, 1976), 33.

138. Tret'iakov's use of "links" is "an obvious rejection of the concepts of classical dramaturgy since an act is normally designated as *акт* or *действие* in Russian." Myong Ja Jung-Baek, "S. Tret'jakov und China" (PhD diss., Georg-August-Universität Göttingen, 1987), 32.

139. M. Zagorskii, "'Rychi, Kitai' (Teatr imeni Vs. Meierkhol'd)," *Zhizn' iskusstva*, no. 6 (1926): 11–12.

140. Sergei Tret'iakov, "O p'ese 'Rychi, Kitai!,'" in *Slyshish, Moskva?! – Protovogazy – Rychi, Kitai!*, 159.

141. Other factographers endorsed *Chapaev* as well. See Sergei Tret'iakov, "Nashi tovarishchi," *Novyi Lef*, no. 10 (1928): 1; and "Zhivoe i bumazhnoe," in *Literatura fakta*, 142. Pertsov too embraces Furmanov in *O chem i kak pisat' rabochemu pisateliu*, 36ff.

142. On the contemporary debates about whether to designate *Chapaev* a novel or an ocherk collection, see Hans-Peter Schneider, *Dokument und Romanform als Problem in D. A. Furmanovs Romanen* Tchapaev *und* Miatezh (Frankfurt am Main: P. Lang, 1977), 45.

143. Dmitry Furmanov, *Chapaev* (Moscow: Foreign Languages Publishing House, 1956), 238.

144. Viktor Shklovsky, *A Sentimental Journey: Memoires, 1917–1922*, translated by Richard Sheldon (Ithaca, NY: Cornell University Press, 1970), 233. Barthes would likewise conclude that "narrative *verisimilitude* is based on the *probable*." "The Sequence of Actions," 144.

145. Viktor Pertsov, "Ideologiia i tekhnika v iskusstve," *Novyi Lef*, no. 5 (1927): 23. Even champions of the novel like Lukács had to admit that "the conclusion can be anticipated from the very beginning" ("Narrate or Describe?," 130).

146. "Mathematical probability and the aesthetic appearance of truth are connected not merely through their common derivation from the logical-poetological term 'probability.' In the eighteenth century, they still belonged to a common space of discussion and thinking." Rüdiger Campe, *The Game of Probability: Literature and Calculation from Pascal to Kleist*, translated by Ellwood H. Wiggins Jr. (Stanford, CA: Stanford University Press, 2012), 197–98.

AFTERWORD

1. Sergei Tret'iakov, "Prodolzhenie sleduet," *Novyi lef*, no. 12 (1928): 3. This line does not appear in the version of this essay that appeared one year later in *The Literature of Fact*.

2. There was sufficient exulting from the opponents of factography at the conference. Grigorii remarked that "Tret'iakov has essentially pulled out by the root the very thing that he once worshipped: he buried the theory of factography, cast away all vestiges of Lefism, and said that we need to study artistic literature. I think that this is the most important thing, and the most valuable thing, not just for Tret'iakov himself but for all of ocherk literature." *Vsesoiuznoe soveshchanie po khudozhestvennomu ocherku* (June 7, 1934), l. 19. Likewise, Bragina stated that "our meeting has shown that the Lefist theory of the literary fact is a problem of the past: we have already moved beyond this phase." *Vsesoiuznoe soveshchanie po khudozhestvennomu ocherku* (June 7, 1934), l. 2.

3. Sergei Tret'iakov, "Briefe an Bertolt Brecht" (September 9, 1934), in *Erfindung und Korrektur*, 263.

4. For an early attempt by a RAPP member to co-opt the ocherk, see A. Diatlov, "Ob ocherke," in *K tvorcheskim raznoglasiiam v RAPP'e. Sbornik statei. K tret'ei Oblastnoi konferentsii LAPPa* (Leningrad: Priboi, 1930), 74–82. The next year RAPP organized the first major conference on the Soviet ocherk in January 1931: see the write-up "Ob itogakh proizvodstvennogo soveshchaniia ocherkistov," *Na lit. postu*, no. 10 (1931).

5. "Na vsesoiuznom soveshchanii po khudozhestvennomu ocherku," *Literaturnaia gazeta*, no. 74 (June 12, 1934): 2.

6. Poltaratskii, quoting Shklovsky's earlier speech. *Vsesoiuznoe soveshchanie po khudozhestvennomu ocherku* (June 6, 1934), l. 24. Here we discover another parallel with photography, where indexical particularism called out for a system to control and manage the accumulation of work. As Allan Sekula once wrote about this archival logic, "bibliographic science provided the utopian model of classification for these expansive and unruly collections of photographs." "The Body and the Archive," in *The Contest of Meaning: Critical Histories of Photography*, edited by Richard Bolton (Cambridge, MA: MIT Press, 1992), 373.

7. *Stenogramma soveshchaniia brigad po khudozhestvennomu ocherku* (March 3, 1934). RGALI fond 631, op. 1, delo 63.

8. Quoted in Forrester, "Thinking in Cases," 1996, 12.

9. Gal', "Pisatel' vsekh zhanrov," 144. For similar reasons, I. V. Rybintsev pointed out that Boris Agapov tends to confuse content with form in his ocherki. *Sovetskii khudozhestvennyi ocherk* (Kiev: Vishcha shkola, 1976), 37.

10. Petr Neznamov, "Na novosel'e," in *Literatura fakta*, 253.

11. Gal', "Pisatel' vsekh zhanrov," 143.

12. "People have been speculating a lot recently about this Socialist Realism. On this point one has to say with utmost clarity: Socialist Realism is anything but a closed style that is already established. Style comes about only at the end: it cannot be imposed on anyone or expounded in a program. . . . Socialist Realism is less of a style than an orientation [*nicht so sehr Stil als Einstellung*]. Tret'iakov, "Der Schriftsteller im Aufbauwerke," 11–12.

13. Boris Agapov, "green fruit," *Nashi dostizheniia*, no. 5 (1934): 144–47.

14. Shklovsky, quoted in a report from the June 1934 ocherk conference,

"Ocherk—boevoe oruzhie piatiletki," *Literaturnaia gazeta*, no. 73 (June 10, 1934): 3.

15. Bekker, "Problema khudozhestvennogo ocherka," 56.

16. I. Zhiga, "Promezhutochnyi zhanr," *Literaturnaia gazeta*, no. 29 (July 15, 1930): 2.

17. Luzgin, "V bor'be za proletarskii ocherk," 30.

18. D. Brown, "The Ocherk: Suggestions Towards a Redefinition," in *American Contributions to the Sixth International Congress of Slavists II* (The Hague, 1968), 31.

19. V. Bogdanov, "Teoriia v dolgu (o zhanrovoi spetsifike ocherka)," *Voprosy literatury*, no. 12 (1965): 46–68.

20. Tret'iakov, *Vsesoiuznoe soveshchanie po khudozhestvennomu ocherku* (June 5, 1934), l. 18. Needless to say, Tret'iakov's skepticism about the ocherk as a non-genre never made it into the printed version of the talk that was published in *Our Achievements*. Other presenters at the conference vehemently denied his claim, which was denounced as an example of factographic recidivism. Thus Bragina: "It is completely obvious to everyone that the ocherk is a phenomenon of great, authentic literature and that the ocherk has nothing in common with factography, with mere notation. . . . People have been talking about what distinguishes this genre. But comrade Tret'iakov, I will still call it a genre, without dismissing the fact that there can be a great diversity of different forms within the genre." *Vsesoiuznoe soveshchanie po khudozhestvennomu ocherku* (June 8, 1934), l. 2.

21. Pertsov, "Novyi tip pisatelia," 29. Like Tret'iakov, Pertsov explained that "for us, a 'genre' is nothing in and of itself; the social function of literature is everything." "Otvety na zapiski," 203.

22. Oswald Spengler, *The Decline of the West*, translated by Charles Francis Atkinson (New York: Viking, 1928), 2:189, 195.

23. Boris Eikhenbaum, "V poiskakh zhanra," *Russkii sovremennik*, no. 3 (1924): 228–31.

24. Boris Eikhenbaum, *Moi vremennik: Slovesnost', nauka, kritika, smes'* (Leningrad: Izd-vo pisatelei, 1929), 125.

25. Tret'iakov, *Vsesoiuznoe soveshchanie po khudozhestvennomu ocherku* (June 5, 1934), l. 18.

26. Iu. P. and V. B., "Literatura v 'tolstom' zhurnale," *Chitatel' i pisatel'*, no. 4 (1929): 4–5.

27. Aleksandr Belenson, "Kino-Eye by Dziga Vertov," in *Lines of Resistance*, 128–30.

28. For a brilliant analysis of Tynianov's debt to Darwin's account of evolution, see Lev Tsyrlin, "K voprosy o 'zhizni' i 'smerti' literaturnogo fakta," in *V bor'be za marksizm v literaturnoi nauke*, edited by V. Desnitskii et al. (Leningrad: Priboi, 1930), 81–116. The most trenchant analysis of the formalist theory of literary evolution remains Pavel Medvedev, "The Formalist Theory of the Historical Development of Literature," in *The Formal Method: A Critical Introduction to Sociological Poetics*, translated by Albert J. Wehrle (Cambridge, MA: Harvard University Press), 159–74.

29. Yuri Tynianov, "Literary Fact," in *Permanent Evolution*, 156.

30. See, for example, *Russkaia proza*, edited by Boris Eikhenbaum and Iurii Tynianov (Leningrad: Akademia, 1926).

31. Iu. Tynianov and B. Kazanskii, "Ot redaktsii," in *Fel'eton. Sbornik statei* (Leningrad: Akademia, 1927), 6.

32. Iurii Tynianov, "Literaturnoe segodnia," *Russkii sovremennik*, no. 1 (1924): 291.

33. Yuri Tynianov, "Interlude," 174.

34. Tynianov and Kazanskii reference the lively polemics on the pages of *The Journalist* in 1926 in "Ot redaktsii," 7. Around the same time, a report in *The Journalist* on "state courses in the technology of speech" describes how Formalists like Tynianov, Tomashevsky, Eikhenbaum, Shcherba, and Iakubinskii were leading seminars on topics like journalism and stenography at Leningrad's Institute of the Living Word: T. Remizov, "Gosudarstvennye kursy tekhniki rechi (pis'mo iz Leningrada)," in *Zhurnalist*, no. 4 (April 1925): 51.

35. Iu. Tynianov and B. Kazanskii, "Ot redaktsii," 7.

36. B. Tomashevsky, "U istokov fel'etona," in *Fel'eton*, 70. On the Formalist conception of the newspaper as a "super-genre," see Aage Hansen-Löve, *Der russische Formalismus: methodologische Rekonstruktion seiner Entwicklung aus dem Prinzip der Verfremdung* (Vienna: Österreichische Akademie der Wissenschaften, 1978), 543.

37. Teodor Grits, "Zhurnal barona Brambeusa," *Novyi Lef*, no. 11 (1928): 20. In his review of Chuzhak's 1924 *"Literatura": K khudozhestvennoi politike RKP*, Petr Neznamov recognized Chuzhak's debt to Tynianov theory of the literary fact: "Na territorii literatury," in *Zhurnalist*, no. 13 (1924): 70.

38. Boris Kushner, "O bol'shom ocherkovom stile," *Nashi dostizheniia*, no. 7–8 (1934): 166.

39. For some of these designations, see Rybintsev, *Sovetskii khudozhestvennyi ocherk*, passim. On the ocherk as an "intervallic genre" specifically, see Ivan Zhiga, "Promezhutochnyi zhanr," *Literaturnaia gazeta*, no. 29 (1930): 3.

40. Aleksandr Kurs, "Kritika 'Nastoiashchego,'" *Nastoiashchee*, no. 9 (1928): 3.

41. Karl Kraus, "Apokalypse," in *Untergang der Welt durch schwarze Magie* (Vienna: Jahoda and Siegel, 1922), 12.

42. Kraus, "Apokalypse," 12.

43. Viktoria Ivleva, "Literary Theory in Practice: Rethinking Jurij Tynjanov's 'The Wax Figure,'" *Russian Literature* 60, no. 2 (2006): 127–57. As Ivleva explains, the "living monster" Iakov represents the genre that "has not yet found his place in life" (147). Likewise Mikhail Iampol'skii writes of the "intervallic phase of the 'monster'" (*промежуточная стадия 'монстра'*) in Tynianov's *Wax Figure*: "Maska i metamorfozy zreniia (Zametki na poliakh 'Voskovoi persony' Iuriia Tynianova)," *Tynianovskii sbornik* (Moscow: Imprint, 1994), 5:50.

44. Iurii Tynianov, "Voskovaia persona," in *Sochineniia* (Moscow: Khudozhestvennaia literatura, 1959), 464.

45. Pertsov, *Maiakovskii. Zhizn' i tvorchestvo (1925–1930)*, 215.

46. Daston, "Baconian Facts, Academic Civility, and the Prehistory of Objectivity," 49.

47. Daston, "Marvelous Facts and Miraculous Evidence in Early Modern Europe," 111. Daston offers some examples of seventeenth-century "facts": "monstrous births, celestial apparitions, cyclones, diamonds that glowed in the dark, and other strange phenomena" (109). Eventually these wondrous phenomena would be stripped of their religious significance to become scientific facts.

48. *Informe* affirms "that the universe resembles nothing." George Bataille, "Formless," in *Visions of Excess: Selected Writings, 1927–1939*, edited and translated by Allan Stoekl (Minneapolis: University of Minnesota Press, 1985), 31.

49. Georges Bataille, "The Deviations of Nature," in *Visions of Excess*, 56, 55.

50. Georges Canguilhem, "Monstrosity and the Monstrous," in *Knowledge of Life*, edited by Paola Marrati and Todd Meyers, translated by Stefanos Geroulanos and Daniela Ginsburg (New York: Fordham University Press), 141, 134.

51. *The Old and the New* was a film that evaded summary. Indeed, when Tret'iakov tried to explain what the film was about, he found that he could not provide a synopsis of the film and so instead he just drew up a list of the facts: "The film tells about how . . . ; about how . . . ; about how . . . ; about how . . . ; about how . . . ; about how . . ." Sergei Tret'iakov, "General'naia liniia," *Pioner*, no. 11 (1929): 15.

52. "S. Tret'iakov," in *Pervyi vsesoiuznyi s"ezd sovetskikh pisatelei 1934*, 344–46. His understanding of translation in 1934 marks a dramatic reversal from his earlier approach to translation, which dwelled on those words and concepts that had no equivalent in other languages. Writing about his current project *Den Shi-Khua*, he noted in 1928 that "it is hard to establish 'equivalent significance' [*дозначность*] in a translation from Chinese everyday life into ours." Sergei Tret'iakov, "O perevode," *Novyi Lef*, no. 7 (1928): 41.

53. Clark, *The Soviet Novel: History as Ritual*.

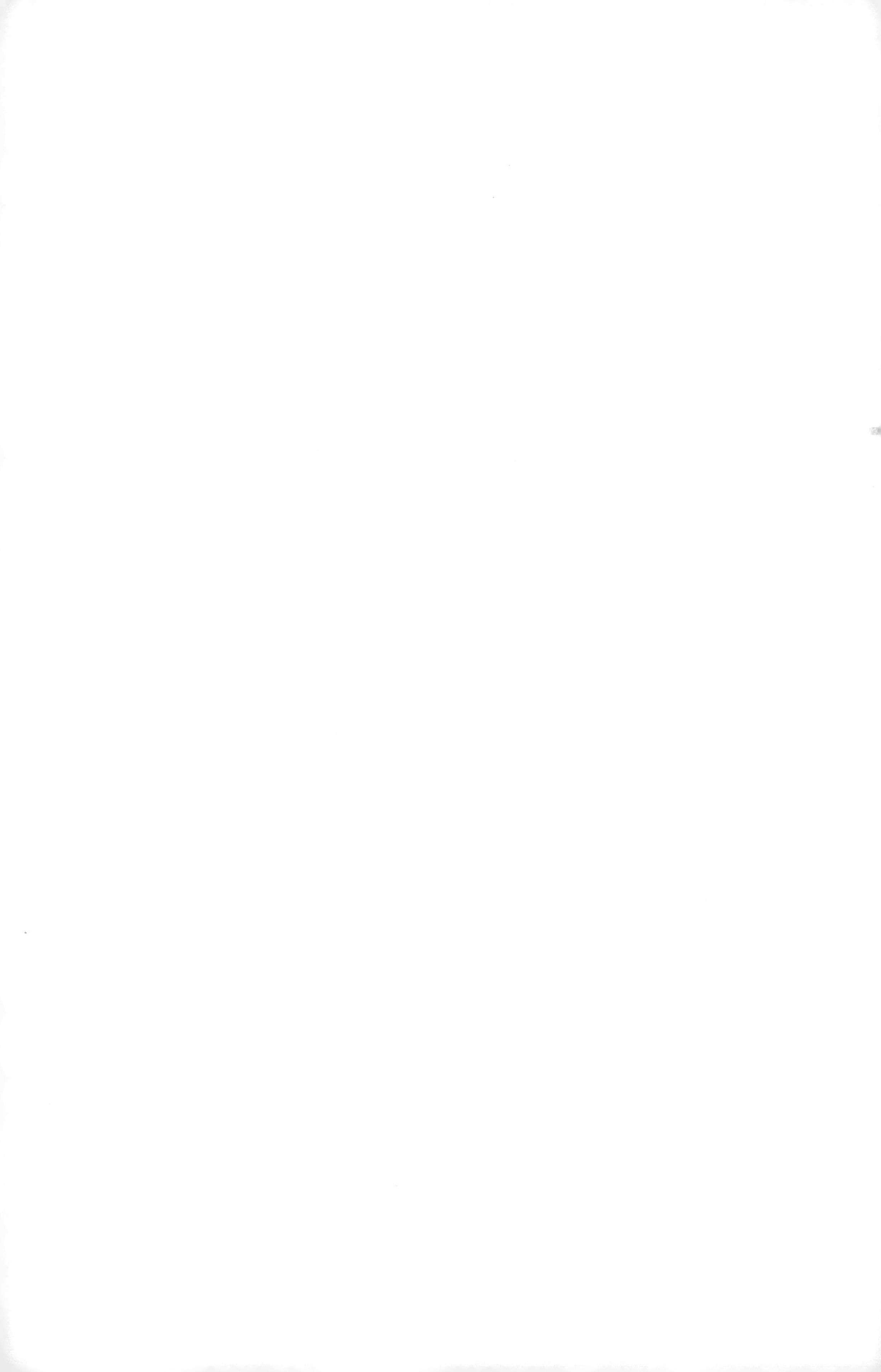

Index

Page numbers in italics refer to illustrations.

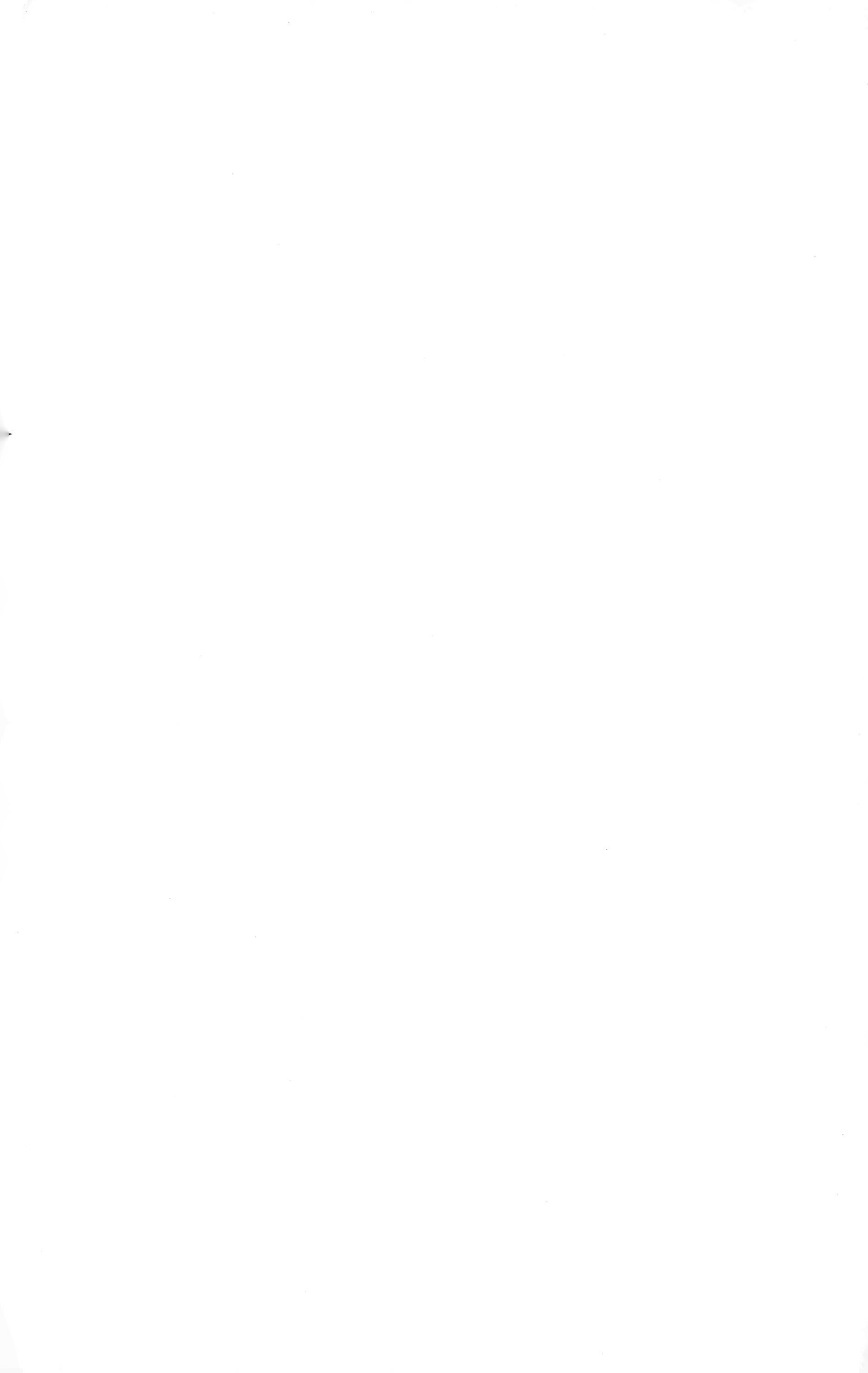